POLITICS AND CUL
VICTORIAN BRIT

COLIN MATTHEW

Politics and Culture in Victorian Britain

Essays in Memory of Colin Matthew

Edited by
PETER GHOSH
and
LAWRENCE GOLDMAN

OXFORD
UNIVERSITY PRESS

OXFORD
UNIVERSITY PRESS

Great Clarendon Street, Oxford OX2 6DP

Oxford University Press is a department of the University of Oxford.
It furthers the University's objective of excellence in research, scholarship,
and education by publishing worldwide in

Oxford New York

Auckland Cape Town Dar es Salaam Hong Kong Karachi
Kuala Lumpur Madrid Melbourne Mexico City Nairobi
New Delhi Shanghai Taipei Toronto

With offices in

Argentina Austria Brazil Chile Czech Republic France Greece
Guatemala Hungary Italy Japan Poland Portugal Singapore
South Korea Switzerland Thailand Turkey Ukraine Vietnam

Oxford is a registered trade mark of Oxford University Press
in the UK and in certain other countries

Published in the United States
by Oxford University Press Inc., New York

© The several contributors 2006

British Library Cataloguing in Publication Data

Data available

Library of Congress Cataloging in Publication Data

Data available

Typeset by Newgen Imaging Systems (P) Ltd., Chennai, India
Printed in Great Britain
on acid-free paper by
Biddles Ltd., King's Lynn, Norfolk

ISBN 0–19–925345–5   978–0–19–925345–6

3 5 7 9 10 8 6 4 2

Contents

1

A Brief Word on 'Politics' and 'Culture'

Peter Ghosh and Lawrence Goldman

The intellectual engagement and respect aroused by Colin Matthew were so great and so widespread across several continents, that there could easily be a series of volumes written in his memory, and we claim no monopoly in that respect. In origin at least, the present volume is no more than a local tribute, though it does of course spring from one of the Victorian institutions to which Colin was so devotedly loyal throughout his adult life: that house of many mansions known as the Oxford History Faculty. Yet if Oxford historians are notorious believers in intellectual pluralism, the local focus of this volume has in fact produced a significant underlying unity of approach. This was in no way an obeisance to editorial command, but was rather the unforced result of asking Colin's friends and colleagues to write on themes suggested by his memory and concerns. We hope, then, that whilst the essays which follow are of course independent works in their own right, they may also be read as a collective statement, a response to a fundamental conundrum which, like Oxford itself, accompanied Colin throughout life.

Colin's central concern, like ours, was how to set about the writing of modern British history taken as a whole—he would of course have dismissed with contempt the idea that the goal of academic training and expertise was mere specialism for its own sake. He further assumed that any properly synthetic account of this history must take politics as its organizing focus. Yet within his academic lifetime the study of British politics experienced challenges to its legitimacy and assumptions of the most radical kind. To understand the scale of this challenge we may go back—and it is some way—to Oxford in the 1970s, when Colin Matthew was making his name by his seminal and provocative work on Mr Gladstone.[1] This was the last time either in academic life or in the wider public culture of the United Kingdom when British political history could be taken to be a subject of self-evident importance and centrality. At that date the principal university

---

[1] For a consideration of Colin Matthew's historiographical achievement the reader must consult the chapters by Ross McKibbin and Boyd Hilton in this volume.

seminar in modern history at Oxford was the seminar on modern English history, which was held on Thursday afternoons in the Old Library of All Souls. (Those who were critical of the speaker, or else simply detached, will recall the contemplative delight of gazing at the white barrel vault of the ceiling, with its apparently simple and yet infinitely sinuous tracery.) It was here that, in 1975, Colin Matthew and Ross McKibbin first presented a typically provocative and now famous study of the role of the 'Franchise factor' in the rise of the modern Labour Party. In addition, for a period of some years in the later 1970s and early 1980s, Colin had his own independent seminar in Christ Church on Wednesdays, which occupied precisely the same terrain of 'English' history—and it was here (to take another seminal case) that Boyd Hilton's first, essay-length construction of 'the Age of Atonement' was aired to an academic public in the year that Mrs Thatcher became Prime Minister.

By a curious paradox, then, the study of 'English' history appeared to have reached a kind of peak within the research life of the university, just as its traditional foundations in the public culture were slipping away. Indeed even today much of our understanding of nineteenth-century British politics (a century which must be read as running through to the demise of the Liberal party in the mid-1920s) is still framed by work published *c.*1965–75. Yet simultaneously there were many people in the university world (though rather fewer outside it) who had been vociferously protesting against the hegemony of 'English' political history for a decade and more: they wished (to put it crudely) to get away from politics, away from England, and perhaps both. It might easily be supposed, then, that the state of affairs we have just been describing reveals Oxford history as deeply conservative—and such it may well have appeared from outside. But the actual course of events was more complex; most certainly so for Colin Matthew and his immediate contemporaries.[2]

One of Colin's central assumptions was that institutions and historical traditions were best reformed from within. If they had had a real presence in the past, then this implied an inner life which might be reworked to suit new circumstances and conditions. By contrast discontinuity and rupture represented a form of defeat. Discontinuity and a 'clean slate' were bad not merely on account of any sentimental valuation of the past 'for its own sake', but because in a purely practical sense the dismissal of accumulated achievement and frameworks, and the breach in human loyalties and energies this caused, were damaging and wasteful. In the case of British politics, Colin had grown up in a world where in the wake of Hitler British and American parliamentary institutions had been acknowledged as uniquely valuable throughout Western Europe, and those institutions continued to constitute a primary point of reference for ordinary people at home. On the other hand, the assumption of a uniquely valid, insular, and British singularity was running

---

[2] The present editors are their juniors and were no more than members of the audience in these developments.

down—not least because of victory in 1945. Victory may perhaps have put an end to Germany's alleged *Sonderweg* or special path to modernity, but it also eliminated much of the perceived gulf between the polities of Britain and Western Europe. Thus academic and intellectual engagement with a past defined in terms of English and British singularity—above all, the study of 'constitutional history'— was also in decay.

However, Colin's reaction to this state of affairs was not to say that one should simply concede the case against the study of English and British politics—as a Scotsman, he had a pertinent understanding of just how interchangeable 'England' and 'Britain' were. He did not accept that one should turn towards 'social' history or the history of the Third Reich (to name some of the more salient options at this date). Rather, he hoisted a flag in favour of reworking modern British history, and its political history, from within. Such was one idea behind his 'alternative' seminar in British history; and if engagement with the subject rose to a quantitative peak in later 1970s Oxford, this was in no way an act of complacency. Colin took it for granted that the foundations of the study of modern British history were historically conditioned and liable to change; but this only made it the more necessary to contribute to change and not to be the mere passive victim of 'external forces'. Given a firm, Scottish Unionist, allegiance to British constitutional tradition at that date, he could have few doubts as to the magnitude of the threat it was under. But though he might have been dubbed a kind of intellectual conservative on account of his Unionist and constitutionalist loyalties, his reaction was conservative only in the sense in which all evolutionary reform is conservative: 'Reform, that you may preserve.' Here was an implicit Macaulayan motto which underlay all his historical work.

Such too was the thinking which underlay his work on Gladstone's *Diaries*, and this, of course, offers a far more specific idea of Colin's response to the potentially annihilating challenges faced by all those who wished, and wish, to expound modern British political history in the late twentieth and early twenty-first centuries. What, on the face of it, could be a more traditional subject than Gladstone, and what less appealing text than his diaries, made up as they were of long catalogues of persons met, letters sent, and books read, with little in the way of Pepysian light relief? Yet the publication of Colin's first long introduction to the *Diaries* in 1974 was not unlike the opening of Tutankhamun's tomb: where once had lain a mummy of a somewhat unappealing kind, to be debunked and demoted at all costs,[3] there now stood a treasure chest, which he would explore for fully twenty years, producing an almost endless series of novelties across an extraordinary range of subjects. ('Homer on Roads' was a favourite early example.[4]) What was not

---

[3] For two important examples of this tendency, which are in their own way 'classics': R. T. Shannon, *Gladstone and the Bulgarian Agitation 1876* (London, 1963); J. R. Vincent, *The Formation of the Liberal Party 1857–1868* (London, 1966).

[4] *The Gladstone Diaries* (Oxford, 1974), iii, 16 Sept. 1852, cf. p. viii.

Pharaonic, however, was the way in which he had recalled one of the great symbolic figures of nineteenth-century British history to life. To breathe life into Gladstone made the entirety of later Victorian politics more plausible and accessible; it became once more part of a continous stream of evolution which in Colin's view not only spoke, but led, directly to the present.

He gave a snapshot of his predicament at the beginning of the *Diaries* project, and of possible ways forward, in a talk given at Oxford after the final volume was published in 1994—this to a seminar by now suitably renamed, the Modern British History seminar. He commented first on what had seemed to him the sheer remoteness of nineteenth-century history over twenty years before—and here we should recall that his original engagement on the *Diaries* project was an accident so far as he was concerned. (Had the chance to stay in Oxford not arisen, he would most probably have developed as a scholar of twentieth-century British imperialism instead.) He then cited two books he had read at the very outset of the project (*c*.1970) which had opened up a quite new dimension to his understanding of Victorian 'politics': Alec Vidler's *The Orb and the Cross: A Normative Study in the Relations of Church and State with Reference to Gladstone's Early Writings* (1945) and Duncan Forbes's prize essay, *The Liberal Anglican Idea of History* (1952). It is a remarkable testimony to the apparent decadence and excessive materialism of modern political history at this time that these works, which would today be seen as essential components of the history of Victorian ideas, should still have been lingering as unexploited and detached curiosities decades after their original publication.[5] However, Colin—and here he may appear as spokesman for a generation—put an end to this. Just as it has become unthinkable for twentieth-century historians to study social 'classes' solely as material phenomena regardless of their attendant (and yet autonomous) 'cultures', so in the case of Gladstone, we no longer envisage a pious individual bereft of any context outside high politics; a man who (in the eyes of the historian) had embarked on an extremely lengthy narrative that appeared hagiographical at best and at worst alien and repugnant. Instead we see him as a properly historical agent: a member of a tightly integrated society, standing in clear relation to deeper, organizing matrices of ideas, and responding to the purely practical problems these ideas outlined with precision, a degree of inner humility, and an immense creative energy.

Even today Colin's 1974 Introduction to the *Diaries* reads almost like a sensational document. In it Gladstone began his public life (as Vidler and Forbes had implicitly suggested) as a man trying to understand his contemporary world through religion; but this attempt collapsed, in public life at least, and he ended up by the early 1850s as the exponent of a surrogate political economy. So far as the materialistic outcome is concerned, Colin was very much a man of his time; but it

---

[5] Students of decadence may observe the placement and treatment of these two books, especially Vidler's, in the *Bibliography of British History 1789–1851: Issued under the Direction of the American Historical Association and the Royal Historical Society of Great Britain* ed. Lucy M. Brown and Ian R. Christie (Oxford, 1977), nos. 753, 3432.

is an intriguing question as to how much further he was prepared to develop the intellectual and cultural inquiries which formed his starting point. This early episode looks very much like the invocation of 'cultures' as external bodies, which, much as they enriched the overall historical picture, did not in fact revivify constitutionalism—the central political culture. By contrast, fifteen years on, when he came to write about Home Rule—much the greatest 'constitutional' episode in Gladstone's career—he was happy to allow that constitutionalism had a profound historical culture of its own, and that this was the ancestor of Gladstone's early political and intellectual formation. On the other hand, by this point the immediate relevance of both Ireland and devolution was so great that they could be treated almost as present-day events, needing little historical enrichment, and most of Colin's comparisons here look forward to the twentieth century.[6] Yet thereafter, particularly in his 'last' years—i.e. when he was more fulfilled and vigorous than ever—he began to develop an interest in British historiography.[7] Here was the true cultural underpinning to constitutionalism, and perhaps it was for this reason he came to lament that, as an undergraduate, he had never taken the famous paper on 'Gibbon and Macaulay' designed by Hugh Trevor Roper in the 1950s.

We cannot be sure just how important this movement was. What is clear is the way in which Colin worked to salvage political history as an organizing focus by dramatically widening—or restoring—its range; above all by exposing its connections to highly evolved schemes of ideas and values in the areas of religion, political economy, and history. In this sense he allied 'politics' to 'culture', where 'culture' is not mere gas and uplift, but something definite. He had recognized that, since the immediate, external characteristic of almost any given historical world is its infinity, real and evidential, one of the most necessary and reliable ordering principles for the historian is precisely that offered by 'ideas': the intellectual and conceptual structures erected by the historical subjects themselves. (However, in his mind this in no way precluded the subsequent intervention of the historian with his or her own priorities.) The personal significance of the linkage between politics and culture can be gauged from the fact that, as the *Diaries* project drew to a close, Colin began to ponder what his next project would be. After fourteen volumes of Gladstone it was going to have to be on a large scale— and here we can see why he and the *Dictionary of National Biography* would prove to be so exceptionally suited to each other. Yet we should not forget his own personal project, sketched in embryo prior to his *DNB* appointment, which was for a multi-volume work entitled the *Making of British Political Culture*.[8] Had he lived, he anticipated returning to this project just now, when the revised *Dictionary* was triumphantly complete.

---

[6] *The Gladstone Diaries* (Oxford, 1990), x, pp. cxxvi–clxi.

[7] Note the paper on 'Victorian Historiography' given in Apr. 1999 to the Annual Ontario Victorian Studies Conference in Toronto.

[8] Outlined to 'the Asa group' (a private discussion group) *c.*1990.

The *Dictionary* is of course a subject in itself: but here too Colin's ability to mobilize a (primarily) national community of contributors, and so to produce a legitimate successor to the great Victorian monument of Leslie Stephen and Sidney Lee, represented a remarkable triumph—perhaps his most remarkable triumph, measured in any visible and outward sense—for the belief in reform and change within a continuous national tradition. There was no renunciation of the past here. Though the new *Dictionary* rectifies all manner of deficiencies in the old one, still it is avowedly a descendant of the original. This was not merely a literal truth—an acceptance that the best material from the Victorian edition should not be thoughtlessly jettisoned—but also informed its basic working assumptions. The splendidly non-bureaucratic formula of 'No flowers by request' (as an advice to authors) encapsulated the idea that there might still be a common approach to writing which is free from lifeless formulae, and Colin was delighted to note 'that contributors, whether working on an early Welsh saint or a recent businessman, have a common understanding of the grammar of a *New DNB* article'.[9] The success of his Kitchener-like appeal for contributor volunteers[10] also showed that there could still be a national community of letters and culture, capable of producing results that, measured by their rapidity, economy, and efficiency, easily surpassed the highest expectations of the new millennium for all its Roseberian commitment to 'business' principles. The new *Dictionary* was to be broad, liberal, and humane in conception: besides the 'stars' of politics and literature—where the term 'star' was a fruit of late Victorian politics—there would now be added a full range of the 'stars' of popular culture and sport; besides businessmen and workers there should be 'a gallimaufry of the eccentric and the bad';[11] and fully three times as many women. Yet this remarkable sense of the national community as a community of individuals was something that Colin had already understood through his work in identifying 20,500 'Dramatis personae' for the *Diaries*. Work on Gladstone was also the seed of several other distinctive features which he sought to highlight as *DNB* editor: the importance of family life, marriage, and children; of hard cash or the lack of it as recorded in probate statements; of portraiture and physical appearance—all these represented a vivid accompaniment to more 'lasting' achievement, whether in Gladstone's life or the lives of the wider nation.

So the presence of 'political culture' at the heart of his thinking was no accident, and the reader will readily see that our title, which also links 'politics' and 'culture', stands in the closest relation to Colin Matthew, the author of a study of 'the ideas and politics of a post-Gladstonian elite'.[12] Yet by the sort of paradox that will rejoice those who do not like their history to be too orderly, this was not a title coined by the editors out of *pietas*. It came rather from reflection on the nature of the individual essays which had been proposed, and in this sense the title and

---

[9] 'Further Down the Road', *New Dictionary of National Biography*, Newsletter 2 (Dec. 1996).
[10] *TLS* (15 Jan. 1993), 17c.
[11] 'How Far have we Got?', *New DNB*, Newsletter 1 (Dec. 1995).
[12] The subtitle to *The Liberal Imperialists* (1973).

scheme of the book are very much those of the individual contributors themselves. The essays which follow do not constitute a formulaic unity. None the less, in their linkage of specific sets of ideas to the public sphere; their reading of politics through the lenses supplied by such 'cultures'; and their retention of a high degree of centrality for the political sphere—a priority which, so far as public life was concerned, any Victorian would both recognize and demand—a group of diverse hands here displays a significant and unprompted consensus. Now this is not a magic potion which, if imbibed, will tell us how to 'do' Victorian and modern Britain; yet it may be a significant, because representative, historical document at the beginning of the new century. Of course, this consensus or sense of position is in no way a local Oxonian property. Self-evidently, the challenge faced by modern British political history today is one which is faced by every student of the subject, in whatever university or literary marketplace. Here the contributors would wish to acknowledge the debt they owe to all those who came from outside Oxford to the conference at St Hugh's College, one of Colin's two Oxford colleges,[13] where their essays were presented and discussed in more plastic form. This was a tangible embodiment of a wider, national context.

It is a context of which Colin remains an assured part. We cannot of course say what he would have thought of our efforts; but we may be sure that if he were sitting in the King's Arms as usual on a Saturday morning, taking coffee and chewing the cud with one or two old friends, he would, after a suitable delay, have uttered a quite definite and suitably pithy dictum. Our best hope is that the discussion, a discussion which he himself did so much to enrich, should continue.

[13] The conference was also generously supported by Christ Church, his other college, and by the Oxford History Faculty. Our sincere thanks to both and to St Hugh's.

I

2

Colin Matthew (1941–1999)

Boyd Hilton

Sudden deaths are always shocking, especially when they result from wholly unsuspected natural causes. Even so, it is hard to convey the depth of the abyss felt by so many at the news that Colin Matthew had died. As Keith Thomas wrote shortly afterwards, 'a sense of shock and desolation ran through Oxford and was rapidly disseminated outwards to all the learned world. Colin Matthew was one of the few wholly irreplaceable people in this University. He played so central a role in the lives of so many of us that, at this moment, our feeling of loss is utterly over-whelming.'[1] In the many hundreds of letters sent to his widow, Sue Matthew, it is striking how often close colleagues recalled him in geological or navigational terms. 'An immovable rock.' 'His rock-like dependability.' 'A great rock of sense and purposeful ambition.' 'One of the fixed points on which to take bearings.' The fact that Colin should have died from a weak heart was in itself hard to take because it subverted the image of someone who seemed invulnerable. 'A fount of wisdom and good advice.' 'We relied on him.' 'We have lost our best man.'

Two-and-a-half years later historians of modern Britain suffered another devas-tating loss in Roy Porter. Both men died in their fifties after suffering massive heart attacks in a public highway while on or beside their bicycles. But if Roy brought Charles James Fox or Georges Danton to mind, Colin's image was in some ways more Cromwellian than cavalier. The Lord Protector's portrait held pride of place above the mantelpiece at home, and he named one of his sons Oliver. He was especially fascinated by the Victorians' own fascination with Cromwell,[2] and saw in it a clue to Gladstone's charisma, will power, and incor-ruptibility. In the first shock of grief friends and colleagues remembered Colin's own 'absolute integrity', his 'sense of justice', 'straightforwardness', and 'invariable faithfulness to a code of personal conduct and integrity of judgment'. It made him, one said, 'an unusual figure in the often feline academic world'. Such

---

[1] Keith Thomas, 'In Memoriam Colin Matthew', *Oxford Magazine*, 172 (1999), 6–7.
[2] He made significant contributions to the 'Nineteenth-Century Cromwell Archive' in the Bodleian Library.

comments hit the mark, but did not by themselves convey the mixture of the man, for the same friends in the same letters described him as tolerant, understanding, compassionate, sympathetic, generous, decent, funny, above all lovable, not characteristics conventionally seen as Cromwellian. His 'wry appreciation of the human comedy involved in any institutional occasion'[3] saved him from solemnity, while the integrity referred to was 'never displayed on his sleeve' or rammed down others' throats. Nevertheless, the key to his unique personality surely lay in the tension between these puritan and liberal sides.

The eldest of three siblings, his earliest years were spent happily with his mother and grandparents in Inverness. (The Highlands would retain a strong emotional pull for the rest of his life.) He later moved to Edinburgh where his father was a distinguished consultant physician. In later life he would often express disdain for that city's upper bourgeoisie and for the medical profession in particular, but such sentiments must be interpreted cautiously since his judgements were often severest about those to whom he felt the strongest tugs of loyalty. There was little ambiguity about his loathing of Edinburgh Academy, however, particularly its militaristic ethos and the harsh physical punishments meted out for academic shortcomings. Probably what embittered him was the perceived injustice more than the harshness in itself. There may have been a minor personal crisis at this time. At all events, in 1954 he was withdrawn from the Academy and sent to Sedbergh School, where the syllabus was less intense. Like many public schools of the day Sedbergh was tough and rather hearty, its ethos as rugged as that of the surrounding North Yorkshire terrain, and there was a heavy emphasis on sport, especially rugger and running. His house master (and also headmaster) Michael Thornely, who later became a lifelong friend, was somewhat bemused by his first meeting with the awkward 13½ year old, delivered by his father some hours ahead of schedule.

Colin was very shy. He had never been south of the border before and I believe that his years at school in Scotland had not been altogether happy. I asked him whether he had a supreme contempt for the 'cursed Sassenach'; very dourly he replied, 'Well no, sir, not a *supreme* contempt', and relapsed into silence. Fortunately, my wife, as so often, came to the rescue, having somehow discovered that Colin was interested in puppets. Together they discussed puppetry and all its works until the arrival of the other 'new boys'.[4]

The words dour and shy recur frequently in memories of Colin at this time. Another epithet, one that has more resonance with those who knew him later, is sardonic. He had an 'impish' sense of humour, but was a fundamentally serious

[3] Obituary in *The Times*, (1 Nov. 1999).
[4] Michael Thornely, headmaster of Sedbergh 1954–75 and housemaster of school house 1954–67, personal communication. Colin's sense of his Scottishness was if anything reinforced by the move to Yorkshire. Addressing the school debating society five years later in support of a proposition that 'the Scot was the backbone of Sedbergh' (carried by one vote), he brought proceedings to a climax by announcing 'that he normally refused to argue with Englishmen, and merely laughed at their stupidity'.

boy who made up his own mind and spoke it. Wary, watchful, and not as yet perhaps very warm, he honoured tribal allegiances but tempered them with common sense.[5] He did not rag, probably because he thought it was pointless, and it can have been little surprise to his fellow juniors when he went on to become a prefect and head boy. He was not exactly a charismatic or heroic leader, but according to a close friend and contemporary, Jamie Bruce-Lockhart, he resembled 'a reliable judge whom others liked and above all respected'. There is much testimony from former fags as to Colin's kindness and consideration, though at least one junior remembers him as a strong disciplinarian, and we can be sure that he was never familiar. Fagging was indispensable, he informed the school debating society in 1959, since 'in schools without fagging there tended to grow up familiarity between senior and junior boys'. The comment lights up the minutes of an otherwise entirely predictable debate, and hints at an originality of perception which was later to become a hallmark, but in most respects Colin's own mindset was at this time fairly conventional. He threw himself into sport, and though lacking the talent of his father, who had played on the wing for Scotland, it is recorded that he 'never flinched a tackle'. His real forte was long distance running.

He had a very particularly high bounce to his run, and seemed indefatigable. I can see him now in my mind's eye running on the back lanes and foothills of Sedbergh, a gaunt figure in a drenched blue jersey in pouring rain when we were prefects taking juniors on what were called 'House runs'. I, not being a good runner, would be at the back whipping up the slackers. Colin would lead from the front, pacing and testing the keenest. Then occasionally he would bounce back to the rear to see how the rest of us were getting on, only to disappear onwards into the streaming rain to catch up with those at the front again.[6]

Maybe he ran so hard for the same reason that Gladstone chopped trees. More likely he cultivated a reputation for keenness at games as a cover for what today would be called his feminine side. As in many such schools, Sedbergh's hearty and aggressive philistinism served (perhaps deliberately) to emphasize its odd pockets of sweetness and light. For Colin one of these was the school library with its fine collection of books donated by Brendan Bracken, an old boy. There was also the debating society, which he seems to have run single (not to say high) handedly for several months, and a small number of intellectual cliques. But above all there was the history sixth, run by his first true mentor, Andrew Morgan, who had fought successfully to distance his department, both physically and symbolically, from the main school by taking over a couple of cottages in which he daringly employed 'Socratic teaching methods'. In those days many of the best students stretched their sixth form years beyond A level to a seventh or eighth term in which they sat the Oxford or Cambridge colleges' scholarship examinations. It was also not uncommon for some boys, especially if they were prefects, to see out the school year even after they had secured their places at university. This meant several

---

[5] Jamie Bruce-Lockhart, personal communication.
[6] Jamie Bruce-Lockhart, personal communication.

months of delicious freedom, to be spent wisely or flippantly according to taste. Colin did well at A level, secured his place but not a scholarship to Christ Church, Oxford, and then opted to fill the shining hours by running the school and reading the collected works of Balzac, which he claimed was a deeply formative experience. He would always remain grateful to Sedbergh and to Morgan, while for his part Morgan judged Colin to be massively able but still a little lacking in flair. It was hard to be sure, however, for Colin did not reveal much, being often 'encapsuled in a tight, almost Calvinistic carapace of non-communication'.

Yet, things were happening. Often they were sharp arrows of critical doubt about the wisdom or accuracy or logic of some proposition I had trawled across his bows. There was clearly a deeply questioning mind at work, but the encounters never developed into fruitful dialogue, still less to a relationship of personal warmth.

Eventually a close friendship would develop between master and pupil, but not until long after Colin had left Sedbergh.

The youth who went up to Oxford in 1960 was independent minded and resilient, but still reserved and at times even tongue-tied. He was immensely moved by the traditions, the grandeur, and the madcap charms of Christ Church, but he had nothing in common with the booming hearties of Peckwater Quad (very audible in those days), and it seems unlikely that his carapace softened much over the next three years. The senior history don was Charles Stuart, an expert in nineteenth-century Britain, whose teaching emphasized high political intrigue to an extent that was then becoming deeply unfashionable in the face of marxisant assumptions about the importance of material interests.[7] Colin always remained thankful to Stuart for the 'Namierite' grounding he received in the published correspondence and memoirs of the period, and it gave him confidence when he came to tackle Gladstone's political career. Despite his respect for Stuart as a tutor, however, he was unhappy about what he saw as the college's amateurish approach to academic work in general. In Stuart's view there was no point in striving officiously to turn a natural third-class man into a second-class one, nor any great shame when an unacademic but otherwise worthy and engaging undergraduate ended up with a Fourth. Such insouciance must have offended Colin's Scottish sense of the seriousness of education. He was also bothered by Stuart's insistence on holding out against the practice, adopted by most if not all other colleges, of laying on individual tutorials for the crucial third-year special subjects. Such matters did not help, but the real reason for Colin's failure to shine in the Schools examinations was his inability to be snappy or glib. Always he liked to chew on problems, venture solutions, and then withdraw and refine them. So, like the vast majority of undergraduates, he took second-class honours, and it must have seemed as though his Oxford career had come to a conventional end in 1963,

[7] The archetype was Asa Briggs, *The Age of Improvement* (London, 1959). Cambridge historians such as Maurice Cowling and John Vincent were to pioneer a revival of interest in high politics in the late 1960 and early 1970s.

when he went to Uganda to take the diploma in education at Kampala's Makerere University.

A much older person, who knew Colin slightly at the time, surmised that he went to Africa because he wanted to help the poor. That may sound uncharacteristically priggish, but the idealism is believable. The Scots had invested in empire emotionally (and often literally) for more than two hundred years, and Colin undoubtedly felt an obligation to serve humanity in some practical way. It helps to explain why John Buchan was one of his favourite novelists.[8] Officially employed as an educational officer in the Tanzanian civil service (1964–6), what he did in practice was teach the constitutional history of Britain to local students at a school in Old Moshi. One can be sure that he taught Magna Charta and the Bill of Rights from a Whig perspective, and with a full conviction of the utility of his lessons for a young country seeking to establish itself following decolonization.[9] Conversely, a fascination with Britain's ever-changing role in world history would later inform his scholarship, making it much less insular than that of most Victorianists. His African experience was formative in many ways, the most important of which was that he met his future wife, Sue Curry, who was teaching at Machame on the slopes of Mount Kilimanjaro. This lithe and beautiful young extrovert from Indianapolis had a number of admirers, but she fancied Colin's Land Rover and she was amused when he turned up at her hospital bedside, where she was recovering from hepatitis, with a bunch of bedraggled flowers and Gibbon's *Decline and Fall*. They were married in America in 1966, and shortly afterwards set up home in Oxford, first in Elsfield (where Colin's ashes are buried, close by Buchan's grave), and then for nearly thirty years on Southmoor Road in Walton Manor north of Jericho, between Kingston Road and the canal. In 1968 Sue gave birth to David, after which Lucy and Oliver followed in fairly swift succession. It was at some point between David's arrival and Lucy's that Ross McKibbin and I got to know 'the Matthews'.

Many people have happy and fulfilling private lives, but his wife and children were so important to Colin, and so central to his developing persona, that they must be given pride of place in any memoir. An observant friend and colleague remarked that 'the Matthews' family life seemed a kind of miracle'. Another commented that it was 'as near to perfection as anyone can hope for'.[10] (Colin's own parents' marriage had ended in divorce.) 107 Southmoor Road was emphatically a home to have fun in, not a house beautiful. Later, once the children had gone off to university, some concessions were made to conventional taste in such matters as tidying up and decorating, but for the first two decades it resembled the state of nature. It was also the most open house I have known. Friends, colleagues, students, children of the neighbourhood, and animals of various sorts seemed free

---

[8] Alongside two other Scotsmen, Walter Scott and Robert Louis Stevenson.

[9] Shortly after independence, Tanganyika and Zanzibar merged to form the nation of Tanzania in 1964. Colin remained to the end a keen member of the Britain–Tanzania Society, on behalf of which a collection of nearly £2,300 was taken at his funeral.   [10] Keith Thomas, 'In Memoriam', 6–7.

to wander in and out. More casual acquaintances, like people the Matthews had met on their frequent travels round the world, as well as people the Matthews had never met but knew someone they knew, seemed constantly to call. Admittedly, the deliciously informal atmosphere owed much to Sue's mid-Western background. It was (to paraphrase D. H. Lawrence) the golden softness of this woman's American flame of life that set the tone—a flame she later put to service as a primary school teacher and legendary head of St Ebbe's School—but in his own gruffer and more whimsical register Colin played his part. Sometimes he would shrug his shoulders smilingly, as if to acknowledge that he had no choice but to go along with his wife's flow. At all events he was a devoted father, both wise and indulgent. He joined in youthful activities with unaffected pleasure, and yet—thanks partly to a slightly abstracted air—managed never to seem *de trop*. I can see him now directing some children's game, absentmindedly turning music on and off perhaps, while at the same time holding forth with the adults present on history, politics, or whatever. He enjoyed games, physical and mental, and he loved talk. Once his children and their friends had turned into adolescents he liked to interrogate them, jovial and serious by turns, occasionally pontificating in a slightly sheepish way, but for the most part genuinely listening. He seemed to think that whatever he discovered about other people's lives and beliefs would enhance his own store of understanding. Eventually the children went about their ways, but the house retained its magnetic qualities for all sorts of people, while Sue and Colin helped to fill the void by an energetic regimen of opera and theatre going. So that, although they always appeared to be consummately relaxed, they never seemed to be still.

I suggested above that the key to Colin's personality lay in the tension between his puritanical and liberal sides. It would be a gross over-simplification to see the distinction in chronological terms. Nevertheless, he once told my wife in the matter of fact yet earnest way he had that he 'thoroughly disliked' the person he had been when young, and that Sue had 'transformed' him. And it may be significant that while in Tanzania he began to pick up some old threads. For example, he corresponded with his old history teacher, Andrew Morgan.

He was now more open and communicative than I had ever known him. Was it Africa? Or was it Sue, who was already on the scene? I was chuffed that this reticent man who had never asked anything of me, now asked for the loan or gift of some of my paperback history books as they had virtually none in his college . . . I was delighted . . . to learn that the relationship at Sedbergh had not been as perfunctory and formal as I had thought.

It would seem that at last Colin began to feel good about himself, enabling him to acknowledge debts he long had been conscious of but had felt shy of expressing. But whether or not his personality changed, his appearance certainly did. He remained medium tall and fairly slim, with a smooth skin and slightly pink complexion, but shortly before I got to know him his hair had turned suddenly from badgerish to Old Testament white. He blamed a dentist who, he said, had been so engrossed in conversation with Sue that he had forgotten to switch off the radiography machine in time. This characteristic dig at the healing professions might have been a joke. Still, the combination of his boyish face and bright white hair was an unforgettable one.

So joyous was Colin's private life, and so successful his later career, that it is easy to forget just how anxious and difficult Colin's early years as a professional historian were. After returning to Oxford in 1966 he embarked on a diploma in economics and politics, but soon exchanged that for research into late Victorian and Edwardian history. His doctorate, written under the deft supervision of A. F. ('Pat') Thompson, was completed in 1970 and published in 1973 as *The Liberal Imperialists: The Ideas and Politics of a Post-Colonial Elite*. As he saw it, Rosebery, Haldane, and Asquith had developed admirable, even noble, plans for domestic and imperial renewal, being far more humane than their Tory counterparts Milner and Kitchener, but they had failed owing to 'incompetence', 'bungling', and a 'lack of capacity for organization'. Ultimately the 'Limps' had lacked the Cromwellian gift for seeing things through. *Liberal Imperialists* is a fine book, but it was neither flashy nor modish, while the academic job market was drying up after the post-Robbins flash floods of the 1960s. Colin did not have a first-class degree, and he had lost years as a result of his time in Africa. When vacancies did come up, more often than not he failed to be shortlisted. At the eleventh hour, in 1970, a lifeline was thrown in his direction when he was appointed assistant editor to M. R. D. Foot on the Gladstone diaries project. This and the associated lectureship at Christ Church kept him in the game, but was widely regarded as a menial appointment with a limited future. He had not even been the front runner for the post, and got it partly because some of the other candidates were thought to be too highly qualified.

Charles Stuart chortled, the day after the appointment, 'if Foot thinks he'll be able to boss Matthew about, he's made a terrible mistake'. In fact it seems likely that Foot knew exactly what he was doing. In 1968 he had published the first fourteen years of Gladstone's diaries (down to 1839) in two exemplary volumes, but his own research interests were now directed towards twentieth-century warfare. The project languished, prompting interested parties at Christ Church, the Rhodes Trust, the Oxford University Press, and not least Lambeth Palace (whose incumbent has ownership of the diaries) to revitalize it. They can hardly have anticipated just how quickly Colin would do this. He was off like a horse out of a trap, enabling Foot to resign from the project within two years.[11] It had been a bloodless and perfectly amicable coup, but this did not stop some of Colin's friends from dramatizing it. We began to portray him as a man of Bismarckian steel, an iron editor prepared to topple anyone who stood in his way. It is possible that Colin secretly enjoyed this myth making, but he did little to stoke it, and

---

[11] Vols. iii and iv were published under joint editorship in 1974, but the riveting 56-page introduction was by Colin alone.

always spoke of Foot with respect. In 1976 Christ Church made him a research student (or senior research fellow), but still he had no security and the Gladstone project would not last for ever. Indeed, the faster he completed it the sooner he would do himself out of a job, but characteristically he did not allow this consideration to slacken his pace. Meanwhile he continued to be passed over for permanent Oxford jobs, a cause of some chagrin and agitation. It surely explains the impatience and even asperity which he sometimes displayed in those years, not with friends but in the wider academic community. He was rarely rude, but could switch off communication when he disapproved of someone, and this could be mistaken for aloofness or even arrogance. He was too stoical and perhaps too proud to moan overmuch about his career prospects, and it was only a much later incident that made me realize just how deeply frustrated he had been. In 1992 he was elected to a professorship, on which I congratulated him. He ruminated for a moment, as was his wont. Then he gritted his teeth, thumped my bookshelves, and said: 'It'll show them!' (I did not press him as to who, precisely, 'they' were.) The expression of pent-up resentment was wholly uncharacteristic and quickly passed over. Nevertheless, one can best appreciate how marvellous Colin's last eight or nine years were by recognizing the toll which his earlier struggles had taken.

The real turning point had come in 1978 when, at the age of 37, he had been elected to a Tutorial Fellowship at St Hugh's College. It was an appropriate appointment, for although he remained attached to Christ Church emotionally, and indeed physically since the Diaries continued to be edited from Gladstone's undergraduate rooms in Canterbury Quad, St Hugh's was much more suited to Colin's open-necked shirt style. (Later, when he became a public man serving on numerous London committees, he would keep a tie in his pocket to be assembled at the last possible moment.) It appealed all the more that he was among the first male fellows of St Hugh's, and he clearly relished the pioneering role. He became a notably conscientious and successful college tutor, balancing the academic and the pastoral with rare judgement, and served for a time as senior tutor. (Later, several of his colleagues hoped that he might become principal.) Meanwhile volumes v to xiv of the Gladstone Diaries came out in batches with a speed that took many academics' breath away—in 1978, 1982, 1986, 1990, and 1994. Although production standards were lavish, the operation itself was largely performed on a shoe-string and was initially low-tech, though when Colin eventually adapted to computers—slightly later than most—he quickly became both avid and expert. (This is evident from the extraordinary fourteenth volume in which a highly analytical index was supplemented by a 'Where was he?' and 'What did he read?'[12]) Another secret was his ability to inspire the loyalty, even devotion, of a succession of assistants and helpers. As an editor he had a knack of knowing just how much explanatory information to impart in footnotes—always there when

---

[12] It won the Library Association Wheatley Medal for an Outstanding Index in 1994.

the reader needed him, never overstaying his welcome. A major transition occurred with volume vii, which dealt with Gladstone's first premiership (1868–74) and in which Colin supplemented the diary with extensive cabinet minutes, memoranda, and several thousands of letters. It was the latter, rather than Gladstone's jejune record of daily events, that made it and succeeding volumes such utterly indispensable tools of research.

But most of all there was the series of masterly introductions. Honed and polished to a degree, but sonorous at the last, they established him as a consummate stylist. Alongside certain running themes, Colin took the opportunity to place each stage of his subject's career within a strong context of interpretation. If this method tended to emphasize discontinuities, it seemed entirely justified by Gladstone's restless and questing nature, his successive obsessions and enthusiasms. Volume iii tackled Gladstone's transition from extreme High Tory with quasi-Tractarian longings to the Peelite and proto-Liberal statesman. Volume v dwelt on the *étatiste* strains in Gladstone's thinking (provoked in part by a period of exclusion from office) and on his work as Chancellor of the Exchequer. Volume vii was about the first-time Prime Minister's sense that his career was approaching its conclusion, and his ability to 'maintain his traditions of private introspection and development, despite the press of public business'. Paradoxically, Gladstone seemed less concerned with the processes of governance than he had during the years of opposition in the 1850s, while his obsessions with Mrs Thistlethwayte and the Vatican estranged him from many of the processes of his own government and of the legislation that ensued. Volume ix saw Gladstone out of office once more, but belatedly moving to take the lead in the Bulgarian agitation. Colin's theme here—the subject of a projected separate study never completed—was Gladstone's role 'in shaping the form and style of British political communication for decades to come'. In volumes x and xii he focused once more on policy and especially on Irish Home Rule, but moved beyond the then current preoccupation with tactics to consider broader imperial developments. In this he was clearly influenced by contemporary debates on European federation and Scottish devolution.[13] These successive theme changes gave Colin's *Gladstone* a continuing excitement that would be difficult to sustain in a conventional linear biography. Most admirable of all, perhaps, was the conviction with which he melded the public and the personal. His most delicate assignment in this respect occurred near the beginning, in the Introductions to volumes iii and iv. Gladstone's rescue work with prostitutes was well known, but his urge for self-scourging was not. I remember Colin bringing a photographed page of one of Gladstone's diaries into the King's Arms and asking me to identify a squiggle shaped a bit like a lop-sided pi-sign. When I was unable to do so he said excitedly, 'It's a whip. Gladstone was a

---

[13] e.g. his surprisingly absorbing account of Gladstone's efforts to secure a just fiscal and financial relationship between the imperial and proposed Irish exchequers may have been informed by Margaret Thatcher's successful campaign for a rebate from the European Union.

flagellant!' I told him he was overwrought, but he was of course correct.[14] However, he wrote about the matter with such exemplary tact that a feature of Gladstone's persona which might have seemed risible (at best) merely added to the reader's sense of the statesman's complexity and greatness: 'Priggish and hypocritical he may have seemed to enemies, foolhardy to friends, but his struggles with his body and his conscience, when seen in the diary in the context of his religious, political and family life, cannot but seem noble.'[15] This and similar comments signified empathy, but left his friends uncertain as to whether Colin actually *liked* Gladstone. When the question was put to Sue recently, she did not answer directly, but revealed that when Colin read to her the passage that he had just written on Gladstone's death and funeral, he was unable to finish it because of the tears rolling down his cheeks.

Colin's two-volume analytical biography of Gladstone, based for the most part on his successive Introductions, was published in 1986 and 1995 and won him the Wolfson Prize for History. Gladstone looms so large in current historiography that it takes an effort to realize that forty years ago he loomed much less so. There was the official *Life* of 1903 by John Morley, the only person before Colin to have had full access to the diaries; there was J. L. Hammond's intellectual study *Gladstone and the Irish Nation* (1938); and there was Philip Magnus's conventional biography of 1954. In all three cases the theme was that of a man who started out in politics with extreme right-wing and High Church views and ended up as an ultra-Liberal. Both the first two authors emphasized the gradual nature of this development, but whereas Hammond described a process of sedimentary growth, Morley's vision was exactly the reverse. For Hammond the secret was Gladstone's emerging 'European sense', and his realization of 'the value and place of self-respect in the life of a nation'; for Morley skins of congenital bigotry simply peeled off one by one as he grew in experience and understanding. Magnus by contrast presented Gladstone's move across the political spectrum as a much jerkier process, and one interspersed by a series of 'mental earthquakes'. The only significant challenge to these three broadly Whiggish interpretations had come from John Vincent. In the latter's opinion, Gladstone suffered from 'a certain bareness of ideas', but despite or because of this inadequacy he was a supreme word spinner or 'casuist', qualities which enabled him to galvanize the public with 'visceral' rhetorical 'thrills' in the 1860s,[16] and to master the linguistic rules of the high political game in the 1880s.[17] Now Colin's intellectualist approach owed something to Hammond, but his unparalleled knowledge of Gladstone's writings enabled him to place the interpretation on a much more sophisticated basis.

[14] Subsequently two younger colleagues of mine discovered a similar squiggle in the manuscript diaries of Lord Morpeth. Further investigation revealed that it occurred every seven days and must have stood for 'Sunday' or 'Sabbath'.   [15] Introduction to vol. iii, p. xlviii.

[16] John Vincent, *The Formation of the Liberal Party 1857–1868* (London 1966), 211–35.

[17] A. B. Cooke and John Vincent, *The Governing Passion: Cabinet Government and Party Politics in Britain 1885–86* (Brighton, 1974).

He accepted Magnus's idea of punctuated progression, but argued that the 'mental earthquakes' or explosive political initiatives only occurred as a result of intense and lengthy cerebral processes. For example, he argued that the young Gladstone reached his views on the proper ends and forms of government as a result of reading and reflecting on Plato and Aristotle. He resisted Vincent's interpretation, partly because it seemed cynical, but mainly because he was committed to the hypothesis that the political *rapport* between Gladstone and the bulk of Liberal voters was based on the latter's fundamentally rational understanding of political and social action.

And yet, paradoxically, Colin's great success in explaining Gladstone perhaps vindicates one element of Vincent's analysis. Although he wrote brilliantly on Church politics and religious culture, as evidenced by his essays on Pusey and the Oxford Movement,[18] theological doctrine was a subject on which I sometimes felt that Colin's antennae were slightly insensitive. In part this may simply have reflected an institutional preference. Whereas work on nineteenth-century Britain by Cambridge scholars such as George Kitson Clark, Owen Chadwick, Maurice Cowling, Edward Norman, Jonathan Parry, and Richard Brent has tended to privilege religious perpectives, the approach of Oxford historians has been predominantly secular.[19] Whatever the reason, Colin had some resemblance to Morley, of whom it was said that he was magnificently qualified to understand Gladstone in every respect except religion. That two historians should have plumbed the depths of the statesman's character so successfully despite this barrier prompts the reflection that A. B. Cooke and John Vincent may have been right after all (for I had not previously thought so) when they wrote that Gladstone was able to 'move rapidly from one world and atmosphere to another and perhaps incompatible one, forgetting for the time all the other contexts in which he operated'.[20] It suggests that he was religious without being introspective. Perhaps those who were born into early nineteenth-century evangelicalism could never be truly introspective, given that their thoughts were constantly fixed on their Maker, conceived as an external force. Gladstone's diaries are the account of a life spent tremulously in a situation of moral trial, but the only self-examination they contain is of a spiritual nature. Likewise, in his late autobiographical memoranda, Gladstone rationalized his past actions but gave little sense of what his younger self was feeling at the time. It seems certain that Colin (who was introspective without being religious[21]) mainly admired this later Gladstone, whom he saw as

[18] H. C. G. Matthew, 'Edward Bouverie Pusey: From Scholar to Tractarian', *Journal of Theological Studies*, 32 (1981), 101–24; H. C. G. Matthew, 'Noetics, Tractarians, and the Reform of the University of Oxford in the Nineteenth Century', *History of Universities*, 9 (1990), 195–225.

[19] Compare, e.g., Jonathan Parry's emphasis on religious issues in his account of Gladstone's First Government with Colin's emphasis on budgets, trade unions, land, foreign policy, and imperial issues. J. Parry, *The Rise and Fall of Liberal Government in Victorian Britain* (New Haven and London, 1993), 227–73.   [20] Cooke and Vincent, *Governing Passion*, 53.

[21] Which is not to say that he was aggressively anti-religious. He was brought up in the Kirk by his devout mother, who was a great influence on him; he accompanied his wife to church on special occasions; and he loved the cadences of traditional Anglican liturgy.

conventionally religious but no longer religiously obsessed as in earlier years, being far more preoccupied (as Colin was too in an intellectual way) with the scope of government action at home, with fiscal relations between the classes, and with the morality of imperial development.

In 1991 Colin was elected a Fellow of the British Academy, and in the following year he attained his personal chair. His work on the Diaries was now virtually complete, and he was an obvious choice to lead the New Dictionary of National Biography, a project of the Oxford University Press with support from the British Academy.[22] 'Still under fifty' and with 'stamina for the long haul', the Managing Director of the Press is supposed to have said. He asked friends for advice as to whether he should take the position, and some demurred, mainly because they hoped that he would devote himself full-time to the big book he wanted to write on nineteenth-century political culture. Fortunately Colin rarely listened to bad advice, and probably he had known all along that he would accept. He may even have seen this enormous new project as a way of filling the void left by Gladstone. To many people's astonishment he undertook to complete the work within twelve years, a staggeringly *short* haul, but there was one condition: no expense was to be spared in making it as wide-ranging and as comprehensive as possible. As a result the *New DNB* contains more than 50,000 articles by about 10,000 contributors, and is the product of a munificence that is all the more remarkable for the fact that it was achieved against a background of academic parsimony.[23] Colin tackled the project with Gladstonian energy, Cromwellian sternness, and—it must be said—just a touch of Sedbergh, the latter characteristic being manifested in one of his early instructions to the troops. 'Contributors should remember that their views must stand the test of time—a test which may last for much of the next century. The preparation of the *New DNB* puts a generation on its mettle. Let that generation show itself liberal, firm, and just!'

His new role brought him into contact with scholars and others from all over the globe, but the centre of the web was 37A St Giles, and the epicentre was Colin's desk. He read everything which came into the building, and was so in control of operations that he always had time to relax with anyone who dropped in. No visitor could fail to be impressed by the high morale of the more than forty staff, or by the extraordinary speed and efficiency of their operations, yet the atmosphere was always utterly calm, not to say jolly.

By this time his career and reputation had really begun to roll. And, as he became seriously distinguished, so he attained in his professional life that serenity which he had long since known in private. I think he was now very happy indeed. As a good-natured but brisk and efficient chair of committees his managerial

---

[22] It is now officially called *The Oxford Dictionary of National Biography*.
[23] That it should have been delivered on time and on budget in 2004 was a credit to Colin, to its second editor Brian Harrison, and to the dedicated team at 37A St Giles.

services were in constant demand.[24] In addition to performing numerous college and faculty duties, he was a Curator of the Bodleian Library, served on the editorial board of the Oxford Historical Monographs, and was for many years a member (later chairman) of the North Oxford Branch of the Labour Party. In London he acted as a vice-president of the British Academy, vice-president and literary director of the Royal Historical Society, a member of the Royal Historical Manuscripts Commission, and—most 'chuffed-making' of all—a trustee of the National Portrait Gallery. There were also numerous international commitments, of which the Bertrand Russell Project at McMaster University was especially dear to his heart. He took his responsibilities very seriously but wore his esteem lightly, without any pomposity or condescension, not that his family would have allowed him to do otherwise. One letter from the Director of the National Portrait Gallery began, 'Dear Professor Matthew, In the absence of the Prime Minister we would like you to open our new twentieth-century gallery'. It at once became a household joke: 'In the absence of the Prime Minister, we would like *you* to do the washing up'.

Clearly Colin was not just one of the premier historians of his generation but also one of the most public spirited. And, now that his generation is passing over the brow of the hill, it becomes possible to put the nature of that public spirit into some perspective. Many of his Oxford teachers and mentors had distinguished war records. Some had risked their lives and had medals to show for it; others, like Charles Stuart, had experienced the intellectual challenge of sifting intelligence at Bletchley Park and elsewhere. Several (again including Stuart) were highly conscientious tutors, and some excelled in research, but many found it hard not to give off a detumescent impression that the most exciting stage of their lives was past. To compensate, many adopted the role of public intellectuals, contributing to broadcast discussions on the BBC's Home Service and Third Programme, or writing on current affairs in national journals and newspapers. A few on the left were committed ideologically, while many more affected a witty and nihilistic Toryism. The 'Thatcherite' generation that followed Colin's has been similarly concerned to reach out to audiences beyond the academy, though its fascination with conditions in American universities, its involvement in publishing and TV blockbusters, and its general media savvy has little in common with the world of the older public intellectuals. Colin meanwhile belonged to a brief intervening generation which took the welfare state and full-cost student grants for granted, assumed that full academic employment was the norm,[25] and regarded teaching and research almost as service industries. To prepare and examine undergraduates was the prime professional duty, but there were many other obligations such as conducting meticulous scholarship with footnotes full and watertight; adjudicating in

[24] On the subject of briskness, a government minister once gave him an afternoon in which to find an appropriate academic history use for some monies that by the morrow would have to be returned to the Treasury. He found one.
[25] An assumption which was, of course, challenged by reality from the 1970s onwards.

research councils between applicants for funds; preparing scholarly editions like the Gladstone diaries for the benefit of other historians; publishing extensive bibliographies on-line and in print;[26] and, *ne plus ultra*, the *New DNB*. This highly professional approach to history did not necessarily exclude a deep interest in national politics, and it certainly did not do so in Colin's case, yet like most left-leaning academics of his generation he did not choose to address a national audience directly.[27] His preferred platform was the long series of articles entitled 'In Vacuo' that he wrote for the *Oxford Magazine*. Most would pick up on some issue of parochial concern, before ranging out onto themes of general political or ideological significance. Likewise most of his historical writing was informed by—and intended to contribute to—present-day debates. He felt it his civic duty to provide accurate and luminous scholarship, which would in turn have tangible political consequences. This Whiggish (and Scottish Enlightenment) sense of the continuity between past and present was in many ways unfashionable, and was one of the characteristics that gave his work its originality. An instinctive Keynesian, who despised 'the dotty nostrums of the monetarists',[28] he was both puzzled and shocked by the populist success of Thatcherism, not simply because it undermined assumptions about the British people's sense of social fairness, but also because it seemed to contradict decades of organic political development. However, it was not enough simply to deprive the Prime Minister of an honorary degree, or to treat her with snobbish disdain and vituperation as so many academics did. Rather, the challenge she presented had to be faced and worked through. While he was pleased by the success of New Labour, he had little confidence that its 'Third Way' had the legs to meet that challenge.

He was greatly exercised in his later years by the financial obstacles which discouraged domestic students from undertaking research in the humanities, with the result that 'what had once been a largely British representation in each new cohort of research students was increasingly being replaced by a pattern in which overseas research students predominated'.[29] This had nothing to do with prejudice against overseas students—no one could have been more eager to embrace new and different traditions—but unless a nucleus of home-grown students could be maintained, all hope of organic *national* development was lost. A similar dilemma had faced Gladstone, who early on was forced to abandon his ideal of a mono-denominational state in favour of one dedicated to religious pluralism. Viewed superficially it was just the first of his many flip-flops, but then, as Colin reminded us, 'Always with Gladstone, it is in the detail that the clarity and

[26] e.g. the Royal Historical Society Bibliographies, on the managing committee of which Colin served.

[27] A collective abstinence which must have contributed to the Labour Party's surrender of the intellectual high ground. A notable exception was Colin's friend Ross McKibbin, noted for a series of hard-hitting but reflective pieces in the *London Review of Books*.

[28] Colin Matthew, 'In Vacuo', *Oxford Magazine*, 169 (1999), 3–4.

[29] Colin's views as reported by Sir Tony Wrigley in his President's Notes to the British Academy Review, Dec. 1999, www.britac.ac.uk/news/reviews/02–99b/04-president.html.

consistency become apparent'. This comment, from a Gladstone centenary address, was one of his final pronouncements on the statesman, and so has a doubly elegiac quality, especially as, in it, Colin came as close as he ever did to revealing part of his own personal code.

No one in our public life has been so radical and so conservative [as Gladstone], radical when he was a conservative, and conservative when he was a radical, and both running together ... Gladstone's life tells us much about the best that a public figure can achieve in representative government, and in our own Oxford context it shows that people and places can change for the better, however irksome those changes may seem at the time.[30]

Never one to shirk things that irked others, Colin was active in helping the University to meet some of the challenges of recent years. In all such discussions he stood for pragmatism and common sense, and yet he remained at heart an idealist. Fully alive to what he once called 'the charm and the danger of Oxford', he was preoccupied in a wholly Gladstonian way with how such institutions might evolve organically to perform newly required duties, without sacrifice of their fundamental purposes. It was characteristic that, in taking over the *New DNB*, he insisted that it should build on Leslie Stephen's nineteenth-century version. There were to be very many more women, more nationals who spent their lives abroad, more foreigners who contributed to life in Britain, and many more people whose obscurity in life belied their subsequent significance,[31] but equally important was his rule that no one who had appeared in the original should be discarded, not even the humblest Victorian cleric. It was a case of evolution by accretion.

Despite all his public activities he never seemed rushed.[32] Still more impressively he did not allow them to stem the flow of original research.[33] The scope of that research may have been limited thematically to nineteenth- and twentieth-century Britain, but he moved effortlessly between scholarly monographs, seminal articles, and broad synoptic surveys intended for a wide readership,[34] and he was equally at home with political, social, cultural, and intellectual history. One of his

[30] Colin Matthew, 'Gladstone and the University of Oxford', a lecture delivered in Christ Church Hall at the Gladstone Centenary Commemoration, 18 May 1998, and reprinted in the *Christ Church Annual Report* (1998), 61–70.
[31] Often when an unfamiliar name of some dead national cropped up in conversation, Colin would scribble it down for checking to see whether the person merited inclusion in the *New DNB*.
[32] As Peter Ghosh has commented, 'Although, for many, the abiding image of Colin Matthew will be of the scholar and the public man, pondering what might become of Britain in the future, for the parents of south Oxford it will be that of the devotedly loyal husband who would always turn out on weekday evenings for events at St Ebbe's School [where Sue was head teacher], and who, as a special treat, would play the bagpipes at the summer fête'. *Guardian* (2 Nov. 1999).
[33] Except perhaps towards the end. After delivering a characteristically stimulating and original seminar paper on 'Gladstone and O'Connell' in Oct. 1998, he admitted to me that he felt that he was 'running on empty'.
[34] Notable among the latter were his contributions to *The Oxford Illustrated History of Britain*, ed. Kenneth O. Morgan (Oxford, 1984) and *The Nineteenth Century: The British Isles 1815–1901*, ed. Colin Matthew (Oxford, 2000).

secrets was to adopt William Hone's dictum that 'an hour before breakfast is worth two in the rest of the day'. For five or six mornings each week, he would make a point of writing sustained historical prose between 7 and 8, often to music and usually to opera, one consequence of which was that, whenever he attended live performances, he would involuntarily pull out a cheque book or some other scrap of paper and scribble away furiously in the dark. Another secret was not to worry about what other people thought. In this sense he was utterly his own man. He was once asked to address a conference on the following theme: 'Between the Mother and the Other: Sub-Texts of Nationhood'. Quite unabashed, he spoke on 'The Criteria for Inclusion in the *New DNB*'. That last talk understandably became a party piece, but otherwise he rarely repeated himself, either on paper, at the lectern, or in conversation. When talking privately on nineteenth-century matters he liked to ruminate and was not afraid of long pauses. I always felt that we were exploring the margins of our knowledge, or, to cite lines from one of his favourite poems, that we were seeking to uncover an old lost road through the woods. It was an exhilarating journey.

The last time I saw Colin was about three weeks before he died, when he and Sue called on us in Cambridge. He was in his usual high spirits. He had just uncovered some long dead plot in the Oxford University archives—a donnish conspiracy to prevent Professor X from being invited to deliver the Ford Lectures—and he regaled us with it over lunch, accompanying the saga with characteristic snorts and chuckles. Afterwards he insisted on visiting Newnham to check out an oak tree which Gladstone had presented to that college in 1887. It was eventually tracked down and duly photographed from various angles.[35] One could infer from these events that Colin loved trivial gossip and that he had an obsessional interest in anything and everything Gladstonian, but this was only part of the truth. With regard to the Ford Lectures, as always he was keen to trace the story's underlying significance, such as what it said about shifting historical fashions and the structures of power within the faculty. As for tracking down the oak tree, in some ways it illustrated Colin's approach to history very forcibly. He admired R. G. Collingwood, and was aware of the philosopher's belief that Hercule Poirot was a better detective than Sherlock Holmes. Rather than chasing scraps of surviving evidence like footprints and cigarette ends, and vainly 'hoping that something will come of it', the 'scientific historian' should seek to understand the big picture in all its details, however apparently irrelevant to the investigation in hand. Only by seeking to know everything will we know which are the important questions to ask. It is a challenging and to some extent unfashionable prescription, but it gives Colin's work its authorial omniscience, its semblance of control over

---

[35] Photography being a late enthusiasm of Colin's. This was the second tree presented to Newnham by Gladstone, the first having been torn down by a maurauding group of Conservative (male) undergraduates.

narrative and insight into character and motive, qualities he may well have imbibed from the novels of Balzac. Although there was nothing remotely bombastic about his historical writing, it had an almost Victorian self-confidence, and it also projected certain values which can also be called Victorian. Those values can be summed up in his own admonition to contributors to the *New DNB*, when he told them to be 'liberal, firm, and just'. At the risk of making him sound much too solemn, let those three words be his epitaph.[36]

[36] I have been advised by many people in writing this memoir. They include Jamie Bruce-Lockhart, Martin Ceadel, George Garnett, Peter Ghosh, Lawrence Goldman, Elspeth Griffiths, Christopher Heber Percy, Sue Matthew, Ross McKibbin, Andrew Morgan, John Morrill, Jon Parry, Margaret Pelling (to whom especial thanks are due), John Robertson, Michael Thornely, and William St Clair.

3

Colin Matthew: A Memoir

Ross McKibbin

I first met Colin Matthew formally in 1970 at the social history seminar then held at St Antony's College, Oxford, and organized by Tim Mason, Raphael Samuel, and Joaquin Romero Maura. This seminar was to have immense influence on the history of Oxford history and the room was always crowded. The occasion was a paper Tim Mason gave on a Durkheimian approach to the study of Nazism, and neither Colin nor I had arrived early enough to get a seat. We stood at the back of the room. We were both completing our doctorates, Colin on the Liberal Imperialists, myself on the early history of the Labour Party, were both supervised by Pat Thompson and had, in fact, passed each other occasionally coming in and out of Pat Thompson's room at Wadham, but without much more than a nod. Squashed together at the back of the St Antony's seminar room, we could scarcely avoid introducing ourselves, and we did. We met again later that year when Colin went to Christ Church, Oxford, as lecturer in Gladstone studies (in effect, assistant editor of the Gladstone diaries to M. R. D. Foot) and I went as a research lecturer (Junior Research Fellow) in history.

We became close friends quickly and began to talk a lot about our work, and history and politics more generally. We were also both preparing our doctorates for publication. I doubt that I gave Colin much help in the preparation of the *Liberal Imperialists*: he was very expeditious in getting his to the OUP, whereas I took longer in order to have another trawl through the Labour Party archives—then for the first time being professionally catalogued. I was in some ways not very happy with the argument of my thesis, and especially the role of the First World War: what part it played in the rapid growth of the Labour Party after 1918. It was Colin who suggested one way out. I gave him a draft of the conclusion to read and he said there was a problem: it assumed the political framework was the same after 1918 as in 1914. He pointed out, however (something obvious in retrospect), that the Representation of the People Act (1918), which almost trebled the electorate and introduced universal manhood suffrage for the first time, could arguably have been the 'factor' that transformed the fortunes of the Labour Party after 1918, while the absence of universal manhood suffrage inhibited them before 1914. The result was a couple of hasty sentences in the conclusion of *The Evolution of the Labour Party* which did not really fit with the rest of the book.

We had at the same time got into the habit—not being proper academics and having some free time—of deriving innocent pleasure from a game we called McCalmont. The Harvester Press had just published a new edition (1971) of F. H. McCalmont's wonderful *The Parliamentary Poll Book of All Elections, 1832–1918* and Colin and I had each bought a copy. The game consisted of ringing the other up and asking, say, which party won Hythe in 1847. The consequence was that both of us acquired a great deal of apparently useless psephological history. It was a combination of playing McCalmont and Colin's comments on the Representation of the People Act which led to the only piece of historical work we did jointly: an article 'The Franchise Factor in the Rise of the Labour Party', which appeared in the *English Historical Review* in 1976. We had decided that it was worth trying to test the hypothesis that the 1918 Act was the crucial 'factor' in the Labour Party's post-1918 success. Much of the basic research was done by Colin's wife, Sue Curry, who had not yet returned to teaching. It was she who discovered that our first strategy—simply comparing the results in each constituency between 1910 and 1918—would not work since the 1918 redistribution had so changed the boundaries of most (though not all) constituencies that comparing like with like was very difficult. It was also clear that what Colin called the 'figures' were probably beyond us. We, therefore, recruited John Kay, then economics fellow at St John's College and expert in psephology, 'to do something with the figures'. This he did. Although Colin and I were agreed on the basic hypothesis—the significance of the 1918 Act to Labour—we were not altogether agreed as to an important sub-argument: why it was the Labour Party and not the Liberals who benefited from the extension of the franchise. I was not quite certain, but thought it was probably the Liberals' overdependence on Nonconformist institutions. Colin argued that it was more their excessive 'rationality': they depended on a relatively narrow, relatively 'educated' electorate, like the 1910 electorate, whereas the post-1918 was more likely to respond to a 'demagogic' party like the Labour Party. I was never convinced by this: as Philip Williams pointed out to us when the 'Franchise Factor' was presented as a seminar paper, the Liberals were not backward when it came to demagogic catch-cries. None the less, Colin's argument we adopted; partly because I was unsure about an alternative, partly because it undoubtedly fitted the general hypothesis. The 'Franchise Factor' was very influential and generated a large literature. The three of us gained enormous pleasure from writing it and we felt something of the satisfaction that scientists—as we imagined—routinely feel from joint creation. There was a brief discussion as to the order in which our names should appear which produced a characteristic Colin intervention. John Kay cheerfully took third place on the grounds that he had 'only' done the figures. I murmured that the phonebook convention was that

Mc came first. Colin said that might be true but that I had now a permanent job
and he didn't: so Matthew came first.

Colin remained very attached to that article and was reluctant to accept any
criticism of it: I think largely because he was not an established scholar when it
was written and it was an important step on his path to later academic celebrity.
My feeling, however, is that it got Colin into something of an intellectual impasse
which his premature death never allowed him to sort out. He had in the early
1970s developed a view of Liberal political rhetoric as peculiarly 'rational' but this
did not seem to me to cohere with his developing view of Gladstone. I had reread
Max Weber's famous essay 'Politics as a Vocation' shortly after Colin became sole
editor of the Gladstone diaries and was struck by what Weber said about
Gladstone and Lincoln as the prototypes of the demagogic political leader of the
twentieth century. Colin then read the essay and was impressed by the argument.
Although it did not provide a rigid framework for his evolving picture of
Gladstone, Weber's argument was always at least in the background. The attention Colin gave to Gladstone's use of the tools of modern democracy (one of the
most innovative aspects of his work on Gladstone)—particularly the press—was
certainly inspired by Weber. But a 'Weberian' view of Gladstone does not fit easily
into an interpretation of the Liberal Party as peculiarly 'rational'. Colin had
decided that resolving this was something he would do (and had no doubt he
could do) after the publication of the *Oxford Dictionary of National Biography*. He
was, of course, unable to do it.

Working on the franchise and on Gladstone had the paradoxical effect of
making him more 'European'. Colin was not a 'little Englander'—he was not after
all English—but he had a very strong sense of the uniqueness of British institutions, and the unique value of these institutions. He had voted in favour of leaving
the Common Market in the 1975 referendum, and was surprised that I had not.
Some years later he said that 'obviously' he would not vote in favour of leaving
'now'. This change of mind was doubtless partly practical—it is not clear how
Britain could actually leave the EU safely—but it was also partly intellectual. We
had made the 'Franchise Factor' explicitly comparative simply to emphasize just
how undemocratic the British franchise was in comparison with most other 'comparable' countries—including France and Germany. And this suggested a less
attractive aspect of the uniqueness of British institutions. Furthermore, Colin
himself demonstrated, as no previous historian had done, how intellectually and
ideologically embedded in European culture (especially German and Italian)
Gladstone was. Colin was also required to teach late nineteenth- and twentieth-
century European history for the Oxford history syllabus and this again suggested
to him how far Britain was in fact a European state. We had indeed begun to draft
a new special subject for the history school on the fiscal crisis of the European state
*c.*1900–14, which was to include Britain, only to abandon it when we realized it
would probably be too difficult for any undergraduate and would not fit easily
into the awkward division between British and European history which the

Oxford history school then prescribed and for the most part still does. In the various reforms to that school which took place during Colin's membership of the History Faculty—and in many of which he was instrumental—he always argued for the abolition of this division, though with little support. In the university classes for the special subject paper on Church and State in English Society, 1829–1854 (of which he was one of the progenitors) his colleague, John Walsh, was struck by the aplomb with which Colin put English Anglicanism into a wider European context.

I think his view of British institutions as almost uniquely benign was also affected by his attitudes to Thatcherism. During most of the period he was editing the Gladstone diaries Thatcherism was at full flood. Colin was always a man of the left, always a member of the Labour Party, even in the early 1980s when he was out of sympathy with much of what it did, and always politically engaged. That, he thought, was part of the historian's moral duty. He did not believe that Thatcherism was just another form of Conservative politics. It was, by British standards, what he called an 'explosion'. Colin, like many, had a somewhat ambivalent attitude to it. He thought that British institutions, by not reforming themselves in the twentieth century as they had done on the nineteenth, had left themselves open to something like Thatcherism. He was, however, unambiguously hostile to its economic and social policies. And this had an influence on his own historical writing. Although he increasingly interpreted Gladstone as a radical politician of the left, he had decreasing sympathy for Gladstone's prudent finances or the conviction, a nineteenth-century common-place, that the finances of the state were fundamentally no different from the finances of the household. He was thus, like a number of trade union leaders in the 1980s, readier to regard the political institutions and written constitutions of the EC states with favour, not simply because they had more active states and generous welfare systems than Britain, but because their more explicitly democratic institutions encouraged social mutuality, unlike the universal 'truculence' (his word) which is what he thought Thatcherism bequeathed to Britain.

We did not write anything more jointly and to some extent our interests chronologically moved apart. Gladstone pulled Colin further into the nineteenth century while my interests for the most part stayed in the twentieth. Both of us were very fortunate, and Colin particularly so, that Boyd Hilton was a junior research fellow at Christ Church when we came, and although Boyd went to Cambridge in 1974 he had a much more direct influence on Colin's work than I did. I read the introductions to the successive volumes of the Gladstone diaries and most of the entries Colin did for the new *Dictionary of National Biography*— but as an educated lay reader whose function was largely to point out things other readers might not follow. Colin was more important to me than I to him—in two respects. He was, first of all, a very good strategic reader; someone who could pick the heart of the argument. As an example: I had become interested in the success of the Conservative Party in the interwar years—partly as a result of our realization when working on the franchise (very late in the day) that the success of the Conservative Party under mass suffrage also needed explanation. In an essay I argued that the Conservatives had achieved their success largely because they were able to mobilize the 'public', a class (the majority) which stood for the national interest, against the working class, a class (the minority) which stood against the national interest. I was not, in fact, the first to argue this; but certainly argued it more strongly than anyone else. I had originally called the essay 'Class and Conventional Wisdom: The Conservative Party in Interwar Britain'. It was Colin who suggested that it be called (as it was) 'Class and Conventional Wisdom: The Conservative Party and the "Public" in Interwar Britain'. Given the focus of the argument and the way the essay has been read that was absolutely the right title: but it was not one that had occurred to me. Colin read all the essays that were later published as *The Ideologies of Class* (1990) and I could always rely on this kind of pointed structural comments.

Second: he was—in ways which are difficult to describe—both a problem solver and an inspirer. An essential element in the way both of us worked was to talk about what we were doing. Discussions between us (of which, for reasons I have mentioned, I was the principal beneficiary) tended to be unwritten 'drafts' and much of the pleasure which I got from writing history actually came from these discussions—which in the last few years tended to become formalized as coffee on Saturday morning in the King's Arms with our good friend and colleague Martin Ceadel. (It was in the King's Arms that the younger Gladstone's apparent habit of self-flagellation was revealed to the world.) Even the prospect of such a discussion seemed to clarify things. In the 1970s I had written an essay on working-class betting but was aware that somehow the argument was not working. I rang Colin and told him that I was coming to see him, and that the argument had to be settled. As it turned out, the argument fell into place just before I got to his room; but Colin said he would claim the credit anyway. His capacity to inspire was not simply part of a scholarly exchange, though that certainly was very important, but also a result of the way he encouraged people to believe that what they were doing was worth doing, was intellectually significant. When his friend and colleague Peter Ghosh, as a young graduate student, went to talk to Colin about nineteenth-century finance, Colin gave him an offprint of his own *Historical Journal* article on that subject inscribed 'From one Gladstonian financier to a better one'—a charming and generous gesture which was typical. Doing history with him was, in both senses, exciting. And since his death I have found that for myself much of the excitement of writing history has gone.

Colin's eventual success as a historian did not come easily. He did not get first-class honours in his undergraduate degree and was not, I think, even very close. There were perhaps several reasons for this: but one was that to him the writing of history was a kind of moral struggle and struggles do not have easy or quick outcomes. He thought the good historian had to 'suffer'—experience a kind of mental strife—and those who had not 'suffered' were unlikely to be good historians. This meant that his historical processes were ruminative. It was a family joke that Colin would suddenly make a pronouncement on a subject everyone else had abandoned half-an-hour ago. He said that one of the good things about going to the opera was that it gave you an opportunity to think. It also meant that his written work went through several drafts; and the last was often very different from the first. The magisterial style and argument of the Introductions to the successive volumes of the Gladstone diaries came after much 'suffering'.

I had wondered what Colin would do when the publication of the Gladstone diaries was complete. He now had a personal chair in Oxford but was still teaching at St Hugh's College where he had been a tutorial fellow. He probably would have returned to teaching and research without too many difficulties, but that would certainly have been anti-climactic, and he felt this. Furthermore, he now had immense standing in the profession. Gladstone had given him a remarkable mastery of nineteenth-century history: he even became a trustee of the National Portrait Gallery largely as a result of his fine essay on Millais's portraits of Gladstone. He was a Fellow of the British Academy (soon to be its vice-president) and was in demand in many parts of the world. The decision was partly made for him when it was decided to prepare a new edition of the *Dictionary of National Biography* and Colin was asked to be its general editor. Although he sought the advice of friends and colleagues as to whether he should say yes, I think he never seriously thought of saying no. I was one of those who, on balance, felt he should say no; but I much underestimated the scale of the exercise he contemplated. And I underestimated how far his conception of the new dictionary made it proof against objections that a collection of biographies was not how history should now be written. In a sense this is what he had done with the Gladstone diaries: when the diaries themselves began to get thin he fleshed them out with correspondence and an elaborate scholarly apparatus—including the remarkable bibliography of Gladstone's reading. And the introductions became longer and more intellectually ambitious. Colin was undoubtedly aware of the objections that could legitimately be made to the new dictionary.[1] Had he not been so, the dictionary would have had a narrower methodological and historical focus. As it stands, via an extraordinarily catholic definition of biography, the sixty volumes of the new dictionary constitute a whole national history.

Colin got tremendous satisfaction from editing the new dictionary. He had marvellous colleagues who were immensely loyal both to him and the dictionary. Even an outsider visiting the dictionary's offices could sense the exceptionally creative and benevolent atmosphere. Now that the dictionary has been published Colin would still only have been 63, and had previously showed no sign of diminishing intellectual power. The question 'what now'—raised when the Gladstone

---

[1] This was the working title of the project in Colin's lifetime, as distinct from the published title, the *Oxford Dictionary of National Biography*.

diaries neared completion—would have been raised again. He hoped his masterwork—aside from the diaries and the new dictionary—would be a study of nineteenth-century political rhetoric, an attempt to uncover the foundations of Victorian political language. As we talked about it over the years its conception, like the diaries and the new dictionary, grew larger. It was never written; and that is a great loss to us. But not as great a loss as it might have been. Much of the argument had been anticipated in the Introductions to the Gladstone diaries; and indeed in other essays. We thus have a pretty good idea of what the argument would have been. On the other hand, I thought there were, as I have suggested, some intellectual inconsistencies within the argument as it had developed which still needed to be resolved. I also felt that although he had been primarily an intellectual historian, he was as much interested in British institutions and their history. Here, it seemed to me, was where his interests increasingly lay—and, specifically, in why these institutions seemed more adaptable, more open to reform, in the nineteenth than in the twentieth centuries. One of his last published works, in fact, was an essay in the *London Review of Books* on the future of the Anglo-Scottish Union.[2] The real loss, I think, is not the unfinished book on nineteenth-century rhetoric but the incomplete nature of his study of British political institutions.

[2] 'The British Way' (5 March 1998), 27, 30–1.

4

Colin Matthew: A Bibliography

Peter Ghosh and Lawrence Goldman

The list which follows is not complete. It does not note book reviews (though we strongly recommend the review of Harshad C. Patel, *Vanishing Herds*, in the *Oxford Times*, 1973, on the East African elephant); letters to the press apart from *Times* newspapers; videotapes; nor miscellanea such as the indices compiled (with Sue Matthew) for *African Affairs*. It is almost certainly incomplete in its coverage of the many occasional pieces delivered by Colin Matthew across four continents as his public reputation escalated in the 1990s.

AS EDITOR

The Gladstone Diaries, 14 vols. (Oxford, 1968–94): vols. i–ii, covering 1825–39 were edited by M. R. D. Foot.; vols. iii–iv (with M. R. D. Foot),1840–54 (1974); vols. v–vi 1855–68 (1978); vols. vii–viii *The Gladstone Diaries with Cabinet Minutes and Prime Ministerial Correspondence: 1869–1874* (1982) the extended title introduced here was regarded by Colin Matthew as the proper description for the *Diaries*—vol. ix, 1875–80 (1986); vols. x–xi, 1881–6 (1990); vols. xii–xiii 1887–96 (1994); vol. xiv, index (1994).

The Oxford Dictionary of National Biography, 60 vols. (Oxford, 2004). Colin Matthew was succeeded as editor by Brian Harrison. Authored contributions: sole or joint author of 148 original articles; revisor for another 630. Original items include those on Queen Victoria (with Kim Reynolds), Edward VII, George V, Edward VIII, George VI; Gladstone and members of his family; Balfour, Asquith, and Macmillan.

With grateful thanks to a wide range of Colin's friends and colleagues, and to Sue Matthew in particular.

BOOKS

The Liberal Imperialists: The Ideas and Politics of a Post-Gladstonian Elite (Oxford Historical Monographs; Oxford, 1973). The Preface is dated July 1971.

Gladstone 1809–1874 (Oxford, 1988). Chapters 3–9 were based on the Introductions to *The Gladstone Diaries*, iii–viii 'with some alterations and additions to suit'; chapters 1–2 covering Gladstone's early life were new.

(edited with Jane Garnett) *Revival and Religion since 1700 Essays for John Walsh* (London, 1993) Authored contributions: 'Preface' (with Jane Garnett), pp. vii–viii; 'Gladstone, Evangelicalism and "the Engagement" ', 111–26.

Gladstone 1875–1898 (Oxford, 1995). Based on the Introductions to *The Gladstone Diaries*, ix–xiii 'appropriately amended'.

Gladstone 1809–1898 (Oxford, 1997). Brings together the two previous *Gladstone* volumes in one.

(edited) *The Nineteenth Century: The British Isles 1815–1901* (Oxford, 2000). Authored contributions: 'Introduction: The United Kingdom and the Victorian Century, 1815–1901', 1–38; 'Public Life and Politics', 85–133; 'Conclusion: *Fin de siècle*', 293–9.

ARTICLES, ESSAYS, LECTURES

(with R. I. McKibbin and John Kay), 'The Franchise Factor in the Rise of the Labour Party', *English Historical Review*, 91 (1976), 723–52.

'H. H. Asquith's Political Journalism', *Bulletin of the Institute of Historical Research*, 49 (1976), 146–51.

(with R. I. McKibbin and John Kay), 'A Footnote to Dr. Clarke's comment' ['Liberals, Labour and the Franchise'], *English Historical Review*, 92 (1977), 589–90.

'Gladstone, Vaticanism, and the Question of the East', in D. Baker (ed.), *Studies in Church History*, XV (1978), 417–42.

'Disraeli, Gladstone, and the Politics of Mid-Victorian Budgets', *Historical Journal*, 22 (1979), 615–43.

'Edward Bouverie Pusey: From Scholar to Tractarian', *Journal of Theological Studies*, 32 (1981), 101–24.

'The Liberal Age (1851–1914)', in Kenneth O. Morgan (ed.), *The Oxford Illustrated History of Britain* (1984), 463–522. Reprinted as the first half of Matthew and K. O. Morgan, *The Modern Age* (Oxford History of Britain, 5; Oxford, 1992), 1–64; and the second half of Matthew and C. Harvie, *Nineteenth Century Britain: A Very Short Introduction* (Oxford, 2000), 64–144. A synopsis under the same title appeared in *Heritage*, 1/2 (1984), 48–53.

'Rhetoric and Politics in Great Britain, 1860–1950', in P. J. Waller (ed.), *Politics and Social Change in Modern Britain. Essays Presented to A. F. Thompson* (Sussex and New York, 1987), 34–58. First given to a conference on Rhetoric at the Oxford Union, 1973, and then as a Founder's Day Address at St. Deiniol's Hawarden in July 1984. The latter text, which is less worked out than the final version, appeared as 'Politica e retorica in Inghilterra 1860–1930', in P. Pombeni (ed.), *La trasformazione politica nell'Europa liberale* (Bologna, 1986), 267–82. The full text is reprinted in Peter Jagger (ed.), *Gladstone* (1998), 213–34.

'Gladstonian Finance', *History Today* (July 1987), 41–5. Reprinted in G. Marsden (ed.), *Victorian Values* (London, 1990), 111–20.

'Tractarians, Noetics and the Reform of the University of Oxford in the Nineteenth Century', *History of Universities*, 9 (1990), 195–225.

'Hobson, Ruskin and Cobden', in Michael Freeden (ed.), *Reappraising J. A. Hobson* (London, 1990), 11–30.

'Charles Harborne Stuart', in Christ Church, *Annual Report* (1991), 37–41. Address delivered at a memorial service in Christ Church Cathedral, 16 Nov. 1991.

'The New DNB', *History Today* (Sept. 1993), 10–13. The original typescript carries the slightly expanded title: 'The *New DNB*: Its Origins and Purpose'.

'Gladstone and the Church of England', *Lambeth Palace Library Annual Review* (1994), 51–63. In the series of annual lectures to the Friends of Lambeth Palace Library.

'Indexing Gladstone: From 5 × 3" Cards to Computer and Database', *The Indexer*, 19 (1995), 257–64.

'Dictionaries of National Biography', *Voices: The Quarterly Journal of the National Library of Australia*, 5/3 (1995), 16–29. Reprinted I. McCalman *et al.* (eds.), *National Biographies and National Identity: A Critical Approach to Theory and Editorial Practice* (Canberra, 1996), 1–18.

Leslie Stephen and the New Dictionary of National Biography (Cambridge, 1997). The 1995 Leslie Stephen Lecture, delivered in Cambridge.

'The British Way', *London Review of Books* (5 Mar. 1998), 27, 30–1.

'Gladstone's Death and Funeral', *The Historian*, 57 (Apr. 1998), 20–4.

'Gladstone and the University of Oxford' (lecture given at the Gladstone Centenary Commemoration, 18 May 1998), in Christ Church, *Annual Report* (Oxford, 1998), 61–70. Reprinted *Oxford Magazine*, Second Week, Michaelmas Term 1999, 3–6; and in Peter Francis (ed.), *The Grand Old Man* (Hawarden, 2000), 6–15.

'Portraits of Men: Millais and Victorian Public Life', in P. Furnell *et al.* (eds.), *Millais: Portraits* (London, 1999), 139–61.

'The Early History of St. Hugh's and the Row', in Helen Ghosh (ed.), *St. Hugh's College in the Twentieth Century* (Oxford, 2000), 15–24.

'Gladstone, O'Connell and Home Rule', in R. V. Comerford and Enda Delaney (eds.), *National Questions: Reflections on Daniel O'Connell and Contemporary Ireland* (Dublin, 2000), 11–29.

'Lord Blake of Braydeston' [Robert Blake], *Guardian* (23 Sept. 2003), 25. This notice was revised after Colin Matthew's death, but only in the formal sense in which any prepepared obituary needs to be completed at the time of the subject's death.

OTHER PUBLICATIONS

Letter, *The Times* (26 Mar. 1976), 15d (advocating compulsory land purchase of white farms in Rhodesia following the models of Ireland and Kenya).

Letter, *The Times* (7 Dec. 1979), p. 15h (in reply to the duke of Buccleuch, on election techniques at Midlothian, 1880).

(with John Walsh and Brian Harrison), Preface to Brian Heeney, *The Women's Movement in the Church of England 1850–1930* (Oxford, 1988), pp. vii–xi. John Walsh was the principal author of the preface whilst Brian Harrison and Colin Matthew did the bulk of the editorial work on an incomplete draft manuscript. (Personal communication from John Walsh).

P. K. Snow, 'History under Siege', *Oxford Today* 1 (Trinity Term 1989), 15. Colin is one of several historians who supply a paragraph to accompany the main text.

'History without Flowers', *The Times Higher* (26 June 1992), 19. Interview after appointment as editor of the new *DNB*.

Letter, *TLS* (15 Jan. 1993), 17c (announcing the commencement of work on the new *DNB*; inviting contributions and suggestions).

'Introduction', to Peter Bell, *Victorian Biography: A Checklist of Contemporary Biographies of British Men and Women Dying between 1851 and 1901* (Edinburgh, 1993), pp. [iii–iv].

'Liberal with the Ink', *THES* (12 May 1995), 16 (on the completed *Gladstone Diaries*).

New Dictionary of National Biography, newsletters 1–4 (1995–8). Published in December of each year, these four-page 'letters' each contain an opening statement by the editor.

Letter, *TLS* (16 Aug. 1996), 17d (inviting contributions and suggestions to the new *DNB* for 'Literature since 1780').

Brief Lives: Twentieth-Century Pen Portraits from the Dictionary of National Biography, selected by Colin Matthew (Oxford, 1997), with a preface, pp. v–vi.

'From the Grave: W. E. Gladstone as Told to H. C. G. Matthew', *New Statesman* (5 Dec. 1997), 48.

'Supplementary Introduction', to Agatha Ramm (ed.), *The Gladstone–Granville Correspondence [1868–1876]* (Cambridge, 1998), pp. v–viii.

'The Country Life Interview', *Country Life*, 193 (4 Feb. 1999), 44.

ARTICLES AND REVIEWS IN THE *OXFORD MAGAZINE*

The *Oxford Magazine* is a journal distributed among 'senior' (permanent resident) members of the University of Oxford, and is concerned with matters of interest to the university community in general. Of venerable antiquity, it was relaunched in 1985 by Colin's friend and neighbour Prof. Jim Reed and Colin quickly began to write for it. In 1987 he started a regular column, 'In Vacuo', which would appear at the end of each vacation. ('Noughth week' is actually the week when the under-graduate term starts; 'Second week' is the second of the eight weeks of term which follow, etc.) These reflective pieces are of interest for a number of reasons. They were often about history, usually trying to relate matters of current university interest to events, issues and parallel situations in the past. They also included Matthew's own thoughts on Oxford and its reform during a period of consistent upheaval and change for the university. And on occasion the essays gave glimpses of Colin's own political views on subjects such as the union of the component nations of the United Kingdom; the European Union; and government education policy. These pieces were well known and frequently discussed in Oxford. However, they are unquestionably of wider relevance and are listed here because of their importance in understanding the intellectual biography of a leading scholar in late twentieth-century Britain.

'All Smiles Again', second Week, Trinity Term 1986, 14–15: a review of Samuel Smiles, *Self-Help*, with an introduction by the Conservative minister Sir Keith Joseph.

'In Vacuo', noughth week, Michaelmas Term 1987, 5–6: on the white papers published in advance of the 1988 Education Bill.

'In Vacuo', noughth week, Hilary Term 1988, 3–4: the 1988 Education Bill.

'In Vacuo', noughth week, Trinity Term 1988, 5: the 1988 Education Bill.

'In Vacuo', noughth week, Michaelmas Term 1988, 5: on the University Funding Council and the assessment of university research.

'In Vacuo', noughth week, Hilary Term 1989, 4: Oxford's Regius professorial chairs.

'In Vacuo', noughth week, Trinity Term 1989, 6: the preparations in Paris for the bicentenary of the Revolution.

'In Vacuo', noughth week, Michaelmas Term 1989, 5–6: on library funding in Oxford; the national curriculum for history in schools.

'In Vacuo', noughth week, Hilary Term 1990, 3–4: reflections on Oxford over the preceding decade.

'In Vacuo', noughth week, Trinity Term 1990, 6: the death of Tim Mason, esteemed by Colin as the most brilliant historian of his own generation.

'In Vacuo', noughth week, Michaelmas Term 1990, 5: on the international crisis over Kuwait; and the publication of the CD-ROM of the British Library Catalogue of Printed Book to 1975.

'In Vacuo', noughth week, Hilary Term 1991, 4–5: the need for greater support for arts research in Oxford.

'In Vacuo', noughth week, Trinity Term 1991, 3: the historical context of the Conservative government's poll tax.

'In Vacuo', noughth week, Michaelmas Term 1991, 2: on the disintegration of the Soviet Union through American eyes.

'In Vacuo', noughth week, Hilary Term 1992, 5: on differential college endowment in Oxford.

'Bodley Matters', eighth week, Hilary Term 1992, 6–7: issues relating to the Bodleian Library.

'In Vacuo', noughth week, Trinity Term 1992, 2: on constitutional relations with the European Union, and those between the nations of the United Kingdom.

'In Vacuo', noughth week, Michaelmas Term 1992, 2: on Britain's relations with the European Union.

'In Vacuo', noughth week, Trinity Term, 1993, 3: on the institutional and historical foundations of economic development.

'Slow Movement', eighth week, Trinity Term 1993, 32–3: review of 'The Oxford Ramble: Songs and Tunes of Oxford', CD by Magpie Lane.

'In Vacuo', noughth week, Michaelmas Term 1993, 4: on changes to the city of Oxford's landscape and buildings.

'In Vacuo', noughth week, Hilary Term 1994, 1–2: a review of the university's relations with government since 1979.

'In Vacuo', noughth week, Trinity Term 1994, 3: reflections on Britain and Europe after a visit to Andalusia.

'In Vacuo', noughth week, Michaelmas Term 1994, 3: on the effects of new electronic resources for arts research.

'Northwards', noughth week, Hilary Term 1995, 1–2: on issues before the North Commission of Enquiry into the structure of the University of Oxford.

'In Vacuo', noughth week, Trinity Term 1995, 2: the introduction of titular professorships and readerships.

'In Vacuo', noughth week, Michaelmas Term 1995, 2–3: the report of the Committee of Enquiry into Oxford's libraries chaired by Sir Keith Thomas.

'In Vacuo', noughth week, Hilary Term 1996, 3: on elections to university bodies in Oxford.

'In Vacuo', noughth week, Trinity Term 1996, 4: on the growth of regulation and the need for expertise in government in light of concerns regarding the safety of foods.

'In Vacuo', noughth week, Michaelmas Term 1996, 3–4: on the aims of the University of Oxford.

''Ere We Go?', noughth week, Hilary Term 1997, 1–2: on the assessment of research and the comparison of universities with soccer teams.

'In Vacuo', noughth week, Trinity Term 1997, 2–3: in anticipation of the 1997 election.

'In Vacuo', noughth week, Michaelmas Term 1997, 7: on monarchy and its reform in the wake of the death of Diana, Princess of Wales.

'In Vacuo', noughth week, Hilary Term 1998, 4–5: a suggested scheme for the sharing of college resources in Oxford by arranging colleges into seven or eight groups.

'End of the Ancient Constitution', Hilary Term 1998, 8–9: a review of the report of the North Commission on the structure of the university.

'In Vacuo', noughth week, Trinity Term 1998, 3: the Belfast Agreement of April 1998 on the future of Northern Ireland.

'All Together Now?', noughth week, Trinity Term 1999, 1–3: on the suggested changes to Oxford's governance and structure made by the North Commission, set in historical context.

'In Vacuo', noughth week, Michaelmas Term 1999, 3–4: historical reflections on the end of the millennium.

MANUSCRIPTS[1]

'Post Gladstonian Liberalism, 1894–1905' (1968): this essay won the Gladstone Memorial Essay Prize in 1968. Typescript, ii + 75 pp.

' "Liberal Imperialists" 1895–1905' (June 1970) Bodleian MS. D. Phil. d.5056, pp. xvi + 427 + 36.

'Saving Time in the Bodleian': a short typescript distributed to new graduate students in modern history at Oxford from 1978 on.

Speech on receiving an honorary degree at McMaster University, 1 June 1999, typescript, i + 6 pp.

MICROFILM

The Papers of William Ewart Gladstone (Research Publications, 1994–8)

TV AND SOUND ARCHIVES

[ITV discussion programme], March–April 1974. This listing is vague but not entirely speculative. What can be said is that volumes iii and iv of the *Gladstone*

---

[1] Colin Matthew kept the considerable academic correspondence he accumulated in the process of editing the Gladstone Diaries, and these papers will be found on deposit at the Bodleian and at the Oxford University Press Archive. A handlist is supplied by the National Archives HMC Report on 'The Historical and Editorial Papers of Henry Colin Gray Matthew (1941–1999)', 5 June 2003. His numerous and seminal statements on the *New DNB* are at present part of the current working stock of that publication, and in any case not a personal archive.

Diaries were published on 13 March 1974 [OUP archives]; that both the text and Colin's Introduction contained the first ever public discussion of Gladstone's sexual anxieties and physical masochism; and that shortly after publication he (and the entire Mathew family) went to a London ITV studio, presumably Thames TV, to appear on a discussion about Gladstone, the Victorians, and sex, where the other participants included Barbara Cartland and John Braine. (Colin came away from this with a high estimation of Barbara Cartland's good sense and competence.) Neither the current ITV archives nor the British Film Institute contain a specific listing of Colin's name relevant to the occasion. However, so far as he himself was concerned, this was much the most memorable of his TV appearances, and for this reason an imperfect listing seems better than none at all.

Tonight [BBC], 22 June 1978, interview with Donald McCormick. C:LCA1950X. 'MATTHEW: talks abt Gladstone's relationships with women from all walks of life, as outlined in "The Gladstone Diaries" recently published.'

A. N. Wilson, *Eminent Victorians*, 5: 'W. E. Gladstone' [BBC], 16 Oct. 1989. NMRL837B. Colin Matthew was one of several contributors.

Nightwaves [BBC Radio 3], 30 Nov. 1995, discussion chaired by Val Cunningham. BDSPROG 1079652. 'As editors of the Dictionary of National Biography work towards a new edition, Valentine Cunningham investigates who's in, who's out and who makes the decisions.'

II

5

Gladstone and Peel

Peter Ghosh

One of the less observed fruits of the decline of the Liberal Party in the 1920s lay in its consequences for the writing of English history. With Liberal decline the classical nineteenth-century party structure and its constitutional agenda were definitively laid to rest. When this happened the historical environment became altogether more congenial for a subject who was not a Liberal, and who had previously been consigned to oblivion on account of his evident inability to adapt to Victorian party politics. In a word, it became possible through the work of George Kitson Clark and later Norman Gash to promote Sir Robert Peel to a central position in early Victorian history as the founder of modern Conservatism—a position which remains well established today in academic life, though it never struck any political root.[1] Of course, scholarship has moved on since then, but Peel's most recent interpreters have accepted the mould cast by their forebears in that they, too, have succumbed to the lure of trying to portray him as a figure central to his era, who represented a gateway to modernity.[2] It is true that the interwar generation saw Peel as the founder of modern Conservatism, whereas today we are asked to view him in mirror image, as the pioneer of 'Gladstonian Liberalism'; what was important for Kitson Clark was, precisely, *Peel and the Conservative*

This paper derives from a personal dialogue with Colin Matthew on the subjects of Gladstone, finance, and politics, going back to 1979, and was originally composed in the summer of 1999 with him in mind. I am indebted to Jon Parry and Ross McKibbin for reading and commenting on it.

[1] N. Gash, 'The Founder of Modern Conservatism' (1970), *Pillars of Government* (London, 1986), 153.

[2] Above all Boyd Hilton, 'Peel: A Re-appraisal', *Historical Journal*, 22 (1979), 612–14; *The Age of Atonement* (Oxford, 1988), esp. chs. 6, 9; 'The Ripening of Robert Peel,' in M. Bentley (ed.), *Public and Private Doctrine* (Cambridge, 1993), 63–84. It should be stressed that Dr Hilton sees Peel only as a gateway to 'Gladstonian Liberalism'; but this has been enough to supply a launch pad for more thoroughgoing modernist teleologies (n. 4 below). So far as Peel personally is concerned, I differ from Dr Hilton in my initial assumption: I suppose that ordinarily Peel meant what he said. Since he has (so far) offered no treatment of any major episode in Peel's life after 1829, I may be allowed here to minute this difference in purely general terms.

Party... 1832–1841,[3] his heyday as a party leader rather than his tenure of office, whereas today the focus is on Peelite political economy as the precursor of varieties of 'liberal' political economy in the late twentieth century;[4] but the ingenuous assumption that there is a teleology between Peelite politics and modernity is the same as before.

In what follows I shall suggest, first, that such views are erroneous; that 'Peel' as we regard him today is an invention and a bubble; that in reality, though undeniably important because of his high official standing, he was profoundly unrepresentative of British politics after 1829, primarily because he was not a party politician.[5] Peel's real interest lies in his individuality and oddity. My second and major concern is with Peel's reception after his death in 1850. One of the most fundamental assumptions underlying our understanding of nineteenth-century politics, although it has never been explicitly worked out, is that Peel remained a central presence in later Victorian England; in particular, that he was a decisive influence on W. E. Gladstone and on the Liberal Party he led between 1867 and 1894.[6] Instead of being represented as a bilateral constitutional and party contest, nineteenth-century politics is more conveniently construed along the single axis supplied by 'Peel–Gladstone'. But if Peel had become an anomaly in his own day, it is unlikely that he should have had any more relevance to succeeding generations, since they, like their predecessors, also believed in a party system as the best means of organizing public opinion in the country and of representing it in Parliament. In fact, after the brief moment of his funeral obsequies, significant reference to Peel largely vanished from considered reflection by later Victorians on their

---

[3] Published in 1929; the subtitle 'A Study in Party Politics' repeats the point. Anna Ramsay's *Peel* (London, 1928) appeared at the same time but is an unrelated work. Miss Ramsay (b. 1894) had reached adulthood by 1914, whereas Kitson Clark (b. 1900) had not. Her work was thus that of a different generation, and as a tariff reformer she had little specific affinity with Peel except in a shared hostility to party. Like the later Victorian biographies of Peel, the book derived from an editorial commission and not authorial *pietas*. By contrast Prof. Gash (b. 1912), like Kitson Clark, was culturally formed between the wars and he identified the centrality of the Peel Papers at this time.

[4] For Peel as the 'reflationary' architect of the mid-Victorian boom, David Eastwood, 'The Age of Uncertainty', *Transactions of the Royal Historical Society*, 6th ser. 8 (1998), 114. On Gladstone as pre-Keynesian, Colin Matthew, 'Disraeli, Gladstone and the Politics of Mid-Victorian Budgets', *Historical Journal*, 22 (1979), 615, cf. idem, *Gladstone 1875–98* (Oxford, 1995), 389.

[5] Peel's difficulty with party has long been recognized, but commitment to his personal importance has caused authors to override the difficulty. For two different and frankly contradictory solutions to this interpretative impasse, both by Norman Gash: 'Peel and the Party System 1830–50', *TRHS* 5th ser. 1 (1951), 47–69; *Reaction and Reconstruction in English Politics 1832–52* (Oxford, 1964), 130–56.

[6] Besides Hilton (n. 2 above) see Colin Matthew, *Gladstone 1809–74* (Oxford, 1986), esp. chs. 3, 5; 'Politics of Mid-Victorian Budgets', 615–43. Matthew's assumptions have been imbibed by a variety of authors: e.g. Richard Shannon, *Gladstone 1809–65* (London 1982), 239, 281, 383 (the 1999 Penguin edn. of this work carries the subtitle, *Peel's Inheritor*); *Gladstone: Heroic Minister 1865–1898* (1999), pp. xii–xvii etc.; Martin Daunton, *Trusting Leviathan* (Cambridge, 2001), 177–8, etc. Jonathan Parry, *The Rise and Fall of Liberal Government in Victorian Britain* (London 1993) is an exception: his view of party and political structure is very different to mine, but his treatment of Peel and Gladstone has something in common with that offered here. Eric Evans's treatment of 'Gladstone's Relationship with Peel' is careful, hard-headed empiricism, but it seeks only to trace that relationship as a

immediate predecessors.[7] To be sure, he was not forgotten by those who knew him well; but they failed to make him a focus of discussion. Because of his oddity, his memory and legacy were not viable resources, and the strangulation of discourse about Peel is observable in a number of contexts: in the failure of his literary trustees, Cardwell and Stanhope, and of their instruments, Goldwin Smith and C. S. Parker, to produce any acceptable portrait of the man for later consumption; in the puzzlement with which he was written off by minor biographers such as Francis Montague and James Thursfield, who tackled him only because the systematic logic of publishers' series demanded it;[8] and above all in his tacit abandonment by Gladstone, the most famous and most articulate, but also the most unusual and least representative, member of Peel's ministerial staff.

I

The radical source of Peel's oddity was his defective grasp of the traditional historical and constitutionalist culture of England. Sometimes referred to as the 'Whig' interpretation of history, this was the near-universal possession of the landed elite and its professional dependants.[9] In this culture the subordination of the executive to Parliament, the absolute priority of constitutional topics relative to material and financial ones, and a long history of party difference defined in these terms were all taken for granted. By Peel they were not. This stemmed from distinct, but mutually reinforcing sources. First, he was the son of a manufacturer, a man who stood apart from the traditional personnel and assumptions of English government. The sons of Parsley Peel (Peel's grandfather) all displayed 'a strong likeness', being 'men of business, reserved and shy, nourishing a sort of defensive pride and lacking all parade, shrinking, perhaps too much, from public service and public notice, and it may be too much devoted to the calm joy of a private station'.[10] Peel's

biographical fact during Peel's lifetime and little more: in D. Bebbington and R. Swift (eds.), *Gladstone Centenary Essays* (Liverpool, 2000), 29–56.

[7] It is commonly believed that Donald Read's *Peel and the Victorians* (Oxford, 1987) showed how 'the cult of Peel became deeply…rooted in middle- and working-class opinion' after his death: Anthony Howe, *Free Trade and Liberal England* (Oxford, 1997), 6; compare, however, Read, 304–12.

[8] F. C. Montague's *Peel* (London, 1888) was part of Lloyd Sanders's 'The Statesmen Series', J. R. Thursfield's (London, 1891) was one of 'Twelve English Statesmen'. Justin McCarthy's *Sir Robert Peel* (London, 1891), one of 'The Prime Ministers of Queen Victoria', was hardly an independent or even biographical work.

[9] For the sense in which 'Whig' history can be equated with an English national view of history: H. Butterfield, *The Englishman and his History* (Cambridge, 1944).

[10] Sir Lawrence Peel, *A Sketch of the Life and Character of Sir Robert Peel* (London, 1860), 21. Lawrence Peel (b. 1799) was a Macaulayan Whig: metropolitan, consciously 'middle class', a lawyer with Macaulay on the Northern circuit in the later 1820s, a Pittite, and an instructed believer in English historical and constitutional culture. He was also Robert Peel's first cousin. As such he had a clear grasp of the position of 'the Bury house' within the extended family, and his was the only biography of Peel written with family knowledge, and which sited him accordingly. It is, then, uniquely valuable, and has been neglected only on the hagiographical principle that little can be learnt from an

retirement into semi-private and politically individual life between 1818 and 1822—an unthinkable step for a party politician—was an innocuous, but significant symptom of this cult of privacy, and distinctly foreshadowed his opting for a similarly individual station as an 'independent public man' between November 1830 and December 1834, or his enjoyment of 'the coolness and impartiality of a spectator' after 1846.[11] This may sound paradoxical for a man who was otherwise so long in office, but, as he explained 'over and over again',[12] he saw office in the same light: as a personal service rendered at the expense of private comfort. This, too, was a mark of his social oddity. Though confessedly a 'public man', a member of the ministerial elite, he continued to identify with his father's class and to approve of its 'apolitical' concentration on wealth-getting—its avoidance of 'the contentions of party' and the 'dissensions of the Legislature'.[13] Thus office was a matter of individual sacrifice, not social obligation. For most MPs, however, the position was just the reverse: they were members of a hereditary governing class who expected to serve in politics, and Peel's preoccupation with his personal comfort, achievements, and sacrifices registered only as 'idle egotism'.[14]

Sir Robert Peel Sr, an autocratic paternalist who ruled over 15,000 men without effective check, sought to 'manufacture' his eldest son in his own image. But though undeniably successful in passing on the habits of command and rule, he also reared his boy with the avowed aim of transcending his own origins and placing him in the governing elite. Peel Jr, felt the trauma of this lonely path long before he encountered the public ridicule to which it exposed him. He 'shrank from strange approach'; 'he would walk a mile round rather than encounter the rude jests of the Bury lads'; whilst his father's 'overtraining' was such that the family remarked upon the son's unhealthy resemblance to 'the tenderness of a forced plant'.[15] These anxieties were compounded by a simple fact: Peel, Sr, was one of the richest men in England. When he died in 1830 his personalty alone was in region of £1,700,000. It was then the highest amount ever sworn, and he was nothing less than the Bill Gates of his day.[16] In consequence a central motif underlying the son's public career was a perpetual search for security for the family property, of which his share was far the largest. Thus his handling of

---

author of Whig politics—though in fact this made him a most discriminating observer of Peel's conduct until 1840 (when he left England for India).

[11] Respectively: *Hansard*, 3 ser. [15]. 370 (7 Feb. 1833), (hereafter *H*); Peel to Prince Leopold 27 Jan. 1847, pr. C. S. Parker, *Sir Robert Peel: From his Private Papers* (1891–9), iii. 479. hereafter *Peel*.

[12] *H* [83]. 92 (22 Jan. 1846); see the whole passage, 90–4.

[13] Respectively: Address to the Electors of Tamworth [18 Dec 1834], pr. *Memoirs by Sir Robert Peel* ed. Lord Mahon and E. Cardwell (1856–7) hereafter *Memoirs*, ii. 59; *Speech of Sir Robert Peel... at the Town Hall, Tamworth, September 4th, 1835* (1835), 8; cf. *H* [15].385–6 (8 Feb. 1833).

[14] *Speech of Sir Robert Peel... at the Merchant Tailors' Hall, 11th May, 1835* (1835), 5. This is a central statement on these issues, see esp. 4–10, 16–18.

[15] Lawrence Peel, *Sketch*, 41, 48–9; cf. 86–7 on public ridicule. Our ignorance regarding Peel's father, even allowing for Peel Jr's destruction of his papers—as a defence of privacy?—is simply disgraceful.

[16] Obituary, *Gentleman's Magazine*, 100 (1830), 556–8, the most accessible brief account of Peel Sr.

the 'constitution' focused on hierarchy, authority, and property—'the maintenance of order and the cause of good government'. 'Liberty', the primary preoccupation of any ordinary politician, was a mere derivative of property: it was the liberty of 'the people...to apply themselves to the honest pursuits of industry', and so to amass property like his father.[17] It was this focus on property which produced Peel's distinctive merger of questions involving political institutions with those of criminality, thereby diminishing the former and elevating the latter. From his first rise to eminence in 1817 until his death in 1850, he was always seeking to allay his 'apprehensions' about perceived threats to the conjoint hierarchy of government and property. Yet given the indefinite expanse of the latter it was evident that any lasting relief for these fears was unattainable.[18]

Property was by no means the only source of Peel's anxieties. Lacking a secure, that is, socially grounded culture,[19] he was especially vulnerable to the anxieties of the wartime era in which he grew up. Of course, this had affected English politics generally but still, given their entrenched libertarian and consensual traditions, it was necessarily ephemeral. For Peel, however, it was perpetuated by a lifelong involvement with Irish politics dating from 1812, and by a marriage which encapsulated both these influences—to the daughter of General Floyd, formerly second–in–command of the 30,000 strong British army in Ireland. These experiences added fuel to Peel's sense of the fragility and artificiality of social order and imbued him with an extraordinary and exaggerated belief in executive power as the shield of that order, above all in its capacity as a policing agency. In fact neither Peel nor Wellington, another freak of the war and his close partner in office after 1828, were ministerial politicians in the traditional mould of the Pitts or Canning. Peel depreciated the younger Pitt, and displayed instead a nostalgia for the era of Walpole or the Pelhams, where ministers could more easily be detached from any party or popular context.[20] Pittite politics may have been formally opposed to the Foxite creed of party, but still they assumed that any defence of government could only be undertaken as part of the defence of traditional institutions as a whole: they thus relied on a basis of popular, and implicitly partisan,

---

[17] Respectively: Address to the Electors of Tamworth, [18 Dec. 1834], pr. *Memoirs* ii. 59; *Speech of Sir Robert Peel... at the Town Hall, Tamworth, on September 4th, 1835*, 7–8.

[18] On 'securities' and 'apprehensions' e.g. *H* 1st ser. [36]. 410–1 (9 May 1817), 3 ser., *H* [15]. 386 (7 Feb. 1833); on criminality, political 'institutions', and property generally, *H* N s. [14]. 1214–39 (9 Mar. 1826). Peel was twice reproved for hysteria regarding his own property at Drayton: in 1831 by Croker and in 1842 by his wife, Parker, *Peel* ii. 190–1, Gash, *Sir Robert Peel* (1972), 345–6.

[19] Peel's Oxford double first, his bookishness, and art collecting were all examples of the pride of an individual intellect (all willingly funded by his father). In politics this led to the extraordinary claim that his private judgement was the criterion of safe institutional reform (to the bishop of Durham, 23 Feb. 1835, *Memoirs*, ii. 78) and to a faith in (his own) 'abstract reasoning' and 'logical deductions' in all spheres (to Croker 3 Aug. 1842, *The Croker Papers* (1884), ii. 382–4). The result of this earnest endeavour was an unstable eclecticism. Peel's 'burglary of intellect' has been a commonplace since Disraeli, but serious analysis of this cultural oddity is wanting.

[20] Peel to Croker, 20 Sept. 1841, *The Croker Papers*, ii. 407; Lawrence Peel, *Sketch*, 52; Gash, *Sir Robert Peel*, 693.

support. The strategy of Pitt in dissolving a hostile Parliament in 1784 and (putatively) of Canning in 1827 was not simply monarchist or ministerialist; it was demotic as well. Peel, however, believed neither in party nor in popular politics. One of the historical enthusiasms of this learned autodidact was an admiration for Strafford—another autocratic improver educated by Irish experience. Like him 'he thought that when once you went into a measure of a despotic character, it was well to err if at all on the side of sufficiency'.[21] Alternatively, he was 'the English Metternich', the authentic reactionary with 'a foreign *tournure de phrases*' who evinced a compulsive and un-English fascination for the French Revolution.[22] The point at which his counter-revolutionary and Irish culture fused was in an equally un-English admiration for Burke.[23] Like Burke, but unlike almost all Englishmen, Peel could see no difference between the ancient constitution of England and the *Ancien Régime* of France. Since he placed no reliance on the 'constitution' as the guardian of liberty and totem of social and political consensus, the threat of a French-style collapse was ever-present:

Do not believe that the bloody miscreants, who chased each other in rapid succession from the slippery heights of power to the scaffold, were monsters peculiar to France; that the Dantons, and the Marats, and the Robespierres, were *lusus naturae*, which other times and other countries can never engender. No, these men were the foul, but legitimate spawn of circumstances. Their murders and their crimes were not the mere wanton gratification of an original, inherent, super-natural thirst for blood. They were the necessary instruments for getting and maintaining power—the arts of self-defence in the time of anarchy. And if you consent to unloose the bonds of authority in a society constituted like ours, you will have the same consequences, the same men, and the same crimes, here as in France.

"The scum will gather, when the nation boils."[24]

---

[21] 20 Jan. 1838, *à propos* Canada: W. E. Gladstone, *Autobiographical Memoranda 1832–45* ed. J. Brooke and M. Sorensen (1972), 92. On Strafford, Peel to Croker, 19 Nov. 1831, *Croker Papers*, ii. 139.

[22] *The Diary of Frances, Lady Shelley*, ed. R. Edgcumbe (1912–13), Jan 1819, ii. 17, 21. Note in the same vein Peel's 'glowing eulogium upon the genius of Napoleon...as a ruler who understood thoroughly, and could animate the mind of the people whom he ruled'—a foretaste of 1846 in 1814: Lawrence Peel, *Sketch*, 61. For Peel's special collections of books on Ireland and the French Revolution—Ireland being the one part of the UK which palpably did not function along English, constitutional lines—Gash, *Sir Robert Peel*, 691.

[23] Peel's study of Burke goes back to 1817 at least, *H* 1st ser. [36]. 415 (9 May), cf. Parker, *Peel*, i. 289, and probably derived from Croker, a kinsman of Burke. Contrary to a widely received opinion, Burke did not enter the pantheon of Conservative or 'English' thinkers until after 1900, by which time the oddity and ferocity of his constitutionalism were easily overlooked.

[24] At Glasgow, 13 Jan. 1837: *A Correct Report of the Speeches delivered by Sir Robert Peel...at Glasgow* (1837), 90–1, cf. *Speech...at the Town Hall, Tamworth, September 4th, 1835* (1835) 5–8. The quotation derives from Dryden's *Don Sebastian* (1689): 'Away ye scum, That shall rise upmost when the nation boils;...' I quote from the edition Peel is most likely to have read: *The Works of John Dryden; Now First Collected* (London, 1808) ed. Walter Scott, vii. 409; for a modern text and location, see *The Works of John Dryden* (Berkeley, 1956–2000), xv, Act IV. iii. 353–4. As a symbolic choice of an author and text to represent a profound alienation from the classical English political culture epitomized by the Revolution of 1688, this could hardly be improved upon.

Consistently with this, he abhorred any appeal to the judgement of electoral or 'public opinion'. He did not deny that 'public opinion' existed, but by it he meant only an irrational frictional element, the impure alloy of 'public feeling and impression' which must, regrettably, be set alongside the 'reason' and 'strict argument' of the minister, with his vastly superior sources of information.[25] Throughout his career his 'great object' was 'to keep out of view all topics calculated to disturb the public mind'—Protestantism before 1829, Reform in 1831, or distress in 1841–2.[26] When Peel insinuated in 1845–6 that the retention of the Corn Laws posed a 'serious danger' to the aristocracy and to English institutions, and that this supplied his primary justification for 'adjusting [those laws] in the time of tranquillity', it was an authentic symptom of a Burkean or Metternichian paranoia of revolution—and one which, like any paranoia, was not to be laid to rest by such a minor fiscal adjustment as that of 1846.[27] Thus in 1846 all consideration of economic advantage was secondary in Peel's mind. *If* Corn Law repeal was to be considered in that light, then the measure was not his at all, but was owing to those who argued '*à priori*, without the benefit of experience', in a word, to 'RICHARD COBDEN'.[28] But for Peel statistics of crime, and in particular 'crimes connected with sedition, discontent and disaffection to the Government', were 'more important considerations than those of either trade or revenue'.[29] It cannot be stressed too strongly that Corn Law repeal was a pre-emptive high political act, and not a necessary measure; it was based not on fact, but on Peel's 'apprehensions' as to the possible consequences of a future food scarcity in England.[30] Once we strip away the *tournure de phrases*, the real point at issue was that, if he did not act pre-emptively as minister, the Corn Laws might become a topic of debate by the adult equivalent of 'the Bury lads', 'the vulgar 10*l.* householder

---

[25] Cabinet memo. 29 Nov. 1845: *Memoirs* ii. 186; see also ii. 166. In opposition Peel went so far as to accept 'an intelligent deliberate public opinion', i.e. one which had nothing to do with 'cheap newspapers', and coincided with the private judgement of members of the House of Lords: e.g. at Glasgow, 13 Jan. 1837, *Correct Report*, 72, 84.

[26] Peel to Arbuthnot 29 Sept. 1841, pr. *The Correspondence of Charles Arbuthnot*, ed. A. Aspinall (1941); cf. *H* N S. [20]. 86 (5 Feb. 1829) on Protestants, and *H* [9]. 539–45 (17 Dec. 1831) on Reform.

[27] Peel to Lord Justice Clerk, Aug. 1846, *The Private Letters of Sir Robert Peel*, ed. G. Peel (1920), 280–1. In 1847 Peel was to be found reading the socialist writings of Louis Blanc, preaching to Frenchmen on the revolutionary dangers they faced (!), and asking 'Is the sun of England herself steadfast?' Comte de Jarnac, 'Sir Robert Peel, d'après souvenirs personnels et des papiers inédits', *Revue des Deux Mondes* 3 Période, (1874) Tom IV, 284–323, here 313–14. Hearing this last remark, Jarnac commented, 'I then understood for the first time both the precipitate abolition of the corn laws and the dominant strain in the particular genius of Sir Robert Peel.' The same counter–revolutionary affinity informs Guizot's *Sir Robert Peel* (Paris, 1856).

[28] Respectively *H* [83]. 70 (22 Jan. 1846), [87]. 1054 (29 June 1846). In January tribute to doctrinaire Free Trade was properly positioned within the overall frame of Peel's argument and was uncontroversial; in June it was apparently unconditional and much resented by Whigs and Peelites. The inference, common to all Peelites, was that Peel spoke out in a bid, paralleling that of Cobden, to smash party structures: Gladstone, *Autobiographical Memoranda 1845–66*, ed. J. Brooke and M. Sorensen (1978), 19–20, 23.   [29] *H* [83]. 73–4 (22 Jan. 1846), cf. [87]. 1048 (29 June 1846).

[30] *Memoirs*, ii. 189, 311, 313–14.

class—the class just above physical force', at the 1847 election.[31] The Corn Laws were repealed in 1846 because Peel could not stomach the free expression of opinion within the unmanaged electoral system created by 1832. It was not the Chartists even but 'a reformed constituency' which he viewed as the threat to England's 'ancient monarchy' and 'proud aristocracy'—so deeply was he entrapped in the mentality of reaction, and so far removed from the ordinary assumptions of English politics.[32]

It was no accident then that the thoroughly anti-parliamentary Carlyle of *Latter-Day Pamphlets* (1850) should identify Peel as the one man who might come, 'Hercules-like', to 'expurgate Downing Street', nor that Peel should previously have responded to his overtures in 1846 with real sympathy.[33] Peel, as much as Carlyle, believed in one-man rule, in Robinocracy, and this was notoriously how he governed. As Gladstone put it, 'Your government has not been carried on by a Cabinet, but by the heads of departments each in communication with you.'[34] Peel himself was equally direct: the Queen's Minister was beholden only to the personal favour of the monarch, whilst it was 'the privilege of power' for him to rule solely 'according to his sense of the public good'.[35] In this way his 'middle-class' belief in purely personal service to the state became allied to a view of monarchical prerogative befitting the eighteenth century. The limit of his adaptation to any post-Walpolean constitutional structure, was, first, to place the repression of discontent, formerly over-reliant on extraordinary and politically vulnerable measures such as the suspension of habeas corpus, on a more regular, statutory, and bureaucratic basis: such is the common thread linking his Irish and English police reforms and his law reforms.[36] A second brainchild of the

[31] Peel to Croker, 15 Apr. 1831, *Croker Papers* ii. 114: strikingly Peel is quoting Orator Hunt. On the need to avoid electoral discussion: *Memoirs*, ii. 164, 166. Dissolution was acceptable only as an ultimate 'sacrifice', in the wholly unlikely case that Corn Law repeal failed to pass the Commons. The threat of revolution due to a retained protection would then constitute 'a greater evil' than that arising from electoral discussion: *H* [87]. 1042–3 (29 June 1846).

[32] *H* [83]. 94 (22 Jan. 1846), cf. [87]. 1053 (29 June 1846). Chartism was effectively dead by 1846, a year of high prosperity; but even when it had been a threat, Peel and Graham looked to Cobden, the 'middle-class' epitome of the new constituency, as its source, reflecting a consistent preoccupation since 1830: *Speech . . . at Merchant Tailors' Hall, 11th May, 1835* (1835), 14; Gash, *Sir Robert Peel*, 353–7. It is clear then that Peel's famous eulogy of Cobden in 1846 *was* ambiguous, something confirmed by his rejection of Cobden's political overtures at the same time, though it was not so perceived by contemporaries.

[33] *Latter-Day Pamphlets* (Centenary edn., 1898), 91, 121, cf. 169–71 (1, 15 Apr. 1850). Peel's letter to Carlyle of 22 June 1846 thanking him for *Cromwell's Letters* indicates a knowledge of Carlyle's work going beyond 'mere courtesy', most obviously of Carlyle's *French Revolution* (1837): J. A. Froude, *Thomas Carlyle: A History of his Life in London* (London, 1884), i. 376–7, cf. J. Seigel, 'Carlyle and Peel', *Victorian Studies*, 26 (1982–3), 181–95.

[34] 13 July 1846, pr. *Autobiographical Memoranda 1845–66*, 29, cf. 26 Feb. 1842 (reporting Graham), 14 Aug. 1845, pr *Autobiographical Memoranda 1832–45*, 172, 280. Peel 'assented' to this judgement, and at no point upheld that principle of Cabinet collegiality which was an original pillar of government based on party.   [35] *H* [83]. 92–3 (22 Jan. 1846).

[36] *H* N S. [17]. 411 (1 May 1827). Gladstone was typically English (and anti–Peelite) in his hostility to state control of the Metropolitian Police: *The Diary of Sir Edward Walter Hamilton* (Oxford, 1972), ed. D. W. R. Bahlman, 31 Mar. – 24 May 1883 *passim*; hereafter *Hamilton Diary (I)*.

eighteen-teens had to wait longer for its enactment: the attempt to buttress political stability by payment of a fiscal Danegeld, imposing a property tax in order 'to take off... taxes on consumption'.[37] Simple repression would be supplemented by that executive finessing of the perceived threat of physical force, which formed a principal motif of the tax and tariff policy of the 1840s. (It also veiled an identification of the national interest with that of cotton textiles fully as ingenuous as that of his father, a Pittite free trader.) However, the roots of his policy in the fever of counter-revolution remain clearly in view, and at no point did Peel recede from a coercive and manipulative understanding of the populace. They, he supposed, could only be moved by the bleak materialism of 'physical enjoyment', restrained by the checks of police and law, or anaesthetized by 'the feelings of habitual reverence'.[38] He was not devoid of compassion, but he could see no way to make compassion prevail over fear, when confronted by the 'innumerable millions of human beings [who] are inevitably doomed to an existence of perpetual labour, absolute ignorance, and suffering as irremediable as it is undeserved'.[39] Nothing could be further removed from the confident assumption of the traditional, landed elite, that social hierarchy was the unforced product of a centuries-old community of ideas or sentiment.[40]

On many, but by no means all, occasions, Peel's legislative and administrative acts were recognized as technically appropriate. However, this did not equip him to function as a politician in post-war Britain. What set him apart from Ultras, Canningites, Whigs, and Liberals alike was an inability to come to terms with the resurgence of party politics in peacetime. In this sense, Peel's predicament after 1832 was no different from that of the oldest and most intellectually sympathetic of his political friends, J. W. Croker;[41] and his experiences within Parliament are a forcible commentary on Croker's decision to abjure it after the Reform Act. Having long been on the lookout for democratic and subversive strains in English society, 1832 appeared to confirm Peel's *idée fixe* and was easy enough to

[37] Peel in *The Journal of Mrs Arbuthnot*, ed. F. Bamford (London, 1950), 12 Mar. 1830. There is no record of him speaking thus before 1830, but the idea was freely canvassed within the ministry in 1819, and it would be surprising if he was unaware of it: Boyd Hilton, *Corn, Cash, Commerce* (Oxford, 1977), 82.

[38] Respectively: *H* [83]. 95 (22 Jan. 1846); [9]. 545 (17 Dec. 1831); cf. Peel at Glasgow 13 Jan. 1837 on society as a 'machine', *Correct Report*, 59– 60.

[39] Conversation of 1847, in Jarnac, 'Sir Robert Peel', *Revue des Deux Mondes*, 4 (1874), 314. This was the obverse of the sentimental peroration in the Commons of 29 June 1846 on 'those whose lot it is to labour': *H* [87]. 1054– 5.

[40] For a later example of this traditional confidence, W. E. Gladstone, 'The County Franchise, and Mr Lowe thereon' (1877), repr. *Gleanings of Past Years* (1879–80), i. 131–70.

[41] Both men were parvenus, who abjured what they held to be a naïve appeal to constitutional prescription in favour of a more modern yet robust outlook adequate to the challenge posed by 1789. However, neither was an original thinker, capable of such an ideological reconstruction—an indirect testimony to the hegemonic power of constitutionalism. Such were the bases of an 'affectionate' friendship which lasted from 1812 (if not before, see *The Croker Papers*, i. 46) until 1846. See, however, Peel's comment in 1834 on their divergence regarding the Reformed parliament: *Memoirs*, ii. 60.

assimilate. But by the same logic he was clear that he owed the new political settlement no more than a verbal acceptance, and that otherwise he should continue to act as before. Such was the meaning of the Tamworth Manifesto of 1834, with its refusal to apostatize from 'the principles on which I have heretofore acted' and its commitment to a depoliticized, executively led, and frankly marginal institutional reform of the kind practised by ministries since 1815.[42] Yet this was whistling in the dark. Party was becoming an all-embracing modality from which there was no escape.[43] It comprised at least three major elements: a politics physically *organized* around party both in Westminster and the constituencies; the acceptance of party as the principal formal expression of public *opinion*; and the definition of significant political contest in terms of a distinctively party *agenda*, centred discursively and legislatively on the reform or defence of 'the constitution', as distinct from the halfway house implied by Peelite administrative rectification. (Regrettably only the first and most mechanical of these features has received much serious study from modern historians.[44]) Given the primacy of party and its foundation in the free representation of opinion, it was impossible for someone who was principally concerned to sustain and promote executive government at a nascent Whitehall to make a significant political input, except as a wrecker—and party wrecking was notoriously what Peel did over Catholic Emancipation and the Corn Laws.

But given the primacy of party, his actions were bound to incur penalties. The effect of party betrayal in 1829 was to disable Peel as an opponent of Parliamentary Reform in 1832—and it must be stressed that failure in 1832 rather than 'success' in 1846 was the central episode of his career. Regardless of the cosmetic exercise performed at Tamworth, by Peel's own, Burkean estimate 1832 was a political 'revolution';[45] or as we might say, the single most radical act of constitutional reform in modern British history, which among many changes annihilated the power of the executive to manage elections[46]—a retrenchment of far greater consequence than that extremely modest, compensatory growth of the

---

[42] *Memoirs*, ii. 61. The Manifesto was anticipated by Peel's speech of 7 Feb. 1833, where in a related case of wishful thinking, he prophesied the decline of party as a result of 1832: *H* [15]. 384–6. For pre-1832 anticipations: e.g. *H* N s. [17]. 411 (1 May 1827); [9]. 545 (17 Dec. 1831). Note that 'Parliamentary reform', the effective disfranchisement of corrupt boroughs, began with Shoreham in 1770.

[43] By the election of 1837 the London papers could at once classify all MPs as Liberal or Conservative with only 2% of 'doubtful' attributions: *Lord Melbourne's House of Commons. Elected in July and August 1837* (1837), repr. from the *Spectator* (19 Aug. 1837): cf. Gash, *Reaction and Reconstruction*, 165 n. 3, Parry, *Rise and Fall*, 167.

[44] Jon Parry has gone so far as to demote the dialectic of party in favour of the unitary construct he calls 'Liberal Government', so tending to abolish post-1846 Conservatism altogether: *The Rise and Fall of Liberal Government in Victorian Britain.* For an alternative deconstruction of party in terms of the short–term interests of individual high politicians, Angus Hawkins, *Parliament, Party and the Art of Politics in Britain, 1855–9* (1987), 1–21, cf. idem: *British Party Politics 1852–86* (1998).

[45] *H* [9]. 543–4. Norman Gash, the originator of the (still tenacious) view that the Reform Act made no essential difference to 'the political scene', has never explained the discrepancy between his judgement and that of Peel: *Politics in the Age of Peel* (1953), p. x, *Sir Robert Peel*, 11.

[46] Peel to Arbuthnot 8 Nov. 183 [9], *Peel*, ii. 368; cf. Gash, *Politics in the Age of Peel*, chs. 12–14; R. Pares, *King George III and the Politicians* (Oxford, 1953), 196–8.

centralized, state bureaucracy in the century after 1800, which was so great an object for Peel.[47] Party betrayal in 1846 meant the end of Peel's career as an active politician, even while he gratified his pique on passing his bills over and above 'the mischievous energies of the House of Commons'.[48] He had, it is true, seriously disrupted orthodox party structures inside Parliament by his actions, but he could not erase them, and still less so out of doors. As a result even his appetite for rule was exhausted and his early death was a real release—both for him and for his increasingly reluctant 'Peelite' followers. With it the last prominent attachment of British politics to the siege mentality of war and counter-revolution was severed.

II

Was it the case, none the less, that after his death the example of this eccentric and unreformed politician supplied the principal legacy of earlier to later nineteenth-century British politics? The obvious test of such an idea lies in the attitude of W. E. Gladstone: the outstanding *rhetor* of the Liberal Party after *c.*1860 but also an original Peelite, who had served under Peel both in 1834–5 and in 1841–6. These external facts of his biography offer an opening for the supposition of modern historians that Peel was the precursor not merely of Gladstone but of 'Gladstonian Liberalism' from the 1860s—though the term with its embedded assumption of Gladstone's ideological centrality to a 'liberal*ism*' is yet another modern construction.[49] From this follows the major proposition: that the

---

[47] For a recent view of 'state formation' in Britain, David Eastwood, *Making Public Policy in Nineteenth Century Britain* (Swansea, 1998). As Prof. Eastwood rightly notes, what really distinguished England was 'representative centralism', i.e. integration via parliamentary consensus rather than by bureaucracy: 21.

[48] Peel to Prince Albert n.d. [1847] cit. Gash, *Sir Robert Peel*, 673 cf. Peel to Hardinge, 4 July 1846, pr. Parker, *Peel*, iii. 471; *H* N s. [17]. 407 (1 May 1827).

[49] The term 'Gladstonian', as a party description, only came into common use in 1886 with the Home Rule split. The first author to posit that Gladstone was central to 'Liberalism', rather than an excrescence, was D. A. Hamer, *Liberal Politics in the Age of Gladstone and Rosebery* (1972); contrast the traditional view of J. L. Hammond and M. R. D. Foot, *Gladstone and Liberalism* (1952), 1–5. Colin Matthew then moved beyond Hamer in suggesting that Gladstone's centrality was not merely personal but ideological: *The Gladstone Diaries*, iii, xlii (Oxford, 1974), hereafter *Gladstone Diaries*; *Gladstone 1875–98* (Oxford, 1995), 307. However, this idea goes back in fact to his Gladstone Memorial Prize Essay of 1968, revealingly entitled 'Post Gladstonian Liberalism, 1894–1905' (TS, in the possession of Sue Matthew), 1–21 (though the earlier, parallel invocation of *Disraelian Conservatism* by Paul Smith in 1966 may also be noted as a product of the same mentality). Hence the rise of the modern shorthand 'Gladstonian liberalism' which is now commonplace: e.g. Hilton, 'Peel: A Re–appraisal', 614; Eugenio Biagini, *Liberty, Retrenchment and Reform* (Cambridge, 1992), index s.v. 'Liberalism, Gladstonian'. For the true contemporary understanding of this phrase, see the pamphlet written before the 1885 election by one George Brooks, a 'Christian Radical', entitled *Gladstonian Liberalism: In Idea and in Fact* (London, 1885). The title is so unlikely that the author has to explain it (p. viii), but its meaning remains conventional, since it is all to do with personality and nothing to do with intellectual or ideological principle. 'The great Liberal party has no creed but Gladstoneism', and when Gladstone retires 'Liberals will learn that it is impossible to rely upon one man, however great, instead of relying upon vital and lofty principles' (p. ix).

trajectory of Victorian liberalism—and implicitly of British politics as a whole—
runs from Peel to Gladstone, and not via the path of a continuous Liberal tradition based on the commitment to 'Civil and religious liberty' from the 1780s
onwards. It is an extraordinary denigration of party and its libertarian and constitutional concerns in favour either of canonically elevated personality or else of
(lower case) 'liberalism' as an ideology of modernity floating free of party,[50] and
may be traced back to the belief, pioneered by Toynbee and the Hammonds, that
the master key to the understanding of nineteenth-century politics lies, just as it
did for most of the twentieth century, in the economy. Hence the emphasis
today on the study of political economy, and the identification of Gladstone with
'fiscal liberalism', defined above all as the liberalism of free trade.[51]

These assumptions may be examined through scrutiny of Gladstone's relationship with Peel. This will illustrate that, regardless of high personal veneration,
Gladstone always maintained an intellectual detachment from Peel, because his
conceptions of politics, of party, and public opinion were radically different;
further that Peel's memory was unusable as a political resource, because Peel was
an executive, not a party, politician. Gladstone had been forcibly and, as he admitted, somewhat unwillingly educated by Peel as to the significance of financial
reform and of good legislative practice; but he really was—or rather he knew that,
despite holding a sophisticated and obviously eccentric set of ideas about political
institutions, he *had* to be—'a party man' from his very first entry into politics.[52]
Party was the necessary channel to effective action in the political world; the fact
that he had considerable difficulty in deciding *which* party would best serve his
purposes only enhances the force of this recognition. (There are obvious parallels
with Disraeli here.) But whatever his doubts, the agenda which primarily moved
him were always religious, and later libertarian. As such he was inseparably
attached to some, at least, of the constitutional issues, which lay at the heart of the
Victorian party agenda: if not so much to Parliamentary Reform, then certainly to
the Church of England and the Union with Ireland. His interest in matters fiscal
and economic was never more than secondary and if ever he appeared to enjoy the
subject, this was precisely because there was less at stake for him in an area which
did not touch on political institutions and was thus intrinsically bipartisan.[53]

It was, however, financial politics which supplied the direct link between
Gladstone and Peel, and Gladstone's prominence as Chancellor of the Exchequer

---

[50] Cf. Colin Matthew's deliberately loose conception of a 'British party of progress, whether
Liberal or Labour': *The Liberal Imperialists* (Oxford, 1973), p. x.

[51] Matthew, *Gladstone 1809–74* (Oxford, 1986), 172, cf. 75, 105, 135. The academic ancestry of
this expansive conception of free trade would include J. Gallagher and R. Robinson, 'The imperialism of Free Trade', *Economic History Review*, 6 (1953–4), 1–15.

[52] Note introducing a volume of 'Secret Political Memoranda', 1833–43, 26 Apr. 1836:
Autobiographical Memoranda 1832–45, 67. See also the emphatic declarations of 9 May 1841, 17
June 1844 (at the expense of Peel and Graham on the Sugar question): ibid., 135–7, 263–4.

[53] For an introductory conspectus: W. E. Gladstone, *Autobiographica*, ed. J. Brooke and
M. Sorensen (London, 1971), 39–65; *Autobiographical Memoranda 1832–45*, 158–61, 196–201,
228–49, 254–5, 265–79.

under Aberdeen and Palmerston would have been unthinkable without his having first served at the Board of Trade under Peel. In this sense the mantle of Peel was his for the taking: but he never chose to assume it. There were some specifically financial reasons for this. Unlike Peel, Gladstone believed that abolition of the income tax and not its preservation would best preserve social hierarchy, even if he accepted its temporary utility as an instrument of fiscal reform. Of course, the period of Peel's ministry was the period of its application to such reform and offered no evidence as to the sincerity of his alleged desire to abolish the tax thereafter. But by 1848 Gladstone supposed that Peel was prepared 'to tolerate every kind of financial error' simply to maintain the Whig ministry in power, and this included its tendency to allow income tax to slide into perpetuity—hardly an example to cherish for the future.[54] Thus his great 1853 budget statement (where income tax was the central subject) made just two, brief references to Peel: one, a purely factual statement noting the reintroduction of income tax in 1842; another, to indicate that Peel's doctrine of imposing income tax on foreigners was mistaken. The only financier to receive an encomium on this occasion was the Younger Pitt. Gladstone went out of his way to quote Mallet du Pan's description of Pitt's speech proposing the introduction of income tax in 1798 as 'a complete course of public economy; a work, and one of the finest works, upon practical and theoretical finance, that ever distinguished the pen of a philosopher and statesman'.[55] But then the Pittite tax, unlike the Peelite one, had been truly extraordinary, and it had been safely abolished.

The same year (1854) the Crimean War triggered a revolution in a previously stable government expenditure, which rose by 25 per cent in the seven years to 1860.[56] In Gladstone's eyes this created a *tabula rasa*, and his reaction was to launch a now legendary and extreme crusade to restore the essential stability of pre-war government expenditure, regardless of economic and fiscal growth, and regardless of the political inconvenience to the Liberal Party—something painfully evident in his quarrel with those *echt* Peelites Cardwell and Goschen in January 1874,[57] which led to an electoral collapse. But on economy too

[54] Memorandum, 12 Dec. 1848 pr. *Autobiographical Memoranda 1845–66*, 38 cf. Sidney Buxton, *Finance and Politics., An Historical Study. 1783–1885* (1888), i. 90–5. For Peel's record on the income tax, S. H. Northcote, *Twenty Years of Financial Policy* (1862), esp. 27–32. Peel to Arbuthnot, 16 Feb. 1830, also shows his sympathy for the imperatives behind income tax differentiation—the basis for all plans to render the tax permanent in the late 1840s and early 1850s: *Correspondence of Charles Arbuthnot*, 124. Martin Daunton's assumption of a seamless fiscal continuity between 'Peel and Gladstone' must be pronounced a mirage, at least so far as Peel and Gladstone are concerned: *Trusting Leviathan*, 85, 104, 149, etc.

[55] W. E. Gladstone, *The Financial Statements of 1853 and 1860 to 1865* (London, 1865) hereafter *FS*: 1853. 15; cf. 14–16, 32–3, 66 on Pitt; 18, 38 on Peel.

[56] On a constant accounting basis, estimated ordinary government expenditure (the politically sensitive measure) was £56.1m for 1853–4 and £70.1m for 1860–1: Northcote, *Twenty Years of Financial Policy*, 237–9, 387; Buxton, *Finance and Politics*, ii. 336.

[57] Cardwell's connection with Peel is well known. Goschen had no direct connection, and made no use of Peel's name. However, he was a university Liberal, a close friend of C. S. Parker, and was

Gladstone could find no Peelite precedents.[58] Peel's views were those of a man brought up in the wars against France, views clearly expressed within Gladstone's official lifetime by his sanctioning a substantial expansion in both army and navy expenditure in 1846, in response to French naval competition—a most un-Gladstonian course of action, when we compare *his* responses to the naval scares of 1859–60 or 1884–5.[59] Indeed one of the cloud of arguments advanced by Peel in favour of pre-emptive Corn Law repeal in November 1845 was to present it as a political sweetener, offsetting this enhanced defence expenditure.[60]

Still, none of these differences touched the question of free trade, and if ever Peel were to supply a traditionary resource for his successors, here was the occasion for it. But though there were no overt obstacles to making Peel the object of some sort of hagiography regarding 1846, this did not happen. Gladstone's budget statements in 1860 and 1861 were both great symbolic occasions, which celebrated the Cobden treaty and the 'winding up' of 'the controversy with regard to Protection'; but in neither was there any mention, let alone celebration, of Peel. The only historical names mentioned were Huskisson and Pitt, and, as in 1853, only the latter received real praise. We know from his private ruminations that Gladstone discerned in Peel a financial and a ministerial descent from Pitt,[61] but this only sharpens the fact of his public silence. To explain it, we need to consider not only the legacy of Peel, but those of Pitt and Cobden also.

Gladstone's use of the Younger Pitt was not just limited to the income tax. No political legacy could be founded on the restricted basis of a single issue, a fortiori that supplied by an extra-constitutional topic. A first link to Pitt, now too easily forgotten, lay in the fact that, until he became a decided opponent of the radical reform of Parliament in March 1831, the young Gladstone was, like his father,

linked thereby to Cardwell and the inner circle of the guardians of the Peelite heritage. Above all, he was typically Peelite in his hostility to party—a central clue to the later vagaries of his political career: A. R. D. Elliot, *The Life of Lord Goschen* (1911), i. 25– 6, 67–76.

[58] For public expression of these views: e.g. 3 *Hansard* [164]. 995–1006 (20 Feb. 1857); *FS* 1860; 14–22; 1861, 31–7, 60–1, 73–5, 1862, 57–62; 1863: 3– 9, 78– 81, etc. When Gladstone looked for an instance of pre–Crimean parsimony, his most frequent allusion was to the Wellington ministry of 1828–30, exploiting the statistical fact of a post–1815 low in expenditure and also the identity of the Premier: e.g. *FS* 1864, 58. An obvious difficulty in Colin Matthew's treatment of Gladstonian finance is that he has so little to say about this crusade over expenditure: implicitly it was negligible, except as an assertion of Treasury control over the civil service: *Gladstone 1809–74* (1984), 111. His assumptions have been carried to a conclusion by Martin Daunton, who seeks to write the history of 'the Gladstonian fiscal state' without reference to expenditure: *Trusting Leviathan*, xi. The GOM would not have been amused.

[59] Parker, *Peel*, iii. 399–412. The 'Gladstonian' at this point was Aberdeen, who wanted to resign over the issue of increased naval expenditure, an episode which clearly foreshadows Gladstone's deep affinity with Aberdeen over foreign and defence policy in the 1850s. Note too the strong military and naval tradition of the Peel family, evidenced by Peel's younger brother General Jonathan Peel, and his favourite son, Capt. William Peel VC (cf. *DNB*).There was nothing in the Gladstone family like this.   [60] 'Cabinet memorandum, November 29' 1845, *Memoirs*, ii. 193–4.

[61] On the financial descent from Pitt, see 'Party. As it was and As it is' (1855), hereafter 'Party'. Add. MS. 44745, 186, 219; cf. *Autobiographical Memoranda 1845–1866*, 29.

an ardent Canningite or Pittite. This, very broadly, was the institutional stance he reverted to after the breakdown in the 1840s of the politico-religious system elaborated *The State in its Relations with the Church* (1838). A second was that, whereas (as we shall see) the memory of Peel was simply nihilistic in respect of party, that of Pitt was benignly catholic: he could as easily be construed the parent of Whigs as of Tories, and so amply covered the ambiguity of Gladstone's own position in the 1850s and early 1860s, as he hovered between the two.[62] However, this same ambiguity also made the Pittite legacy over-complicated for most contemporaries, whose party loyalties were so much more straightforward. When the lineal head of Pittite Whiggism, the 3rd Marquis of Lansdowne, and the glittering recipients of his patronage—Macaulay as much as the 14th Earl of Derby—died out in the decade 1859–69, the claims of ambiguity and historical refinement fell away, and in the next generation Pitt was colonized as a Tory, pure and simple.[63] By the same token, Gladstone ceased to make any significant use of him after this time.

If and when free trade was celebrated as one of the foundations of mid- and later Victorian Britain, it was celebrated not as a Peelite or Pittite, but as a Cobdenite achievement.[64] This was no doubt a predictable position for ordinary Liberals to adopt after 1859, when Bright and Cobden became more or less reconciled to the two-party system, but Gladstone's case was far from ordinary. Of course Peel himself had given a remarkable impetus to Cobden's future fame when he stated in June 1846 'that the name which ought to be chiefly associated with the success of [Corn Law repeal] is the name of RICHARD COBDEN'.[65] Gladstone, like many of Peel's supporters, was shocked by this: 'All that he said was true, but he did not say the whole truth: and the effect of the whole was therefore untrue.' Peel's statement was true, given the evident fact that Cobden had proposed and Peel had opposed a doctrinaire free trade between *c*.1837 and 1845. However, as Gladstone knew full well, Peel's conversion to a dogmatic free trade had been 'belated' because it was primarily determined by a concern for social stability and not by enthusiasm for the truths of political economy *per se*.[66] Yet Cobden had fomented precisely that subversive class hostility which most appalled Peel, having 'throughout argued the corn question on the principle of holding up the landholders of England to the people as plunderers'. For Peel to acknowledge him as

---

[62] *FS* 1860; 32, 36–7; cf *FS* 1862; 25, where he again referred to Pitt as 'that greatest of all our Peace-Ministers'.

[63] Macaulay d. 1859; Lansdowne d. 1863; Derby d. 1869. For Whiggish and moderate Tory versions of Pitt *c*.1860, consider Macaulay, Lawrence Peel (above n.10), and Lord Mahon, Peel's trustee, who sought to account for the transformation of his Stanhope ancestors from 18th-century Whigs into moderate 19th-century Tories, in his *History of England from the Peace of Utrecht to the Peace of Versailles* (1836–53) and its continuation, the *Life of Pitt* (1861–2). For the later, whole–hogging Tory appropriation of Pitt, T. E. Kebbel, *The History of Toryism* (London, 1886).

[64] For a detailed demonstration, Tony Howe, *Free Trade and Liberal England* (Oxford, 1997).

[65] *H* [87]. 1054 (29 June 1846).

[66] 'Party' (1855) Add. MS 44745, fos. 181, 189b–190.

the architect of a reform proposed for quite opposite reasons was thus 'most improper and practically untrue'.[67] So strongly did Gladstone feel that he attempted publicly to rewrite Peel's declaration in November 1852. The Derbyite party had formally renounced protection in the summer election of that year, and the vast majority in Parliament was now prepared to bury the hatchet and vote for the principle of free trade, without reference to past controversy. Such was the gist of the moderate resolution proposed to Parliament by Palmerston. By contrast the doctrinaire free traders, especially C. P. Villiers and Cobden, refused to accept this, and insisted in effect that the Tory rump acknowledge its error in opposing Peel in 1846. This was too much for Gladstone. He lamented 'the extraordinary prolongation of the contest which we are now closing' and wished, so far as he honestly could, to promote that reunification of the Tory Party, which Peel's 1846 declaration had been designed to prevent. As a result he attached strict conditions to any eulogy of Cobden, admitting only that the benefits of free trade were 'in no small part at any rate due to labours in which he [Cobden] has borne so promin-ent a share'. In a further denial of his old leader he also claimed, contrary to all probability, that in voting against Villiers and Cobden, the Peelites were 'taking the course which would have been the course of Sir Robert Peel himself'.[68]

Over the next decade, Gladstone and Cobden would discover many points of sympathy on foreign policy, armaments expenditure, and the Anglo-French trade treaty of 1860. Yet they never became intimate. Gladstone would continue to declare that even on arms and foreign policy he was no Cobdenite;[69] and at the root of this distance lay his suspicion of the doctrinaire mentality which had led Cobden into the fundamental heterodoxy of querying the legitimacy of English social hierarchy, and of the landed elite at its apex. None the less, at Cobden's death in 1865 Gladstone prophesied that 'Cobden's name is great: & will be greater.'[70] Certainly, he helped fulfil this prophecy. When free trade came under the challenge of the McKinley Tariff in 1890, his use of Cobden's name was comprehensive, whilst that of Peel had almost disappeared. Corn Law repeal, he pronounced, 'was the work of Mr Richard Cobden entirely; and when Sir Robert Peel, at the close of his Ministry, made that remarkable acknowledgement in 1846 that the great tri-umph that had been achieved was due not to a political party but to Richard Cobden, he placed on record a simple fact, which coming generations will acknowledge'.[71] On the face of it, this was a complete reversal of his position in

---

[67] Memo, 9 July 1846, *Autobiographical Memoranda 1845–66*, 19; cf *Gladstone Diaries*, 30 June 1846.   [68] *H* [123]. 680–5, here 683, 681, 684 (26 Nov. 1852) cf. 695–6.

[69] Gladstone to Palmerston, 2 May 1862, *Palmerston and Gladstone* (1928), ed. P. Guedalla, 212–13.   [70] *Gladstone Diaries*, 7 Apr. 1865.

[71] Gladstone at Prince's Hall, Piccadilly, *The Times* (13 May 1890), 13a. See also *Autobiographica*, 73: 'It was Cobden who really set the argument [for free trade] on its legs: and it is futile to compare any other man with him as the father of our system of Free Trade.' (1894). For an earlier statement, *FS* 1860, 56; here Gladstone accepts Cobden as the author of 1846, without making any explicit contrast with Peel.

the decade after 1846: the element of truth in Peel's eulogy of Cobden was no longer offset in his mind by a greater untruth. Why was this?

One possible suggestion is that Gladstone changed his tune when he joined the Liberals in 1859, but this is unlikely. As the above quotation shows, he could never, either in his Peelite or Liberal days, regard the fiscal and extra-constitutional issue of free trade as constituting a party dividing line.[72] No; the reason why Gladstone ceased to defend Peel against himself, and why he yielded up the free trade legacy unreservedly to Cobden, lay not in his relatively distant relationships with Cobden or the Liberal Party, but in a close, but far more ambiguous relationship with Peel. Unqualified acceptance of Cobden was in fact the result of his abandonment of the attempt publicly to sustain Peel's memory. This had occurred in 1855 with the collapse of the Aberdeen coalition, an event which prompted the definitive formulation of Gladstone's views on Peel and the Peelite legacy in the manuscript entitled 'Party. As it was and As it is'.[73] Originally intended for publication as an anonymous pamphlet, this is not merely a lengthy piece (*c.*25,000 words) but a most important one. As is suggested by one of its subtitles—'A Sketch of the Political History of Twenty Years', from 1835 to 1855—it is a complete survey of Gladstone's career as a 'Peelite', and quite the most significant of his autobiographical writings with the exception of *A Chapter of Autobiography* (1868).[74] The latter surely deserves its priority as a comment on Gladstone's ideal and theoretical concern with the role of the Church in politics; but the earlier piece casts a flood of light on the sphere of 'Parliamentary Government' (another subtitle). Of course, Gladstone always placed secular politics below the Church, but still it was his work in this 'lower' sphere which constituted his historical distinction—both in his day and in ours.

As we have seen, even in the 1830s Gladstone had recognized the inescapable nature of party. Although he had (after persuasion) supported Corn Law repeal in 1846—which might look like an anti-party move—he had been a persistent critic of Peel's determination 'to individualise himself' at the expense of party action from July 1846 onwards, going so far as to describe it in 1849 as 'false and in the

---

[72] See e.g. the treatment of free trade in his speech at Manchester, 18 July 1865, the first he gave 'unmuzzled': *Speeches and Addresses delivered at the Election of 1865* (1865), 2–4. Also the 'Address . . . to the Electors of the Southern Division of the County of Lancashire', 18 July 1865, ibid., 38–9; *H* [183]. 151 (27 Apr. 1866). For pre-1859 denials of the relevance of fiscal and financial issues to party, 'Party' (1855), Add. MS 44745, fos. 175–7, 'The Declining Efficiency of Parliament' *Quarterly Review*, 99 (1856), 562; *H* [164]. 986 (20 Feb. 1857), etc.

[73] Add. MSS 44745. fos. 173–222. It was written during the Easter recess, 30 Mar.–12 Apr. 1855: *Gladstone Diaries*, ad loc.

[74] The full title, pencilled in on 12 Apr. 1855, is: 'Party. As it was and As it is.—A Sketch of the Political History of Twenty Years.—Retrospect and Prospect of Parliamentary Government.' Add. MS 44745, L. 222 b. On f. 216 b, Gladstone described himself as 'an anonymous pamphlet writer', but then crossed out the word 'pamphlet'. The principal previous user of this MS is Richard Shannon, whose concerns are, however, largely psychological: it was an attempt to confer 'spurious dignity' upon Gladstone's 'sense of inadequacy', *Gladstone 1809–65* (1982), 309.

abstract almost immoral'.[75] The years of party disorganization between 1846 and 1859 were a bleak and even disastrous period for Gladstone, and it is a comment on the triumphalism of modern biography that it manages largely to overlook the fact.[76] His own view in 1859 was that 'For thirteen years, the middle space of my life, I have been cast out of party connection, severed from my old party, and loath irrecoverably to join a new one.'[77] Not only was he cast out from his party, but from office. The only relief to an otherwise uniform misery lay in the two years of the Aberdeen Coalition. Then Gladstone was able to serve as Chancellor of the Exchequer, so satisfying the desire to render public and ministerial service; he could also hope that an avowed coalition of Peelites and Liberals might ultimately 'have grown into union',[78] and supply him with the party basis which would be necessary in the long term. However, any such hopes perished in 'the rout of January–February 1855'. By this he meant a whole sequence of events: the end of the Aberdeen ministry in January; the unexpected failure of Derby to form a Conservative ministry at the beginning of February—a ministry which, regardless of his previous 'Peelite' incumbency, Gladstone would have been happy to join; and then the framing of a third, broadly conservative ministry under Palmerston, which Gladstone joined, albeit reluctantly, but then left after fifteen days.[79] In this way he returned to the wilderness of political isolation and futility. Such was the context of his reflections on 'Party' the following Easter.

Peel was the centrepiece of these reflections because he was 'the great historical figure of recent politics'—a renewed suggestion of Peel's Carlylean aura from one who had nothing in common with Carlyle.[80] But his legacy was deeply ambivalent. For whilst Gladstone accepted a most favourable estimate of Peel's claims to political greatness up to the end of 1845, there followed a respectful, yet ultimately annihilating criticism of Peel and Peelism in the decade 1845–55. The difference between the two periods lay, of course, in the destruction of the Tory Party over the Corn Laws, and the political disorganization which ensued as a result. By 1855, in contrast to 1846 or 1852, Gladstone found himself in agreement not only with the more dispassionate of Peel's opponents, but also with Cobden and Disraeli,[81]in that he was now convinced that Peel bore the primary

[75] Conversations with Peel, 13 July 1846, Aberdeen, 19 Oct. 1849 , *Autobiographical Memoranda 1845–66*, 27, 46.

[76] Colin Matthew demotes the discussion of party allegiance to the realm of 'tactics', whereas 'strategy' is supplied by the teleology of free trade liberalism, to which (in his view) Gladstone had been progressively committed since 1841. So by 1853 'the great crises of his public and private life... had been largely resolved', and the years that followed were largely ones of 'tranquillity': *Gladstone 1809–74*, 104.

[77] Gladstone to Heathcote 16 June 1859 , pr. Morley, i. 627; the idea is repeated in Gladstone's review of '*The Life of the Prince Consort*. Vol. III' (1877), repr. *Gleanings of Past Years* (1879), i. 127.

[78] 'Party', Add. MS 44745, fo. 221b.

[79] Because the crisis was so important to him, Gladstone kept near daily records of it: *Autobiographical Memoranda 1846–1866*, 153–92.

[80] 'Party', fo. 187 b; cf. *Autobiographical Memoranda 1845–6*, 30 (1846).

[81] On Cobden, 'Party', fo. 189; cf. *H* [112]. 856 (Hume), 859 (Inglis), 894 (Russell): 3, 4 July 1850.

responsibility for the prevalent anarchy, by his wilful destruction or 'sacrifice' of his party in 1846. (The idea that Corn Law repeal was a necessary part of the economic 'education' of the Tory Party, and thus that it was really the *opponents* of repeal who were somehow responsible for its destruction, is a further example of the twentieth-century anachronism which identifies the fortunes of party with a fiscal and economic agenda.[82])

Before the struggle began he seemed to have so much of cheerful faith in human nature, and in the good sense of Englishmen, as to form sanguine anticipations of its end. His expectation then was, that the adamantine necessity would constrain those, whom the claim of Justice could not win, and that the Act [for Corn Law repeal] when passed would leave him with his whole party, except a few malcontents and grumblers, still in the ranks. [However] . . . when in the midst of the struggle, he began to feel its real intensity, he seems in his own mind to have substituted indifference to the destruction of the party which was so eminently HIS, for his previous excess of confidence in its being preserved. And it seems as if at the last, when he hurled his eulogy of Cobden in the teeth of his former friends and combined with this panegyric some sharp & very plain expressions against the hypocrisy of selfish monopolists, for one single moment at least this recklessness had almost passed into ferocity, a temper little worthy of the man, uncongenial to his high tone of patriotism . . . The strict party order & organisation of which Sir Robert Peel had been morally as well as materially the cause, he had now been the instrument of destroying.

Ecce novus saeclorum nascitur ordo.[83]

Thus for Gladstone the national good of Corn Law repeal need not have involved the party evil of Conservative break-up and collapse. Quite consistently with this, he was reluctant—like most of his contemporaries, but unlike many more recent writers—to allow that there might be an antithesis between loyalty to party and loyalty to country, at least so far as active politicians were concerned. Loyalty to country was predicated on loyalty to party, and in a quite specific fashion.[84] Given the premium he placed on ministerial service and on good executive government, it is clear that Gladstone was well capable of looking beyond the confines of party. However the central tenet, which runs throughout the tract on 'Party', was that good government in the national interest was not merely compatible with, but was the product of, a polarized and balanced two-party system, for only stringent

---

[82] Norman Gash introduced this idea, showing that the diffused Keynesianism of the 1950s and 1960s affected him almost as much as it did his juniors: *Reaction and Reconstruction in English Politics*, 153–4.

[83] 'Party', fos. 184–5 cf. Virgil, *Eclogue* IV. 5. Contrast the milder judgement on Peel's conduct in 1851: *Autobiographical Memoranda* 1845–1866, 78.

[84] Gladstone allowed two partial exceptions: after Peel's 'official death . . . the idea of his Country *now* became the stewardess of the inheritance of his fame': 'Party', fo. 186b. Again at fo. 201b he invokes the idea of loyalty to country to defend Peel's moral character against charges of trickery and cunning, regardless of the political character of his actions. This may seem a somewhat unreal separation, but it is reflected in the later dual verdict that while Peel kept 'an enormous conscience', his 'reputation as a statesman stands somewhat too high'. L. Tollemache, *Talks with Mr Gladstone* (1898), 126 (13 Jan. 1896). The duality would seem to reflect a moral and religious absolutism operating regardless of the claims of politics.

party competition could stimulate and regulate efficient government. The enduring source of Gladstone's reverence for Peel lay in his idea of Peel's good governance; but the same idea also made Peel's conduct in causing his party to shatter deeply culpable.

In Gladstone's view the session of 1846 formed the beginning of a new and consistent pattern of conduct, with Peel 'playing a part he had never played before'. He was determined to let his enemies beat him on Irish Coercion as soon as he possibly could, and he was determined to resign, rather than to try and reconstruct the Tory Party. This, in turn, was a repudiation of the Duke of Wellington who, despite his opposition to Corn Law repeal, had supported Peel because he believed that it was only under him that the Queen's government could properly be carried on: yet at Peel's behest that government was now to be given up.[85] Here again Gladstone's belief in the link between loyalty to party and to government is manifest. Thereafter Peel was possessed of two central ideas: 'The first of them was an intention never to resume the exercise of power. The second was a belief that the grand danger of the country, against which it was his first duty and his peculiar vocation to guard, would lie in a desperate struggle that must sooner or later come for the restoration of Protection.'[86] The only way to guard against this was to ensure that the Derbyite party never came into power. But these ideas led (in Gladstone's view) to a further series of entanglements and errors. Given his first resolution, Peel should have quit Parliament entirely: few would believe that he was no longer a candidate for office, and by remaining he was in 'a false position'. The Peelites could not legitimately act without his 'participation or countenance' and were paralysed as a result: Goulburn could not rejoin the Tories in 1846–7, whilst Graham and Herbert could not link up with the Liberals.

Peel's second idea was still more damaging. He sat on the Opposition side of the House and yet he rendered Russell's ministry a systematic support, recording a series of votes against his own personal opinions. The moral falsity of this was in itself repugnant to Gladstone, but in any case this strategy rested on an intellectual fallacy. Peel was 'self-duped'. Unlike Cobden and Bright, who, Gladstone now accepted, enjoyed the 'paternity' of Corn Law abolition, Peel displayed 'maternal' qualms and apprehensions:

The young law of 1846 was an infant Hercules and was strong enough even in its cradle to strangle, not one serpent only, but if necessary two. It is not probable that the Whigs and Derbyites united could have repealed that Act. The idea that Derbyites alone could do it has now proved to be so futile and childish, that there is a difficulty in realising the fact that anybody entertained it.[87]

(It is unclear how Gladstone could uphold this robustly confident doctrine regarding England's social and political stability, whilst at the same time accepting

---

[85] 'Party': quotation, fo. 190 b; on Irish Coercion and Wellington, fo. 186b.
[86] Ibid., fo. 189b.   [87] Ibid., fo. 192.

Peel's own case for a pre-emptive Corn Law repeal as a means of averting constitutional subversion;[88] but this is one of the few instances where he remained constrained by past loyalties.) The consequences of such 'childishness' were, first, that the life of protection was artificially prolonged—this despite the fact that it had never been a significant ground of dispute between the parties, and was in fact a mere oppositional 'cry' and not a viable governing 'principle'. Secondly, by maintaining the Peelites in existence as an independent third force in Parliament, Peel was responsible for 'preventing Parliament from resuming its natural and usual organisation in the form of two political parties[,] a Government and an opposition'.[89] The result was an opposition (the Derbyites) who were too weak to oppose, and a government which became lethargic and inefficient as a result. The most evident symptom of this degeneracy lay in the trickery and flippancy of Disraeli—although Roebuck, the immediate cause of the downfall of the Aberdeen coalition, was also mentioned, whilst in subsequent years Gladstone would come to see Palmerston, too, as a sign of the same disease.[90]

This overwhelming indictment rested on blank incomprehension of Peel's attitudes to party. Gladstone accepted, as many later historians have done, that Peel's conduct before 1846 was that of a legitimate party leader; but this brought him up against a brick wall in explaining Peel's supposed change of course in that year:

Why did he keep [the Peelites] hanging between earth and heaven, between wind and water?... Did he mean them to be eternally divorced from their old friends and eternally prohibited from making new? Did he contemplate the dying out of party connection altogether and the substitution of philosophical for Parliamentary Government? Could the practical mind of Sir Robert Peel overlook the necessity of working the Parliamentary Government by means of one or other of the great and stable subsisting combinations, and the impossibility of mere eclectic contrivance?... It is not possible to find a satisfactory answer to these questions.[91]

Disagreement on party epitomized disagreement on the entire structure of politics. Gladstone shared to the full Peel's desire for efficient government; but whereas for Peel government was the executive function of the Queen's Minister guided by private reason and supported by a centralized bureaucracy, with Parliament as a necessary but sometimes inconvenient hurdle, for Gladstone government was, precisely, 'Parliamentary Government'. Its concerns lay with efficiency and economy rather than bureaucracy, and with legislation rather than administration, whilst it only possessed meaning and legitimacy when conceived as the apex of a social and party political hierarchy. Government could only function because at the base of that hierarchy there lay 'the good sense and marvellously tempered self-command of the English people'.[92] Like Peel or any ministerialist, Gladstone could see that popular or public 'opinion' was not pure or infallible—as more naive and doctrinaire Liberals might suggest—and that it

---

[88] Ibid., fos. 189b–190.   [89] Ibid., fo. 192b.   [90] Ibid., fos. 203–215.
[91] Ibid., fo. 194b.   [92] Ibid., fo. 178.

was subject to temporary distortion, inflammation, or even worse; but unlike Peel, he took it as axiomatic after 1841, when the election of that year vindicated *both* the conservative loyalty of the people and the viability of the Reformed settlement of 1832, that in the last analysis one had to rely on national opinion conceived in the widest and most popular sense as the basis for high political action.[93] Parties then functioned as a middle term, mediating between executive and people, supplying the means of uniting 'men by the common bonds of opinion and feeling to their friends', both inside Parliament and out of doors.[94] This reliance by both parties on common opinion and feeling was, of course, none other than the celebrated doctrine commonly associated with Gladstone's later Liberal phase: that one should 'Trust the people'.[95] However, this populism or nationalism was also accompanied by an hierarchical (and supposedly Tory) insistence that social and political leaders should lead. Hence the well-known formulation at the end of his life regarding his most 'striking gift' in politics: it was not 'the simple acceptance of public opinion', but rather 'an insight' on the part of a political leader 'which generates in the mind a conviction that the materials exist for forming public opinion, and directing it'.[96] Opinion was a *datum*, but leaders led and shaped it all the same. Both these emphases, the popular and the hierarchical, were with Gladstone for almost the entirety of his career, and in this profoundly social and ultimately consensual conception of Parliamentary Government he was, like most Englishmen, radically at variance with the administratively centred *étatisme* of Peel.[97]

Gladstone was unaware that his differences with Peel were as great for the years 1833–46 as thereafter, whilst his ignorance of the man before 1832—Peel's real heyday—was self-confessed and total.[98] None the less, throughout their relationship he had always maintained his personal detachment—Church politics alone were sufficient to ensure that before 1846[99]—and this was what set him apart

[93] See e.g. Gladstone's distinction between the 'spurious public mind' and the true one in 'The History of 1852–60', *EHR*, 2 (1887), 282. This is the language and concept of Macaulay and Mackintosh. [94] 'Party', fo. 195 b. On 1832, fos. 196–197b.

[95] e.g. Gladstone's answer to the question posed by Andrew Reid to Liberal luminaries in 1885, *Why I am a Liberal* (1885): 'The principle of Liberalism is TRUST IN THE PEOPLE qualified by prudence: the principle of Conservatism is MISTRUST OF THE PEOPLE qualified by fear' (13) The fear Gladstone had in mind was the fear of democracy and popular revolution he himself had displayed regarding Parliamentary Reform in 1832, but which was then allayed by the Conservative recovery of 1837–41: 'Party', fo. 178. This was why he considered the idea of 'Trust in the People' as Liberal in origin, to be traced back to Althorp and Russell: 'The History of 1852–60', *EHR*, 2 (1887), 281. But though the idea had been voiced by Reformers in 1831, it also accorded with the English nationalism espoused in *The State in its Relations with the Church* (1838).

[96] Memorandum *c.*1895 pr. *Autobiographica*, 136; cf. *A Chapter of Autobiography* (1868), 12–13.

[97] Cf. Matthew, *Gladstone 1809–74*, 117–20, 125, 169–70.

[98] Gladstone's late, oral remark to C. S. Parker that 'there were two Peels, one before, the other after, Parliamentary Reform' is, like the chronology of the MS on 'Party', an effective admission that Peel's career before 1832 was a kind of void so far as he was concerned: *Peel*, ii. 209 and n. 1. He could never have said this of Canning.

[99] To this should be added his proposed resignation over Corn in 1842 which, given the date and the issue, was a remarkable declaration of personal autonomy: *Autobiographica*, 45–6, 234–5.

from the other Peelites who, with the partial exception of Aberdeen, were epigones, unable to function as independent politicians without a leader. And regardless of its historical inaccuracy, Gladstone's 1855 analysis was decisive in drawing a practical moral for the future: that henceforward a Peelite third party at Westminster, and with it any overt Peelite legacy, should cease to exist. Such is the verdict pronounced by the mythical justice of 'Rhadamanthus' upon a guilty Peelite in the final section of of the manuscript on 'Party'.[100]

The effect of this judgement on Gladstone's subsequent conduct is plain to see. Before 1855, despite obvious differences, he would make use of Peel's name on occasion because the exigencies of Peelite 'or Aberdeenite' politics demanded it. An outstanding example is his speech against Disraeli's budget in December 1852, although even at this most emotionally charged moment, when the split of 1846 was in some sense renewed, Gladstone still expressed a clear preference for Conservative Party reunion, and did not fail to address the Derbyite fraction as legitimate descendants of 'the party of 1842'.[101] Again in 1853 Gladstone might still describe himself as Peel's 'pupil and follower in politics', even if all he meant by this was the notorious fact that he was part of the Peelite fraction in Parliament.[102] But after 1855 Peel ceased to feature in his pedigree.

Here was the reason why the tract on 'Party' was first conceived under the guise of anonymity and then not published. If, to use modern terminology, the aim of the tract was to lay a Peelite discourse to rest, there was nothing to be gained by presenting that discourse in a newly systematic and more elaborate fashion, however hostile the tendency behind such a presentation. Here was the 'tender ground' which he shunned when refusing invitations to review biographies of Peel on distinct and widely separated occasions—by Guizot in 1857 and by James Thursfield in 1891.[103] The nearest he came to breaking his silence was occasionally to restate the anti-Peelite conclusions of 1855 in covert and largely impersonal form. This was most obvious in his 1856 *Quarterly Review* article, 'The Declining Efficiency of Parliament', which rehearses the conclusions of the tract on 'Party', but under heavy disguise. Parliament's 'declining efficiency' is held to date, as before, from 1846, but Gladstone is silent as to why this pivotal change took place: he merely refers to 'the time when Sir Robert Peel's Government was driven from office', without inquiring who or what did the driving. The catalogue of Peel's sins and errors after 1846 is then reduced to two sentences on 'the four last, and perhaps most questionable, years of his political life'—although there really was no 'perhaps' in Gladstone's mind. Meanwhile the article was rendered topical, and attention diverted away from the sensitive point, by the concentration of its

---

[100] The final section, beginning fo. 216 b, was '8. The Peelites: Their Arraignment and Apology'.
[101] *H* [123]. 1691 cf. cols. 1678–84, 1691–3. Given this premiss, Gladstone argued that the Derbyites should vote against Disraeli's budget. For the usage of 'Aberdeenite' *vice* 'Peelite': 'Party', fo. 217.   [102] Gladstone at Manchester, *The Times* (13 Oct. 1853), fo. 7c.
[103] Gladstone to Elwin, 27 Mar. 1857, cit. *Gladstone Diaries*, 17 Mar. 1857 n. 4, cf. 17–21 Mar. 1857, 16 Apr. 1891.

energies in a twenty-page attack on Palmerston as one of the *symptoms* of declining efficiency and party disorganization.[104] A still more covert allusion to Peel occurred at the opening of his budget statement of 1861. We saw that this would seem to have been a most natural time to celebrate the triumph of free trade and its apostles, especially if one were to suppose that 'Gladstone's chancellorships represent the politicization of Peelism'; but instead the Chancellor described the termination of the mid-Victorian tariff controversy in the following cryptic terms: '[1860–1] was a year, in which the controversy with respect to Protection, so long the leading cause of agitation in the country, and of political disorganisation in this House, may be said to have been at length finally wound up'.[105] This looked like a simple hit at protection, but it was also a secret repudiation of Peel—the architect and support of 'political disorganization'.

A final, tacit rebuke to Peel is offered by Gladstone's course of conduct in 1886. On the face of it, his desire to pass Home Rule even at the cost of splitting his party bears some resemblance to Peel's behaviour in 1846.[106] But this is superficial only. Unlike the Corn Laws, Home Rule was a party issue, a constitutional issue, 'a Magna Charta for Ireland', which Gladstone urged on the most elementary and elemental Liberal grounds: the desire to create 'free institutions' based on 'the essential principles of liberty'.[107] It is true that there was also a case *against* Home Rule which Liberals could genuinely believe in—that political liberty was not to be had except at the expense of social hierarchy in Ireland, and of the sovereignty of Parliament in Westminster; but this only made Gladstone's desire to monopolize party legitimacy the more intense. Unlike Peel in 1845–6,[108] he sought desperately to persuade his backbenchers to support him between January and June 1886, because he knew that it was only by party support that Home Rule would be carried; unlike Peel he did not effectively retire from politics thereafter, but strove for another eight years to identify the Liberal Party irrevocably with the Home Rule cause; and unlike Peel, he carried the majority of his party with him. The crisis appeared to create a third force or 'public nuisance' with the potential for disorganizing politics, though it was supplied by the Liberal Unionists and not the Gladstonians;[109] but in fact politics were not disorganized after 1886 as they had been after 1846, because the Liberal Unionists behaved almost exclusively as allies of the Tory Party, in contrast to the diffuse voting patterns of the Peelites after 1846 and the wider party decadence which resulted. Gladstone was well aware of his distance from Peel in all this. Talking in 1888 he 'got upon the subject of Home Rule and how some of his past colleagues would have regarded the

---

[104] Quotations, 'Declining Efficiency', 526, 533 respectively; for the attack on Palmerston, ibid., 535–55.   [105] *FS* 1861: 1; cf. Matthew, *Gladstone 1809–74*, 114.
[106] Matthew, *Gladstone 1875–1898* (Oxford, 1995), 234, 307–8.
[107] *H* [304]. 1059, 1038, 1043 (8 Apr. 1886).   [108] *Memoirs*, ii. 18–24.
[109] Gladstone applied the term 'public nuisance' both to himself and the Peelites in the 1850 s and by implication to the Liberal Unionists in the 1880s: e.g. 4 Feb. 1857, *Autobiographical Memoranda 1845–1866*, 213; 'The History of 1852–60', *EHR*, 2 (1887), 285.

question. The statesman of whose agreement with Home Rule he felt most confident was Lord John Russell; . . . the man about whom he felt most doubtful was Sir Robert Peel'.[110] The immediate reference here was specific, to Catholic Emancipation, a part of that Irish policy which 'constituted a black page in [Peel's] history',[111] and which was separated by such an immeasurable gulf from the policy of 1886 that any comparison was odious. However, the mention of Russell shows that there was also a more general set of ideas at work here, for it reminds us of the urgency of Gladstone's desire to site himself within Liberal Party tradition;[112] and it was party and the conception of political and social structure which it implied which, even more than the specific divergence over Ireland (immense though that was), lay at the root of his divorce from Peel.

We may then dismiss the idea of any Peelite transition into Liberalism (or liberalism). It is true, for example, that Gladstone's previous history must always be borne in mind in interpreting his later conduct as a Liberal leader, since it implied the retention on his part of a set of Conservative (rather than Peelite) attitudes on a whole host of constitutional questions, of which the congeries of issues raised by the political position of the Church of England was the most notorious. But such continuities hardly suggest that Gladstone's curious past was of any significance for the Liberal Party; rather they cast the severest doubt on any claim made for him as a shaper of its identity. Why should a man who, notoriously, entered the Liberal ranks at the age of 50 and even then (as he proclaimed to the world) 'in *pauperis formâ*', have any rights or say in the matter? Why should 'an outcast' seek to foist his old identity onto those who took him in, not least when they were an entire party with a continuous, constitutionally defined identity going back to the era of Charles Fox?[113] (Note here that Gladstone never presented Peel in the way he did Canning, for example, as a closet Liberal.) Not only was Peel, as Gladstone well knew, 'a member until his death of the Carlton Club', but his 'fearlessness in regard to administrative changes' was combined 'with no small dread of constitutional innovation'—the hallmark of the Tory.[114] In this most basic sense, when Gladstone crossed the floor of the House in 1859, he left Peel, even the pre-1846 'Tory' Peel, behind him.

This is almost the end of the story, but not quite. Gladstone *did* make one important, if anonymous, public statement on Peel in later life; however, it was not a statement on Peel and the Liberal Party, but on Peel and the Tory Party.

[110] *Hamilton Diary (II)*, 14 Dec. 1888.
[111] Ibid., 19 Feb. 1894; cf. Lionel Tollemache, *Talks with Mr Gladstone* (1898), 127 (13 Jan. 1896).
[112] Invocation of the Foxite precedent of 1782 and of Russell on behalf of national self-determination within the United Kingdom were central to Gladstone's promulgation of the Home Rule case in Apr. 1886: *H* [304]. 1044–67, 1542–5 *passim* (8, 13 Apr. 1886).
[113] Speech on the Second Reading of the 1866 Reform Bill: *H* [183]. 130 (27 Apr. 1866); cf. *A Chapter of Autobiography* (1868), 8. Gladstone's marginality to 'traditional' Liberal identity is powerfully urged by Parry, *Rise and Fall*, Part IV.
[114] 'Party', fo. 221; 'The Declining Efficiency of Parliament', 565. Cf. Gladstone at Manchester 18 July 1865, *Speeches and Addresses Delivered at the Election of 1865* (1865), 2, where Peel is described as 'the leader and head of the Conservative party'—the type of all subsequent references to him, however polite.

Not the least remarkable feature of the 1855 manuscript on 'Party' had been its treatment of Disraeli, alongside that of Peel. Disraeli was a 'genius',[115] but it was genius expressed through a complete departure from orthodox Conservatism: he was one of the worst fruits of the disorganization that Peel had so inexplicably caused. Twenty-five years on, under the provocations of 'Beaconsfieldism', Gladstone returned to this train of ideas—above all in a *Fortnightly Review* article, 'The Conservative Collapse: considered in a letter from a Liberal to an old Conservative', published anonymously under the name of 'Index' in May 1880.[116] Put most simply, Gladstone was trying to do what Goldwin Smith (the chosen instrument of Peel's trustees) had first attempted in 1868, though with far greater subtlety: to discredit Disraeli's 'Conservatism' by reference to the earlier and more wholesome brand of Peel.[117] Disraeli (he argued) had been pioneering a new and illegitimate 'pseudo-Conservatism' ever since 1844. The penalty for such behaviour in 1880 was an electoral rout greater than at any time since 1832, but this precedent also suggested the means of Conservative recovery: the exercise of 'a prudence and sagacity like those with which Sir Robert Peel, between 1832 and 1841, lifted his party out of the mire and set it on the hill-top'.[118] Of course, the idea of a once and future Liberal leader offering advice on the reconstruction of the Tory Party was extraordinary to a degree. Informed readers at once recognized the text as 'unmistakeably the product of the pen of Mr. G.',[119] and the episode stood as a further revelation of his eccentricity in relation to the rank and file of the Liberal Party. But there can be no doubt that this was an authentic reflection of Gladstone's views on Peel, and that in this perspective Peel's principal bequest to the later nineteenth century (if he had one at all) lay in his conduct before Corn Law repeal, and as an exemplar to Conservatives, not to Liberals.

III

So Gladstone's relationship with Peel was deeply ambivalent. He revered Peel's moral probity, and had a warm sympathy for what he took to be Peelite ideas

---

[115] 'Party', fo. 181 b.
[116] Vol. [27 NS] 33 (1880), 607–24, dated 17 Apr. 1880; cf *Gladstone Diaries*, 13–17 Apr. 1880 . It was preceded by two brief references in the same vein at Midlothian: *Political Speeches in Scotland*, 27, 210. The 'status quo' position of 1859–79 had of course been to say virtually nothing about either Peel or the proper role of the Tory Party. One exception, however, is the brief remarks delivered at Wakefield in 1871 (triggered by a visit to an old Eton school chum and retired Peelite, James Milnes Gaskell). Here he hailed 'the leaders and members of the Conservative party', even under Disraeli, as Peel's 'successors'; from this derived the health of the two-party system: *The Times*, (6 Sept. 1871), 3d.
[117] Cf. 'Peel', *Macmillan's Magazine*, 19 (1868), 97–106. Goldwin Smith had been appointed Peel's official biographer by his trustees (Cardwell and Stanhope) at the end of the 1850s, but he was too much of a journalist and polemicist to produce anything more than interpretative sketches: cf. C. S. Parker, *Sir Robert Peel* (London, 1891), i. London [10]. However, he was also a violent opponent of Gladstone—another instance of authentic Peelism marooned in no man's land: e.g. *Hamilton Diary (I)*, 23 Nov. 1881; Tollemache, *Talks with Mr Gladstone*, 29 Jan. 1894, 108–9.
[118] 'The Conservative Collapse', 623.   [119] *Hamilton Diary (I)*, 1 May 1880.

about good executive government and for Peel's supposedly orthodox party leadership of 1833–46. On the other hand, he became increasingly aware of a fundamental divergence from Peel after 1846. This became final in 1855, when he privately resolved that Peelite politics, as distinct from Conservative politics, were a dead-end. Party and the contempt shown for it by Peel were located as the root of their differences. Despite his own, well-documented eccentricity, Gladstone had always recognized the necessity of party to effective political action; he recognized, too, that the energizing root of party politics lay in dispute over institutional or constitutional issues. Trying to make fiscal and economic issues the test of party allegiance, as Peel had done in 1846, could lead only (in Gladstone's view) to party dissolution and chaos, and so to the degradation of 'Parliamentary Government' as a whole.

The immediate implication of these findings is that any attempt to construct nineteenth-century politics around a lineage from Peel to Gladstone, or around a 'liberal' tradition defined primarily in terms of tariff and economic policy, is untenable. However, we should not rest content with a simple negative. Prima facie there is indeed cause for despondency. Writing in 1974 Colin Matthew made the striking remark that Victorian Liberalism was 'an undefined standard', and so it has remained since.[120] Despite or because of the best efforts of historical scholarship, synthetic conceptions of Victorian politics have remained in a state of near perfect competition. Indeed, there is no agreement here even on the object of study. Is it 'Liberalism', a definite ideological construct? Within this category, free trade liberalism is the dominant, but by no means the only, runner.[121] Is it the 'Liberal Party', which since the 1960s has commonly been viewed as a coalition of forces with no essential unity?[122] Or is it the one-party hegemony christened 'Liberal Government', where the identity of Liberalism rests on its social assumptions and parliamentary *modus operandi* rather than on specific political doctrines or policies?[123] Here is an extraordinary yet explicable state of affairs. Extraordinary because no Victorian, at least before 1885, was ever seriously troubled by such questions as *Why I am a Liberal* or what was *The Meaning of Liberalism*.[124]

---

[120] *The Gladstone Diaries* (Oxford, 1974), iii, p. xlii; cf. Parry, *Rise and Fall*, 20, writing in 1993.

[121] e.g. Lawrence Goldman, *Science, Reform and Politics in Victorian Britain: The Social Science Association 1857–1886* (Cambridge, 2002), esp. ch. 2; Eugenio Biagini, *Liberty, Retrenchment and Reform: Popular Liberalism in the Age of Gladstone 1860–1880* (Cambridge, 1992). Dr Biagini incorporates free trade (ch. 2) within a much wider range of Liberal causes.

[122] John Vincent's *The Formation of the Liberal Party 1857–1868* (1966) was a pioneer here, and it was in reaction to this book that Matthew made the remark quoted in the text: cf. *The Gladstone Diaries* (Oxford, 1978), v, p. xliv and n. 1.

[123] Jon Parry's definitions of the Liberal Party ('the party of wisdom, property and rational parliamentary debate') and its ideals ('integration, establishment, reason, consensus, law, parliamentary government') plainly do not allow for the existence of viable Conservative competition: *Rise and Fall*, 223, 260.

[124] The titles of books ed. A. Reid (1885) and J. M. Robertson (1912). The 1885 Reform Act signalled clearly that the agenda of constitutional politics was becoming exhausted, and the first discussions of what was to follow, and of 'new Liberalism' (though really the first Liberal 'ism') followed at once.

Explicable because, since party identities were taken as self-evident, there was little contemporary reflection on the subject. (It is no accident that the first great analytical tract on the British parties should be written by Ostrogorski, a Lithuanian Jew.) Hence one root of our modern uncertainties.

Yet if the Victorian discussion of party lacks reflective depth, it compensates by its unanimity. Whatever the degree of his eccentricity, Gladstone perceived this. He did not, unlike Peel, reject party, and he was (of course!) quite right to see it as the sole effective means to conduct politics during his lifetime. First, because at that date there was no effective discourse of 'country' apart from 'party', such as would become prevalent in the twentieth century.[125] He was also right to suppose that 'party' implied a competitive struggle between the two parties. Contrary to the practice of many modern scholars, there was no such thing as a history of the Liberal Party without that of the Tory Party, and vice versa. He was right, thirdly, to suppose that parties were united by the primary object of their struggle—the 'constitution' or the 'organic institutions' of the country. It is a point upon which the great majority of textbook definitions of party prior to 1885 (and even some which reject the idea of party) are agreed.[126] Textbooks aside, the parliamentary constitution formed a matrix of such power that neither radicalism and Chartism could escape from it, and its command over electors and non-electors was fully as great as that over high politicians.[127] The historical root of this extraordinary magnetism lay in the fact that 'the constitution' had been the central concern of a fundamentally consensual English politics ever since 1688. In the nineteenth century the constitution ceased to be the '*ancient* constitution', being washed by an historicist tide of ideas about progressive reform that had hardly existed hitherto; but the focus of attention was the same.

So a Liberal was first and foremost a constitutional reformer; a Conservative, a constitutional defender. However, neither party had an 'ideology'—a term unknown to nineteenth-century Britain except as a faint and dismissive memory of France in the later 1790s, but which, if it has any precise meaning, implies a total and exclusive system of ideas, and hence the kind of socio-cultural rivalry between blocs or 'pillars' such as the 'Socialisms', 'Liberalisms', and 'Catholicisms' which divided the nations of Western Europe in the nineteenth and much of the

---

[125] Graham Searle, *Country before Party* (1995) dates the rise of such a discourse to the period after 1885: chs. 3–4.

[126] e.g. T. B. Macaulay, *The History of England from the Accession of James II* (1848), i. ch. 98–102; T. Erskine May, *The Constitutional History of England 1760–1860* (1861–3), ch. 8; W. E. H. Lecky, *History of England in the Eighteenth Century* (1892 edn.), i. 2–7, ii. 93–7 (1878); T. E. Kebbel, 'The Spirit of Party', *Nineteenth Century*, 11 (1882), 378–88; for the 1830s see Gash, *Reaction and Reconstruction*, 131–3. Goldwin Smith, Peel's official biographer designate, was a notorious assailant of the English party system, but even he could reproduce an orthodox definition of a Conservative as one opposed to 'organic change': e.g. 'Peel', *Encyclopaedia Britannica* (1859), xvii. 363b, 'Peel and Cobden', *Nineteenth Century*, 11 (1882), 869–89, here 877.

[127] Gareth Stedman Jones, 'Rethinking Chartism', in *The Languages of Class* (Cambridge, 1983), esp. 168–78; Patrick Joyce, *Visions of the People* (Cambridge, 1991), ch. 2; J. Vernon (ed.), *Re-reading the Constitution* (Cambridge, 1996).

twentieth centuries.[128] By contrast, the two British parties—British in composition but wholly English in their ruling ideas—were united at the level of first principle: their shared belief in the intrinsic goodness of the constitution, a goodness also defined as the uniquely English marriage of political liberty with social order, in contrast to the horrors of continental despotism and revolution. If the English have ever had a modern ideology, it was this ideology of England. But though it rendered the identity of the parties doctrinally weak, still 'party' was an outlier of constitutionalism, and so remained inevitable as a practical tool. Thus Gladstone was right—lastly—to perceive that party existed within, and to serve, a wider bipartisan consensus; to see that the maintenance and the reform of 'institutions' were but two sides of the same coin; and to locate the foundation of Victorian politics not in any party principle but a national one: 'the good sense...of the English people'.[129] He was indeed unusual in being able to see himself at work either as a Liberal or a Conservative; but he was not unrealistic, because his understanding of what it took to be a Liberal or Conservative was, unlike so much else in his thinking, surprisingly ordinary.

[128] The terminology of *Verzuiling* or 'pillarization' derives from A. Lijphart, *The Politics of Accommodation* (Berkeley, 1968), but its usage has far outstripped its original Dutch and benignly pluralist roots. For an accessible outline of what continentals understood by 'ideology', see Karl Mannheim on 'the total conception of ideology', *Ideology and Utopia* (1936), ii. 1–3.

[129] 'Party', fo. 178.

6

Gladstone and a Liberal Theory of
International Relations

Martin Ceadel

A distinctive feature of the political culture of nineteenth- and twentieth-century Britain was its receptivity to the liberal or idealist approach to international relations, which assumed that 'the unruly flow of international politics could be canalised into a set of logically impregnable abstract formulae inspired by the doctrines of nineteenth-century liberal democracy'.[1] Such were the dissenting words of E. H. Carr, who dubbed it 'utopianism' in the second half of the 1930s and pioneered an explicitly realist alternative. Thus, even as liberalism collapsed as an autonomous force in domestic politics during the 1920s and early 1930s, its optimistic vision of international relations gained broad acceptance in the form of what Carr termed 'overwhelming paper support for the League of Nations'.[2]

That W. E. Gladstone anticipated this internationalist idealism was asserted as early as the interwar period. In 1928, when the League of Nations still seemed to be making headway, Herbert Gladstone recalled his father's *Edinburgh Review* article of October 1870 which had asserted, despite the fact that the Franco-Prussian War was then raging, that 'a new law of nations is gradually taking hold of the mind, and coming to sway the practice of the world'. He commented: 'Truly a prophetic saying. Nearly fifty years later these words crystallised in the Covenant of the League of Nations.'[3] In 1935, by which time the League was facing evident challenges, Paul Knaplund published a classic defence of Gladstone's foreign policy as an enlightened alternative to the Bismarckian *Realpolitik* which he blamed for the First World War, noting that 'in this age of uncertainty, distrust, depression, and war scares, it may be well to study how [Gladstone] hoped to lead mankind in the path of justice and peace'.[4] And the following year, in a contribution to a *Festschrift* for the League of Nations Union activist and classical scholar

---

[1] E. H. Carr, *The Twenty Years' Crisis 1919–1939* (2nd edn., London, 1946), 31.
[2] Ibid., 15.   [3] Viscount Gladstone, *After Thirty Years* (London, 1928), 107.
[4] Paul Knaplund, *Gladstone's Foreign Policy* (London, 1935), p. xviii.

Gilbert Murray, J. L. Hammond asserted that Gladstone 'had what we would now call a League of Nations mind. He . . . was concerned before everything else for the spirit and principle of public law.'[5] After the Second World War this idea of Gladstone as a prophet of twentieth-century liberal internationalism established itself as an orthodoxy. In 1954 Alan Bullock and Maurice Shock argued that

the ideas to which he gave currency, far from losing their hold upon the Liberal imagination, have gained in strength since 1914. In the hopes placed in the League of Nations and the United Nations, in the attempt to organise collective security and the disappointed but constantly renewed appeals to world opinion against injustice and aggresssion . . . Gladstone's beliefs have found a frustrated but passionate confirmation.[6]

And in an otherwise revisionist work published in 1977 Michael Bentley stated that Liberal support for the League of Nations 'reflected Gladstonian preconceptions of international relations as the discourse of moral personalities which were potentially conformable to moral law'.[7]

Colin Matthew accepted this orthodoxy, writing that Gladstone offered 'a vision of international legitimacy and order which, as later developed and institutionalized in the League of Nations and the United Nations, represented the best hope of twentieth-century Liberalism'.[8] Characteristically, Matthew also clarified, refined, and qualified it, specifying the contribution which Gladstone made to liberal internationalism as an ideology, distinguishing this from his contribution to embedding it in British political culture, and drawing attention to his failure to attempt its institutionalization. However, because Matthew was writing his Introduction to the Gladstone diaries over many years and addressing many other themes, he understandably did so only through scattered *aperçus*. My essay begins by drawing these together and in certain respects fleshing them out. It then examines the progress made by Gladstone's 'vision of international legitimacy and order' in the decades between its definitive expression in the Midlothian Campaign and its coming to fruition in the First World War.

In order to identify Gladstone's contribution to the debate about peace and war we must first understand how that debate had evolved by the time he became Liberal leader. It had always been dominated in Britain, as in most countries throughout the modern political era, by what Matthew called 'the "national interest" view'[9] and students of international relations such as E. H. Carr have termed 'realism'. Because this was the ideology justifying the defence expenditures and defence policies which have been the constant target of the peace activists whom I have spent much of my time studying, I have labelled it 'defencism'. Its core assumptions have been that countries have both an unfettered right to fight

[5] J. L. Hammond, 'Gladstone and the League of Nations Mind', in H. A. L. Fisher *et al., Essays in Honour of Gilbert Murray* (1936), 98, 99–100.

[6] Alan Bullock and Maurice Shock, *The Liberal Tradition from Fox to Keynes* (1956), p. xl.

[7] Michael Bentley, *The Liberal Mind 1914–1929* (Cambridge, 1977), 150.

[8] H. C. G. Matthew, *Gladstone 1809–1898* (Oxford, 1997), 272.   [9] Ibid., 186.

defensively and a duty to maintain strong defences as a contribution to international order.[10] Defencism is thus a more moderate ideology than militarism, which believes that war is a principal mechanism of human progress and therefore allows aggression. It is also more restrained than crusading, which allows aggressive war when this promotes a political reform intended ultimately to further the cause of peace. Although normally taken to be a self-evident truth requiring no explanation, defencism was influentially expounded by the Anglican theorist of the common wisdom, William Paley, whose writings were to receive frequent critical citations in early peace literature. In a best-selling primer first published in 1785, Paley dissented from the Quaker view that 'it is unlawful for a Christian to bear arms', and insisted:

The justifying causes of war are deliberate invasions of right, and the necessity of maintaining such a balance of power amongst neighbouring states, as that no single state or confederacy of states, be strong enough to overwhelm the rest. The objects of just war are precaution, defence, or reparation. In a larger sense, every just war is a *defensive* war, in as much as every just war supposes an injury, perpetrated, attempted or feared.

Paley also warned that 'it is unsafe for a nation to disband its regular troops, whilst neighbouring kingdomes retain theirs'.[11]

Defencists such as Paley believed that international conflict could be prevented for substantial periods by prudent diplomacy and balance-of-power policies, but assumed that the international system could not evolve beyond an armed truce. This was too negative for those of a more progressive cast of mind, whose belief in the achievability of international 'peace' of a positive kind caused a peace movement to emerge in Britain during the mid-1790s in reaction to the Napoleonic Wars and to institutionalize itself at the end of those wars.[12] From the outset this movement was an uneasy alliance of pacifists (absolutists who believed that war could be abolished by a mass act of conscientious objection) and *pacificists* (reformists who believed it could be abolished by structural reform either in the international system or in the states composing it). Pacifist writings within mainstream Anglicanism and Nonconformity, as distinct from smaller sects such as the Quakers, began to appear from 1796 onwards; and a pacifist-led body, the Peace Society, founded twenty years later when Gladstone was a 6 year old, was still the best-known peace association at the time of his death. Yet because pacifism opposed all use of military force, it was always very much the minority viewpoint even among peace activists. And with very few exceptions pacifists did

---

[10] Defencism is examined in more detail in Martin Ceadel, *Thinking about Peace and War* (Oxford, 1987), ch. 5.

[11] William Paley, *The Principles of Moral and Political Philosophy* (London, 1785), 637, 641, 644–9, 653, 655.

[12] See J. E. Cookson, *The Friends of Peace: Anti-War Liberalism in England 1792–1815* (Cambridge, 1982); Martin Ceadel, *The Origins of War Prevention: The British Peace Movement and International Relations, 1730–1854* (Oxford, 1996), chs. 6–7.

not expect their absolutist perspective to be regarded as practical politics for the foreseeable future. After Henry Richard, secretary of the Peace Society from 1848 to 1885, became a Liberal MP in 1868, he invariably argued in his parliamentary speeches from *pacificist* rather than pacifist premises. For example, in 1882, while acknowledging that his own opinions remained those of a Christian pacifist, Richard reminded the Commons that he 'never obtruded those views on his House', because 'no one would be safe from ridicule here who would attempt to bring our national policy, and especially our foreign policy, to the test of a severe Christian morality.'[13] John Bright and his fellow Quaker MPs adopted the same tactics.

Therefore only *pacificism*, which allowed military force provided it was both defensive and politically progressive, stood a chance of influencing the political classes. But even it could do so only to the extent that its recipe for abolishing war struck a chord. In the 1790s radicals such as Tom Paine and William Godwin argued that war was caused by monarchies and aristocracies and would disappear once a republican or popular government was established; but, though anticipating much of the democratic peace theory which became fashionable almost exactly two centuries later,[14] this was too revolutionary a view to achieve support from the electorate of the time. From the mid-1830s the free-trade campaigner and future Liberal MP Richard Cobden popularized the 'Manchester School' view that international commerce was 'the grand panacea'[15] which would create economic interdependence among nations and progressively reduce the incidence of war. But, popular though this critique proved to be, its utility as a guide to foreign policy was reduced by the isolationism with which Cobden associated it. In his early writings, as is well known, Cobden advocated 'withdrawing ourselves from foreign politics', and hoped, in a reformed political system, 'to see the test of "no foreign politics" applied to those who offer to become the representatives of free constituencies'.[16] Admittedly, from 1848, when he committed himself to the peace movement, he softened his opposition to diplomacy to the extent of supporting arbitration, disarmament, and trade agreements, including the negotiation of the Cobden–Chevalier treaty of 1860 with Gladstone's encouragement. Yet he and associates such as John Bright were still perceived as isolationists because of their commitment to non-intervention. This was in large part a reaction against the policies of the long-serving Whig Foreign Secretary, Lord Palmerston, which were grounded upon an expansive view of British national interests but were often justified to progressive opinion as being motivated by concern for the liberties of Europe: in other words, Palmerston was a truculent defencist who was prepared for domestic-political purposes to use crusading rhetoric. In the 1850s and 1860s crusading—against

[13] *Hansard*, CCLXXII, cols. 1766–7 (25 July 1882).
[14] For a seminal exposition of this theory, see Michael W. Doyle, 'Kant, Liberal Legacies, and Foreign Affairs', *Philosophy and Public Affairs*, 12 (1983), 205–35, 323–53.
[15] Richard Cobden, *Political Writings* (2 vols., London, 1867), i. 45.   [16] Ibid., i. 43.

Russia, particularly following its suppression of the Hungarian revolt against the Habsburgs in 1849, or in support of Italian nationalism—was at a peak of popularity in British progressive circles, as evidenced by the remarkable reception Kossuth received in 1851 and which Garibaldi would have enjoyed in 1864 had the government not quickly spirited him out of the country. For *pacificists* at this time the susceptibility of many of their fellow radicals or liberals to at least the rhetoric of crusading was a major worry, and helps to explain why so many of them became dogmatic non-interventionists. Admittedly, there was a more engaged *pacificist* approach, pioneered by Jeremy Bentham, systematized by James Mill, and publicized by American peace activists William Ladd and Elihu Burritt, which called for a congress of nations to codify international law so that a court of nations could apply it; but still it saw no need either for a permanent international organization or for the enforcement of court decisions.[17] The engaged strand in *pacificist* thought was thus both less popular and less developed than the isolationist one.

We can now consider Gladstone's contribution to the peace-or-war debate. Colin Matthew's observations on this subject can be grouped together to form three intuitions. The first was that, having established common ground with the Manchester School by accepting its economic vision, Gladstone offset its political isolationism by expounding a form of 'moderate interventionism'[18] which could not be confused with Palmerstonian meddling. In consequence, although Gladstone's own thinking 'stopped short of the classic Liberal position',[19] when blended with Cobdenism it resulted in a mature liberal internationalism. The second intuition was that Gladstone did much to give this viewpoint 'a popular base in the era of the extended franchise'.[20] The third was that, even so, Gladstone and his contemporaries did less to institutionalize liberal internationalism than their political successors would do during the First World War, with unfortunate long-term consequences for their own political movement: 'The generation of British Liberals which played so prominent a part in the founding of the League of Nations was, for Liberalism, perhaps a generation or two generations too late.'[21]

Consider the first intuition as Matthew adumbrated it. After being converted to free trade in the 1840s, Gladstone was by the early 1850s 'extolling the mid-century Liberal solution: "free and unrestricted exchange . . . with all the nations of the world", with Britain "the standard bearer of the nations upon the fruitful paths of peace, industry and commerce" '.[22] Even so, in 1854 he supported British entry into the Crimean War, which Cobden and Bright opposed, and continued to justify it after most other supporters had ceased to do so. Moreover, he did not rule out British involvement in the Franco-Prussian War. In consequence,

---

[17] As emphasized in F. H. Hinsley, *Power and the Pursuit of Peace: Theory and Practice in the History of Relations between States* (Cambridge, 1967).   [18] Matthew, *Gladstone*, 410.
[19] Ibid., 272.   [20] Ibid., 273.   [21] Ibid., 570–1.   [22] Ibid., 81.

throughout his first government he 'differed sharply from traditional Mancunian isolationism embodied in the Cabinet by John Bright. In addition to the precept of intervention, he supported a traditional priority of the "national interest" view of Continental affairs', namely a concern for the Low Countries.[23] Matthew was in effect saying that, according to Gladstone, British military involvement could be justified anywhere in Europe on principled grounds, to uphold what he called the public law of Europe, as had been attempted in the Crimean War. It could also be justified in Western Europe on prudential grounds too, because of Britain's defensive interest in preventing the Low Countries falling into the hands of a power which might use the Channel ports to invade or blockade it, something he would have been prepared to do had Belgium been menaced during the Franco-Prussian War.

In associating him with 'the "national interest" view' and its 'traditional priority' of maintaining the independence of the Low Countries, Matthew recognized that, despite Gladstone's move via Peelism into the Liberal Party, the intellectual baggage which he had retained from his Conservative past included defencism and one of its geostrategic orthodoxies. Matthew further recognized that Gladstone's defencism was of a particular kind because of the 'High-Church ideology of the Concert of Europe'[24] which was another survival from his youthful high toryism. Matthew understood that the Concert of Europe, an 'essentially monarchic' institution working through 'the essentially aristocratic structure of European embassies',[25] originated in a realist and conservative vision: 'It recognized the differing interests of states, it accepted that some states were more powerful than others, and it worked through the existing social structure of Europe, the continuing power of the aristocracy being exemplified in its control of the embassies and the chancelries through which the Concert system was worked.'[26]

Yet Gladstone assumed that coexistence among the European powers was part of the divine purpose, and to that extent saw the international system as having some of the characteristics of a society. This placed him in what some modern international-relations theorists term the 'international society' school and others the 'liberal realist' one, which holds that order is maintained in part by diplomatic norms and institutions such as the Concert of Europe; it separated him from the 'classical realist' school, which contends that it is maintained by power resources alone.[27] As Matthew noted, Gladstone's faith in the Concert's aristocratic diplomacy conflicted with the radical *pacifism* of Paine and Godwin and their successors: 'Foreign policy was not, as it was for the Radicals, corrupt dealings between landed castes, but rather the means by which European nations communicated for the public good.'[28] However, his international-society or liberal-realist

[23] Ibid., 186.   [24] Ibid., 271.   [25] Ibid., 274.   [26] Ibid., 271.
[27] The most famous expression of the international-society view is Hedley Bull, *The Anarchical Society* (London, 1977). For the varieties of realism, see Timothy Dunne, 'Realism', in John Baylis and Steve Smith (eds.), *The Globalization of World Politics* (Oxford, 1997), 109–24.
[28] Matthew, *Gladstone*, 183.

assumptions brought him close to liberal *pacificism*. He viewed the Concert of
Europe as compatible with 'the Liberal belief in the benefits of free trade in
promoting international harmony': indeed, he 'saw free trade as the partner of the
Concert'. He also saw the Concert as compatible with nationalism as a basis for
state legitimacy: in doing so, he 'found himself apparently on common ground
with the Liberals, though his nationalism was primarily religious rather than
liberal in origin; he had been a nationalist before he had been a liberal'.[29]

The most controversial aspect of Gladstone's Concert of Europe ideology was
its 'precept of intervention'.[30] In Matthew's words: 'Within the context of the
Concert, coercion by arms was, in its proper context, a proper instrument of
policy which would in most cases achieve its result without war.'[31] Famously,
Gladstone called in 1876–8 for the European powers to threaten action against
Turkey in response to its atrocities against the Bulgarians, and did the same two
decades later in response to its atrocities against the Armenians. However, he
derived the Concert's right of intervention in such cases not from the military
preponderance of the great powers that constituted it but from its moral authority
as an agent of the divine will. The Concert was allowed to interfere in the affairs of
other states and sometimes even coerce them only 'because it represented the best
available institutional representation of Christian morality in international
affairs'.[32] In other words Gladstone believed that, even for the great powers acting
together, might did not make right: their intervention in the affairs of other
countries had to be morally justifiable.

This emphasis on morality was the bridge that enabled the conservative and
defencist idea of the Concert of Europe to cross over into the liberal and *pacificist*
idea of international organization. Admittedly, not all liberals accepted that
the Concert was capable of evolving as Gladstone envisaged. Thus the historian
J. R. Seeley, one of the few British nineteenth-century intellectuals to advocate an
international federation on the American model, did so because he was of the
opinion that 'The international system wanted is something essentially different
from, and cannot be developed out of, the already existing system by which
European affairs are settled in Congress of the great powers.'[33] But many believed
that, despite evident limitations at present, the Concert had the potential to
become an idealist institution. During the 1880 general election the campaigning
journalist W. T. Stead described it in a Liberal leaflet as the 'germ of a United
States of Europe'.[34] In 1884 a contributor to the *Contemporary Review*, though
warning that the Concert was often 'only another name for the predominance of
one power which has the means, or knows the art, of making a majority of the rest
subservient to its wishes', conceded: 'Nevertheless, it is a fruitful idea. Arguments

---

[29] Matthew, *Gladstone*, 271–2.   [30] Ibid., 186.   [31] Ibid., 274.   [32] Ibid., 275.
[33] *Herald of Peace* (Jan. 1871), 197. For Seeley's lecture to the Peace Society advocating an international federation on the model of the United States, *see Herald of Peace* (Apr. 1871), 197–9.
[34] *Elector's Catechism* (1880), cited in W. T. Stead, *The United States of Europe on the Eve of the
Parliament of Peace, Being the 'Review of Reviews' Annual 1899* (London, 1899), 33.

based on justice, or drawn from considerations of common interest, cannot be urged wholly in vain. They must in decency be either admitted or refuted, and the most cynical statemen may in the end be shamed into doing what is right.'[35] As late as 1911 a writer in the *Fortnightly Review*, whilst recognizing its past failings, claimed that, when compared with the alternative mechanism of the balance of power, 'the Concert is perfect in theory and quite possible in practice, and has, moreover, the supreme merit of responding to certain ideals which are calculated to dignify and elevate the otherwise often squalid machinery of international politics'.[36] Moreover, as secularization gathered pace, the notion of 'the public law of Europe', though derived by Gladstone from Christian ideas of natural law, was increasingly associated with positivist conceptions of international law. And as the idea of democracy spread, the great powers lost the near-monopoly of international legitimacy that they had possessed in the heyday of the Concert of Europe, and settled merely for privileged representation on the Council of the League of Nations and the Security Council of the United Nations, organizations with partially democratic procedures whose authority rested primarily on their representativeness of the international community as a whole. Gladstone thus contributed to the 'transition of the concert system from the club of monarchies which it had been since the eighteenth century to a wider base of popular legitimacy'.[37]

Because Gladstone believed in concerted action, he disliked unilateral action, even by Britain. He thus feared that Disraeli's purchase of Suez Canal shares in 1875 would have adverse consequences 'if not done in concert with Europe'.[38] In respect of the Eastern Question during 1877–8 he 'held that an independently British policy towards the Straits, separate from the Concert's concerns at civilized standards of behaviour in Turkey was unnecessary, undesirable, and dangerous. There was no unique "British interest", and there should therefore be no unilateral British action.'[39] His consequent opposition to unilateral British intervention on Turkey's side, which caused a jingo mob to attack his London home in February 1878, was welcomed by peace activists. They already appreciated his decision to refer the Anglo-American dispute over the *Alabama* claims to arbitration. Admittedly, this dispute was in reality solved by a bilateral diplomatic compromise in 1872, which was publicly presented as the quasi-judicial decision of an arbitration tribunal sitting in Geneva largely to protect it from domestic hawks on both sides of the Atlantic; but Matthew was right to argue that Gladstone appreciated the exemplary value of being seen to arbitrate the issue, because it showed how 'two civilized nations could settle differences without either having to admit being in the wrong'.[40] The peace movement also appreciated Gladstone's desire to limit imperial expansion and reduce defence expenditure. On the armaments issue in particular Gladstone moved beyond a desire to economize to a motivation

---

[35] Henry Dunckley, 'Egypt, Europe, and Mr Gladstone', *Contemporary Review* (July 1884), 13.
[36] Diplomaticus, 'Sir Edward Grey's Stewardship', *Fortnightly Review* (Dec. 1911), 964.
[37] Matthew, *Gladstone*, 410.   [38] Cited ibid., 266.   [39] Ibid., 276.   [40] Ibid., 188.

akin to *pacificism*. In particular, before resigning in 1894 from his fourth and final government in opposition to its naval programme, he composed what Matthew rightly called 'a memorandum remarkable in the annals of British radical writing'. It included the statement: 'I cannot & will not add to the perils & the coming calamities of Europe by an act of militarism... which excuses thus the militarism of Germany, France or Russia. England's providential part is to help peace, and liberty of which peace is the nurse; this policy is the foe of both.'[41]

By thus dissociating interventionism in support of the public law of Europe from interventionism based on a my-nation-right-or-wrong jingoism whilst also linking it to the curbing of armaments expenditure and to anti-militarism, Gladstone made it palatable to many of those who had supported Cobden until his death in 1865. For a while even Henry Richard became as enthusiastic a Gladstonian as a pacifist and close associate of Cobden could be. Thus he cited with approval Gladstone's speech of 9 December 1869 to the Lord Mayor's banquet which asserted that 'a standard of international conduct higher than the particular standard which each set itself' was emerging among nations and that, whilst forswearing 'impertinent interference', Britain should construct 'a sentiment of true brotherhood with those countries with which we are connected by so many kind ties'.[42] Although Richard's pacifism required him still to support non-intervention, he now specified that this meant 'not as is sometimes most untruly alleged, non-intercourse with other nations, or want of interest in the general affairs of the world, but simply abstaining from meddling in the affairs of others'.[43] Moreover, by the early 1880s he was explicitly endorsing 'Gladstonianism',[44] though he was to be disillusioned by Gladstone's intervention in Egypt in 1882. Predictably, some *pacificists* found the breaking of the link between liberalism and isolationism hard to get used to. The veteran radical MP Sir Wilfred Lawson criticized Gladstone's Egyptian policy as 'an abandonment of all the principle of non-intervention, of which we had heard so much when the Ministry were in Opposition', prompting Gladstone indignantly to deny that he had ever been 'a general apostle of non-intervention' and to point out that on the contrary his charge against the previous government in respect of Turkey had been 'that we had not intervention enough'.[45]

If Matthew's first intuition was thus that Gladstone offered 'a vision of international legitimacy and order' which anticipated the international organizations of the twentieth century, his second was that he found himself 'newly associating [this vision] with a popular campaign'.[46] Having in revulsion against the Bulgarian atrocities 'experienced a conversion of Evangelical intensity' in the summer of 1876, he discovered that his campaign of protest had nurtured 'real empathy' between 'certain sections of the Victorian ruling classes and "labouring

[41] Cited ibid., 603.   [42] Cited in *Herald of Peace* (Jan. 1870), 4.
[43] *Herald of Peace* (June 1875), 249.   [44] *Herald of Peace* (Mar. 1882), 26.
[45] *Hansard*, CCLXII cols. 169, 174–5. See also Matthew, *Gladstone*, 376.
[46] Matthew, *Gladstone*, 272.

men", as Gladstone called them'.[47] The Eastern crisis of 1877–8 with its attendant novelty of jingoism, and the profligate imperialism of the Beaconsfield government, enabled him to broaden his support into 'a Popular Front of moral outrage'[48] and to launch the Midlothian campaign of 1878–80 which both 'pointed the way towards the secular humanitarianism of twentieth-century Liberalism' and 'formulated a politics that was both charismatic and rational'.[49] Because Gladstone developed this new 'politics of "The Platform" '[50] in respect of the need for morality in foreign policy, he helped to give this issue a place in public life unmatched by any other country other than perhaps the United States and Scandinavia.

Moreover, he did much to establish the lasting pattern whereby the left in British politics has adopted *pacificist* rhetoric and aspired to an ethical dimension in foreign policy and the right has been overtly defencist. Admittedly, this ideological alignment required the collusion of Disraeli, whose views had become notably more bellicose since the Crimean War when he had been praised by the Peace Society for his 'moderate and pacific counsels'.[51] During the 1870s he had adopted Palmerston's spirited foreign-policy style to such an extent that by 1879 the Peace Society was denouncing Disraeli as 'a tool of the Jingoes and of sycophantic Imperialists',[52] and by the 1880 general election was identifying as 'the only issue' in that contest the question: 'Are we to have a warlike or pacific foreign policy?'[53] After Gladstone emerged victorious the historian E. A. Freeman not only exulted that 'The act which the English nation has just done rises to the height of historical sublimity', but claimed that the Bulgarian-horrors campaign had 'acted as an education of the national conscience. I suspect that many men then practically learned for the first time that there was such a thing as a right or wrong in public affairs.'[54] Even so, the long-term beneficiary of this polarization of British politics between a *pacificist* left and defencist right was the latter. As Matthew noted: 'Conservative pre-emption of patriotism was, appropriately modified to suit the occasion, to have a long and effective life.'[55] Progressivism has generally found international relations less amenable to its analysis than the domestic arena.

This brings us to the third and most provocative of Matthew's intuitions, namely that Gladstone did not do all he might have done to develop the liberal internationalism which he and his party had seemingly embraced in the Midlothian campaign. He was negligent in two respects, the first being that he and his colleagues failed to create an international association of Liberal parties:

It was an important consequence of the Home Rule preoccupation that British Liberalism did not in these years play a more active role in encouraging the sort of institutional development of internationalism implicit in Gladstone's campaigns during . . . the 1870s.

---

[47] Ibid., 282, 287.   [48] Ibid., 294.   [49] Ibid., 294, 312.   [50] Ibid., 642.
[51] *Herald of Peace* (Jan. 1856), 3.   [52] *Herald of Peace* (May 1879), 233.
[53] *Herald of Peace* (May 1880), 66.
[54] E. A. Freeman, 'The Election and the Eastern Question', *Contemporary Review* (June 1880), 958, 962.   [55] Matthew, *Gladstone*, 268.

When Gladstone came to challenge British armament expansion, as he did in 1892–4, he was able to do so in the context of national politics only: the liberal movement had neither associated itself with the Second International (formed in 1889), nor provided an alternative international institutional structure. As the leader of world Liberalism in its political form, this failure was a perhaps surprising blot on the British liberal record between the 1880s and 1914.[56]

It is a pity that Matthew did not expand this suggestion, as it is not clear what a 'Liberal International' would have consisted of or what its prospects would have been.

The second respect in which Gladstone was negligent was that, for all his enthusiasm for the Concert of Europe, he 'offered no structural proposals to improve or advance upon' its effectiveness, and that despite doing much to popularize the cause of international arbitration, he 'did not personally suggest means of institutionalizing' it.[57] This is undeniable: Gladstone seemed content with the Concert of Europe and arbitration arrangements as they stood. And, as already implied, a mere handful of British liberal intellectuals argued for the creation of an international organization during the second half of the nineteenth century. (Apart from J. R. Seeley, whose international federalism has already been noted, only the historian Frederic Seebohm, who published a book calling for 'an international police force',[58] and James Lorimer, an international jurist in the natural-law tradition, whose legal writings called for a fully fledged international government with its capital at either Byzantium or Geneva, seem to have done so in a systematic way.[59]) The overwhelming majority of liberals pinned their hopes on the steadily increasing number of bilateral treaties containing arbitration clauses, which they assumed would be enforced by world public opinion. This attitude was summed up by Britain's Lord Chief Justice who in 1896 told the International Law Association that the absence of a 'League of Nations of the Amphictyonic type' did not matter because the 'sanctions which restrain the wrongdoer'—namely 'dread of war and the reprobation of mankind'—were 'not weak', and were moreover growing stronger every year.[60]

Matthew's account of Gladstone enables us to identify a number of characteristics which limited his capacity to promote and institutionalize liberal internationalism. His 'transparently extraordinary' character, his 'powerful individualism', his 'highly complex and eclectic' mind, and his 'curious lack of self-awareness'[61] made him personally and intellectually too idiosyncratic to be a model liberal-internationalist educator of the kind Gilbert Murray and others were to be in the era of the League of Nations. His speeches in response to the inoffensive *pacificist* resolutions which Henry Richard introduced in the

---

[56] Matthew, *Gladstone*, 570.   [57] Ibid., 274.   [58] *On International Reform* (1871), 135.
[59] *Institutes of the Law of Nations* (2 vols., Edinburgh, 1883–4), ii. 275–88.
[60] Lord Russell of Killowen, *Arbitration: Its Origin, History and Prospects* (London, 1896), 30.
[61] Matthew, *Gladstone*, 2, 51, 337.

Commons on 8 July 1873, 15 June 1880, 29 April 1881, and 19 March 1886 were sledgehammers to crack nuts; and John Vincent was right to observe in respect of the first of these that Gladstone treated Richard no better than Palmerston had treated Cobden.[62] And his insistence on the efficacy of the Concert of Europe, even though it was being undermined as early as Bismarck's conclusion of the Three Emperors' Alliance in June 1881, was less than wholly persuasive.[63]

Furthermore, as Matthew pointed out, Gladstone's 'radical conservatism, which fused at times with an advanced liberalism... deeply perplexed conservatives and often disappointed liberals'.[64] An example of a fusion of ostensibly contradictory political principles was his belief in the possibility of 'reconciliation between the "equal rights of all nations" and the requirements of international order'.[65] Another care which perplexed liberals was his unapologetic attitude to coercion: 'He saw intervention as a natural part of the maintenance of the civilized order of the world. He used military and naval force coolly and without embarrassment.'[66] And despite being a politician who 'understands the popular impulse', as the artisan George Howell observed early in the Bulgarian-horrors campaign,[67] he had surprisingly little appreciation of the weight which common-sense morality attached to defensiveness as a justification for the use of force. Believing that validation by the Concert of Europe was justification enough, Gladstone did not bother to present it as extended self-defence. Thus although he could seem *pacificist* when opposing unilateral inverventions, he could appear to be a crusader when advocating interventions in the interests of European order.

These contradictory appearances were exacerbated by his habit of expressing moderate and qualified sentiments in language so vivid as to imply a more extreme position. As Matthew noted:

'Bag and baggage', the catch-phrase of the *The Bulgarian Horrors* pamphlet, helped popularize the campaign but it was a misleading distillation of Gladstone's view of a Balkan settlement, which in fact saved as much as it could for the imperial power. 'Bag and baggage' was—like 'the pale of the constitution' in 1864—a phrase whose fame sharpened its author's radical reputation while ignoring the surrounding qualitifications.[68]

Gladstone's anti-Turkish rhetoric alarmed peace activists as much as did Disraeli's anti-Russian inclinations. During 1876–8 they saw themselves as combating 'two strong opposing impulses' both of which were 'tending in the direction of general war'. One, mainly found among Conservatives, was inspired by defencism: 'the

[62] John Vincent, *The Formation of the Liberal Party. 1857–1868* (London, 1966), 248 (which however misdated Richard's first resolution to 1870).

[63] As argued in W. N. Medlicott's classic work, *Bismarck, Gladstone and the Concert of Europe* (London, 1956).   [64] Matthew, *Gladstone*, 1, 2.

[65] Ibid., 376.   [66] Ibid., 375.

[67] 'Working Men and the Eastern Question', *Contemporary Review* (Oct. 1876), 868.

[68] Matthew, *Gladstone*, 280.

traditional policy of this country, which was supposed to bind us, for the sake of British interests, to maintain at all costs the integrity and independence of the Turkish Empire'. The other, mainly found among liberals and radicals, was inspired by crusading: 'the feeling of uncontrollable indignation caused in the popular heart by the revelations... of the hideous brutalities committed by the Turks in Bulgaria... which begot a desire in some quarter for armed intervention—to suppress such outrages, and to establish good Government in Turkey'.[69] Henry Richard was thus in a difficult position when he joined Gladstone as a speaker at the St James's Hall meeting of 8 December 1876 at which an Eastern Question Association was formed. Although Richard expressed enthusiasm for the meeting and the new association, he made it clear that he did 'not want to go to war against Turkey any more than for it' and indeed considered crusading ('a war waged in the interests of philanthropy') even more objectionable, because of its humanitarian pretensions, than a war fought on defencist principles.[70] In 1895–6, moreover, Gladstone's powerfully expressed protest over the Armenian massacres—most notably, his last great political speech, delivered at Liverpool on 24 September 1896, which urged that Britain 'take into consideration the means of enforcing, if force alone is available, compliance with her just, legal and humane demand' upon Turkey[71]—worried the peace movement again.

In between these two indulgences in crusading rhetoric Gladstone had gone to the opposite extreme of creating excessive *pacificist* expectations. As George Brooks, a Congregationalist minister who had at the time been an enthusiastic Gladstonian, later noted of the Midlothian campaign: 'When a man speaks in such a spirit of peace, retrenchment and reform; of responsibility, progress and justice, common people may be forgiven if they expect him to achieve great results.' For Brooks the 'orator of Midlothian' had given people 'faith that a brighter day had dawned. Wars would now cease, and the nation would have a season of rest. England would no longer play the part of a bully among the nations, but would respect the rights of others, and do as she would be done by.' Yet, after making a promising start to his foreign policy, Gladstone had dashed expectations by an Egyptian policy which a disenchanted Brooks condemned as 'an unbroken and lamentable series of mistakes, blunders, crimes'.[72] Matthew noted in Gladstone's defence that at the time of the occupation of Egypt he 'was simply outnumbered and outflanked in his Cabinet and was anyway physically and mentally exhausted by his constant work in the Commons on the Irish Crimes and Arrears bills'.[73] Yet Matthew also acknowledged that the Egyptian

[69] *Herald of Peace* (June 1877), 246–7.
[70] Eastern Question Association, *Report of Proceedings of the National Conference at St James's Hall London December 8th 1876* (n.d.), 30–2, 83. *Herald of Peace* (Jan. 1877), 156.
[71] *The Times* (25 Sept. 1896), 5.
[72] George Brooks, *Gladstonian Liberalism in Idea and in Fact* (London, 1885), 75, 84.
[73] Mattthew, *Gladstone*, 386.

intervention was no aberration. Despite Gladstone's Cobdenite principles on commerce and empire, whenever he was in office 'his executive itch, his sense of the immediate, of what seemed to be "practical" encouraged imperial action eventually as bold as that of any other Victorian'.[74] He was motivated by an aversion to 'disorder', which in the Egyptian case affected his personal interests as a 'bondholder at second hand'; and he agreed to the bombardment of Alexandria 'without an expression of regret as Britain began the imposition of "order" on behalf of the international community'.[75]

Matthew also hinted that Gladstone's heart was never in the internationalist cause as much as it was in religious pluralism, free-trade minimalism, executive *étatism*, or new means of political communication—'the four great themes' which he identified in the definition and summary of 'Gladstonism' at the end of chapter 4 of his biography. Indeed, acknowledging that his 'locating of these four compass points has omitted discussion of foreign and imperial policies, the very issues which brought [Gladstone] again to form a government in 1880', Matthew explained:

In foreign policy, his High-Church concept of the Concert of Europe … represented a continuation and extension of the policies of his youth, and brought him into sharp conflict with 'the Manchester School'. It was, Gladstone felt, an interest forced upon him by events and, important and distinctive though his contribution was, it was not what he would have seen as a positive interest.[76]

I interpret this highly condensed remark as a suggestion that Gladstone's proto-internationalism was the improvised result of religious duty in the face of Turkish cruelty combined with political opportunity in the face of unexpected mass enthusiasm for a non-materialistic cause; and that it did not constitute a premeditated commitment to the reform of international relations.

Gladstone's limitations as an expositor of liberal internationalism cannot alone explain why this doctrine made such modest progress between the early 1880s and 1914 even among members of his own party. Four international developments also served as inhibitors. The first was the occupation of Egypt from 1882, which, as already noted, alienated the peace movement and the radical wing of the Liberal Party. Admittedly, Gladstone adroitly neutralized the Anti-Aggression League, a peace association which Herbert Spencer, John Morley, and others had just launched. Having invited Spencer to breakfast, he praised the League's *pacificist* moderation as compared with the pacifist dogmatism of the Peace Society, and promised that he and Bright would ensure that the government behaved with as much restraint as circumstances allowed. Spencer was won over; and in consequence the Anti-Aggression League was stillborn.[77] But the Peace Society, in what proved to be its last act of real courage, accused 'the Liberal Party' of a 'humiliating'

---

[74] Ibid., 350.   [75] Ibid., 387, 389.   [76] Ibid., 350.
[77] Martin Ceadel, *Semi-Detached Idealists: The British Peace Movement and International Relations, 1854–1945* (Oxford, 2000), 119.

attempt 'to rehabilitate what some think its waning popularity, on a foundation of pure Jingoism' a mere two years after having gone to the country on 'a cry of indignant protest against the prevailing Jingoism'.[78] And radicals made the post-Cobdenite and proto-Hobsonian discovery that some economic interests actually favoured aggression. According, for example, to Randal Cremer, secretary of the Workmen's Peace Assocation and later not only a Lib–Lab MP but the first British winner of the Nobel Peace Prize: 'The men who formerly made wars were generally monarchs and unscrupulous statesmen, but our modern warmakers are financiers'.[79] The implications of this new version of radical pacificism were isolationist: Britain should stay out of the quarrels into which financial vested interests were trying to push it. Thus intervention in Egypt not only tarnished Gladstonism in the eyes of peace activists but, by encouraging isolationism in radical circles, impeded the development of an engaged liberal *pacificism*.

A second development was the scramble for Africa and Asia, which led Gladstone's successor, Lord Rosebery, to try to move the Liberal Party away from *pacificism* and towards defencism. This was partly because defencism offered the more plausible analysis of great-power competition. But it was also for domestic reasons: particularly after Gladstone dedicated his third and fourth governments to the cause of Home Rule for Ireland, the Conservatives could advantageously deploy what an official Liberal publication admitted to be 'a common charge against Liberalism (made in direct contradiction of the facts) that the Liberal party is indifferent to the safety of the Empire and whilst in power neglects the Imperial defences'.[80] Wanting to take external relations out of party politics, Rosebery's 'Liberal Imperialists' called for continuity in foreign policy, on the grounds that national interests and international constraints were the same for Liberal as for Conservative governments. As Matthew put it in his first book:

The concept of continuity suggested that those who professed it were not looking for a specifically 'liberal' foreign policy. The Liberal Imperialists denied that this was either desirable or possible, thereby annoying the radical wing of the party, which saw what the Liberal Imperialists regarded as a lack of options as a conspiracy by the 'governing classes'.[81]

Although the Liberal Imperialists failed to capture the party, they succeeded in muting its *pacificist* message.

The third event was Turkey's massacring of the Armenians in 1895–6 and crushing of the Greeks in 1897, which exacerbated Liberal divisions. As already

[78] *Herald of Peace* (Dec. 1882), 154.
[79] *Arbitrator* (Sept. 1882), 2. For Cremer's career see Martin Ceadel, 'Sir William Randall Cremer', in Karl Holl and Anne Kjelling (eds.), *The Nobel Prizes and the Laureates: The Meaning and Acceptance of the Nobel Peace Prize in the Prize Winners' Countries* (Frankfurt, 1994), 167–92.
[80] *Liberal Magazine: A Periodical of Liberal Speakers and Canvassers* (Feb. 1896), 35.
[81] H. C. G. Matthew, *The Liberal Imperialists: The Ideas and Politics of a Post-Gladstonian Elite* (London, 1973), 196–7.

noted, Gladstone repeated his call of two decades previously for action by the European powers against Turkey. However, Lord Rosebery's defencism inclined him to a less emotive view; and he resigned the party leadership in protest at Gladstone's oratorical swansong of 24 September 1896 at Liverpool. Liberals became polarized over the feasibility or otherwise of a moral foreign policy, the *Daily Chronicle* attacking Rosebery's advocacy of 'the dogma of "British interests" against the interests of humanity', and the *Daily News* taking the opposite view.[82] Gladstone still sought to legitimate his crusading by invoking the Concert of Europe, causing a contemporary to note: 'The keynote of Mr Gladstone's policy was, not for isolated action, but for shaming the Powers into united pressure on the Porte.'[83] Yet the European powers refused to act against Turkey, thereby tarnishing the Concert idea in the eyes of many Liberal moralists. For example, a spokesman for the 'Liberal Forwards', though acknowledging the 'fascination' of the Concert of Europe—'It raises the thought of the Great Powers leaguing together to prevent war, acting, in short, short as the Police of Europe... — condemned it as 'the cant phrase of modern diplomacy' which in practice 'substitutes for our British policy a policy "made in Germany" '.[84] This discrediting of the Concert weakened the connection between a moral foreign policy and an internationalist one.

The fourth international factor was the Boer War, which further intensified Liberal disagreements over the Empire. It prompted the radical economist J. A. Hobson, already a critic of 'a "spirited" commercial policy',[85] to argue that imperialism had an 'economic taproot', namely the domestic underconsumptionism which led capitalists to seek alternative outlets for their surplus finance.[86] And it so blatantly split the party between pro-Boers and imperialists that the annual report of the National Liberal Federation in March 1900 conceded:

It would be affectation to deny that great and considerable differences exist in the Liberal Party as to the true interpretation to be placed upon the events which culminated in war. There are some who hold that the war is just and necessary, some that it is just but unnecessary, some that it is not unjust but unnecessary, some that it is both unjust and unnecessary.[87]

The continuing 'controversy between Imperialists and other Liberals' was attributed by the journalist J. A. Spender to a profound ideological cleavage:

On the one hand is a feeling that Liberalism must not be an enervating creed which unfits its adherents for their part in the world struggle, or a cosmopolitan creed which saps the

---

[82] Cited ibid., 25.

[83] James Annand, 'Armenia and Home Politics', *Progressive Review* (Jan. 1897), 333.

[84] P. W. Clayden, 'Great Britain and the Concert of Europe', *Progressive Review* (Apr. 1897), 72, 76.

[85] J. A. Hobson, 'Free Trade and Foreign Policy', *Contemporary Review* (Aug. 1898), 169.

[86] J. A. Hobson, 'Capitalism and Imperialism in South Africa', *Contemporary Review* (Jan. 1900), 1–17, and The Economic Taproot of Imperialism', *Contemporary Review* (Aug. 1901), 284–93.

[87] National Liberal Federation, *Proceeedings in Connection with the 22nd Annual Meeting of the Federation held in Nottingham, March 26–29 1900* (1900), 35.

foundations of common patriotism. On the other is the desire to moralise mankind in its international relations and to resist the primitive instincts and passions which inspire both national pride and racial prejudice, and which can be played upon by unscrupulous statesmen with such fatal ease... The excess of one side is jingoism, that of the other side anti-patriotism.

Spender concluded that the only solution to this disagreement was to alter the British constitution so that 'Imperial and domestic questions are allotted respectively to Imperial and domestic legislatures.'[88] Few Liberals were so pessimistic; yet most accepted that their party handled external issues badly. For example, in a Liberal counterpart to the 'dozen handbooks describing the principles and purpose of socialism', which Herbert Samuel published in 1902, he acknowledged that 'there are some Liberals who seem inclined to neglect this side of politics'. In particular, he argued, Liberals overlooked the fact: 'The motto "Peace, Retrenchment and Reform" does not cover the whole sphere of politics. Security is needed as well; and a policy is clearly incomplete which fails to give prominence to the need of maintaining an armed force powerful enough to defend the national rights if attacked, and to secure the fulfilment of the national duties if opposed.' Samuel's attempt to produce a statement of positive foreign-policy principles on which all members of the party could agree was necessarily vague on the subject of interventionism:

At various times and in various circumstances Liberals may hold different views as to the desirability of intervening in this part of the world or that, of co-operating with this power or that power; but the doctrine that the foreign policy of England should aim at promoting the welfare, not only of England, but of the world at large is a permanent and characteristic article of their creed.[89]

Although this formulation was more engaged than isolationist, it made no mention of any aspiration to develop an international organization.

However, soon after Gladstone's death there was a slight but significant increase in the calls for an international organ of governance. One reason for this was the Hague Conferences of 1899 and 1907, which although mainly encouraging the cause of arbitration were also seen by a few liberals as themselves constituting an international organization in embryo. It was during preparations for the 1899 conference that W. T. Stead claimed that a United States of Europe 'may be much nearer than even the most sanguine of us venture at present to hope'. This was because the continent needed to remove 'the artificial impediments' that handicapped its capacity to compete with 'the virgin resources of the new world'. A United States of Europe would need an armed force; but it 'will be an international police rather than an international soldiery'. The existing Concert of Europe was not only the germ of a future United States, Stead asserted, but

[88] J. A. Spender, 'Why I am a Liberal', *New Liberal Review* (Nov. 1902), 479–80, 482.
[89] Herbert Samuel, *Liberalism: An Attempt to State the Principles and Proposals of Contemporary Liberalism in England* (1902), pp. xv, 347, 363, 364.

already 'the realization, though still very imperfect, of the conception of a federal centre of the continent'. To achieve its full potential, however, it needed to introduce majority voting.[90] Similarly, in 1907 the economist H. Stanley Jevons considered it 'obvious that the Hague Conference, which has met for the second time this year, is the institution which will be shaped step by step into a world-wide federal government'.[91]

But the main reason for the new interest in international organization was a fear of war resulting from the challenge of the Central Powers to the status quo. Only a few years previously it had been suggested that in Britain 'the very notion of war has been lost' because since Napoleon's defeat 'no inhabitant of these islands had felt the actual touch or stress of war, or so much as the apprehension of either',[92] and that in consequence 'our habit as a nation in outward relations is apathetic unconsciousness'.[93] Now, as concern about the European situation increased, the debate about war prevention became more intensive; and most schools of thought gained converts from the ranks of the previously apathetic. Militarist rhetoric, previously almost unknown in Britain, made an appearance.[94] Defencists reaffirmed their confidence in the balance of power, with the editor of the *Observer*, J. L. Garvin, asserting: 'The equilibrium of great armaments gives stability to peace and prevents a plunge into the dread unknown of conflict. Any country which weakened its relative force would diminish the whole world's security.'[95] Defencist thinking also appeared to win over the Liberal government which Sir Henry Campbell-Bannerman had formed in December 1905. Although the new Prime Minister was a loyal Gladstonian and his administration was 'in its whole character . . . a Gladstone government without Mr Gladstone', in the words of a contemporary,[96] they felt obliged to continue the entente with France, negotiate an agreement with Russia, and intensify the naval arms race with Germany.

For their part, *pacificists* offered an unprecedented array of diagnoses. Radicals blamed the apparent conversion of the Liberal front bench to defencism on declining parliamentary control over the executive—a diagnosis which was soon described as 'one of the commonplaces of politics'[97] and which paved the way for the formation of the Union of Democratic Control as the first new peace association of the First World War. In place of 'entanglement' they urged 'isolation',

[90] Stead, *United States of Europe*, 12, 24, 25.

[91] H. Stanley Jevons, 'The Development of an International Parliament', *Contemporary Review* (Sept. 1907), 323.

[92] Thomas Gibson Bowles, 'The Lost Notion of War', *Contemporary Review* (Mar. 1899), 351.

[93] J. S. Phillimore, 'Liberalism in Outward Relations', in Six Oxford Men, *Essays in Liberalism* (London, 1897), 134.

[94] e.g. Harold F. Wyatt, 'God's Test by War', *Nineteenth Century* (Apr. 1911), 591–606.

[95] J. L. Garvin, 'Imperial and Foreign Affairs: A Review of Contemporary Interests', *Fortnightly Review* (Feb. 1909), 197.

[96] Calchas, 'The Ebbing Tide of Liberalism', *Fortnightly Review* (Aug. 1907), 177.

[97] Sidney Low, 'The Foreign Office Autocracy', *Fortnightly Review* (Jan. 1912), 1.

defined as being 'friends with all, and partners or confederates with none, as we were under Lord Salisbury';[98] and they also launched a campaign against a new target, the international arms trade. Socialists called for a general strike against capitalist war. For their part, liberal *pacificists* fought their corner harder than for more than two decades, Norman Angell's *The Great Illusion* providing the most famous rebuttal of radical and socialist claims that aggressive war could ever make financial sense even for a capitalist elite.[99]

Admittedly, some peace activists failed to comprehend the symbiotic relationship between their own increased support and the deteriorating European situation. For example, the Liberal MP Arthur Ponsonby commented in 1912 that 'the pacifists, together with other groups closely interested in foreign questions, are bewildered at the amazing contradiction between the enlightened and rationalizing movement on the one hand and the reckless competition in aggressive preparations on the other'.[100] Others, however, understood that peace schemes were being proposed because international relations were deteriorating and not because they were becoming more susceptible to reform. For example, even while making his own optimistic prediction that the Hague Conferences would evolve into world-wide federal government, Jevons accused some of his fellow countrymen of 'underestimating the feelings of insecurity and distrust of one another which in reality still animate the European nations', and suggested that 'the desire for international peace and security' had become so strong 'that the wish has become father to the thought'.[101]

As the First World War drew near, references to 'federation' and 'juridical order' started to appear in peace literature.[102] The phrase 'league of peace' or 'peace league' also began to be used. For example, in his rectorial address to St Andrew's University in 1905 the Scottish-born industrialist Andrew Carnegie employed it to describe a group of states prepared to pledge 'non-intercourse' with—or trade boycott of—a state in breach of an arbitral ruling. Carnegie even suggested that this 'League of Peace . . . also might reserve to itself the right, where non-intercourse is likely to fail or has failed to prevent war, to use the necessary force to maintain the peace, each member of the League agreeing to provide the needed forces, or money in lieu thereof, in proportion to her population or wealth'. Moreover, although expecting 'more than one great holocaust of men to be offered up before the reign of peace blesses the earth',[103] Carnegie continued to advocate a 'Peace League' in subsequent years.[104] Campbell-Bannerman used a similar

[98] Diplomaticus, 'Isolation or Entanglement?', *Fortnightly Review* (June 1912), 984, 985.

[99] Angell's thesis was first expounded as a pamphlet entitled *Europe's Optical Illusion* in 1909, and was developed into a book the following year.

[100] Arthur Ponsonby, 'Foreign Policy and the Navy', *Contemporary Review* (Sept. 1912), 305.

[101] Jevons, 'Development of International Parliament', 309.

[102] *Herald of Peace* (Mar. 1906), 186; (June 1910), 68; (Jan. 1911), 76.

[103] Andrew Carnegie, *A Rectorial Address Delivered to the Students of the University of St Andrews, 17 October 1905* (St Andrews, 1905), 38–9, 40.

[104] See Carnegie's *War as the Mother of Valour and Civilization* (Peace Society, 1910), and 'Arbitration', *Contemporary Review* (Aug. 1911), 169–76.

phrase in the Albert Hall rally which celebrated his appointment as Prime Minister, though he did not make clear what he meant by it. Warning of the excessive level of armaments, he argued that

as the principle of peaceful arbitration gains ground, it becomes one of the highest task for statesmen to adjust those armaments to the new and happier condition of things. What nobler role could this great country assume than at the fitting moment to place itself at the head of a league of peace, through whose instrumentality this great work could be effected?[105]

Some internationalists envisaged an explicitly European organization: in 1909 a German-born industrialist, Sir Max Waechter, began a campaign for a federal Europe, the first step towards which would be a free-trade agreement because the necessary 'community of intererests' could 'only be established by a common tariff and the free intercourse of the different nations'.[106] Others anticipated a global body: in March 1914 Hobson outlined the functionalist case for a 'world-government, conformable to the full necessities of economic internationalism'.[107]

Even so, international organization had in general been neglected prior to the First World War. As the Peace Society was to acknowledge soon after its outbreak: 'Of the two parts of the political machinery of peace, greater attention has been given to International Arbitration...But the other, and really more important section, International Union or Federation, has been overlooked.'[108] It was only after diplomacy failed in August 1914 that most liberal *pacificists* concluded, in the words of Willoughby Dickinson: 'It is clearly no use to concentrate all [our] efforts, as hitherto, on treaties of arbitration and such like, so long as such treaties are and cannot be made binding...What is needed is a common entente based on common goodwill and common sacrifice, and enforceable by common action.'[109] Demands for 'some sort of international authority' were 'continually upon the lips or pens of a large number of more or less intelligent persons of every variety of political belief', as Leonard Woolf, commissioned to research the subject of international government for the Fabian Society, soon noted.[110] Thanks mainly to the Cambridge political scientist Goldsworthy Lowes Dickinson, this international authority became known as the League of Nations. And thanks mainly to President Woodrow Wilson, it became practical politics.

Did Gladstone contribute to the creation of international organizations such as the League? The danger of exaggerating posthumous influence is illustrated by

---

[105] *The Times* (22 Dec. 1905), 7.
[106] *European Federation: A Lecture Delivered at the London Institution on the 25th February, 1909* (n.d.). See also two articles by Waechter: 'The Federation of Europe: Is it Possible?', *Contemporary Review* (Nov. 1912), 621–30; and 'England, Germany and the Peace of Europe', *Fortnightly Review* (Mar. 1913), 829–41.
[107] 'The Limits of Nationalism', *War and Peace: A Norman Angell Monthly* (Mar. 1914), 155–6.
[108] *Herald of Peace* (Jan. 1915), 24.
[109] 'The War and After', *Contemporary Review* (Sept. 1914), 331–2.
[110] L. S. Woolf, *International Government* (1916), 7—originally published in the *New Statesman* (10 and 17 July 1915).

Lord Robert Cecil's implausible but politically understandable attempt to claim his own father, the Conservative Prime Minister Lord Salisbury, as a prophet of the League of Nations on the strength of his having invoked Tennyson's phrase 'the Federation of Mankind' in one speech and expressed a vague wish for 'some international constitution' in another.[111] It should also be recognized that politicians other than Gladstone nurtured the engaged strand of liberal thought: in particular, Sir Edward Grey's capacity to retain the respect of the majority of backbenchers and also of intellectuals such as Gilbert Murray helped to stop the mainstream of his party turning its back on European affairs; and by the end of the First World War, when Grey became the first president of the League of Nations Union, the erstwhile Liberal Imperialist had rebranded himself as a liberal internationalist. Moreover, British military involvement itself encouraged a more engaged attitude. For example, although originally a neutralist, Norman Angell had concluded before the end of 1914 that 'doctrines which have been held very tenaciously in the past: non-intervention, no military alliances with foreign countries, etc' had been rendered obsolete because Britain had through its entry into the war 'become an integral part of the European system and it is outside the domain of practical politics to go back'.[112]

However, Gladstone's colossal personal reputation ensured that the progressive aspects of his international thought were remembered by his political successors. As Campbell-Bannerman put it at the Albert Hall rally of December 1905:

We Liberals, let us not forget it, are the heirs of a great and inspiring tradition; that tradition was forged when public opinion was opposed to any attempt to regulate differences by an appeal to the reason and conscience of mankind. Mr Gladstone [cheers] defied the public opinion of his day. He took his stand on higher ground, and by referring the Alabama dispute to arbitration he established a precedent of priceless value to mankind.[113]

And it is well attested that Gladstone's international vision directly influenced that of President Wilson.[114] It therefore seems reasonable to conclude that, although Gladstone was never a fully fledged or wholehearted liberal internationalist, and although the First World War would have produced demands for an international organization even if he had never expounded his Midlothian vision, still without the Gladstonian legacy of moderate interventionism and faith in the public law of Europe which Matthew so shrewdly analysed, British Liberalism would have been either more Cobdenite or more defencist in the late nineteenth and early twentieth centuries and to that extent less enthusiastic about the League idea.

---

[111] Viscount Cecil, *A Great Experiment* (1941), 14–15, 22.

[112] *Prussianism and its Destruction: With which is Reprinted Part II of 'The Great Illusion'* (London, 1914), 236, 239.   [113] *The Times* (22 Dec. 1905), 7.

[114] Harley Notter, *The Origin of the Foreign Policy of Woodrow Wilson* (Baltimore, 1937), 29–31, 89; J. W. S. Nordholt. *Woodrow Wilson: A Life for Peace*, tr. H. H. Rowen (Berkeley, Calif., 1991), 13–15, 50.

7

The Enfranchisement of the Urban Poor in Late-Victorian Britain

John Davis

Colin Matthew's first published article would prove one of his most influential pieces. In his celebrated 1976 essay on the role of franchise extension in the rise of the Labour Party, Colin, writing with Ross McKibbin and John Kay, argued that the then little studied fourth Reform Act of 1918 had, by enfranchising the 30 per cent or so of adult men previously beyond the political pale, provided the impetus for the growth of Labour and the replacement of the Liberals as the party of the left.[1] The authors invoked Werner Sombart's contemporary argument that the established political institutions of Western Europe had failed adequately to reflect the emerging social 'fact' of conflict between capital and labour, and that in Britain, specifically, the growth of a party of labour had been inhibited before 1918 by an exclusive electoral system, so denying many of Labour's natural supporters the right to vote. Matthew, McKibbin, and Kay argued that the bulk of the missing 30 per cent before 1918 were working class. They showed that in the pre-1918 system urban, industrial boroughs had the lowest proportion of their male population registered to vote, prosperous county towns the highest.

The 'Franchise Factor' article looked forward into the twentieth century. Colin Matthew, at least, was much influenced in writing it by the then prevalent view of the steady emergence of class as the basis of political allegiance during the course of the twentieth century.[2] I do not intend here to approach the arguments about

I am grateful to Professor Duncan Tanner for many helpful suggestions and much of the spadework behind this essay, to the participants at the conference held at St Hugh's College, Oxford, in Sept. 2002 for their comments on an earlier version of this piece, and to the editors for their perceptive criticisms of the early drafts. I should also mention the help provided by the staff of the London Metropolitan Archives for making it possible for me to view the critical 1883 Bethnal Green register at a time when it was still in a very fragile state.

[1] H. C. G. Matthew, R. I. McKibbin, and J. A. Kay, 'The Franchise Factor in the Rise of the Labour Party', *English Historical Review*, 91 (1976), 723–52.

[2] Colin once spoke to me of the influence of the idea of class-based politics upon his early work. The Franchise Factor authors speak of D. Butler and D. Stokes's *Political Change in Britain* (London,

the explanatory value of class in political analysis I have always doubted that franchise played the dominant role attributed to it in 1976, yet I have also considered it perverse to deny that Labour gained enormously from franchise extension. What interests me is the closing section of this extremely ambitious article, which made claims about the nature of pre-1914 British politics going some way beyond the psephological parameters of the rest of the essay. The authors argued that the Liberal Party faced peculiar difficulties in adjusting to the political world created in 1918 because their style of politics had been tailored to a limited electorate. Theirs was a cerebral and unemotional politics, based on the core liberal value of the appeal to reason.

This section was largely written by Colin Matthew. That it represented more to him than a passing *aperçu* is shown by his development of the idea in a provocative essay on political rhetoric published eleven years later. In 'Rhetoric and Politics in Great Britain, 1860—1950', Colin described the distinctive qualities of a large but limited electorate, 'a half-way house between the very limited electorate of the 1832 Reform Act and the achievement of what was effectively (though not completely) universal suffrage for men in 1918'.[3] The process of partial democratization shaped the political etiquette of the period: 'the extension of the franchise made extra-parliamentary speechmaking necessary; the continuing limits on the electorate made it effective'.[4] Victorian political oratory was, in other words, anything but demotic in tone, but rather 'long, serious, detailed, well-informed— rarely demagogic, with few concessions to the audience in simplification of matter, style or language'.[5] It was addressed to an audience defined by the electoral system, comprising the 'employed adult male, of some substance, the head of a household with the initiative to get himself registered'.[6] The 'vast new electorate' of 1918 swamped these discerning citizens, and, along with the popularization of the press, silenced the elevated extra-parliamentary debate that had prevailed before the war.[7]

My own work on local politics in late-Victorian London left me uncomfortable with this picture of an urban electorate refined by virtue of its exclusivity. Previously, in conjunction with Duncan Tanner,[8] I have sought to show how blunt an instrument the 1867 franchise was in practice, and how the confidence of the 'Franchise Factor' authors that the foreman of Robert Tressell's Ragged Trousered Philanthropists might have been enfranchised while the rest of his gang were not, or that the 1867 franchise filtered out the 'classic slummies' from the electorate,[9] did not square with my experience of the random incidence of the

1969), the *locus classsicus* of class-based analysis, as 'this most important book', while criticizing its lack of a historical dimension. Matthew *et al.*, 'Franchise Factor', 735 n. 4.

[3] H. C. G. Matthew, 'Rhetoric and Politics in Great Britain, 1860–1950', in P. J. Waller (ed.), *Politics and Social Change in Great Britain: Essays Presented to A. F. Thompson* (Brighton, 1987), 36.

[4] Ibid., 39.   [5] Ibid.   [6] Ibid., 36.   [7] Ibid., 54.

[8] J. Davis and D. Tanner, 'The Borough Franchise After 1867', *Historical Research*, 69 (1996), 306–27.   [9] Matthew *et al.*, 'Franchise Factor', 724–5.

1867 system in London. Moreover, the depiction of the late-Victorian electorate as a sophisticated 'national debating society' appeared at odds with my impression of the London electorate in that period.

It is surely impossible now to gauge empirically the political awareness of the late-Victorian electorate, but it is possible to test the assumptions about its refinement and exclusivity on which the thesis of the 'Rhetoric' essay rested. Here I shall attempt to look at the electorate that the 1867 reform actually produced in urban areas, and to see how far it was true that 'the classic slummies' were successfully filtered out by the 1867 system. To do this I have looked at a number of sample slum areas, defined as such by the local authorities which scheduled them for clearance under the 1875 Artisans' and Labourers' Dwellings Act and the 1890 Housing of the Working Classes Act. Clearance under this legislation required that a substantial proportion of the houses in the area be certified as unfit for human habitation by the local medical officer of health. It was always likely that fit houses stood along side uninhabitable ones, and it is, of course, by no means certain that dwellers in insanitary accommodation were *ipso facto* destitute or even disadvantaged, let alone that they were not 'respectable', but the choice of areas designated for clearance appears to me to offer the most objective means available of identifying the late-Victorian slum. The selection of precise sample areas from all the slum clearance schemes of the late nineteenth century depended largely upon the survival of electoral registers covering the districts concerned, if possible for years close to the census years of 1871, 1881, and 1891. Eight sample areas emerged from this process, in Bethnal Green, East London, in Birmingham, in Brighton, in Devonport, in Newcastle-upon-Tyne, in Nottingham, in Salford, and in Sheffield.[10]

Table 1 shows that, by the last two decades of the nineteenth century, the number of registered voters in all but one of the sample areas represented between 35 and 60 per cent of the male population of voting age shown in the census. The levels shown are generally below the national average of around 60 per cent, but these are all areas of concentrated poverty, with no middle-class presence beyond the occasional clergyman. It should be acknowledged immediately that the impression of precision given by calculations to two decimal places is deceptive. Table 2 shows the proportion of those appearing in the registers for the sample areas appearing in the nearest census, and indicates that, in all the instances chosen, a significant proportion of registered electors was absent from the census, even in census years. Some of these omissions will be explained by inaccuracies in the census itself: enumerators were exploring areas conventionally regarded as

---

[10] For an account of the Crofts area some twenty years before demolition, see 'The Sanitary State of Sheffield, XI', *Sheffield and Rotherham Independent* (13 Feb. 1872); for the Edward St area, see the reports of Council discussions in *Brighton Examiner* (6 June, 3 and 10 Oct. 1890); the discussion of the clearance scheme for the Pandon groups is reported in *Newcastle Daily Chronicle* (9 Sept. 1876) and that of the clearance of the Milk St/Little Ann St area in *Birmingham Daily Gazette* (2 May 1894).

John Davis

Table 1. Sample area statistics

Bethnal Green, London: Boundary Street area

	1871		1881		1891	
Pop.	7686		6998		6497	
Houses	835		737		676	
Men 21+	1879		1711		1574	

	1873	1876	1881	1882	1883	1885/6
Electors	286	436	457	425	852	798
% 1871	15.22	23.20				
% 1881			26.71	24.84	49.80	46.64

	1887	1888	1889	1890	1891	1892
Electors	749	772	721	777	638	756
%1891	47.59	49.05	45.81	49.36	40.53	48.03

Birmingham: Milk St/Little Ann St area

	1871		1881		1891	
Pop.	290		282		290	
Houses	66		66		65	
Men 21+	62		63		77	

	1868	1872	1878–9	1881–2	1887	1891
Electors	14	26	37	36	33	31
% 1871	22.58	41.94				
% 1881			58.73	57.14		
% 1891					42.86	40.26

Brighton: Edward St area

	1871		1881		1891	
Pop.	1191		1311		1200	
Houses	176		198		201	
Men 21+	486		484		450	

	1868	1872	1878	1882	1886	1890
Electors	19	51	80	69	93	99
% 1871	3.91	10.49				
% 1881			16.53	14.26		
% 1891					20.67	22.00

Devonport: James St area

	1881
Pop	498
Houses	43
Men 21+	118

	1885
Electors	42
% 1881	35.59

Newcastle: Old and New Pandon Groups

	1871
Pop.	1396
Houses	106
Men 21+	330

	1867/8	1868/9	1871	1872	1876
Electors	18	138	30	131	181
% 1871	5.45	41.82	9.09	39.70	54.85

Table 1 (*Continued*)

Nottingham: Greyhound Street, etc., area

	1871	1881
Pop.	558	455
Houses	136	114
Men 21+	136	131

	1871	1881
Electors	76	62
% 1871	55.88	
% 1881		47.33

Salford: Brown Street/Garden Street/Wood Street area

	1871	1881	1891
Pop.	954	970	824
Houses	185	186	163
Men 21+	222	242	244

	1868/9	1871	1876	1881	1885–6	1891
Electors	87	120	117	103	80	74
% 1871	39.19	54.05				
% 1881			48.35	42.56	33.06	
% 1891						30.33

Sheffield: Crofts Insanitary area

	1881	1891
Pop.	1529	1536
Houses	303	343
Men 21+	439	487

	1881	1886	1891
Electors	181	164	156
% 1881	41.23		
% 1891		33.68	32.03

Note: The areas used were defined by property scheduled under the clearance schemes concerned and shown in the deposited plans in the House of Lords Record Office. Figures for area populations, for houses and for men aged 21+ are taken from the census street returns. Electoral registers were consulted either in the British Library collection or in the appropriate local history libraries. NB that the Bethnal Green area used here omits the five scheduled streets in Shoreditch.

perilous for middle-class interlopers, and it would be unsurprising if their inquiries were not always as exhaustive as they should have been. Sometimes the missing men would have been present at the addresses for which they were registered on the qualifying date (31 July of the year before the register came into force) but would have moved or died by the time of the census. Some such movements were inevitable in any significant sample, and urban working-class communities were traditionally given to frequent short-range movements. Some of the absentees were doubtless the products of errors in the registration process. In working-class areas, where local authorities frequently collected local taxes

Table 2. Percentage of registered electorate identifiable in census (sample areas)

Newcastle 1872	74.81%
Birmingham 1872	69.23%
Birmingham 1881–2	83.33%
Nottingham 1871	69.74%
Nottingham 1881	70.97%
Bethnal Green 1882	77.18%
Bethnal Green 1883	63.15%
Bethnal Green 1892	90.99%
Sheffield 1891	87.18%

from landlords rather than occupiers, the registration authorities depended upon landlords to supply the names of their tenants, as the payment of local rates made the occupiers eligible for the vote if otherwise qualified. Landlords were frequently ill-informed about the identities of their tenants, particularly where sub-tenancies had arisen, and their ignorance posed a substantial obstacle to the compilation of accurate registers: the 'large number of misnomers and omissions' noted in the 1870 register for Nottingham as a result of 'the making of inaccurate rating returns'[11] was a characteristic feature of the early years of the system; Table 2 suggests that accuracy levels increased over time.

In other words, of the group of men captured by the registration authorities but missed by the census enumerators, some will have been missed by enumerator error, some will have moved or died after the register was compiled, and some will never have existed. It is impossible to know how many fell into each group; all we can say is that those men who appear on both lists are likely to be 'real'. What can we say about them?

Though much of the franchise debate has revolved around questions of class, little is to be gained by seeking a class basis to the franchise in the sample areas. The areas chosen were slum clearance areas and were consequently almost exclusively working-class in composition. That much is obvious from the census, but further fine tuning is impossible. We can only hope to infer class from occupation, but census occupational categories tend to be crude, partly because the definitions are themselves impressionistic—is a 'general dealer' a shopkeeper or a costermonger?—and partly because the categories used tell us nothing about income or regularity of employment. The Bethnal Green sample was, on the face of it, predominantly artisanal rather than labouring, but it would be wrong to attribute either greater prosperity or superior status to a community that was in fact enduring a process of de-skilling and pauperization.[12] Table 3 is therefore of

---

[11] *Nottingham and Midland Counties Daily Express* (28 Sept. 1870).
[12] D. R. Green, *From Artisans to Paupers. Economic Change and Poverty in London, 1790–1870* (Aldershot, 1995), esp. chs. 2 and 3.

Table 3. Census occupations of all men and of identifiable voters, Bethnal Green sample area, 1882, 1883, and 1892, and Sheffield sample area, 1892

Bethnal Green: Occupation	All (1881)	1882 Voters (%)	1883 Voters (%)	All (1891)	1892 Voters (%)
Labourers	288	33 (11.46)	66 (22.92)	333	114 (34.23)
Hawkers, etc.	294	44 (14.97)	83 (28.23)	201	113 (56.22)
Carmen, drivers	46	3 (6.52)	13 (28.26)	53	14 (26.42)
Clothing, footwear	109	24 (22.02)	36 (33.03)	137	40 (29.20)
Furniture, woodwork	366	75 (20.49)	122 (33.33)	378	159 (42.06)
Building	94	9 (9.57)	23 (24.47)	60	26 (43.33)
Metalwork	81	14 (17.28)	22 (27.16)	55	24 (43.64)
Other artisans	217	48 (22.12)	79 (36.41)	69	25 (36.23)
Shop, publicans	104	53 (50.96)	48 (46.15)	143	74 (51.75)
Service, shop assts	35	1 (2.86)	5 (14.29)	32	7 (21.88)
Other/not known	77	13 (16.88)	19 (24.68)	113	40 (35.40)
Total	1711	317 (18.53)	516 (30.16)	1574	636 (40.41)

Sheffield: Occupation	All (1891)	Voters (%)
Labourers	173	47 (27.17)
Miners	25	9 (36.00)
Hawkers, etc.	14	4 (28.57)
Carmen, drivers	17	7 (41.18)
Clothing, footwear	36	11 (30.56)
Furniture, woodwork	14	5 (35.71)
Building	40	4 (10.00)
Metalwork	111	29 (26.13)
Other artisans	7	2 (28.57)
Shop, publicans	21	10 (47.62)
Service, shop assts	5	1 (20.00)
Other/not known	24	7 (29.17)
Total	487	136 (27.93)

limited value. Its two most striking features—the low enfranchisement level for labourers and the high level for shopkeepers—could both be anticipated without resort to the census street returns. Labourers were most likely to be residentially mobile and therefore most likely to fall foul of the one-year residence requirement for the vote. Shopkeepers, so far as they can be distinguished from street sellers, were less likely to move, and they were also more likely to be direct ratepayers and thus registered directly by the local authorities.

A quite different variable is age. Evidence of the relationship between age and the vote is also familiar from the work of Childs.[13] Table 4, drawn from the

---

[13] M. Childs, 'Labour Grows up: The Electoral System, Political Generations, and British Politics 1890–1929', *Twentieth Century British History*, 6/2 (1995), 126–7.

Table 4. Bethnal Green sample area: enfranchisement rates by age, 1882–3

Age	Men, 1881 census	Identifiable voters (percentages in brackets)	
		1882	1883
21–29	428	29 (6.78)	53 (12.38)
30–39	484	92 (19.01)	143 (29.55)
40–49	379	91 (24.01)	148 (39.05)
50–59	253	71 (28.06)	117 (46.25)
60+	166	34 (20.48)	55 (33.13)
Totals	1,710*	317 (18.54)	516 (30.18)

* Differs from total in Table 1 because one head of household was enumerated without age recorded.

Bethnal Green sample area before and after the electoral expansion of 1883, shows a clear bias against the young. Young adults were, once again, more likely to be mobile, to live as sub-tenants or to live with their parents, in which case the father was likely to be registered for the property (or a widowed mother rated and nobody registered). This was a feature of the pre-1918 franchise in general, not simply in poor areas, as is demonstrated forcefully in Portland Place, one of London's most exclusive residential streets, in 1892. There the percentage of men of voting age in the 1891 census who appear on the 1892 electoral register is surprisingly small at 37.75 per cent (57 out of 151).[14] The percentage figure is, of course, deflated by the army of servants who had clearly gained little from the 1885 service franchise: there was only one service voter in the entire street.[15] The non-registered were not all servants, however: those missing included four bankers, four merchants, two barristers, two solicitors, two officers in the armed forces, a dental surgeon, a law student, and five men of private means. In most cases they lived with their parents or elder brothers and lost the vote as a result. The 30-year-old solicitor Percival Hardy and the 25-year-old Reginald Hardy, whose father and brother were registered,[16] were doubtless articulate members of the 'national debating society' made possible by the electric telegraph,[17] but they could not vote. The 23-year-old clerk at the Bank of England Ernest Harvey[18] would play a prominent role in one of the twentieth century's most important national debates during the 1931 financial crisis, by which time he was Deputy Governor of the Bank, but in 1892 he had no vote.

[14] These figures calculated from the 1891 census (RG 12/90, 91, and 93) and the electoral register for Marylebone East, 1892, London Metropolitan Archives, LCC/PER/B/172. The Chinese and Persian embassies were omitted from the calculations.

[15] Though the raw figure has also been deflated—and rendered largely meaningless—by the large number of absentees or non-residents on the register: only 33 out of 57 registered electors were visible in the census, a far smaller proportion than in the working-class sample areas.

[16] 92 Portland Place, RG 12/93.   [17] Matthew, 'Rhetoric', 48.

[18] 59 Portland Place, RG 12/93.

The young were also more likely to be found in the common lodging houses which mushroomed in slum areas: the lodging house dwellers picked up in the sample areas were preponderantly below the age of 35. Whatever liberalization was effected in electoral law after 1867, no household franchise could embrace this rootless and room-sharing group. Of the working-class sample areas analysed here, only Birmingham was without common lodging houses; registration levels for all the other areas are depressed by their presence. This factor above all explains the very low level of enfranchisement in the Brighton sample. This area was known for its cluster of common lodging houses, whose notoriety was, indeed, one of the main reasons for the area's clearance.[19]

The Brighton evidence offers, though, an extreme indication of a pattern evident from these census figures: that a man of voting age was most likely actually to gain the vote if there were no other adult men living under the same roof. It is not going too far to suggest that the physical size of the houses in an area was the greatest single determinant of that area's enfranchisement level. Franchise law and registration practice were least problematic in cases where one household occupied one separate dwelling. In such areas an adult male of voting age who did not change his address or claim poor relief stood a very good chance of getting the vote. Neither a humble occupation nor a humble dwelling was in itself a disqualification for the franchise, and the samples in slum areas with small houses, in Birmingham and Nottingham, where the ratio of adult men to houses stood little higher than 1:1, show high levels of registration.

The 1867 Act had intended, of course, to place a further substantial barrier in the way of poorer occupiers, in the form of the requirement that they pay local taxes in person: Disraeli's adviser Montagu Corry had considered 'personal payment of rates . . . *the* one thing to be insisted upon'.[20] This entailed the abolition of the practice of compounding, by which local authorities had collected rates from owners rather than occupiers in poor areas. This practice had developed because it offered the authorities the only practicable means of getting their money in, and its removal threatened local authority revenues as well as alienating occupiers who suddenly became rateable.[21] In 1869 Gladstone's first government legalized compounding once again. This made it impossible for occupiers of compounded property to pay the rates in person even if they wished to, but their civic rights were protected by a requirement for the landlord to pass their names to the rating authorities, who would register them so long as the rates were actually paid. In

[19] One Brighton alderman claimed that 'of the population assigned to this area, it was not overstating the matter to say that fully one-third was made up of the shifting class inhabiting common lodging houses', *Brighton Examiner* (3 Oct. 1890), for a report of the debate in Brighton Council on adoption of the scheme.

[20] Corry to Disraeli, 29 Mar. 1867 (original emphasis), Disraeli Papers, Bodleian Library, Oxford, B/XI/J/13.

[21] A. Offer, *Property and Politics, 1870–1914: Landownership, Law, Ideology and Urban Development in England* (Cambridge, 1981), 286–7.

Birmingham, Brighton, and Salford, where it can be tested, the boost given to registration levels by the 1869 legislation is very clear. The basis of the system that would survive until the First World War was thus established: the bulk of the occupiers' list would consist of direct ratepayers and compounded tenants whose names were provided by landlords, augmented at the annual revision courts by local political associations enlisting those of their own supporters not otherwise registered. Individuals could claim on their own behalf, and each year's revision courts would include a handful of such claims, but it was not generally the case that 'the head of a household' needed 'the initiative to get himself registered' if he wished to vote.[22] Most household voters arrived on the register automatically as ratepayers or through the actions of their landlords.

After 1869 the greatest difficulty in securing the vote was faced by tenants of multi-occupied property. The 1867 Act explicitly denied the vote to joint occupiers. The meaning of this clause was contested from the start: men sharing a room were clearly ineligible, but men sharing a building might include Oxford dons, resident barristers in the Inns of Court, and dwellers in purpose-built flats, none of whom took kindly to disfranchisement. Attempts to reconcile established ideas of a 'dwelling house' with the new rating requirement, produced much awkwardness—'a cellar opening into the open air, without any common staircase, or communication with the rest of the house, would be considered a dwelling house if it was rated'.[23] After much confusion in the courts, the law was changed by stealth in 1878, to enable even a room in a shared house to confer the vote if it was occupied separately as a dwelling. A further ruling in 1881 established that the occupiers of such rooms could qualify as householders rather than lodgers if their landlords did not live on the premises.[24]

The initial uncertainty surrounding tenement occupiers is demonstrated vividly by the oscillating Newcastle figures (Table 1). The Old and New Pandon blocks were divided into flats, as was common in the North-East. These flats were clearly separate from one another in a manner that did not apply in multi-occupied premises elsewhere, and when the 1867 Act made the personal payment of rates a requirement of the household franchise, the local authorities in this area faced the question of who should be rated in such blocks. Whereas in a normal multi-occupied house, with a principal tenant and several sub-tenants, only the former stood much chance of being rated, a purpose-built block of flats did not usually allow the overseers to distinguish between tenancies. The enfranchisement level for 1867–8 suggests that the Newcastle authorities simply rated the owners of the whole blocks rather than the occupiers of tenements within them. This practice was apparently sanctioned in such cases by section 7 of the 1867 Act and appeared

[22] Matthew, 'Rhetoric', 36.

[23] Evidence of Leofric Temple, revising barrister on the northern circuit, Select Committee on the Registration of Voters, Parliamentary Papers 1868–9, VII (294), Q. 3216, 24 June 1869.

[24] J. Davis, 'Slums and the Vote', *Historical Research*, 64 (1991), 386–7.

to be vindicated by a decision in July 1868 in favour of six Sunderland tenement occupiers who objected to being rated. But the Sunderland decision related to a house built for one family and subsequently divided, and the arguments supporting the decision implied that the occupiers would have been rateable in a purpose-built tenement block.[25] A legal fog enveloped the North-East of England: 'the intentions of the Legislature... appeared clear enough till learned gentlemen of the Crown went wandering over the country to obscure them', as one local newspaper complained.[26] Overseers in the area remained in a state of 'the greatest possible confusion' as to who ought now to be rated and consequently registered.[27] In Gateshead, Sunderland, Newcastle, and South Shields the tenement occupier was granted the vote in 1868—the Newcastle sample area's electorate rising eightfold—while in Tynemouth and Berwick he was denied it.[28] The 1869 Act tidied up this mess, removing unequivocally the link between personal payment of rates and the right to vote, and the enfranchisement level in the Pandon groups shot up to nearly 42 per cent, but doubts remained as to what constituted a house for franchise purposes. Overseers consequently resorted to *ad hoc* definitions of a dwelling house, under which an occupier might be denied the vote by the shared use of a kitchen or a common staircase.[29] Everything now depended upon the revising barrister's view of this issue at the annual revision court: in the 1874 Newcastle revisions for the 1875 register (which appears not to have survived), for example, 'holders of one or two rooms having no separate entrances into the street... were disallowed on the ground that they could not be considered separate dwellings.'[30] The enfranchisement level of the Pandon groups thus became largely unpredictable, falling to 9 per cent in 1871 but rising almost to 40 per cent in the following year. The blocks would not survive long enough for their tenants to benefit from the 1878 legislation, but before demolition their enfranchisement level had passed 50 per cent. In this grim slum, with a mortality rate of 57.6 per 1,000 in 1873,[31] it was possible for more than half the adult male population to be registered whenever the law was interpreted in their favour.

London was the pre-eminent city of multi-occupation, and the effects of the evolution of electoral law are evident in the figures for the large Bethnal Green sample. Although the registration level moves upwards there as elsewhere as the 1867 reform is put into effect, while the practical difficulties of registering multi-occupiers were reinforced by doubts as to their legal entitlement, this level remained relatively low, and there is no obvious leap attributable to the 1869 Act. The impact of the 1881 ruling is, though, transparently clear in the 1883 register, the first to be affected by the decision. The legal position of multi-occupiers had

[25] *Stamper* v. *The Overseers of Sunderland-near-the Sea, Law Reports, Common Pleas*, 3 (1867–8), at 399–400 (Byles), 403 (Montague Smith.)   [26] *Newcastle Daily Chronicle* (2 Oct. 1868).

[27] S. Smith, registration agent in the City of London, and T. F. Hedley, overseer of Sunderland, in Select Committee on the Registration of Voters, QQ. 1360 and 1678, 27 Apr. 1869.

[28] *Newcastle Daily Chronicle* (2 Oct. 1868).   [29] Davis, 'Slums and the Vote', 381.

[30] *Newcastle Daily Chronicle* (10 Oct. 1874).   [31] *Newcastle Daily Chronicle* (9 Sept. 1876).

become much less dubious; all that remained in doubt was the capacity of the registration authorities to identify them. London authorities, faced with the task of listing an elusive tenement population, had reacted with horror to the 1878 Act,[32] but London overseers found themselves under pressure from local political associations to do their legal duty.[33] The process of registering tenement occupiers as lodger voters had proved dauntingly expensive to the associations. In 1869 it had cost the Marylebone Liberals over £300 to get 5,400 lodger voters enrolled;[34] once it became arguable that the local authorities had a legal duty to register them as householders, the associations clearly preferred to put pressure on the authorities. In August 1879 Joseph Chamberlain drew the attention of the Home Secretary to the problem of bureaucratic resistance and asked if local authorities were liable to penalties for the omission of eligible names.[35] The result was a Home Office circular to vestry clerks twelve days later, repeating Chamberlain's claim and requesting 'that you will favour the Secretary of State with your observations thereon'.[36] Their observations are not hard to infer, and a Home Office reproof to the Hackney Vestry Clerk in 1880, following a further complaint about 'the non-registration of voters under the Parliamentary and Municipal Registration Act, 1878',[37] suggests that bureaucratic foot-dragging continued. Vestry obstructionism could not, though, survive the 1881 decision.

After that decision, and a further Home Office circular spelling out its implications, resistance in principle dwindled. *The Times* warned that 'the whole of the "residuum" will be swept into the net of registration', and revising barristers in London mocked a law which meant that 'half a house is to be considered as a whole (laughter)',[38] but the state of the law was now beyond challenge and the local authorities set about implementing it. Some limited themselves, like the Hackney overseers, to issuing 'placards...over the whole parochial area, and circulars...setting forth the facilities which the law now gives for the acquisition and exercise of voting rights and privileges',[39] but St Pancras claimed to be the first authority to carry out the demands of the 1878 Act to the letter, engaging 100 staff in 1881 to survey what was a very large parish, and adding 11,000 names to the list in the process.[40] The practice spread to the parishes comprising the Southwark parliamentary borough (where 'the canvassers found the people unwilling to believe in the alteration'[41]) and elsewhere; Islington Vestry employed

---

[32] See H. M. Bompas's letter 'The Vestry Clerks and the Franchise', *Echo* (31 July 1879).

[33] e.g. in Lambeth, *South London Press* (9 Oct. 1880).

[34] Evidence of W. R. Cremer to the Select Committee on the Registration of Voters, Q. 2207, 30 Apr. 1869.   [35] *Hansard*, 3rd ser., CCXLIX, vols. 53–4 (4 Aug. 1879).

[36] Circular, Liddell to Vestry Clerks, 16 Aug. 1879, Home Office Domestic Letter Books, National Archives, HO/43/131, p. 228.

[37] G. Lushington to Vestry Clerk, parish of St John, Hackney, 14 Oct. 1880, HO/43/133, ps. 658–9.

[38] *The Times* (26 Nov. 1881); Hurrell, revising barrister at Southwark, *South London Press* (1 Oct. 1881).   [39] *Hackney and Kingsland Gazette* (5 Aug. 1881).

[40] *St Pancras Guardian* (27 Aug. 1881).   [41] *South London Press* (1 Oct. 1881).

agents to visit tenement houses, eliciting 1,534 new names for the register 'of whom otherwise the overseers could have had no knowledge'.[42]

The more active authorities took pride in their work, but the drawbacks were obvious. In the first place, the lack of prior knowledge of the new voters implied a lack of knowledge of other details relevant to their right to vote, in particular whether they satisfied the one-year residence qualification and whether they had received poor relief during the qualifying period. Enforcement of these provisions was in any case widely thought to be lax. The impossibility of recovering the movements of voters generally prevents the historian from testing contemporary doubts about the residence qualification, though evidence from one East London case study suggests that evasion of the qualification ran at a significant level. Katherine Buildings in Whitechapel was a model dwelling owned by the Improved Industrial Dwellings Company, the residents of which were 'for the most part casual workers, dock labourers, carmen, employés of the building trades, fish porters and hangers-on to the numberless small industries which exist in East London'.[43] Beatrice Potter and Ella Pycroft, acting as rent-collectors for the corporate landlord, kept notes on the inhabitants, including information on the duration of each tenancy. Of 134 men identified as residents of the buildings at the end of the qualifying period for the 1888 register (31 July 1887), 83 appeared in that register. Of these 27 appear not to have occupied the qualifying accommodation for the whole year. Thirteen had moved from elsewhere in the Tower Hamlets parliamentary borough, and would therefore have been eligible as successive occupiers. Whether the authorities could actually have known of their entitlement, however, seems doubtful.[44]

The disqualification of paupers should have been easier to enforce in practice, in that the Poor Law guardians were required to provide the registration authorities with lists of those who had received poor relief during the qualifying period, and the tightening of Poor Law practice in the larger cities from the late 1870s meant that fewer able-bodied males were receiving relief in the first place. None the less, the Bethnal Green Conservatives were able to remove around a quarter of the electorate from the borough's register in 1891 by wholesale challenges to the draft register on the ground of having received poor relief—a purge which shows up clearly in the figures for the Bethnal Green sample area. The revising barrister chided the overseers for the large number of names successfully objected to on the grounds of receipt of poor relief. They promised better behaviour in future, but their explanation—that 'there had not been sufficient time for them to find out these cases'[45]—suggests that lax enforcement was the

---

[42] Islington Vestry, *Twenty-Ninth Annual Report* (1884–5), 38, London Metropolitan Archives.

[43] B. Potter, 'A Lady's View of the Unemployed at the East', *Pall Mall Gazette* (18 Feb. 1886).

[44] The Potter/Pycroft notebooks are in the archives of the British Library of Political and Economic Science, Misc Coll 43; the 1888 Whitechapel register is the London Metropolitan Archives, MR/PER/B/182.

[45] *Eastern Argus and Borough of Hackney Times* (30 Aug., 27 Sept., and 4 Oct. 1890); *Star* (22 Aug. 1890).

norm. The politically inspired Bethnal Green purge was in any case unusual: once a pauper appeared on the draft register, the political associations were normally reluctant to seek to remove him at the revision courts. Even in flagrant cases, once on the draft list a poor relief recipient had to be objected to individually to be removed, as revising barristers frequently made clear.[46] This procedure entailed certain expense and likely political odium.

In general, tenement canvasses involved local authorities in considerable expense for limited results. The 1,500 tenement occupiers discovered by Islington's canvass amounted to under 6 per cent of the total electorate, suggesting that this category remained seriously under-represented. Though the improvement in the Bethnal Green figures is striking, they did not, even in 1883, match the highest provincial levels. A similar pattern is evident in Devonport, included here as a port town with a similar degree of multi-occupation to London. The electorate in Devonport rose by 38 per cent between 1881 and 1883,[47] but the one surviving register shows an enfranchisement level little higher than one in three by the mid-1880s.

In 1885 the Liberal government tacitly acknowledged the difficulties faced by local authorities charged with registering multi-occupiers, spelling out in that year's Registration Act that they could discharge their duty by collecting occupiers' names through landlords,[48] although it was universally understood that returns made by landlords—especially non-resident landlords, who were the only ones relevant under the 1881 decision—were 'not implicitly to be relied upon'.[49] As the Bethnal Green sample shows, the effect by the late 1880s was perhaps to deflate the figures somewhat from the levels of 1883. Suggestions after the 1878 Act that democracy had been clandestinely created in London proved unfounded: extending the entitlement to the vote did not entail a proportionate increase in the electoral registers. The law had changed, and with the rights of tenement occupiers legally settled, local authority pressure on landlords,[50] the increasing efforts of the political parties to get their supporters registered and, perhaps, a growing demand from individual claimants had ensured that levels remained far higher than before 1881. But they had never—even in 1883—risen above 50 per cent.

[46] e.g. W. Ribton at Southwark in 1884, *South London Press* (20 Sept. 1884), A. Bathurst at Tower Hamlets, *East London Observer* (8 Oct. 1881).

[47] From the tables in *PP* 1881 LXXIV (HC 174) and *PP* 1883 LIV (HC 72); the electorate of neighbouring Plymouth rose by 45% in the same period.

[48] 48 Vict c. 15, Schedule 2, II, 'Form of Requisition by Overseers requiring Names of Inhabitant Occupiers'.

[49] Algernon Bathurst, revising barrister at Hoxton, *Borough of Hackney Express and Shoreditch Observer* (8 Oct. 1887). Bathurst still urged that 'there ought to be made house-to-house inquiries by the Overseers'.

[50] 'By Section 9 of the "Poor Rate Assessment and Collection Act", every owner of small tenements rated, or liable to be rated, is required to deliver to the Overseers whenever required, a list of the Occupiers of such tenements, and is liable to a penalty of Two Pounds for every omission or misstatement in respect of such list', Notice to Owners to Return Names of Tenants, Hackney, dated '188_', London Borough of Hackney Archives, L/V/115.

The practical obstacles to a tenement franchise remained immense, and the common-sense assumption that the ratio of men to buildings in a given area would influence its enfranchisement levels is borne out by the figures. Thus in Birmingham between 1881 and 1891 and in Salford between 1871 and 1881 a rise in the proportion of adult men to houses is associated with a fall in the enfranchisement level. Conversely in Brighton between 1881 and 1891 a drop in the ratio of men to houses, probably caused by the local authority's closure of lodging houses, is accompanied by a rise in the level of enfranchisement (See Table 1).

The remainder of this essay deals with the evidence from London, and in particular from the Bethnal Green sample area. This is partly because London, with its extensive multi-occupation, stood at the frontier of working-class enfranchisement, but largely because the East End of London was so exhaustively analysed in the late nineteenth century that it is possible to use survey material—particularly that of Charles Booth—to go beyond the raw aggregate figures that I have used in the other sample areas.

The 'Nichol'—the area of Bethnal Green centred upon Old Nichol Street—was probably the most notorious slum colony of the Victorian age. It was poorly built in the first place, with refuse lime from a soap works substituted for proper quick-lime in the construction of the houses, with the result that these properties absorbed moisture unduly and 60 per cent of the houses in the eventual clearance area suffered from damp. The Bethnal Green medical officer found in 1890 that only 9 per cent of houses were structurally sound, while 45 per cent were completely beyond repair.[51] These inadequate receptacles for population were none the less excessively crowded: the area's density of 373 persons per acre was more than double the overall level of Bethnal Green, itself more crowded than London as a whole, although almost all the houses in the Nichol area were of no more than two storeys. From the early Victorian period the area became something of a sump for the East End, gaining notoriety as a result. John Hollingshead highlighted 'Old Nichols [*sic*] Street . . . a specimen of an east end thieves' street' in 1861,[52] while Arthur Morison produced a celebrated fictional account of the area in his *A Child of the Jago* (1896). The area was, of course, surveyed by Charles Booth in his initial account of East End poverty, and additional material, provided by two local clergymen, survives in the Booth archive.[53] The Housing Committee of the London County Council chose the Nichol as the site of its first major housing

[51] Bethnal Green Vestry, *Medical Officer of Health's Report for 1890*, 37–8; Adjourned Report of the Housing of the Working Classes Committee, London County Council *Minutes*, 28 Oct. 1890, 909–10, London Metropolitan Archives.

[52] J. Hollingshead, *Ragged London in 1861* (London, 1861), 81 ff.

[53] Particulars from the notebooks of Revd A. O. Jay, Holy Trinity Shoreditch, Feb. 1889 Booth Collection, British Library of Political and Economic Science (BLPES), B80; Further Notes for the Household Survey, compiled by Revd Rupert St Leger, Curate of Holy Trinity, Shoreditch, BLPES Booth Collection, A2.

slum clearance scheme under the 1890 Housing of the Working Classes Act. Finally, it was described briefly but vividly by Arthur Harding, then 'probably the last man alive to have been brought up in the "Jago" '[54], recounting his life story to Raphael Samuel in the 1970s. If any area could be seen as 'residual', in the terms of the legislators of 1867, it was the 'Nichol'. Its occupiers had not been intended to benefit from the second Reform Act, and indeed did not do so in large numbers for fifteen years, but the enfranchisement of the tenement dweller by the 1878 Act and the 1881 *Bradley* v. *Baylis* decision was bound to affect the area. The doubling of the electorate in 1883 was the immediate result.

It is not altogether clear how this was achieved. The Bethnal Green overseers certainly considered it their duty to increase enfranchisement levels, but they appear not to have undertaken the kind of *ad hoc* survey used in St Pancras, so much as a campaign of assiduous persuasion of landlords, backed by notice of legal penalties. It was an approach better calculated to yield names than to establish their validity, and the suspicion remains that checks upon entitlement to vote suffered in the rush to enrol voters. The one-year residence requirement, in particular, was hard to enforce, as landlords were unlikely to know the precise date of a tenancy's commencement. Of 473 names from the Nichol appearing on the register for the first time in 1883, no fewer than 226 (48%) do not appear in the 1881 census, though all voters were required to have lived in the parliamentary borough since 1 August 1881. Some will have moved into the area between April (the census date) and August, and several were doubtless living elsewhere in Bethnal Green,[55] but it is hard to escape the conclusion that the residence qualification was not being strictly enforced.

Whatever the methods used to expand the register, the effect was clearly to diminish status distinctions within the electorate. Measuring the census classifica- tions of identifiable voters shows a significant rise in the proportion of labourers and street-sellers in the electorate between 1882 and 1883, one which has become still more marked by 1892. Census occupational classifications are, of course, a blunt instrument, but a similar pattern emerges from analysis of enfranchisement levels by street, graded by Booth's poverty colour scheme. The 1873 and 1882 registers show a broad inverse relationship between poverty levels and enfran- chisement, but by 1883 that pattern is far less clear. The biggest gainers in the mean-time had been the two 'poorest' colours, dark blue and black. The blackest street of all, Old Nichol Street, described in Booth's notebooks as 'an awful place, the worst in the [School Board] division', saw its electorate jump from fifteen in 1882 to fifty-eight in the following year (it would peak at eighty-five in 1887). In 'black' streets over the area as a whole, the enfranchisement rate trebled.

---

[54] R. Samuel (ed.), *East End Underworld: Chapters in the Life of Arthur Harding* (London, 1981), p. vii.

[55] The residence qualification did not bar men who moved within the parliamentary borough, if otherwise qualified.

But analysis by street colour also shows that these 'black' streets—the very poorest streets—remained at a disadvantage. Table 6 suggests that the reason for this lay, as with the provincial slum clearance areas discussed above, in the markedly higher levels of crowding. Part of the explanation, admittedly, lay once again in the concentration of common lodging houses in 'black' streets, accounting in fact for 29 per cent of the area's adult male population, but even when lodging houses are stripped from the calculation, the higher crowding levels in these streets remain apparent. However tolerant the law might have become towards those living in multi-occupied buildings, in practice they faced greater difficulties than single occupiers in getting registered. Analysis of identifiable voters on the 1883 register in Table 5 shows that a man's chances of getting registered were inversely related to the number of households sharing his house. The effect of the legal change *is* evident in the Bethnal Green sample—whereas in 1882 no house contained more than three voters, in 1883 there were forty-three houses with four or more registered voters, and one house, in Collingwood Street, contained no fewer than nine—but overall multi-occupiers remained under-represented. The fundamental explanation has been demonstrated by Marc Brodie's painstaking analysis of the Mile End electorate.[56] In practice multiple occupation entailed the sub-division of tenancies, with a principal tenant paying most or all of the house rent to the landlord and recouping this expenditure by sub-letting parts of the building. The principal tenant would be known to the landlord but the sub-tenants, in all probability, would not. In a system dependent upon landlord information for the registration of occupiers, this reduced the chances of sub-tenants' names finding their way onto the register. This in turn reintroduced a degree of social discrimination into a system which had threatened to lose it: principal tenants were more likely to be sufficiently comfortably off and securely employed to allow them to take on responsibility for an entire house rent, while sub-tenants were likely to be poorer and more probably in casual employment. Overall, moreover,

Table 5. Bethnal Green sample area: enfranchisement rate by number of households per inhabited house, 1883

Separate households per house	1	2	3	4	5	6+	Lodging houses
Resident men	400	381	346	213	97	142	132
Identifiable voters	184	132	85	52	22	34	7
Registration level (%)	46.00	34.65	24.57	24.41	22.68	23.94	5.30

Note: This table is to be read thus: '400 men belonged to a household which did not share accommodation with any other household; 184 of them (46%) were identifiable as voters, 381 men belonged to a household which shared accommodation with one other household, etc.

[56] M. Brodie, *The Politics of the Poor: London's East End, 1885–1914* (Oxford, 2004), ch. 2, 'A House Divided'.

Table 6. Bethnal Green, sample area: enfranchisement rates by colour of street in Booth poverty map (%) for all registered electors except non-residents

Electoral Register	1873	1882	1883	1891	1892
Black	11.25	12.79	32.40	27.18	31.74
Dark Blue	15.02	25.00	61.68	41.81	62.28
Light Blue	17.30	25.43	52.85	44.91	52.78
Purple	9.52	50.79	41.94	50.82	57.38
Pink	22.16	30.71	55.00	57.94	57.94

Note: The street descriptions are in the Booth collection at the British Library of Political and Economic Science, notebook B43 (**black** = lowest class. Vicious, semi-criminal. **dark blue** = very poor, casual. Chronic want. **light blue** = poor. 18s. to 21s. a week for a moderate family. **purple** = mixed. Some comfortable others poor. **pink** = fairly comfortable. Good ordinary earnings. **red** = middle class. Well-to-do. **yellow** = upper-middle and upper classes. Wealthy). There were no red or yellow streets in the Boundary St area. Booth did not ascribe colours to Inkhorn Court, Maidstone Place, Myring's Place, Reform Square, or Shepherd's Court.

Table 7. Bethnal Green sample area: men of voting age per inhabited house, 1881

	All	Excluding lodging houses
Black	3.36	2.91
Dark Blue	2.08	1.88
Light Blue	2.00	1.93
Purple	1.58	1.58
Pink	1.76	1.76

there was a direct relationship between the crowding level of a street and its poverty level, as Table 7 shows.

The point is confirmed in Bethnal Green through the contrast offered by the one purpose-built tenement block in the sample area. The model dwellings called Charlotte Buildings, owned by the Improved Industrial Dwellings Company, had been built as flats and did not present the regular problems associated with multi-occupation. Thirty adult men occupied the building in 1881, and thirty voters duly appear for the building in the 1883 register.[57] The occupiers were 'all very poor, mostly casual workers', according to Booth,[58] who coloured the block dark blue—the second poorest shading—on his 1889 poverty map, but with structurally separate tenements and an institutional landlord facilitating registration, a notional 100 per cent enfranchisement level was achieved.

The pattern in Bethnal Green is therefore one of a massive increase in the electorate brought about by the legal changes of 1878/1881, removing any hope that 1867 had tailored a selective, 'respectable' franchise, yet producing a system

---

[57] Not the same thirty, of course, though twenty-one of the thirty are identifiable in the 1881 census.   [58] Booth Collection, BLPES, B43.

in which the single occupier of a house, or the principal tenant who sublet to others, was more likely to gain the vote. Frustratingly, the Booth notebooks do not allow us to go much further for the East End, for the simple reason that the individuals analysed in Booth's survey are not identified by name. Analysis of degrees of poverty is therefore only possible by resort to the broad-brush, and rather impressionistic, categorization of whole streets on the coloured poverty maps. It is possible to go further only in one small area, comprising a few streets in the West Lambeth School Board division, where a pilot study was undertaken in late 1890 for the extension of the East End survey to the rest of London, and local clergymen and others provided details of identifiable individuals. In six streets or parts of streets it is possible to identify individuals both by name and by Booth's individual poverty categories, on an A–H scale. Though close to one another, these streets are not contiguous and do not form an 'area' in the way that the earlier samples do: the six streets actually come from four different parliamentary constituencies, one of them in the parliamentary borough of Wandsworth rather than Lambeth. They were not self-defining 'black spots' in the manner of the slum clearance areas, but they display well above average levels of poverty. It is fortunate that the streets were surveyed in November and December 1890, only four months before the 1891 census was taken, and that the relevant electoral registers all survive.

These Lambeth streets included 301 adult men who were put into poverty categories by Booth. 124 of them (41%) appear on the 1891 electoral register—a level comparable to that of Bethnal Green at the same time. Breakdown by Booth's poverty categories—see Table 8—reinforces other evidence that enfranchisement correlated inversely with poverty: 57 per cent of those above his informal poverty line were voters, against 33 per cent of those below it. It is necessary, though, to note that no class was visibly excluded. Of the very poorest, 27 per cent of Booth's class B, 'a deposit of those who from mental, moral and physical reasons are incapable of better work' were registered, as were four of the nine in his tiny class A, consisting of 'some occasional labourers, street-sellers, loafers, criminals and semi-criminals'.[59] It is important also to remember that Booth's poverty scale is very finely calibrated. Henry Pettitt, a Lambeth compositor with a wife and six dependent children, often out of work and 'more or less starving', could reach the dizzy level of class C; he was no labour aristocrat but he was a voter.[60]

In both Lambeth and Bethnal Green, *ad hoc* notes compiled by local clergymen provide some descriptive evidence about the late Victorian electorate that the statistics cannot convey. They indicate that in one house in Bethnal Green a 'wretched room—walls & ceiling damp & mouldy & room full of dense smoke', another 'wretched room—paper hanging from ceiling in ribbons—2 large holes

[59] C. Booth, *Life and Labour of the People, i. East London* (London, 1889), 37, 44.
[60] A lodger voter, moreover, for 3 Benfield St, 1891 Register, Battersea, London Borough of Wandsworth archives.

Table 8. West Lambeth School Board Division, 1890–1. Selected streets: analysis by Booth poverty category

Category	A	B	*A + B*	C	D	*C + D*	E	F	*E + F*	Total
No. identified by Booth	9	52	*61*	46	94	*140*	79	21	*100*	301
On 1891 register	4	14	*18*	17	32	*49*	49	8	*57*	124
% registered	44.44	26.92	*29.51*	36.96	34.04	*35.00*	62.03	38.10	*57.00*	41.20

Note: A = The lowest class which consists of some occasional labourers, street sellers, loafers, criminals and semi-criminals. B = Casual earnings, very poor. C = Intermittent earnings. 18s to 21s per week for a moderate family. D = Small regular earnings. poor, regular earnings. E = Regular standard earnings, 22s to 30s per week for regular work, fairly comfortable. F = Higher class labour and the best paid of the artisans. Earnings exceed 30s per week. G = Lower middle class. H = Upper middle class, servant-keeping class. The streets included in this analysis were Nealdon (or Neildon) St (Lambeth, Brixton division), Henry St and Portland Cottages (Lambeth, Kennington), Bond Court and Doon St (Lambeth North) and Benfield St (Battersea). Nobody from classses G and H was listed in these streets.

in floor—very smokey [*sic*]', and a third 'wretched home—windows broken, floor rotten, walls crumbling, eaten alive with bugs' could each confer the household vote upon their occupiers.[61] They tell us that the electorate included not only the 'intelligent and friendly' street-seller of coloured prints, 'well disposed to religion except the Salvationist form', whose son went to Sunday school and daughter to the girls' club,[62] and the church-going, abstaining fishmonger annoyed by 'the number of loafers about the street',[63] but also the 'idle and dissolute' fishmonger, of 'thievish stock' and on remand at Stratford on a charge of horse-stealing,[64] the firewood dealer who had trained his six children to sell wood from his barrow 'while the man was in the public house',[65] the drunkard dustman who epitomized Booth's class A ('the hound won't work. He says to his wife "I won't knock you about because you will have me and I won't desert you because the authorities will have a claim." '[66]), and the octogenarian silk weaver whose second wife had left him and who still lived in the room where his first wife had hanged herself.[67] It included

[61] Descriptions of the three rooms in 26 New Nichol St, Bethnal Green, by Revd A. O. Jay, May 1889, Booth Collection, B77. The occupiers of all three rooms appear on the 1889 electoral register, LMA MR/PER/B/185.

[62] Thomas Lacey, 28 Half Nichol St, Bethnal Green, described by Jay in Booth Collection, B80, Feb. 1889, and registered in 1889 (the house then being numbered 15) in LMA MR/PER/B/185.

[63] William Blackhall, 36 Boundary St, Booth Collection, B80, registered at 38 in LMA MR/PER/B/185.

[64] Charles Burdett, 18 Boundary St, described by Revd Rupert St Leger in Jan. 1891, Booth Collection, A2, registered in 1891 in LMA LCC/PER/B/75.

[65] William Martin, 11 Portland Cottages, Kennington, described by ?Mrs Wood in Dec. 1890, Booth Collection, B72, and registered in 1891 in LMA LCC/PER/B/106.

[66] James Padley, 17 Bond Place, Lambeth, described by Mr Wheeler in ?Nov. 1890, Booth Collection, B72, and registered for 1891 in LMA LCC/PER/B/103.

[67] James Cocquard, 20 Half Nichol St, described by Jay in Booth Collection, B80, and registered in 1889 in LMA MR/PER/B/185.

not only the painter who earned 40*s*. per week from jobbing, rent-collecting, and appearing at the music hall as 'the Scotchman in Ally Sloper's troupe'[68] but also the builder's labourer without work for months, the dock casual forced out of trade as a cigar box maker 'owing to use of paper packets made by females',[69] and the failed doll maker turned shoe-black, driven out of business by import penetration, who 'said he "shd be busy when the Germans were all dead." '[70] These were amongst the members of the audience to whom, in the late-Victorian period, the disciples of T. H. Green, the advocates of a scientific tariff, and the defenders of marriage with a deceased wife's sister sought to sell their political goods.

'I shall give up business until you are quiet', the St Pancras revising barrister warned a rowdy group of lodger claimants in 1881: 'the House of Lords and the House of Commons thought you were respectable or they would never have given you the franchise'.[71] The assumption that possession of the vote was an indicator of respectability was apparently entrenched even in the mind of a revising barrister, more familiar than most, one assumes, with the system's loopholes. It was an idea that could hardly have had much currency under the incoherent complex of franchises that had existed before 1832. It was doubtless rooted in the introduction of a uniform £10 borough franchise in 1832—even though the county franchise remained far less exclusive and, in practice, distinctly porous, thereafter[72]—and in the debates over franchise extension from 1852 onwards. Ironically, though, it was the abandonment of the £10 borough franchise in 1866–7 that reinforced the association of voting rights with respectability in political rhetoric. The abandonment of the £10 rating requirement carried manifest political risks. With the two parties competing to enlarge the electorate, and with each of them vulnerable to criticism from conservative dissenters within its ranks, the rhetorical need for a qualitative distinction between voters and non-voters became clear, and the assertion that the vote was a badge of respectability became commonplace, even as it became more implausible. Perhaps by 1881 the fiction was wearing thin, as the remarks of the St Pancras revising barrister provoked 'derisive laughter', but the reporter present none the less attributed this response not to the quaintness of the barrister's views but to the indignation of aspirant voters who 'did not relish the idea of being pent up behind barriers and tended by policemen'.[73]

[68] Joseph Poulter, 11 Neildon St, Brixton, described by Revd C. E. Escreet in Booth Collection B72, Dec. 1890, and registered for 1891 in LMA LCC/PER/B/104.

[69] William Royston, 18 Boundary St, described by Jay in Feb. 1889, Booth Collection B80, and registered for 1889 in LMA MR/PER/B/185.

[70] Edward Read, 18 Half Nichol St, described by Jay in Feb. 1889, Booth Collection, B80, and registered for 1889 in LMA MR/PER/B/185.

[71] J. N. Goren, quoted in *Marylebone Mercury* (24 Sept. 1881).

[72] For the Anti-Corn Law League's switch of emphasis from boroughs to counties in 1844, see N. McCord, *The Anti-Corn Law League, 1838–1846* (London, 1958), 151, and J. M. Prest, *Politics in the Age of Cobden* (Basingstoke, 1977), 81. [73] *Marylebone Mercury* (24 Sept. 1881).

Colin Matthew was, of course, right to claim that the 1867 and 1884 Reform Acts 'had as their aims the enfranchisement of what Gladstone called the "capable citizen" '.[74] What cannot be shown is that this aim was realized. The principal social safeguards in the 1867 law had been the requirement for personal payment of rates and the assumption—not actually spelt out in the Act—that a householder needed to occupy a physically separate dwelling. The first of these safeguards was removed in 1869, the second in 1878–81, and thereafter the boundary lines of enfranchisement were unpredictable and often irrational. The practical difficulty of registering men in multi-occupied areas did work in such a way as to entail a degree of social filtration in those areas, but any impression of the 1867 electorate as socially exclusive should be very heavily qualified: the sample areas studied here were all slum communities, but all showed relatively high levels of enfranchisement, even if 'pink' streets had more voters than 'black' streets. By extension it was surely impossible to engineer an electorate with the political sophistication to provide the sort of educated forum that many Victorian Liberals sought and that Colin Matthew depicted.

It is perhaps unsurprising, then, that a canvasser's account of doorstep responses in Southwark in 1880 has a modern—and markedly uncerebral—tone: ' "don't 'ee come again. My old man says he don't want no vote—he can get along very well without voting; and he do say that they be all a lot of sharks what gets into Parlymint—don't matter what they call theirsels" '; 'I ventured to ask one man why he was a Conservative and another why he was a Liberal. From each I received the same reply—"I don't know. My father was, and so am I, and I shall always be the same" ', though it is equally noteworthy that 'when working men were at home, [the canvasser] found most of them anxious to learn his allegiance and argue the point'.[75] Working-class voters might have been no more politically open-minded than, say, the grand Whiggery of the early nineteenth century, and they did not display great political sophistication, but it would be wrong to assume that they were impervious to political discussion.

This reminds us that the questions posed in Colin Matthew's essay on rhetoric remain suggestive, even if his answer to them might appear insecure. If electoral law could not produce a refined and articulate political nation in the Victorian liberal image, how *was* it that 'a university-educated, intellectual élite succeeded in coordinating the working of a great political movement in a predominantly industrial and commercial state'?[76] In due course, and even before 1918, the implications of the enlarged electorate began to assert themselves, so that by the 1900s politicians of both major parties thought it advantageous to advocate social politics. During the last quarter of the nineteenth century, though, the political class was able to push a number of apparently undemotic causes to the head of the

[74] Matthew, 'Rhetoric', 36.
[75] 'Looking up the Voters [By One Engaged in It]', *South London Press* (11 Sept. 1880).
[76] Matthew, 'Rhetoric', 53.

political agenda, whether by charismatic leadership or through the device of the caucus. An electorate often taken as prone to jingoism could be wooed by Gladstone's ethical foreign policy precepts in 1876–8 and his attack on empire in 1879–80. The somewhat fastidious Radicalism of Chamberlain's Unauthorized Programme and the still more arcane proposals of the 1891 Newcastle Programme could be presented, if not always plausibly, as the will of the people. As late as the 1890s, issues such as Welsh disestablishment, agricultural rating relief, and the problems of the Church schools could still dominate the parliamentary schedule at the expense of old age pensions and the legal position of trade unions.

In this respect Colin Matthew's work on political rhetoric opened more doors than it closed. The questions of how policies are promulgated and how they are received remain fertile today, and one wonders how a historian of Colin's sophistication and technical skill would have developed the arguments expressed in 1987. In the event the tasks of finishing Gladstone's diaries and launching the new *Dictionary of National Biography* prevented him from doing so. That is our loss.

8

The Defection of the Middle Class: The Endowed Schools Act, the Liberal Party, and the 1874 Election

Lawrence Goldman

I

In a famous letter of 6 February 1874 to his brother Robertson, William Gladstone explained the Liberal electoral débâcle at the recent general election as the combination of several factors: the hostility and indiscipline of ' "independent" liberals' on his own back-benches and in the Liberal Party more widely, the religious controversy over the 1870 Education Act, and the famous 'torrent of gin and beer' set in motion by the unpopularity of the 1872 Licensing Act.[1] Many contemporaries also saw it as the inevitable result of the administration's ambitious (and hence controversial) programme of reforms since 1868, or in Disraeli's phrase, their 'incessant and harassing legislation'.[2] According to one London newspaper, 'the nation has wearied of restless legislation and administrative bungling'.[3] Reform had incited opposition: as Lord Halifax, formerly the leading Liberal minister, Sir Charles Wood, wrote to Gladstone on 12 February, 'The feelings of those who suffer from the removal of abuses are always stronger than those of the general public who are benefited'. But Halifax went further and deeper in his analysis, divining 'unreasoning fear' caused by class and denominational tensions between masters and men and churchmen and nonconformists as the reason why many voters had 'taken refuge in conservatism'.[4] This essay will examine the effect of one largely neglected piece of educational legislation, the 1869 Endowed Schools

---

[1] W. E. Gladstone to Robertson Gladstone, 6 Feb. 1874, quoted in John Morley, *Life of William Ewart Gladstone* (London, 1903 edn., 2 vols.), ii. 103–4. See K. T. Hoppen, *The Mid-Victorian Generation 1846–1886* (Oxford, 1998), 611: 'In thirty-four constituencies unofficial candidates stood against official Liberals and a dozen or more seats were lost as a result'.

[2] Robert Blake, *Disraeli* (London, 1966), 534.   [3] *Pall Mall Gazette* (7 Feb. 1874), 1.

[4] Halifax to Gladstone, 12 Feb. 1874, quoted in Morley, *Gladstone*, ii. 102.

Act, on the 'unreasoning fear' of propertied voters, though it will conclude, *pace* Halifax, that there were reasonable and understandable grounds for the political reaction against Liberalism that this particular measure and its administration created.

A generation ago historians' explanations for the Liberals' defeat in the 1874 general election tended to focus on one aspect of the contemporary analysis to the exclusion of other factors—the disaffection of crucial sections of Liberal support. Nonconformists were opposed to the 1870 Education Act, the trade unions were hostile to the 1871 trade union legislation, and brewers and landlords were in uproar over the 1872 Licensing Act. The explanation was predicated on a narrow and unimaginative model of political history, one that framed politics merely in terms of interest groups and their expectations. Indeed, in many ways this was closer to a later twentieth-century conception of politics as the reflection of the material interests of groups demanding favours from governments as the price of electoral support, than the more nuanced nature of mid-Victorian politics where the vote was not a bargaining chip but a badge of status, manhood, and independence.

More recently, however, several historians have shown, in different ways, that this manner of explaining 1874 may be only partially effective. Terry Jenkins has made the point that it is difficult to verify the claim later made by Francis Adams in his *History of the Elementary School Contest in England* in 1882 that 'abstentions by supporters of the National Education League had cost the Liberals twenty seats'.[5] Harry Hanham and Brian Harrison both 'warned against exaggerating the shift of [political] support generated by the [Licensing] Act' as the drinks trade had never been united in its view on licensing reform or in its party-political affiliations.[6] The old interpretation was most comprehensively upended by Jon Parry in *Democracy and Religion*. He showed very clearly that religious sectionalism was not the main problem, and may not have been much of a problem at all, as the Liberals actually seem to have performed better in elections in those areas where nonconformity was strong.[7] According to Parry, Liberal victories in school board elections in 1873 had largely taken the heat out of nonconformist grievances over elementary education because nearly all Liberal candidates 'at that time advocated an unsectarian policy of bible-reading or teaching, but with no further religious instruction'.[8] Far more important was Liberal electoral failure among the middle classes who had more generalized concerns about the radical measures and direction of Liberalism in government. It was 'propertied Anglican disaffection' (rather than the opposition of nonconformists and 'abstentions on the "left" of the party') which made the difference.[9]

[5] T. A. Jenkins, *Gladstone, Whiggery and the Liberal Party 1874–1886* (Oxford, 1988), 40 n.

[6] H. A. Hanham, *Elections and Party Management. Politics in the time of Gladstone and Disraeli* (London, 1959), 222–7; Brian Harrison, *Drink and the Victorians* (London, 1971), 279–85. This point is made in Jonathan Parry, *Democracy and Religion: Gladstone and the Liberal Party, 1867–1875* (Cambridge, 1986), 403.   [7] Ibid., 397–8

[8] Ibid., 398.

[9] Ibid., 401. Jonathan Parry, *The Rise and Fall of Liberal Government in Victorian Britain* (London and New Haven, 1993), 272.

   This position is substantiated in Mark Curthoys's monograph on the trade unions, the labour laws, and the state in the period 1865–76, which argues that the infamous falling out between organized labour and the Liberals over the Criminal Law Amendment Act of 1871 had been patched up by the end of 1873. By this time Robert Lowe at the Home Office had worked out a draft legislative scheme which largely determined what the Conservatives put in place in 1875–6. According to Curthoys, the election of 1874 did not display organized labour's disaffection with the Liberals, but demonstrated, on the one hand, a public recognition by Liberal candidates that the 1871 trade union settlement had to be revisited and revised, and on the other, the general endorsement of Liberal candidates by the unions.[10] And he agrees with Jon Parry that propertied Anglican disaffection rather than defections by organized labour accounted for the defeat of the Liberals, who actually managed to retain much of their strength in the Northern boroughts.[11] As we shall see, it wasn't in the North, but in the southern shires and London that the Liberals lost the election. Curthoys also provides further evidence, *inter alia*, to support Paul Smith's much earlier argument that Conservative social legislation between 1874 and 1877 owed everything to Liberal plans and measures already drafted or in processs.[12]

   However, there is the lurking presence of another cause of the dissociation of the middle classes from Liberalism, the Endowed Schools Act of 1869, which has not received very much attention, having been largely overshadowed by the political controversy over the 1870 Elementary Education Act and its clause 25. This essay aims to bring the Endowed Schools Act, which was designed to reform facilities for secondary, or as it was known, tellingly in this case, 'middle class education', into the limelight, and present it in a political context. It is also intended to bring together different literatures on Liberal politics and secondary education which are generally unconnected.[13] If the influence of the latter on the former can be demonstrated the essay will have vindicated the approach applied to 'political culture' in this volume as a whole by enlarging our sense of what 'the political' is or was, and showing how an apparently apolitical question concerning the reform and redeployment of educational endowments had very considerable consequences for the philosophical attachment of men of property to late Victorian Liberalism.

---

[10] M. Curthoys, *Governments, Labour and the Law in Mid-Victorian Britain. The Trade Union Legislation of the 1870s* (Oxford, 2004), 189–207.   [11] Ibid., 208–212.
[12] Paul Smith, *Disraelian Conservatism and Social Reform* (London, 1967), *passim*.
[13] One of these literatures concerns the place of the Endowed Schools Act and its interpretation by the three Endowed Schools Commissioners charged with overseeing this programme of reform in the history of girls' education in Britain. The Commissioners used their powers to offer opportunities for secondary education to girls as well as boys and were responsible for the formation of several girls' schools in the 1870s. Because this was not a subject for national political controversy (as opposed to purely local disaffection over the use of endowments for girls) it does not form a theme in this essay. For further information, see Sheila Fletcher, *Feminists and Bureaucrats: A Study in the Development of Girls' Education in the Nineteenth Century* (Cambridge, 1980).

In fact, the Endowed Schools Act, or rather its repeal, is not without its place in British history. It was Colin Matthew himself who drew attention to it in his work on Gladstone, because Gladstone believed that its legislative amendment by the incoming Conservative administration in 1874 in the form of the Endowed Schools Act Amendment Act was the first deliberate attempt to nullify the measures of a preceding administration in his long political experience, and hence might be seen as the first piece of nineteenth-century legislation to have been repealed. Gladstone described it as

a Bill for undoing part of the work of the last Parliament . . . the first instance on record, so far as I have been able to ascertain, of any deliberate attempt being made by a Ministry of retrogression . . . The majority of this Parliament is invited to undo the work of their Predecessors in office in defiance of precedents which I would weary the House by enumerating, so great are their number and uniformity.[14]

Gladstone's memory and understanding of the bill were probably both faulty. As Gathorne Hardy replied, the Endowed Schools Commission had been appointed for a finite period only and a decision had to be taken on its future in any event.[15] The Tories did not scrap the Endowed Schools Act in 1874 but really did *amend* it so that it no longer threatened Anglican interests; it was to be administered in a different manner by the Charity Commissioners rather than the Endowed Schools Commissioners. Depending on what is understood by 'retrogression', we can surely think of other acts 'repealed' in this or a similar manner before the 1870s.

But the political implications of the 1869 statute go further than this: many sources, but above all members of the political class themselves, queued up after the election to make the claim (which has largely been ignored by historians) that controversy over the act and its implementation contributed directly and largely to the Liberal defeat. Indeed, the case was made as early as 1873, when one MP warned in the House that disagreement with the measure 'will exercise considerable influence at the next General Election, if, indeed, it has not had some effect in one or two of the more recent contests'.[16] In the second reading debates in the Commons on the amending bill of July 1874 after the Conservatives had come in, several Tories attributed their recent victory at the polls to the Endowed Schools Act, and Gladstone, in a particularly bad-tempered speech, seems to have agreed with them. Viscount Sandon, introducing the amending legislation, justified the Tory measure as 'in accordance with the feelings widely expressed at the late General Election, for he believed the verdict of the country was as much against the late Government upon this subject as it was upon others'.[17] In the resumed second reading debate on the bill, Sandon added that 'it was well known that the

[14] *Hansard*, 3rd ser. CCXX (14 July 1874), 1707–8. See also Gladstone's similar comments *Hansard*, CCXXI (21 July 1874), 476. H. C. G. Matthew, *Gladstone 1809–1874* (Oxford, 1986), 175–6.
[15] *Hansard*, CCXX (14 July 1874), 1710.
[16] Sir James Lawrence, *Hansard*, CCXV (13 May 1873), 1911.
[17] *Hansard*, CCXX (14 July 1874), 1643.

verdict of the nation at the late General Election was in some degree based on the proceedings of the Government under the Endowed Schools Act... Was it a question which hon. Gentlemen opposite would care to have tried upon the hustings? He believed they would sooner think of flying.'[18] William Wheelhouse, Conservative MP for Leeds, contended from the backbenches that 'amongst the causes that led to the downfall of the late Government, no feeling was stronger than the one which induced everybody to distrust the action of this most unfortunate Endowed Schools' Commission'.[19] To this Gladstone replied: 'According to him [Mr Wheelhouse] it appears that our passing this Endowed Schools Bill, far more than some more vulgar causes and considerations we heard of at the time, influenced the elections... Well, that is a view the truth of which I will not contest.'[20] If this was, in the manner of the man, slightly ambiguous, other contributors to these debates were in no doubt. Sampson Lloyd, the banker and Conservative MP for Plymouth, 'never remembered any public act which had caused more unpopularity than the appointment of the Endowed Schools Commission... The country having been appealed to by the right hon. Gentleman (Mr Gladstone) had pronounced against his policy.'[21] Nor was this an exclusively Conservative interpretation of Liberal conduct. When H. A. Bruce, formerly Home Secretary in the Liberal administration (and now Lord Aberdare), came to preside at the Social Science Association's 1875 congress, he reviewed the sorry history of the recent reform of endowed schools and emphasized its political impact for 'an opposition arose throughout the country, which not only had a great effect in crippling the action of the Commissioners, but, he believed, had a very important influence in the complete overthrow of the late government which brought forward the measure'.[22]

Political opposition to the Liberals in 1874 was especially notable in the City of London, whose corporation had been embroiled in a dispute with the Endowed Schools Commission over the remodelling of the educational endowments of the Emanuel Hospital foundation since 1871. Arthur Hobhouse, who played a pivotal role in the whole episode as one of the three Endowed Schools Commissioners, reflected many years later in 1904 in a letter to his nephew, the political theorist L. T. Hobhouse, that problems over the reform of educational endowments by the Commission lost the Liberals the support of the City—and hence of men of property—for all time. Writing about the Emanuel Hospital scheme (which will be discussed below) Hobhouse reflected that

a violent agitation was set on foot, supported by the whole Tory party in the House of Lords. It took all Gladstone's strength to maintain the law. The City, which had been

---

[18] *Hansard*, CCXXI (20 July 1874), 323.   [19] *Hansard*, CCXX (14 July 1874), 1663.
[20] Ibid., 1707.   [21] *Hansard*, CCXXI (21 July 1874), 427.
[22] *Transactions of the National Association for the Promotion of Social Science*, 1875 (London, 1876), 448. Another Liberal who took a similar view was William Torrens, MP for Finsbury. See *Hansard*, CCXXI (22 July 1874), 523–4.

Liberal for long periods of time, has been Tory ever since that interference with its 'property'. The position of its wealthy members and their cries of 'Robbery' had a great effect in the election of 1874.[23]

Liberal MPs representing London constituencies had voted against the government on issues relating to the reform of endowments during the life of the administration, no doubt responding to the strength of feeling among their electorates.[24] In the 1874 election, the Liberals lost seven seats in London, 'three in the City, one in Westminster, in both cases by immense majorities'.[25] After the election, one Liberal MP, Lord George Cavendish, rebuked Gladstone for 'pouring out the vials of his wrath' on the City corporation and the supporters of the unreformed Emanuel foundation in a Commons debate in May of the previous year, 'for he thought to himself at the time that the seats of the sitting Members for London . . . were sure to go at the next election'.[26]

This testimony is not altogether surprising if we recognize that the issue at stake—the remodelling of ancient charitable endowments—was a significant and controversial problem in a mid-Victorian age notable for varied attempts at the reform of many different outmoded institutions in church and state. Morley referred to 'the burning question of the sacrosanctity of endowments' in the politics of the period. [27] His subject, Gladstone, held particularly radical views on the question: he had criticized the 'habit in this country to treat private interests with an extravagant tenderness' in a letter to Lyttelton in 1861.[28] Two years later he suffered a notable parliamentary defeat when his proposal in the budget to extend income tax to charities met with widespread opposition and had to be withdrawn.[29] Nevertheless, he continued to believe in the right of the national government to regulate the affairs of charitable endowments. Defending the proposed reform of the Emanuel Hospital foundation in 1873, he argued that the proposals were not dangerously innovatory but merely in keeping with the trend of the time: 'For the last twenty years we have been dealing with Governing Bodies of all kinds'.[30] Trollope focused one of his most famous novels on the question.

---

[23] L. T. Hobhouse and J. L. Hammond, *Lord Hobhouse: A Memoir* (London, 1905), 44–5.

[24] 'Nine London Liberal MPs and eight others voted with the Conservatives in favour of Crawford's motion of May 1873 defending the existing management of Emanuel Hospital and opposing the Commissioner's second scheme for its reorganisation'. Parry, *Democracy and Religion*, 380.

[25] Morley, *Gladstone*, ii. 99. The other seats lost were in Chelsea, Tower Hamlets, and Southwark. The Liberals also lost a seat in Middlesex.

[26] *Hansard*, CCXXI (20 July 1874), 316. See the similar remarks by the Conservative MP, Mr Locke, in the adjourned debate two days later, *Hansard*, CCXXI (22 July 1874), 509. According to the account of Gladstone's speech in the Commons on 13 May 1873 in *The City Press*, 'There was something fierce, if not actually ferocious, in his attacks upon the Corporation' (17 May 1873), 5. *The Saturday Review* accused Gladstone of 'displaying his characteristic quality of reckless impetuosity', 'Emanuel Hospital' (17 May 1873), 644.   [27] Morley, *Gladstone*, i. 946.

[28] Ibid.

[29] *Hansard*, CLXX (16 Apr. 1863), 224d–h; (4 May 1863), 1072–1102. *The Gladstone Diaries*, ed. H. C. G. Matthew, vi (Oxford, 1978), 24 Apr. 1863, 199. Matthew, *Gladstone 1809–1874*, 139.

[30] *Hansard*, CCXV (13 May 1873), 1895.

The Warden, published in 1855, was loosely based on actual cases, including well-publicized disputes over the use of historic endowments involving the Rochester cathedral chapter and the cathedral school, the Hospital of St Cross in Winchester, and Dulwich College.[31] Trollope depicted the religious, social, and personal conflicts when the inefficient disposition of funds from an ancient endowment controlled by the church for the maintenance of a dozen aged men of Barchester became a public issue and the focus of a reforming campaign.

Such conflicts in real life made the question of the reform of endowments intrinsically political in the widest sense. Setting to one side the particular local interests of boards of trustees, the attempt to alter the instructions of benefactors in any time or place throws up various philosphical problems and issues of political temperament. The temperament of the radicals was to reject the authority of the past—or what was known disparagingly as 'the dead hand', stretching from the grave and controlling the distribution of endowments decades and centuries after they were laid down—especially if the endowments were no longer serving an obviously useful social purpose, and to reorganize them in light of the needs of the present and future.[32]

Hobhouse thought it absurd to allow 'the dead to have anything to do with the regulation of property when their wishes conflicted with the welfare of the living'[33]—though he was to discover how difficult and controversial it was to break with so-called 'founder's intentions' and assign a new definition and meaning to welfare in the present. Conversely, the temperament of the conservative—and one thinks of Burke in this context—was and is to remain more faithful to the past, and respectful of tradition, even at the expense of social and financial efficiency. Yet even Burke accepted that reform might be required, so long as it was not innovation for its own sake: 'a state without the means of some change is without the means of its conservation.'[34]

Certainly, the question of educational endowments gave political men an opportunity to advance their different philosophical positions. As the Endowed Schools bill began its passage through Parliament, several tried their hand at advising the government. Robert Lowe advocated the kind of *laissez-faire* solution contemporaries had learnt to expect from him. In a pamphlet at the end of 1868 entitled *Middle Class Education: Endowment or Free Trade?* he argued that endowments for secondary education were ultimately pernicious in that they created lazy and ineffective teachers guaranteed an income, and lackadaisical pupils sure of an education for which they did not have to pay. The monies should be diverted by the state to other and more productive uses. Meanwhile a true market for

---

[31] Anthony Trollope, *The Warden* (London, 1855; Oxford World Classics edn., 1980), ed. David Skilton, introduction, p. xiii.

[32] See Arthur Hobhouse, *The Dead Hand: Addresses on the Subject of Endowments and Settlements of Property* (London, 1880).

[33] *Sessional Proceedings of the National Association for the Promotion of Social Science* (1868–9), 644.

[34] Edmund Burke, *Reflections on the Revolution in France* (1790; London, 1865 edn.), 259.

secondary education should be established in which the good schools, attracting the fee-paying middle classes, would drive out the bad.[35]

He was answered by two progressive educationists, Joshua Fitch and James Bryce, who had both served as assistant commissioners for the Taunton Inquiry which had investigated the state of secondary education in the mid-1860s and which recommended that the nation's educational endowments be consolidated and reapportioned in the construction of new and better schools. Fitch pointed out that the market for secondary education had not worked up to that point and showed no signs of improving the quality of schooling, while parents who were unable to make informed choices sent their children to schools of dubious standard. He urged in *Fraser's Magazine* in January 1869 that the reform of the endowed schools be the kind of precise, universal, and efficient programme of change that we might expect this type of man to call for, welcoming the 'prospect held out here of consolidation, of method, of improvement, of economy in national resources, of unity and clearness in national aims'.[36] Bryce, later an MP, minister, and diplomat, argued in *Macmillan's Magazine* that endowments, wisely used, could ensure a higher standard of education than would otherwise be possible on the basis of fees paid alone. But to be used wisely 'these endowments should be dealt with in no timid or shrinking spirit'; they should be treated 'as so much public money, to be disposed of as public wisdom thinks best'. This was the radical solution adopted under the 1869 Act, with unforeseen political consequences that we have already encountered.[37]

Meanwhile John Stuart Mill, writing in April 1869 in the *Fortnightly Review*, made the kind of arguments that we might expect from this source as well. He welcomed the radical triumph over the 'dead hand' that he believed he saw in the disendowment of the Irish Church in 1869, but he cautioned against a radical uniformity—an undeviating radical systematization of secondary education of the sort Fitch wanted—for reasons we associate with Mill in other contexts: that he generally feared the social effects of uniformity and wanted to encourage social and institutional diversity. Afraid that if the the public claimed control over private beneficence, charity itself would dry up, he advocated a fifty-year period of grace during which endowments were to be used as the donor intended, after which they might be altered to suit changing public needs—an utterly impractical solution, no doubt, but a compromise between individualism and state control that is suggestive of Mill's general political philosophy at the end of his life.[38]

[35] Robert Lowe, *Middle Class Education: Endowment or Free Trade?* (London, 1868). See D. W. Sylvester, *Robert Lowe and Education* (Cambridge, 1974), 144–61.

[36] J. G. Fitch, 'Educational Endowments', *Fraser's Magazine*, 79 (Jan. 1869), 1–15.

[37] [James Bryce], 'The Worth of Educational Endowments', *Macmillan's Magazine*, 19 (Apr. 1869), 517–24.

[38] J. S. Mill, 'Endowments', *The Fortnightly Review*, NS 28 (Apr. 1869), 377–90.

II

Why had the issue of educational endowments become a subject for legislation and debate in 1869? To answer this question we have to stretch back some years, for the Endowed Schools Act originated in the work of the Taunton (or Schools' Inquiry) Commission which had been established by Palmerston's administration in 1864 to investigate the state of middle-class proprietary and endowed schools, a vexed public issue since the mid-1850s at least. The Commission came to see its main purpose as the reform of middle-class schooling by adapting and re-employing educational endowments no longer fulfilling a useful educational or philanthropic function. In essence—and this proved to be among the reasons for the controversy—the Taunton Commission recommended that endowments given for free education, usually of the local poor, should be redeployed to solve the problem of secondary education for the middle classes. In the Commission's view, free secondary education, except for talented children from poor families awarded scholarships, wasted available funds in an essentially arbitrary distribution. Quite specifically they argued that educational benefactions, whatever their provenance or purpose, were, in essence, the property of the wider community: to quote their report, 'The whole country has an interest in these endowments, and has a right to know how the property is used, and whether the results produced are commensurate with the means'.[39] But this nationalizing solution to the problems of secondary education was clearly in conflict with another of the Taunton Commissioners' observations that 'schools have been regarded as subjects of special trusts of a precisely limited character, not as local contributions to the higher education of the country'.[40] If the reformers thought in terms of national needs and of a national system of secondary schooling, inevitably they would clash with the local and limited interests of boards of trustees and governors who hitherto had controlled the schools. The scene was set for another Victorian drama between centralization and localism.

In accordance with these findings, the subsequent Act, introduced by W. E. Forster, Vice-President of the Council, was intended to facilitate the reorganization of the old grammar schools to supply the needs of the middle classes.[41] Under it, an

[39] *Schools Inquiry Commission* (1867–8), pt. 1, 619.

[40] Ibid., 115. See David Owen, *English Philanthropy 1660–1960* (Cambridge, Mass., 1965), 252.

[41] 32 and 33 Victoria c. 56, An Act to Amend the Law relating to Endowed Schools and Other Educational Endowments in England, and otherwise to provide for the advancement of Education. On the Act and its implementation see John Roach, *A History of Secondary Education in England 1800–1870* (Harlow, 1986), 278–90; idem, *Secondary Education in England 1870–1902* (London, 1991), 3–13. On the equally controversial reform of endowed schools in Scotland, see Robert Anderson, *Education and Opportunity in Victorian Scotland. Schools and Universities* (Oxford, 1983), 162–201. See also Brian Simon, 'Systematisation and Segmentation in Education: The Case of England'; Hilary Steedman, 'Defining Institutions: The Endowed Grammar Schools and the Systematisation of English Secondary Education'; and David Reeder, 'The Reconstruction of Secondary Education in England 1869–1920', all in D. K. Müller, F. Ringer, and B. Simon (eds.), *The Rise of the Modern Educational System* (Cambridge, 1987), 99–101, 111–34, 137–41.

Endowed Schools Commission was created, comprising three commissioners, with the power to make 'schemes' and regulations 'as may render any educational endowment most conducive to the advancement of the education of boys and girls', and present them to Parliament for approval. The remarkable powers given to the Commissioners under section 9 to alter, remodel, and consolidate endowments as they saw fit, and under section 10, to dissolve a school's governing body, or change it in any manner, were to be the source of the controversy. The powers given to the Commission were so wide that it was said to be able to 'convert a boys' school in Northumberland into a girls' school in Cornwall'.[42] Under the terms of the Act, religion could no longer be used as a test of membership of a governing body (section 17), nor had masters in endowed schools to be in holy orders (section 18), though in cases where the religious character of the school as laid down by the founder was clear and unambiguous, section 19 allowed for these conditions to be waived. The Commissioners were also given powers to apply non-educational charities established before 1800 and no longer considered to be fulfilling a useful social function, which were generally for different forms of poor relief, for educational ends.[43] Overall, the Act gave the Commissioners remarkable powers but very little guidance on what was to be done.

As things turned out the Endowed Schools Commission joined the Poor Law Commission of the 1830s and the General Board of Health between 1848 and 1854 as one of the most controversial administrative agencies of the nineteenth century. Given its sweeping powers, the vested and also the legitimate interests that opposed it, and the sheer technical and legal complexity of remodelling outmoded endowments into workable as well as publicly acceptable 'schemes', its rapid notoriety should not have been surprising. It did not help that the three men invested with this power and charged with such a difficult task were avowed Liberals and already closely associated with the controversial process they were now called upon to administer impartially. Lord Lyttelton, the conscientious, high-minded, intellectual chief commissioner, had been a member of the Taunton Commission, was one of Gladstone's brothers-in-law, and was notably close to the Prime Minister. Arthur Hobhouse, later Baron Hobhouse, was a highly successful barrister and also a Charity Commissioner.[44] Canon Hugh Robinson, a barrister as well as a priest and so doubly qualified for his role, had been principal of the York and Ripon Diocesan Training College between 1854 and 1864, and was a friend of W. E. Forster.[45] Meanwhile the Secretary of the Commission (and after 1872, a full member) was Henry Roby. He had also been secretary to the Taunton Commission, and was variously a Cambridge don, a distinguished classical scholar, a schoolmaster, cotton manufacturer, and eventually a Liberal MP.

[42] R. L. Archer, *Secondary Education in the Nineteenth Century* (1921: London, 1966 edn.), 170.
[43] P. H. J. H. Gosden, *The Development of Educational Administration in England and Wales* (Oxford, 1966), 62–3.
[44] L. T. Hobhouse and J. L. Hammond, *Lord Hobhouse: A Memoir* (London, 1905).
[45] F. Boase, *Modern English Biography* (1892: London, 1965 edn.), iii. 226.

In addition to the problem of who the commissioners were and what they believed, there was the yet more inflammatory issue of what they actually did. Structurally, the Commission lacked a vital tier of administrative assistance: Lyttelton explained to the Select Committee of 1873 which investigated the 1869 statute, that the failure to establish provincial authorities with expert local knowledge and contacts, which Forster had originally planned but had then withdrawn, had slowed the process of remodelling endowments, thrown an enormous burden on the Commissioners in London, and incited opposition to what seemed like central dictation.[46] In a statement of their principles in 1872 the Commissioners explained that they had taken the recommendations of the Taunton Commission 'as their principal guides on those points on which the Act itself does not speak'.[47] But in following the recommendations of this 'radical-collectivist document' (as W. L. Burn called it in the 1960s) they were bound to incite opposition, for it deliberately sought to disrupt the religious, social, and educational customs and traditions which it held responsible, in part, for the parlous state of secondary education.[48]

In their attitude to the remodelling of hitherto exclusively Anglican foundations the Commissioners were accused of a bias against the Established Church, and of being part of a much wider Liberal campaign against establishment between 1868 and 1874.[49] The Commissioners 'refused to recognise many schools as Church of England foundations'—though in truth the 1869 Act made it rather difficult to uphold the identity of Anglican foundations, whatever their own views in each case—and they thus ran into obstruction in the House of Lords which rejected a number of their schemes which sought to end the exclusive association of certain schools with the Established Church.[50] The Commissioners drew fire from angry rate-payers whose local elementary schools, before 1869, had been supported by endowments drawn from charities originally established to subsidize secondary education. This cross-subsidy was no longer possible under the terms of the Endowed Schools Act, and thus meant levying a higher rate to support elementary education after the 1870 Education Act was passed. This in turn had religious implications, since many Anglican elementary schools had been supported in this way. Now they would require rate support, and so come under non-Anglican influence, if not outright control.[51]

---

[46] Gosden, *Development of Educational Administration*, 63–4.

[47] 'General Statement of Principles', Report of the Endowed Schools Commission, *PP* (1872), xxiv, appendix 2, 45.

[48] W. L. Burn, *The Age of Equipoise: A Study of the Mid-Victorian Generation* (1964: New York, 1965 edn.), 201.   [49] Fletcher, *Feminists and Bureaucrats*, 121–4.

[50] F. E. Balls, 'The Endowed Schools Act 1869 and the Development of the English Grammar School in the Nineteenth Century, Pt. 2. The Operation of the Act', *Durham Research Review*, 5/20 (Apr. 1968), 219–20. The problem lay with s. 19 of the Endowed Schools Act. Under this, for a school to obtain exemption from those sections of the Act designed to end religious exclusivity, its founder or founders had to have expressly laid down its denomination, and the school had to have educated children in this given faith without interruption. Given that founders often did not specify the denomination of religious worship and education, and that few schools could prove uninterrupted practice of the specified religious form, many customary Anglican foundations fell foul of the legislation.   [51] Ibid., 222–3.

There were problems also whenever a scheme involved lowering the status of an endowed school. Parents who aspired to an education that might fit boys for the professions could not accept the deliberate downgrading of a local school and the dilution of its curriculum to a level below that required for university entrance.[52] In addition, the remodelling of ancient endowments in accordance with the ideas of the Taunton Commission deprived some children of a free education, and those affected were not necessarily from poor families. Rather, they tended to be the sons of the lower middle class, whose parents could not afford fees at the new grammar schools, and who did not want to send their children to the local elementary schools and lose social status. In effect, the Endowed Schools Act accentuated the trend towards fee-based secondary education which had accelerated markedly in the course of the nineteenth century. It thus contributed to the further exclusion of the children of the petit-bourgeoisie from secondary schooling.[53] It was easy, and not inaccurate, to present this as taking away the historic entitlements of the poor and middling sorts, and applying them to the greater benefit and comfort of the rich. Noting that the wealthy could rely on the public schools and the poor on grant-aided elementary schools, Lyttelton admitted in debate in the Lords in 1871 'that it would be the effect of the work of the Commission to give the lion's share and the chief advantage of the endowments under their control, taken as a whole, to the middle class'.[54] His characteristic candour made him an easy target for the many different interests who came to oppose his actions as chairman of the Commission.

The crisis over the legislation and the actions of the Commission broke out in 1871 when the Commissioners turned their attentions to the Emanuel Hospital Foundation in Westminster. This had been established by Lady Anne Dacre at the end of the sixteenth century for the education of boys of the borough, and also for the maintenance of twenty aged men. In the early seventeenth century, the Mayor and Aldermen of the City of London had been appointed the trustees of the charity. By the mid-nineteenth century the foundation had an income of over £2,000 per annum and was educating several dozen boys—64 in 1871—on these funds.[55] There was no hint of misappropriation: according to *The City Press*, which loudly supported the Corporation through the controversy, 'There is no allegation of the perversion of the endowment from its legitimate uses, none of malversation, none even of weakness or corruption.'[56] However, the Endowed Schools Commission believed, not unnaturally, that it could do very much more with the money and put forward a scheme to combine the Emanuel Hospital with

---

[52] Ibid., 220. The issue turned on the teaching of Greek, which was required for entrance to Oxford and Cambridge. The Taunton Commission had decided that lower grade schools should not offer Greek. If a school was regraded and fell out of the first tier, local parents had therefore to find the fees to send their sons to distant first grade or public schools.

[53] Michael Sanderson, *Education, Economic Change and Society in England 1780–1870* (London, 1983), 34.   [54] *Hansard*, CCV (24 Mar. 1871), 1567.

[55] *The Times* (1 Apr. 1871), 12; (17 Apr. 1871), 4.   [56] *The City Press* (29 Apr. 1871), 4.

three other foundations, and out of them make three new boys' schools, two for day pupils and one for boarders, none of which was to provide free education, to educate fully 900 children. The scheme would also have removed the Court of Aldermen of the city of London as the governing body.[57] Given the existing apprehensions of city men in regard to the Liberal administration's plans for the reform of the governance of the capital, and the wounded *amour propre* of men of property now accused of mishandling funds, the issue was an explosive one and the adversary powerful. As W. E. Forster ruefully observed three years later, 'The difficulties of the Commission had arisen in a great measure from the fact that it had ventured to attack the City of London.'[58] Nor were city men without popular backing: they could count on the support of groups like the London Tradesmen's Club, of Fleet Street, whose members had rather more direct reasons for opposing the arrogation of funds originally given 'for the education of the poorer classes of the community'.[59]

If we consider the arguments raised at the 'great public meeting' in the Mansion House on 21 April 1871, convened by the Lord Mayor to protest against the Commission's scheme, and according to *The Times* 'imposing in point of numbers and influence', and listen also to the case made by Salisbury in the Lords at this time, we can hear the authentic voice of propertied men taking fright. The Mansion House meeting was consciously organized as a focus for 'the trustees of every charity in the kingdom likely to be affected by the principle on which the Commissioners appear to proceed'.[60] The crucial issue at the meeting was opposition to the principle, enunciated by the Commission, 'that there shall be no gratuitous education except as the reward of merit'—that the meritorious should take precedence over the needy and the *deserving* in another sense. Propertied men who liked to salve their consciences by dispensing charity opposed the use of the funds they had hitherto controlled for the benefit of the poor to reward merito-cratic ability. It smacked too much of high liberal doctrine for R. W. Crawford, one of the twenty MPs present, though he was a Liberal himself, a Director of the Bank of England, and MP for the City of London: he told the meeting that 'he did not like the application of philosophical principles to the common concerns of life'. The meeting opposed centralization: according to the Lord Mayor, 'the people declined to be governed by a central Board and . . . they had the same ability and desire as in former times to manage their own affairs'. The issue was taken as another example of over-zealous, interfering government by the Liberals—the 'incessant and harassing legislation' of which Disraeli complained and which filled Conservative election addresses in 1874.[61] Those present supported loudly the principle of fidelity to founders' intentions—'the peculiar

---

[57] Owen, *English Philanthropy 1660–1960*, 257–9.
[58] *Hansard*, CCXX (14 July 1874), 1654.
[59] 'The Threatened Extinction of Emanuel Hospital', *The City Press* (29 Apr. 1871), 5.
[60] *The Times* (17 Apr. 1871), 4.   [61] Parry, *Democracy and Religion*, 389.

sanctity with which bequests for pious uses and for the benefit of the poor had ever been regarded'. Upholding these intentions was a responsibility owed by the living to the dead. Moreover, without that fidelity, the very sources of charity would dry up: as Lord George Hamilton, Conservative MP for Middlesex, put it, 'people of means in future would hesitate before they bequeathed funds for charitable uses'. The matter was also presented in terms which clearly anticipate a fundamental spiritual cleavage of modern British politics, separating left from right. According to J. G. Talbot, Conservative MP for West Kent, the 'theory' that guided the Endowed Schools Commissioners 'was that they had to collect together and cut and carve existing institutions as they pleased; but he held that institutions around which the feelings of the country had grown up could not be dealt with as if the object was to obtain a site for a railway station'.[62]

At the same time Salisbury took up the Emanuel Hospital affair in the Lords. In speeches in April and June he, too, complained that the Commission acted independently of any parliamentary scrutiny or responsibility. He speculated that entry based on merit would hand over a school founded for the poor to the offspring of 'the higher middle classes'. He complained that members of both Houses had thought that in 1869 they were acceding to a measure designed to redeploy the funds of badly managed or obviously outmoded endowments. But in reality the measure was being used to remodel charities that were being managed responsibly. He worried also about the effects of such interference on the act of giving itself. If donors could not be certain that their gifts 'will not be devoted to some philosophical crotchet of the day there will be no more bequests or endowments'. And Salisbury vindicated local self-government in contradistinction to 'the practice of other countries. It has been our practice to trust to local enthusiasm and local zeal. We have not collected up all the strings into a single knot to be placed in the hands of central Commissioners.'[63]

For many of those caught up in opposition to the Endowed Schools Act, the crucial issues concerned the threat to the Anglican character of certain schools rather than to property rights and to local as opposed to centralized administration. The lower house of Convocation passed a motion in May of 1873, for example, which almost literally told the Endowed Schools Commission to take its hands off endowments left to the Church 'for the Christian education of her children'.[64] It is evident that those clauses in the Conservatives' original amending bill in the summer of 1874 which were designed to redress changes to specifically Anglican foundations made by the Endowed Schools Commissioners, and to try to ensure that they could never be attacked again by establishing the presumption

---

[62] 'The Corporation of London and the Endowed Schools Commissioners', *The Times* (22 Apr. 1871), 11.

[63] *Hansard*, CCV (24 Apr. 1871), 1549–58; CCVII (30 June 1871), 862–9. For a summary of the Conservative case against the Commission, see [George C. Hodgkinson], 'Education, Endowments, and Competition: Strictures on the Proceedings of the Endowed Schools Commission', *Blackwoods Magazine*, 110 (July 1871), 81–99.   [64] *The Times* (9 May 1873), 8.

that endowed schools were all Anglican foundations, created a furious denominational argument which dominated the second reading debates. In A. J. Mundella's words, the new bill 'converted the school of the community into the dead school of the sect'.[65] It was, *inter alia*, a party-political miscalculation by the Tories to make the bill needlessly controversial and thus assist the reunification of the battered and demoralized Liberal Party in a defence of religious freedom. But those clauses—numbers 4 to 7—were withdrawn during the course of debate and scrutiny, and the religious controversy died down.[66] The amending Act, as finally passed, was in essence an administrative change that transferred the Endowed Schools Commission's functions to the Charity Commission, a body much less assiduous and confrontational, and certainly more cautious, in the slow progress it made in the coming years to regroup endowments to create new secondary schools.

The anxieties caused by the withdrawn clauses of the 1874 Tory bill have further encouraged historians to believe that opposition to the Endowed Schools Act and the work of the Commission was essentially religious (Anglican) in inspiration. While this is part of the story, no doubt, it should not be allowed to obscure the fundamentally secular issues also thrown up by the reform of endowments in mid-Victorian Britain. Indeed, there is plenty of testimony that religion was but an ancillary question. In the debates on the amending bill Gladstone himself made a clear distinction between the secular and ecclesiastical duties of the Commission and contended that their unpopularity 'did not grow out of the manner in which they adjusted differences between Churchmen and Nonconformists, but from the practical reforms they endeavoured to carry into effect—their efforts to put down monopoly, to bring in the elective principle, to displace old and imperfect systems'.[67] In the same debate he was joined by the radical Torrens, a long-term opponent of 'the communistic vagaries of the Endowed Schools Commission', who deprecated 'the substitution of sectarian for social, and polemical for political considerations' and noted that in their opposition to the reform of local educational endowments, his constituents in Finsbury, Anglican and nonconformist alike, had united: 'Men who agree in little else— clergymen and dissenting ministers, employers and employed, Liberals and Conservatives—concur in a feeling of detestation of the policy of the Commission.'[68] And *The Economist* criticized those who had tried to use the 1874 amending bill to settle old denominational scores and 'return to an exclusive Church policy'. The Endowed Schools Commission's mistakes 'such as they were, have not borne upon that question at all. They have borne on the administrative question as to who are the best persons to remodel the old endowments, and on that alone'.[69]

[65] *Hansard*, CCXXI (20 July 1874), 360. [66] *Hansard*, CCXXI (24 July 1874), 645–6.
[67] *Hansard*, CCXXI (22 July 1874), 562–3.
[68] *Hansard*, CCXXI (22 July 1874), 522, 528–9. See also William Torrens, 'Localism and Centralism', *Contemporary Review* (June 1871), 399–413. [69] *The Economist* (25 July 1874), 901.

III

Because historians have concentrated on the religious difficulty, it has been easy to overlook the significance of the Endowed Schools Act of 1869 and its subsequent history. If presented as another educational schism between the establishment and its opponents the whole affair looks very similar to that played out on an even larger scale over elementary education at the same time. Thus the reform of endowed schools has been subsumed into a political narrative which does not fully explain the issues in dispute over secondary education in the early 1870s, nor highlight the implications of that dispute for the political parties and their subsequent electoral fortunes. In actuality, the religious question was only one among several problems that bedevilled the reform of educational endowments. The others were essentially secular issues about property, including its ownership, control, and use; and about the way nation was to be governed—whether (as many saw it) by unelected, central boards, staffed by supposed experts and answerable to themselves only, or by the good will and civic pride of local worthies gathered into properly constituted local bodies. As *The Times* diagnosed the Liberals' problem, 'The late Government were not fortunate in selecting their agents. They seemed to prefer scholars, lawyers and jurists to men of the world and of business, and there were more important matters than this Endowed Schools question which were mismanaged in consequence'.[70] Indeed, one of the many consequences was that 'men of the world' began to drift to the Tories in the 1870s. And beyond these questions were issues transcending the particulars of the reform of endowed schools entirely: whether ancient institutions were to be preserved and venerated, or whether they should be subject to a continual process of reform to keep them in step with current social thought and new public requirements; whether society should place the needs of the present and future above fidelity to the past.

'Men of the world' opposed the Endowed Schools Commission on eminently practical grounds concerning its disruption of educational and social arrangements that had hitherto functioned effectively. There was little need to develop more philosphical arguments when a local school was threatened or a board of trustees dissolved. But at the heart of these disputes were fundamental differences over the very nature of social arrangements and social institutions, and between conservative and liberal temperaments, that transcended their immediate context. These differences occasionally emerged in exchanges between the contending parties, as at a meeting of the Social Science Association in London in July 1869. Here Arthur Hobhouse laid out the reformers' case in a paper 'On the limitations which should be placed on dispositions of property to public uses' which would have denied the right of testators to control their property and its use beyond the grave

---

[70] *The Times* (23 July 1874), 9.

and deliberately broke the link between past and present.[71] He was answered in discussion by the Revd Dr William Irons, prebendary of St Paul's Cathedral, vicar of Brompton, and the author in 1869 of the *Analysis of Human Responsibility*, who set forth an alternative social philosophy:

If they were to cut themselves off, and say they had nothing to do with the past, and nothing to do with posterity, they would only intensify the selfishness of the present generation, and threaten the progress of all civilisation. It should never be forgotten that they owed all they had to their forefathers, and were morally bound to transmit all the advantages they could to those who came after them.[72]

'Men of the world' rarely expressed themselves in these terms. Yet many of them, in their defence of 'founders' intentions' and traditional local arrangements, were led by an unacknowledged impulse to conserve existing social institutions which seemed to be threatened by a new and dangerous form of radical Liberalism. And many of them voted Conservative in 1874, therefore. As the *Saturday Review* speculated at the time, 'If the secrets of the ballot-box were revealed, it would probably be found that an unprecedented number of the most intelligent and conscientious Liberals have either recorded their votes for Conservatives, or abstained from the polls.'[73]

When we think about the accelerating haemorrhage of Liberal men of property out of the party in the late nineteenth century—a crucial aspect of our modern politics, for it ultimately sank the Liberals, helped form the modern Conservative Party, and established that national politics from the 1880s until the 1980s would be class politics—we might think also of the humble role played by the Endowed Schools Act in dramatizing the radical shift in Liberalism after 1868 and the reaction to that shift among the middle classes which contemporaries believed to have had a significant effect on the outcome of the 1874 general election. We might also think of the shift from political history to the history of political culture which forms the theme of this volume. For the Endowed Schools Act and the philosophical questions it threw up have lacked a place until now in the more limited definition of 'the political' which many historians recognize and with which they work. A technical question about educational administration—and an educational question of the second order, coming well below elementary education in supposed historical importance—did not seem to matter much to the history of politics, and could be safely left in the hands of educational and administrative historians. But expand the scope, draw in other literatures, above

[71] Arthur Hobhouse, 'On the Limitations which Should be Placed on Dispositions of Property to Public Uses', *Sessional Proceedings of the National Association for the Promotion of Social Science* (1868–9), 583–608. For the subsequent discussions, in which the speakers included Lords Lyttelton and Stanley, Joshua Fitch, and Edwin Chadwick, ibid., 608–46.
[72] Ibid., 631. *Oxford Dictionary of National Biography*, 29, 355. William Josiah Irons (1812–83) was a notable writer on theology and Bampton Lecturer in Oxford in 1870. See W. Irons, *Analysis of Human Responsibility* (London, 1869).
[73] 'Moderate Liberals and the Government', *Saturday Review* (7 Feb. 1874), 167.

all, put yourself in the shoes of a local gentleman, parson, or solicitor whose conduct and place as a trustee of a grammar school foundation was suddenly under threat from a Liberal Board, including a garrulous radical like Hobhouse, that had existed for a matter of months only—in short, take a wider view of the political culture of the 1870s—and the matters at issue become fundamental. In this wider view, it is not hard to understand why a local worthy whose public conduct was scrutinized in this manner, or who was dispossessed of a historic responsibility, freely borne and unremunerated, might never vote Liberal again.

9

Liberal Passions: Reason and Emotion in Late- and Post-Victorian Liberal Thought

Michael Freeden

For most of those schooled in recent political thinking, liberalism is regarded as the epitome of a rational political theory. It is based on notions of human autonomy, reflective self-direction, considered judgement, and purposiveness. It has employed formal and carefully controlled models of human relationships embodied in the device of the contract, both among individuals and between individuals and society, a contract to which the participants are conscious and willing signatories. It has furthermore entertained a range of pleasure-, happiness-, or welfare-maximizing formulae represented by various calculating utilitarian strands to which it has been indebted. Lately, it has endorsed a range of models exploring free, equal, and transparent communication as applied to deliberative democracy, from which a shared or common good may emerge. In addition, it has subscribed to a set of social ends in which harmony is predominant; it has attempted to contain the vulgarities of whim and outlaw the sins of violence; and it has carefully constructed a framework of human conduct in which reasonable constraint on excessive behaviour is paramount.

Much of this is uncontentious. But were this to be the entire story, it could hardly explain the political and ideological successes of British liberalism over the past century and a half, nor do justice to the self-understandings of liberals. On the surface that success is far from obvious. While rival political movements, such as conservatism or socialism, could appeal to the rousing symbols of nation, patriotism, and a landlocked heritage, or to those of class, community, and the assured promise of a future paradise on earth, liberals could hardly have hoped to make similar political gains through the diffusion of Yellow Books or even—as was already clear at the time—through the extension of the franchise. Successful ideologies require powerful emotional symbols or, at the very least, a language that invokes strong sentiment, even passion. Without those ingredients, the mass mobilization of support that necessarily must accompany modern politics, and the implementation of ideas and programmes, is virtually impossible. Volatile as the reliance on emotion is, it is also an effective short cut to securing recruitment to political causes. But that on its own would be too cynical a view. The ability and the need to express emotion are defining features of the human condition, the pleasure taken in group bonding is a core facet of individual identity, and a politics devoid of emotion would be a desiccated politics indeed.

A closer look at liberalism suggests that, like many of its non-liberal and illib-eral counterparts, it too is engaged in purveying emotion. Liberalism is no excep-tion to the rule that ideologies dress up their arguments in emotional garb, not always intentionally, and that they are genuinely passionate about their core beliefs and principles. Moreover, contrary to the conventional understandings of liberalism, it too consciously recognizes that emotions need to be factored into political discourse. As the editor of the liberal *Nation*, H. W. Massingham, observed in 1909: 'Socialism has great power of emotional and even religious appeal, of which it would be wise of Liberalism to take account.'[1] True, liberalism has had to compete with masters of emotional manipulation throughout the twentieth century from a position of weakness. In particular, its institutional forms have not succeeded in exciting the effervescent enthusiasm of large groups—indeed, they have rarely attempted to do so. But the question at hand here is not the mere presence of emotion and passion in liberal debate, or its effi-ciency. It is, rather, the role emotion adopts and the weight it accrues in relation to other aspects of liberal discourse.

If we attempt to excavate from liberal argument the vein of sentiment that most of its manifestations have produced, the following may be noted. Far from depict-ing liberalism as a set of logical deductions from universal ethical principles—pro-ducing the kind of rationally and ethically unchallengeable super-theory that late twentieth-century philosophers have made it out to be—liberals have almost without exception understood their position to constitute a particular creed, a set of beliefs; and this has to be fought for in a political and ideological struggle, the outcome of which is not necessarily guaranteed. At one level this is only to say that liberals have been keenly conscious of the real-world dimension of their views and the practices associated with them. But at another level they have regarded their beliefs as dependent on persuasion, not demonstration—hence persuasive, even rhetorical, tools became a crucial feature of the intellectual equipment they relied on. In Colin Matthew's pioneering piece on the role of rhetoric in Liberal public discourse, he remarked on the 'craving' liberals felt for public discussion and argument.[2] Later he would observe of Gladstone's Midlothian Campaign, that 'a sharp awareness not merely of the ideological importance of rhetoric, but also of the mechanics of its presentation in the context of nineteenth century

---

[1] H. W. Massingham, 'Introduction', to W. S. Churchill, *Liberalism and the Social Problem* (London, 1909), pp. xvii–xviii.

[2] H. C. G. Matthew, 'Rhetoric and Politics in Great Britain, 1860–1950', in P. J. Waller (ed.), *Politics and Social Change in Modern Britain: Essays Presented to A. F. Thompson* (Brighton, 1987), 51.

technology ... characterized Gladstone's approach to public speaking'.[3] Efficient persuasion, with its aura of commitment, sways the emotions quite as much as the rational faculties, and so did Gladstone's visceral yet calculated dressing up of his oratory in a manner that was 'both charismatic and rational'.[4]

I shall examine these contentions with regard to a specific period in British history—the late nineteenth and early twentieth centuries—in which reflection on the nature of liberalism was particularly prevalent, though prior reference to John Stuart Mill must also be included in such an investigation, if only because of his towering position among British liberals in the generation after his death.

I

When liberalism was characterized as a creed, as it frequently was, this meant no single thing. A creed could be equated first of all with a theory embracing broad principles: this was the equation made by the liberal politician and thinker R. B. Haldane, writing in 1888. On the other hand, the work of liberals could also 'arouse the greatest enthusiasm', and bearers of a creed needed to disseminate it. The 'Nottingham Conferences and abstract resolutions' of the Liberal Party, he asserted, taken by themselves, were 'empty forms, entitled to and commanding no influence and respect. They are only of value in so far as they express pent-up opinions.' This revealing image of blocked and frustrated attitudes calling out for release was further underscored by Haldane's observation that public opinion 'is stimulated and shaped out of a mass of sentiment, which requires moulding by men occupying commanding positions in the public imagination and confidence'.[5] Note these final terms, which state that liberal political argument had to address the imagination, rather than the rational faculties pure and simple, and that its success was predicated on the psychological establishment of trust and authority, more than on the content of the arguments.

Nevertheless, the view of liberalism put forward by members of the liberal intelligentsia was typified above all by its immediate relation to political action. To that end a creed could be presented in more religious terms, which suggested the need for what the social reformer G. F. Millin saw as a combination of principle, policy, and 'the ability to inspire ... with that faith ... which comes of honest conviction and earnest purpose'.[6] As Herbert Samuel put it in his early work on *Liberalism* in 1902: 'the principles that permeate a true liberalism are nothing else than the application to public affairs of the religious spirit itself'.[7] The power and inspiration of liberalism as a faith was a dominant metaphor. Much liberal

[3] H. C. G. Matthew, *Gladstone 1875–1898* (Oxford, 1995), 48.   [4] Ibid., 60.
[5] R. B. Haldane, 'The Liberal Creed', *Contemporary Review*, 54 (1888), 462–4, 472–4.
[6] G. F. Millin, 'The New Liberalism', *Fortnightly Review*, 69 (1901), 636.
[7] H. Samuel, *Liberalism* (London, 1902), 387.

language was steeped in this type of rhetoric, none more so than that of the liberal writer and politician C. F. G. Masterman, who referred to the liberal faith as enlarging 'the common sympathies of humanity'; as 'promoting understanding and friendship', and bringing 'reason and compassion'—a crucial mixture—into the 'common life of man'. The liberal faith was nurtured by 'exultations; and agonies; and love; and man's unconquerable mind'.[8] Purple prose though this was, it simply restated the more generally felt emotional commitment and devotion of liberals towards their beliefs. Yet such sentiments did not entail an abandonment of rational tests, of self-criticism and self-assessment; indeed, those methods and intellectual technologies became a part of the core belief system itself. All this recalls Max Weber's notion of value-rationality, according to which social action is 'determined by a conscious belief in the value for its own sake of some ethical, aesthetic, religious, or other form of behaviour'. Weber emphasized the uncondi-tionality of the demands made by a belief system.[9] Put differently, no trade-offs could occur between its core concepts and other, alternative values: the core beliefs of liberalism were, like those of all of the major ideologies, non-negotiable. Its impetus and enthusiasm would arise from 'certainty of conviction'.[10]

A third way of portraying liberalism was to deny its status as a creed, and to refer rather to a habit of mind or spirit, for which hindrances to human growth were 'perpetually obnoxious'.[11] This invoked a psychological disposition rather than the cognitive embrace of an ideological stance. As the liberal free-thinker, writer, and politician J. M. Robertson contended, 'Liberalism is not so much a creed or body of doctrine as a state of mind, an attitude towards men and towards civic life, which in a manner predetermines one's political judgments'—as indeed was conservatism. Was one born liberal, then? No, decided Robertson, gesturing towards the then widespread nature versus nurture debate: minds were 'in large measure formed by training and usage', through 'social and general education, and only partly... [reflected] an innate temperament'. However, 'whether innate or instilled, a temper or frame of mind is established which makes a man broadly prone to either Conservative or to Liberal views and courses'.[12] This social psychology reinforced the specific, even partisan, nature attributed to liberalism by its advocates, as distinct from the common fashion of today that identifies its universal roots in abstract reason and unassailable notions of the good.

A slightly different way of distinguishing between the conservative and the lib-eral temperament was to assert that, whereas conservatives had instincts, liberals had cool heads,[13] or that they were motivated by a moral impulse that was itself quasi-religious. If the Liberal Party appeared to be on the wane as the twentieth

---

[8] C. F. G. Masterman, *The New Liberalism* (London, 1920), 34.
[9] M. Weber, *Economy and Society* (Berkeley, Calif., 1968), 24–5.
[10] Editorial, 'Party and Principles', *Monthly Review*, 1 (1900), 32.
[11] W. Lyon Blease, *A Short History of English Liberalism* (London, 1913), 7.
[12] J. M. Robertson, *The Meaning of Liberalism* (London, 1912), 5–6.
[13] Haldane, 'Liberal Creed', 464, 472.

century dawned, it was because 'the Liberal party, if the forces comprised in it are to be directed to a single and practical end, requires as leader a man who possesses sufficient spiritual and emotional sympathy to awaken a response in all his followers'. The problem of liberalism, as seen by the editor of the *Monthly Review*, was that the principle of political equality advanced by liberals had lost much of its impetus because 'the thrilling and personal interest is gone out of such questions' and the constitutional reforms did not have 'so magical a power as was hoped'.[14]

These general characterizations supply three diverse approaches to the dissemination of liberal thinking. The first is action through persuasion which, as in J. S. Mill's case, appeals directly to the intellect, but is significantly supported by harnessing the emotional and imaginative dimensions of such discourse. The second is action through proselytizing, which regards its messages as the adoption of a fundamental and embracing *Weltanschauung* that would be spread through a kind of conversion. The third is action through confrontation, which assumes entrenched positions that cannot easily be changed and involves the political vanquishing of opponents. All three often appeared in conjunction—in the same texts or formulated by the same individual—but they are analytically distinct. The first two conjure up a very different view of ideology from the third. They imply a universalizing model: not the instant universal logic of analytical philosophers but the contingent and creeping universalism of a spreading set of ideas that crowds out inferior alternatives, a 'crusade for freedom'[15] very much in tune with the civilizing mission that liberals prided themselves on furthering.[16] The third, however, implies the permanence of conflict, engrained in dispositions that can never be conclusively changed. Here liberal ideology is at battle stations, competing offensively and defensively with other equally powerful ideological forces. Rather than being conceived as a truth, whether philosophical or quasi-religious, it is then plausibly called a 'bias'.[17]

Now this is an interesting extension of J. S. Mill's position. Almost all ethical creeds and religious doctrines, Mill maintained, are 'full of meaning and vitality to those who originate them . . . so long as the struggle lasts to give the doctrine an ascendency over other creeds'.[18] At the point of victory, however, the dullness of acquiescence would take over from the vitality of mental activity. What is striking here is Mill's resort to this uplifting style of contrast. The argument relates to the intellect but the rhetorical tone is emotional, just as life and vitality were prevailing terms of discourse in liberal debate in the period under consideration. In the same way T. H. Green referred to the constancy of progressive, yet combative, human emotions: 'The passion for improving mankind, in its ultimate object, does not vary . . . those who will think a little longer about it can discern the same old cause of social good against class interests, for which, under altered names,

[14] Editorial, *Monthly Review*, 1 (1900), 29–32.

[15] 'A Plea for a Programme', *Independent Review*, 1 (1903–4), 5.

[16] See M. Freeden, 'Twentieth-Century Liberal Thought: Development or Transformation?', in M. Evans (ed.), *The Edinburgh Companion to Contemporary Liberalism* (Edinburgh, 2001), 21–32.

[17] Robertson, *Meaning of Liberalism*, 17.   [18] J. S. Mill, *On Liberty* (London, 1910), 99.

liberals are fighting now as they were fifty years ago.'[19] This was a gloss on Green's commentary on Hume, when Green differentiated between the calm and the violent passions, the former—more appropriately called emotions as distinct from desires—conflicting with but often prevailing over the latter, their calmness not to be confounded with weakness.[20] Likewise, Massingham linked liberalism with 'the movement of life, which when it overtakes parties condemns and destroys them'.[21]

For a variety of reasons, then, the liberal blend of reason and emotion needs to be looked at more closely. In particular, the starkness of that conventional dichotomy needs to be softened. Mill's *On Liberty* may well be read as an avowal of the duty of a thinker 'to follow his intellect to whatever conclusions it may lead'. But at the same time, the cautionary tale of his Utilitarian father, James Mill, remained etched on the younger Mill's memory until his death. 'For passionate emotions of all sorts', so the son wrote of his father in his *Autobiography*, 'and for everything which has been said or written in exaltation of them, he professed the greatest contempt. He regarded them as a form of madness.' But, as Mill junior perceptively noted, 'his aversion to many intellectual errors, or what he regarded as such, partook, in a certain sense, of the character of a moral feeling... he... threw his feelings into his opinions; which truly it is difficult to understand how any one, who possesses much of both, can fail to do'.[22] Consequently, Mill reflected, 'the cultivation of the feelings became one of the cardinal points in my ethical and philosophical creed'.[23] Indeed, the younger Mill's language was often emotive, and he was far from blind to the need to 'kindle enthusiasm' for a discussion of important public issues, so as to stir up the mind of a people and to offer the 'impulse... which raised even persons of the most ordinary intellect to something of the dignity of thinking beings'.[24] Ideas could not travel on their own unless the ground for their emotional reception had been prepared. The role of character was crucial here, boldness and conviction being the vehicles without which original thought could not be spread.[25]

However, while many passages in *On Liberty* are an exhortation to the restraint of passions, Mill's *Utilitarianism* occasionally strikes a different note. In discussing the motives supporting morality, Mill wrote: 'Good for good is also one of the dictates of justice; and this, though its social utility is evident, and though it carries with it a natural human feeling... is the source of the characteristic intensity of the sentiment.' A principle, especially, could be a 'proper object' of such intensity of sentiment, attracting as it did a stronger sentiment than the 'milder feeling which attaches itself to the mere idea of promoting human pleasure or convenience'.[26] Yet even in *On Liberty*, many commentators ignore a remarkable passage nesting in one of the essay's most famous paragraphs. Arguing against the

[19] T. H. Green, *Works* (London, 1908), iii. 367.   [20] Green, *Works*, i. 349.

[21] Massingham, 'Introduction', p. xxii.   [22] J. S. Mill, *Autobiography* (Oxford, 1969), 31–2.

[23] Ibid., 86.   [24] Mill, *On Liberty*, 94–5.   [25] Ibid., 94, 96–7.

[26] Mill, *Utilitarianism* (London, 1910), 56, 57.

use of compulsion as a means to impose paternalist, utilitarian, and conventional views of the good life on that area of individual conduct that concerns the individual alone, Mill let slip the following observation: 'These are good reasons for remonstrating with him, or reasoning with him, or persuading him, or entreating him, but not for compelling him . . .'.[27] In this medley of intellectual and emotional appeals, what stands out is the use of terms such as remonstration, a protest with clear emotional resonance, and entreaty, an exhortation with a passionate edge. These too, though Mill does not formally recognize it, are effective forms of power, and they endorse a reading of Mill in which the emotional strength of partisan beliefs may legitimately be expressed and used in a liberal society in order to influence and change human conduct.

II

In the generation after Mill the commentaries of J. M. Robertson deserve closer scrutiny, and may serve as a test case in locating the more passionate aspects of liberalism. As he was a radical freethinker and secularist one would expect—and one finds—a strong defence of liberal rationality in his social and political writings. But in *The Meaning of Liberalism* (1912) Robertson employed an interesting turn of phrase—intellectual sympathy—by which he meant 'depending on a certain concurrence of power of imagination with concern for logic and consistency'.[28] This was in line with the nineteenth-century acknowledgement of the role of sympathy in the approving of, and identifying with, others, and their converse—feelings that Bentham, for example, regarded as establishing the standard of right and wrong.[29] But it differed in its specific reference to the human imagination as the gateway to a form of altruism, while insisting that such a capacity be tempered by means of the rational faculties. To that extent Robertson, rationalist that he was, demanded the substitution of 'an intellectual for a passional impulse and attitude'. Zeal in the liberal cause was permitted; passion that could lead to prejudice and malice was not. Sympathy was a matter of temperament among the young, but in the longer run it required a more detached intellectual reformulation.[30] In a weak reflection of new psychological fashions, Robertson held that the intellect could build on, and evolve from, the impulses—a theme that is given far fuller treatment by L. T. Hobhouse. In fact, the liberal emotions could exhibit a transition from benevolence to pugnacity: 'The Liberal movement or impulse starts in a simple desire for "better life" for those who lack it; and only when the movement is resisted by the classes who already have the best of things, does a class feeling against them tend to fix itself.'[31]

---

[27] Mill, *On Liberty*, 73.
[28] Robertson, *Meaning of Liberalism*, 19.
[29] J. Bentham, *An Introduction to the Principles of Morals and Legislation* (Oxford, 1960), 137–40.
[30] Robertson, *Meaning of Liberalism*, 25, 28–9.   [31] Ibid., 27.

In an earlier work, *Letters on Reasoning*, written for the instruction of his children, Robertson was far more explicit and revealing. 'There can be no great "movement" of an intellectual kind without its emotional side', he wrote; '. . . *every* judgment, every process of reasoning, has its quantum of emotion . . . one's first sense of the justice and the irrefragability of a great philosophic or scientific doctrine is a marked emotion.'[32] The elation consequent upon the excitement of discovery or insight was also linked to the longer term reasonable advocacy of arguments and beliefs. After all, 'a logical mind may easily be more emotional and imaginative than an illogical. The love of truth and rectitude *is* an emotion; the recognition of a good argument is a solidly pleasurable feeling; and it is an observable fact that the habit of self-criticism, to the end of attaining consistency, can expand imagination by widening sympathy.'[33] Thus the process of critical reassessment at the heart of liberalism straddled reason and emotion. At the same time Robertson was quick to remind his young readers that the wrong argument and beliefs (frequently identified by him as conservative) possessed their emotions just as the the right ones did, and that emotion could also blind people to truth.

Clearly, then, the persistence of sentiment was carefully held in check by liberals. In an early piece, J. A. Simon, the future liberal leader, warned against excesses of liberal feelings for too zealous change:

The emotional Liberal, remembering the glorious traditions of his party, and carried away by a sympathy which is as indispensable for the noble inspiration of a policy as it is inadequate for the prudent determination of its content, is ready to recognise the features of the old Liberalism in every misshapen offspring fathered upon it by the new . . . But a party of progress is betrayed no less by the stolidity of the Smug than by the flightiness of the Sentimentalist.[34]

But his colleague J. S. Phillimore, writing in the same volume, had his ear close to the ground when commenting on the success of Gladstone's Midlothian speeches, frequently referred to by liberals as a triumph of impassioned rhetoric combined with moral earnestness: 'The whole body of citizens is capable at least of the passions of friendship, hatred, sympathy, jealousy; and shares in the sensations of pride and humility, collective strength and common weakness.' These were natural feelings to which the speeches had catered and had to be distinguished from the jingoism that distorted them. The Jingo was 'a ludicrous representative of instincts, sentiments, aspirations in themselves essentially sound, natural and wholesome'. A recognition of the kind of liberal nationalism that had motivated Mazzini is also evident here: 'A nation is sick or decaying in which the pride and satisfaction in its own strength and resources are dormant or extinct.'[35] That important liberal message could of course be projected on to the imperial enterprise. The point, however, is that here it was directed inwards.

[32] J. M. Robertson, *Letters on Reasoning* (London, 1935: abbreviation of 2nd edn, 1905), 86–7.
[33] Ibid., 10.   [34] J. A. Simon, in *Essays in Liberalism by Six Oxford Men* (London, 1897), 102.
[35] J. S. Phillimore, *Essays in Liberalism*, 140–4.

Three distinct features in the congruence of liberalism and emotion become patently clear. First, liberals were emotionally attached to their own ideas and ideology. Second, liberals as well as non-liberals recognized the central function of emotion in political discourse and in attaining political ends. And third, liberals started to be at ease with new understandings of the emotional nature of political conduct, because they began to subscribe to subtler, more holistic, conceptions of human nature, in which emotion was not a private, slightly embarrassing if not outright effeminate, characteristic to be kept out of the public arena but a valuable constituent human attribute. The culturally eventful transition from Victorian to Edwardian England saw a series of changes in approaches to emotion in politics. A passionate commitment to principle and the approval of sociable sentiments were joined by a greater awareness of the pervasiveness of unruly fervour in group conduct, and by a keener scientific—or, more specifically, psychological—recognition of the ineliminable, even desirable, role of emotion and its expression in individual behaviour. The impact of continental studies of the herd instinct was considerable among liberals, particularly in their anxious confrontation with the 'psychology of jingoism' during the Boer War. The perversion of group mentality when subjected to powerful populist and hysterical appeals had the holistic vitality of the group as its counterpart, a holism subscribed to by the new liberals. While the passions produced by the herd were pathological, the emotions of groups displaying solidarity were healthy and constructive. Thus, the impact of the French social psychologist Gustave Le Bon led to a focus on the irrationality of the group instincts that were salient in particular during periods of warfare, but also—and in the long run more significantly—to the highlighting of the production of group thoughts and emotions in general. As J. A. Hobson, initially one of Le Bon's disciples, wrote, 'Do we not know that the contagion of emotion will give a moral life, a character, even to a casual throng of citizens, inspiring beliefs and impelling actions which do not reflect the mere activity of the separate minds?'[36] These tendencies reinforced the liberal discovery of group dynamics that identified a necessary mixture of rational and emotive ties, sustaining social groups and giving them a sense of purpose, while warning against the perils of vicious irrationalism. This inward channelling of beneficent emotion had already been assumed by Mill, when he wrote: 'Education, habit, and the cultivation of the sentiments will make a common man dig or weave for his country, as readily as fight for his country.'[37] The organic view of society, too, found room for human feeling, as Samuel implied in an early talk to the Rainbow Circle: the root idea of the new liberalism 'must be the unity of society—complex in its economic, cooperative, ethical and emotional bonds'.[38] However, these ties of community were to be

---

[36] J. A. Hobson, 'Rich Man's Anarchism', *The Humanitarian*, 12 (1898), 391–3. See also M. Freeden, 'Hobson's Evolving Conceptions of Human Nature', in M. Freeden (ed.), *Reassessing J. A. Hobson: Humanitarianism and Welfare* (London, 1990), 54–73.   [37] Mill, *Autobiography*, 138.
[38] H. Samuel, 'The New Liberalism', in M. Freeden (ed.), *Minutes of the Rainbow Circle 1894–1924* (London, 1989), 28.

distinguished from the inherited and accumulative cultural frameworks that conservatives took for granted. They assumed, by contrast, a continuous participatory and reformist activity among the members of the group.

Hobson later applied these insights to the future of liberalism more directly. Writing after the Liberal Party returned to power in 1906, he argued:

While to Protectionists and Socialists politics are real, positive, and fervent gospels, stirring the imagination and evoking a fanatical energy, the zeal of Liberalism is everywhere chilled by doubts and difficulties . . . Does this mean that coldness and placidity of purpose belong essentially to Liberalism as a middle course, and is Liberalism committed to an embarrassing and disheartening opportunism? No such thing.

Hobson called for a more constructive and evolutionary idea of liberty to 'give the requisite *élan de vie* to the movement; and every cause of liberation, individual, class, sex, and national, must be recharged with the fresh enthusiasm of this fuller faith'.[39] Liberalism was construed as a warm discourse; the dynamics of evolution could lend it the momentum that would inspire a vision for crucial social groups; the metaphor of recharging was employed to depict liberalism as nurturing and exuding an organic energy; and, finally, Hobson singled out liberty, above all, as the emotional catalyst through which liberalism as a movement would be revitalized. Thus he berated the Liberal Party for lacking not only principle but passion[40] and dedicated his arguments to restoring the two components simultaneously.

In a more contemplative work, Hobson elaborated on the movement from instinct to reason—here reflecting the professional findings of his close colleague L. T. Hobhouse (of which more presently). Some progressive voices, though by no means all, had been emphatic in their resistance to reason. The socialist and Labour activist J. M. McLachlan had written in 1908 that 'Students of human nature . . . scarcely need to be reminded that men are stirred to action by their emotions, not by cognition or reason'.[41] The leading new liberals did not see it that way. Instinct and reason were not antithetical. Instead, social reason was an evolution from individual instinct, bringing 'the individual man into vital communion of thought and feeling with the thoughts and feelings of the race, of humanity'. Following the social psychologist William McDougall, Hobson maintained that the directive instincts of animal organisms 'must be accredited with some related emotion, and this emotion, regarded as an act in consciousness, must be accredited with some measure of intelligence'. Reason, in sum, was an intellectual process nourished on fundamental emotions. But given that nations were not yet in an advanced state of evolution, 'the wise statesman would keep his ear to the ground so as to learn the instinctive movements of the popular mind which would yield the best freight of political wisdom at his disposal'.[42]

[39] J. A. Hobson, *The Crisis of Liberalism* (London, 1909), 92, 93.   [40] Ibid., 135.
[41] Quoted in D. Tanner, *Political Change and the Labour Party 1900–1918* (Cambridge, 1990), 51.
[42] J. A. Hobson, *Work and Wealth: A Human Valuation* (London, 1914), 355–8.

L. T. Hobhouse's liberalism, too, lacked emotion neither in personal commitment nor in an appreciation of its concrete function in socio-political life. Indeed it is difficult to imagine a contemporary liberal philosopher today capable of ending a book on liberalism in the way that Hobhouse did in 1911, his prose reverberating with Millite zeal and elevating rhetoric. Mill had written dotingly of his wife that 'the passion of justice might have been thought to be her strongest feeling',[43] but Hobhouse waxed still more lyrical. Praising the realization of liberty through social harmony, mutual restraint, and mutual aid, he reflected: 'The advice seems cold to the fiery spirits, but they may come to learn that the vision of justice in the wholeness of her beauty kindles a passion that may not flare up into moments of dramatic scintillation, but burns with the enduring glow of the central heat.'[44] Substantively, Hobhouse combined the view of liberalism as a proselytizing force with that of liberalism as confrontational. On the one hand, he reinforced the view of liberalism as a crusade. 'The passion of men must be aroused if the frost of custom is to be broken or the chains of authority burst', he stated. On the other hand, reverting to the contingent universalism of liberalism, in ideological competition with other world views, he insisted that people 'must convert others, they must communicate sympathy and win over the unconvinced'. And he concluded: 'the philosophies that have driving force behind them are those that arise ... out of the practical demands of human feeling. The philosophies that remain ineffectual and academic are those that are formed by abstract reflection without relation to the thirsty souls of human kind.'[45] Liberal ideas, for these theorists, had to be carried by liberal institutions—in particular political parties—into the cut and thrust of politics. Passion was not an optional extra in that battle but the engine through which argument and principle would secure a public hearing.[46]

Underlying this view was a grander theoretical apparatus that regarded the concept of justice as the pivotal ethical concept—the 'response of feeling to the elements of a rational order'; hence 'the rational feeling'. Such feeling was related to sympathy, which was determined in turn by an unreflective 'pre-existing affection for the individual'. Approaching the issue from the other side of the equation to Robertson, for whom rational principles were emotions, Hobhouse insisted that feelings *were* rational, in that they reflected fundamental desires and impulses and directed them to constructive, purposive, and social ends.[47] All this was biologically underpinned: 'The sympathetic desires and feelings are in the first place the conscious renderings of the instincts tending to the maintenance of the

---

[43] Mill, *Autobiography*, 113.   [44] L. T. Hobhouse, *Liberalism* (London, 1911), 127.
[45] Ibid., 30.
[46] A few of the passages in this and the preceding two paragraphs have appeared in M. Freeden, 'Dynamics and Sentiment: The Evolution of British Liberalism', *Mélanges de l'école française de Rome: Italie et Méditerranée*, (2002), 657–71.
[47] L. T. Hobhouse, *Development and Purpose* (London, 1913), 79, 177.

species.'[48] As for the rationality of social rules, Hobhouse teased out a complexity many contemporary moralists ignore:

The one thought-factor that is indispensable is the universal judgment by which a rule is apprehended and applied. But a rule that is to be operative in action and to be sustained as a custom must awaken a response in feeling... This sentiment... arises in response to the necessities of... [the social] order, just as other feelings arise in response to the necessities of life.[49]

In sum, 'the psychological evolution then involved in the bare formation of human ethics may be conceived as the growth of a synthesis of the impulsive forces of our nature in response to the requirements of a social life'.[50] Reason also assisted in mediating among feelings, employing the principle of harmony as the guideline.[51]

Hobhouse's naïve holism reproduced an ambivalence in the liberal tradition, one that acknowledged the importance of feelings and of an expressive spontaneity, but then smoothed their edges and presented them in a snugly fitting container. That ambivalence was exacerbated by the First World War and liberal disillusionment with the dismal cultural messages it was constructed to impart. Reason was again contrasted not with emotion, but with irrationality and unreasonableness. War, after all, itself evokes passionate responses, even among liberals. Inasmuch as man remained a rational animal, Hobhouse wrote, the ideals of 'unreason and immoralism' propagated through the war were a threat to civilization. Yet the alternative promised land was itself suffused with a counter-sphere of sentiment: 'We shall find that tranquillity and repose have their part to fill in a desirable life. We shall be more ready to see the true romance that lies buried in all the prosaic detail of... social reconstruction'. The end result would be 'the conception of a common humanity, not as the dream of a philosopher, but as a popular emotion which has tested and proved itself in the hardest of schools'.[52]

In parallel with Hobhouse's developmental socio-psychology, another brand of empirical analysis was making its mark through the writings of Graham Wallas. For the purposes of this essay I have no hesitation in co-opting the Fabian and moderate socialist Wallas into the broad liberal tradition, even though in terms of ideological minutiae he occupies a slightly different place in the configuration of ideas and concepts.[53] In regard to human nature, Wallas's scholarship had none of the scientific finesse of Hobhouse, nor much of the imaginative fertility of Hobson. But what strikes the reader of his celebrated *Human Nature in Politics* is the down-to-earth character of his analysis, unencumbered with grand theory, yet no less plausible for that. Wallas had already reacted unfavourably to Moisei

[48] L. T. Hobhouse, *Mind in Evolution* (London, 1901), 364.
[49] Hobhouse, *Development and Purpose*, 178–9.   [50] Ibid., 180.   [51] Ibid., 278.
[52] L. T. Hobhouse, *The World in Conflict* (London, 1915), 73–4, 104.
[53] One scholar writes of Wallas's 'passionate attachment to Liberalism' (M. J. Wiener, *Between Two Worlds: The Political Thought of Graham Wallas* (Oxford, 1971), 49).

Ostrogorski's book, *Democracy and the Organization of Political Parties*, in a review published in 1903. It included a criticism of Ostrogorski, not for extolling reason, but for failing to understand its complexities. 'After hundreds of pages showing how ignorant and passionate men are, and how easily their opinions can be formed and exploited by any one who will take the trouble to surround them with crude illusions, he is still able to use the words "free reason", and "individual conscience", in an almost religious sense.'[54] This focus on the false worship of the intellect was at the centre of *Human Nature in Politics*, and with it the resurrection of the proper study of the emotions as crucial to comprehending the world of politics and theorizing about it. 'We are apt to assume that every human action is the result of an intellectual process, by which a man first thinks of some end which he desires, and then calculates the means by which that end can be attained.' That intellectualist fallacy was most misleading in the 'forecasting of the action of large communities'—or in other words, the political sphere itself.[55] Rather, Wallas claimed, harking back to Aristotle, affection and other impulses and emotions such as loyalty, fear, humour, the desire for property, or the fighting instinct, were common to the whole human race.[56] Using language close to our current understanding of ideology, Wallas observed: 'It is this... relation between words and things which makes the central difficulty of thought about politics. The words are so rigid, so easily personified, so associated with affection and prejudice; the things symbolised by the words are so unstable.'[57] Political concepts, he realized, were strongly decontested, their meaning held in place through emotional as much as intellectual fiat, as a counter-measure to the indeterminacy and malleability of events, practices, and ideas. And the realm of politics was also in need of broader, more evocative messages than those of words and concepts. Wallas recalled the suggestion that money collected to commemorate Gladstone should be spent on composing a marching tune, 'which should be identified for all time with the Liberal Party'.[58]

The distinctive feature of Wallas's conception of the world, in conjunction with so many progressive liberals of the period, was that thought and feeling were inextricably linked. 'Thought', he wrote, 'is a true disposition, it, like all the other dispositions, has not only its appropriate group of stimuli and its appropriate course of action, but also its appropriate emotion—an emotion which may be heightened into passion and harmonised by the sense of ordered beauty.'[59] Echoing the fashionable holism of the times, he asserted that 'the mind of man is like a harp, all of whose strings throb together; so that emotion, impulse, inference, and the special kind of inference called reasoning, are often simultaneous and intermingled aspects of a single mental experience'.[60] Like most progressives

[54] G. Wallas, 'The American Analogy', *Independent Review*, 1 (1903), 507. Quoted in Wiener, *Between Two Worlds*.
[55] G. Wallas, *Human Nature in Politics* (London, 1948 [1908]), 21, 29.　　[56] Ibid., 30–8.
[57] Ibid., 75.　　[58] Ibid., 84–5.　　[59] G. Wallas, *The Great Society* (London, 1914), 232.
[60] Wallas, *Human Nature*, 99.

he wished the emotions to be subject to 'the control of deliberate reasoning', but not through a monopoly of reason. As long as the impulses were not 'hot and disturbed', Wallas offered 'the co-ordination of reason and passion as a moral ideal'.[61] This last phrase rings truer of the liberal tradition than any attempt at a purging of the emotions in the name of a rationalist mirage.

III

To conclude, I certainly do not wish to suggest that liberalism is not a rational ideology; that it does not regard the application of introspective, carefully considered, and appraised human will and purpose as fundamental to its world view; or that it does not emanate from a strong European rationalist tradition. But I would like to suggest that liberalism has rarely been rational in the narrow, controlled, rule-bound, calculating, and abstract way that some of its adherents as well as detractors believe it to be. Rationality does not exist in a zero-sum relationship with emotion, nor is it to be found in a pure form—were such a pure form conceivable— in any ideology. Liberal reason is not necessarily incompatible with emotion, sentiment, and passion, though obviously not with all of their manifestations; and it is quite proper, as well as inevitable, for a healthy political ideology both to display and to embrace emotion as a rich and creative force in political life. Put more emphatically, no political theory or ideology—inasmuch as it aspires to have an impact on its socio-political environment it—can survive, let alone flourish, without a display of fervour and a conviction of its own virtue. The evidence provided by British liberalism in this case study—and also, I would suggest, by other Western liberalisms in this and in other periods—points decidedly in that direction.

[61] Ibid., 190–1, 194.

III

10

The Church of England and Women's Higher Education, *c*.1840–1914

Janet Howarth

Anglican resistance to the beginnings of women's education at the universities of Oxford and Cambridge has a special place in social memory. Muriel Bradbrook, Mistress of Girton at the time of its centenary, entitled her history of the college '*That Infidel Place*'—struggle with Christian prejudice against a women's college is written into Girton's founding myth.[1] At Oxford it was the opening of undergraduate examinations to women that gave rise to clerical protests.[2] Dean Burgon's sermon, delivered in New College in 1884, 'To Educate Young Women like Young Men and with Young Men—a Thing Inexpedient and Immodest', has become a classic statement of conservative gender theology. It figures in Monica Furlong's portrait gallery of church stereotypes of women based on the story of Eve.[3] Burgon himself was ridiculed in Oxford at the time as an extremist, yet church people of similar views are not hard to find among his contemporaries. 'After all,' wrote the founder of the Woodard schools, 'we all know what women are for, and to draw them from these purposes and put them into conflict with men in universities, the Forum, and the public streets can only have an un-Christian ending'.[4] For a colonial parallel to the Oxford controversy, we have Marjorie Theobald's account of the fulminations of an evangelical bishop, Charles Perry, against the admission of women to the University of Melbourne.[5]

---

[1] M. C. Bradbrook, '*That Infidel Place': A Short History of Girton College, 1869–1969* (London, 1969).

[2] J. N. Burstyn, *Victorian Education and the Ideal of Womanhood* (London, 1980), 97–110; B. Heeney, *The Women's Movement in the Church of England, 1850–1930* (Oxford, 1988), 7–9.

[3] M. Furlong, *A Dangerous Delight: Women and Power in the Church* (London, 1991), 24. On Burgon, see E. M. Goulburn, *John William Burgon, Late Dean of Chichester* (2 vols., London, 1892); J. Howarth, ' "In Oxford But...Not of Oxford": The Women's Colleges', in M. G. Brock and M. C. Curthoys (eds.), *The History of the University of Oxford*, vii, *Nineteenth-Century Oxford, part 2* (Oxford, 2000), 252–3.

[4] N. Woodard to E. C. Lowe, 9 Oct. 1884, quoted in B. Heeney, *Mission to the Middle Classes: The Woodard Schools, 1848–91* (London, 1969), 108.

[5] M. Theobald, *Knowing Women* (Cambridge, 1996), 10–12.

Yet in England (unlike Melbourne) the church—if we take that term to embrace its clergy and committed lay members of both sexes—had become a major provider of both public secondary and university education for girls and women by the turn of the last century. At Cambridge, Oxford, and London the non-denominational women's colleges—Newnham, Somerville, Bedford College—coexisted with colleges representing various shades of Anglicanism. Girton itself, a broad church and liberal foundation, provided religious instruction and services (for those who chose to attend) 'in accordance with the principles of the Church of England as by law established'.[6] Three out of four Oxford women's colleges—Lady Margaret Hall, St Hugh's, and St Hilda's—had a 'definite' and more or less High Church basis.[7] Constance Maynard's Westfield College in Hampstead was an evangelical version of Girton, providing a liberal education accompanied by religious teaching that was theologically distinctly conservative—'strictly Protestant in conformity with the principles of the Reformation and in harmony with the Doctrines of the Church of England (as now by law established), which are defined in the 39 Articles and which are to be interpreted according to the plain and natural meaning thereof'.[8] A second London Anglican foundation of the 1880s was King's College Ladies' Department (as it was first known), an offshoot in Kensington Square of the broad church King's College in the Strand.[9] They were nearly joined by a third. Though intended by its founder Thomas Holloway to be undenominational, Royal Holloway opened in 1886 with a board of governors (appointed after his death) that was wholly Anglican, the archbishop of Canterbury among them. It took more than a decade of lobbying by Nonconformists to get this regime changed.[10] Of the exact number of Anglican girls' public schools we cannot be sure—no contemporary list of such schools exists. Much better documented is the history of the non-denominational Girls' Public Day School Company, with its thirty-four high schools by the turn of the century.[11] But a mid-twentieth-century survey provides some suggestive figures. In 1967 nearly two-thirds (97 out of 152) of the schools regarded as 'girls' public schools'—belonging to the Governing Bodies of Girls' Schools Association, the body equivalent in standing to the Headmasters' Conference—described themselves as 'Church of England'. Among the 96 girls' schools in England and Wales that were then direct-grant grammar

---

[6] B. Stephen, *Emily Davies and Girton College* (London, 1927), 263.

[7] Howarth, 'Women's Colleges'. 'Definite' in contemporary terms meant 'dogmatic'.

[8] The reference to the 39 Articles in Westfield's Trust Deed was removed in 1919: J. Sondheimer, *Castle Adamant in Hampstead: A History of Westfield College, 1882–1982* (London, 1983), 39, 84.

[9] For its role in promoting the study of theology by women, see H. D. Oakeley, 'King's College for Women', in F. J. C. Hearnshaw, *The Centenary History of King's College, London* (London, 1929), appendix A, 490, 494.

[10] C. Bingham, *The History of Royal Holloway College, 1886–1986* (London, 1987), 73–4, 84–5.

[11] J. Kamm, *Indicative Past* (London, 1971); J. Sondheimer and P. Bodington (eds.), *The Girls' Public Day School Trust 1872–1972* (London, 1972). The company became a trust in 1906 and survives today as the Girls' Day School Trust.

schools, a third were Anglican foundations.[12] Most of these schools had existed in some shape or form since before the First World War.[13]

The secular processes that lay behind the transformation of female education in the nineteenth century are by now well understood: a profound change in attitudes, affecting both sexes, to formal schooling and qualifications, driven by professionalization and by the formation of an internally stratified and status-conscious middle class.[14] All religious traditions contributed to the movement for women's higher education and all harboured some reservations about it—indeed, Alison Mackinnon has commented that in Britain and America 'resistance more often than advocacy came from the churches'.[15] Historians have already begun to explore Nonconformist perspectives and the role of the Roman Catholic teaching orders in England.[16] This essay offers a review of the church's record and the issues that complicated its engagement with the movement before 1914.

There is a relatively straightforward story to tell about the decades before the Schools Inquiry Commission (1864–7), when the state played no part in the provision of secondary education. A leading role has long been claimed for the church in developing female education in that period. The church's mission in national education was taken seriously. The National Society's elementary schools for the working classes catered for both boys and girls, and the Revd J. Llewelyn Davies (brother of the founder of Girton, Emily Davies) was to suggest that the church had—perhaps inadvertently—inaugurated the movement for women's education when it created 'the pupil-teacher system and . . . training colleges equally for both sexes'.[17] Of the twenty church teacher-training colleges for women that survived in England and Wales in the 1920s, all but three dated from the years 1841–61.[18] These colleges attracted a few middle-class students training to be governesses, but the elementary schoolmistresses for whom they were primarily intended were recruited from the lower middle and upper working classes.[19]

[12] K. Ollerenshaw, *The Girls' Schools* (London, 1967), 112, 125. See also B. M. Gay, 'The Church of England and the Independent Schools: A Survey', in L. Francis and D. W. Lankshear (eds.), *Christian Perspectives on Church Schools* (Leominster, 1993).

[13] G. Avery, *The Best Type of Girl: A History of Girls' Independent Schools* (London, 1990).

[14] G. Sutherland, 'The Movement for the Higher Education of Women: Its Social and Intellectual Context in England, *c.*1840–80', in P. J. Waller (ed.), *Politics and Social Change in Modern Britain* (Brighton, 1987).

[15] A. Mackinnon, 'Educated Doubt: Women, Religion and the Challenge of Higher Education', *Women's History Review*, 2 (1998), 245.

[16] C. Binfield, *Belmont's Portias: Victorian Nonconformists and Middle-Class Education for Girls* (London, 1981); R. Watts, *Gender, Power and the Unitarians in England, 1760–1860* (London, 1998); K. Allen and A. Mackinnon, ' "Allowed and Expected to be Educated and Intelligent": The Education of Quaker Girls', *History of Education*, 27 (1998); S. O'Brien, ' "*Terra Incognita*": The Nun in Nineteenth-Century England', *Past and Present*, 121, (1988).   [17] C[hurch] C[ongress] R[eport] (1874), 507.

[18] L. G. E. Jones, *The Training of Teachers in England and Wales: A Critical Survey* (Oxford, 1924), appendix B. Bishop Otter College, Chichester, was founded as a college for men but became a women's college in 1872.

[19] C. de Bellaigue, 'The Development of teaching as a Profession for Women before 1870', *Historical Journal*, 44 (2001), 970–1; F. Widdowson, *Going up into the Next Class: Women and Elementary Teacher Training, 1840–1914* (London, 1983).

Demand for schooling for middle-class girls was still largely met by private venture schools: many of these in fact had church affiliations and scripture lessons were often given by visiting clergymen.[20] But church schools of various types were founded in this period that would later take their place in the girls' public school community.

One was the public boarding school, supported by subscribers, for the daughters of the poorer Anglican professional families. The earliest such school for the daughters of Anglican clergymen, St Margaret's Bushey, was an eighteenth-century foundation, but half a dozen date from the 1820s to 1850s.[21] Other schools of this kind, run on strictly Anglican principles, were the Adult Orphan Institution (1820, later Princess Helena College, Ealing), the Royal Naval Female School in Richmond (1840), and the Royal School for Daughters of Officers of the Army in Bath (1864). The Woodard Society's High Church boarding schools for boys were aimed at a similar middle-class market. Rather against Nathaniel Woodard's better judgement, the society acquired its first girls' school, St Michael's Bognor, in 1864; four others had joined it by 1914.[22] Then there were schools run by Anglican sisterhoods for middle-class girls and 'young ladies', the earliest dating from the 1850s and 1860s (among them St Anne's, Rewley House in Oxford, St Agnes's School at East Grinstead, and St Stephen's College, Clewer in Windsor). Perhaps two dozen such schools existed by the early twentieth century.[23] Well-known examples are two schools run by the Wantage sisters— St Mary's School, Wantage (1873) and St Helen's in Abingdon (1903, later St Helen's and St Katharine's).

These church boarding schools and sisterhood schools, like the more ambitious girls' private schools of the period, belong to the hinterland of the movement for women's higher education. That movement, as it developed in the 1860s, was above all about provision of high-quality public day schools for girls and university education for women. On the quality of education in church boarding schools, Sarah Grand's account of 'St Catherine's Mansion, the Royal School for Officers' Daughters' in *The Beth Book* was not much more favourable than Charlotte

---

[20] D. Beale (ed.), *Reports Issued by the Schools Inquiry Commission on the Education of Girls* (London, 1869), 3, 34, 133.

[21] Casterton School (originally at Cowan Bridge), 1823; St Brandon's, Bristol (originally at Gloucester, 1831); St Mary's Hall, Brighton 1836); St Elphin's, Darley Dale (originally at Warrington, 1844); St Michael's, Limpsfield (1850, originally the Church Missionary School in London). Walthamstow Hall (1838) began as an interdenominational Evangelical school for the daughters of missionaries. Schools for the daughters of Nonconformist ministers were founded rather later: Milton Mount College (Congregationalist, 1873) and Queenswood (Wesleyan, 1878).

[22] St Mary's and St Anne's, Abbot's Bromley (1874); St Winifred's, Bangor (1885); Queen Margaret's, Scarborough (1901); Queen Ethelburga's, Harrogate (1912).

[23] The most detailed survey is M. E. Boddington, 'The Part Played by Anglican Women's Religious Communities in the Education of Children in England', (M.Ed. thesis, University of Hull, 1974). It is not always possible to be sure whether sisterhood schools were really secondary schools. Some schools founded by Emily Ayckbowm's Kilburn sisters, such as St Hilda's, Sefton Park, in Liverpool and the Old Palace School, Croydon, began as higher grade schools.

Brontë's portrayal of the Cowan Bridge Clergy Daughters' School in *Jane Eyre*. The Association of Headmistresses did not admit heads of sisterhood schools as members until the early twentieth century, and even then only in cases where the head could give evidence of 'her personal independence in the management of the school'.[24] But three Anglican foundations of the period do have an acknowledged place in the prehistory of women's higher education: Queen's College, London (1848) and the schools associated with two of its most distinguished alumnae, Frances Mary Buss's North London Collegiate School for Girls (1850) and Cheltenham Ladies' College (1853), effectively refounded when Dorothea Beale became its principal in 1858. Queen's, first projected by the Governesses' Benevolent Association but shaped by F. D. Maurice and the professors of King's College who provided most of the teaching, made the case for a liberal higher education for women—and set an important precedent by securing royal patronage for it. The NLCS and CLC showed how it could be provided effectively—and at a healthy profit in areas with a high concentration of professional and business families—in large schools run by powerful headmistresses. Four of the nine heads present at the foundation of the Association of Headmistresses in 1874 were 'Old Queens'—Miss Buss and Miss Beale, Elizabeth Day of Manchester High School, and Mary Eliza Porter, head of the GPDSC's first school in Chelsea. So was Royal Holloway's first principal, Matilda Bishop, and (in a later generation) the founder of Wycombe Abbey, Frances Dove.

These three schools are also of interest for the circumstances of their foundation, and the different ways in which they negotiated denominational issues. As Margaret Bryant has shown in the case of London, processes of local, parish reform drew the clergy into provision of middle-class education, and where new boys' schools were founded a demand for sister schools often followed.[25] Queen's College was the sister school of King's College School. The NLCS (though it remained a private school until the 1870s) was founded alongside a more short-lived North London Collegiate School for Boys under the sponsorship of the parish clergy. All were by-products of the reorganization of the vast London parish of St Pancras. CLC, the first girls' proprietary school in England, was founded in a town in the throes of Evangelical Revival by a group in which clergymen predominated, to cater for the same genteel families as its 'elder brother' Cheltenham College.[26] Anglican religious instruction was provided in all three schools but none excluded non-Anglicans (as was the usual practice in church boarding schools). In harmony with the broad church belief that it was the business of the church to educate, not to proselytize, attendance at theology lectures at Queen's

---

[24] AHM report (1903), 19; Warwick University Modern Records Centre, MSS 18/4/1/2.

[25] M. Bryant, *The London Experience of Secondary Education* (London, 1986), 184–213, 311–19.

[26] A. K. Clarke, *A History of the Cheltenham Ladies' College, 1853–1953* (London, 1953). Like other exclusive Victorian proprietary schools, the Cheltenham colleges did not admit tradesmen's children; see J. Roach, *A History of Secondary Education in England, 1800–1870* (London, 1986), 160, 300.

was optional. At CLC religious instruction was compulsory, but Nonconformist pupils were excused from the catechism lessons given in the junior classes; as Miss Beale told the Schools Inquiry Commission in a nicely ambivalent phrase, 'we do not make our teaching (may I use the word?) "sectarian" '.[27] At NLCS, on the other hand, where there were Jewish as well as Nonconformist pupils, parents could withdraw their daughters from religious instruction. It was often the case that Anglican teaching proved acceptable to Nonconformist parents, provided extremes of High or Low Church doctrine were avoided.[28] A 'conscience clause' was however widely adopted in later nineteenth-century church day schools. This satisfied opponents of religious tests while leaving teachers free to give distinct-ively Anglican instruction without watering it down for the sake of non-Anglican pupils.[29]

In the years after the Schools Inquiry Commission, the climate changed in some respects quite significantly. For women's higher education as a whole the change was entirely positive: the eleven years after the Endowed Schools Act of 1869 were the most productive period of the nineteenth century in the creation of endowed and proprietary girls' schools and women's university colleges.[30] For the church, however, this was a period of stress—of challenge to its monopoly of educational endowments, pressure for undenominational religious teaching (as required in board schools under the 1870 Education Act) and anxiety, in some quarters at least, about the post-Darwinian crisis of faith. In girls' secondary education, schools were now being founded in large numbers by bodies outside the church's control.[31] Some national response on the part of the church seemed called for—above all, to the undenominational high schools of the GPDSC. But Anglicans were divided about *how* to respond, and the issues involved were often about denominational politics rather than the politics of gender. This is best illustrated by the experience of Church of England women's university colleges, institutions set up at this time by voluntary initiatives.

There is not much evidence that women's colleges were ever regarded as by definition 'infidel places'. The phrase is taken from a story told by a Girtonian, Anna Lloyd, a Quaker student who joined the college when it first opened at Benslow House in Hitchin in 1869 (it moved to the Girton site on the outskirts of Cambridge in 1873). Sharing a railway carriage with a clergyman travelling to London with two ladies, she heard him remark, 'This is Hitchin, and that I believe

---

[27] Beale, *Reports*, 203–4.

[28] See, e. g. F. R. Gray, *And Gladly Wolde He Lerne And Gladly Teche* (London, 1931), 164.

[29] For Edward Benson's defence of the conscience clause on these lines against High Church objections see Benson to Heywood (copy), [Aug. 1883], Benson MSS vol. 2, fo. 145, Lambeth Palace Library.   [30] Sutherland, 'Movement for Higher Education of Women', 92–3.

[31] On the 94 girls' grammar schools founded by the commissioners who implemented the Endowed Schools Acts, see S. Fletcher, *Feminists and Bureaucrats* (Cambridge, 1980). Some were Anglican schools, depending on the terms of the original endowment, but all were required to have a conscience clause.

is the house, where the College for Women is—that *infidel* place'.[32] Anna Lloyd recorded the exchange that followed:

I remember the fire that flushed my face as I said 'Oh, no! not infidel; why do you say that?' And then how I explained that the College for Women was founded on the same principles as the men's Colleges of Cambridge, & did not their founders desire and provide for religious observance? I can recall the recoil with which the ladies eyed me, but the clergyman shook hands as he left the train, and said he was glad I could give such a good account of affairs.

The most controversial feature of Girton was, in fact, its claim to be just like the ancient university colleges for men—a claim studiously avoided by other early women's colleges—and this aspiration was recalled when Girton acquired a purpose-built chapel in 1902.[33] But it seems likely that the clergyman in this story (as distinct, perhaps, from his lady companions) was dismayed less by a college for *women* than by the influence of '*infidel*' colleges. It was after all in this same year, 1869, that T. H. Huxley coined the term 'agnosticism'.[34] A year earlier a new scheme of lectures for ladies had been launched in connection with that 'godless institution of Gower Street', University College, London (once described by Edward Irving as 'the Synagogue of Satan').[35] Oliver Lodge, who lectured to women at the undenominational Bedford College at about this time, notes that the local clergy frequently spoke of it, too, as a 'godless institution'.[36] At least Anna Lloyd's clergyman was willing to be convinced that her college might be different. Some years later Constance Maynard found rumours in London evangelical circles that Girton 'believed in Darwin' and was 'very atheistical'.[37] But one might suspect, again, that these were based on assumptions about the general state of religious belief at the universities in the 1870s.[38]

Such concerns did however create a genuine 'religious difficulty' for the early women's colleges. Any college that lacked a definite religious basis was apt to be regarded in church circles as 'godless'. This was clearly not the view of all committed Anglicans. For some, religious liberty was a paramount consideration and the repeal of the University Test Acts in 1871 entirely welcome. Emily Davies's insistence on linking Girton to the Established Church in the college's Memorandum of Association disappointed some of her Anglican allies. Emily Shirreff protested against 'binding our infant institution to the Church of England, fastening upon

[32] E. M. Lloyd, *Anna Lloyd (1837–1925): A Memoir with Extracts from her Letters* (London, 1925), 57–8.
[33] *An Address given by the Rev. J. Llewellyn Davies at a service held on the inauguration of the chapel at Girton College, Cambridge, May 23 1902* (London, 1902), 5. G[irton] C[ollege] A[rchive], GCAR 6/4/2.   [34] H. McLeod, *Religion and Society in England, 1850–1914* (London, 1996), 179.
[35] N. Harte, *The University of London 1836–1986* (London, 1986), 64, 132. The undenominational UCL was a college for men until 1878, when it became coeducational.
[36] O. Lodge, *Past Years* (London, 1931), 160–1.
[37] C. B. Firth, *Constance Louisa Maynard* (London, 1949), 168.
[38] CCR (1872), 298–324; and on agnosticism at Cambridge, D. Newsome, *Godliness and Good Learning* (London, 1961), 27.

it the trammels that older institutions are struggling to cast off'.[39] Nor were the non-denominational colleges without notable Anglican supporters: Somerville's first chairman, John Percival, was a future bishop; Gladstone's daughter Helen became vice-principal of Newnham. But for many Anglicans, the religious basis of a residential women's college was essential as a guarantee that it would have a Christian ethos. And yet in the 1870s and 1880s, the years when women's university education was taking off, a religious foundation that commanded general acceptance was all but impossible to devise.

Girton's ethos was ecumenical and tolerant. The committee that launched it included the bishops of Carlisle, Peterborough, and St David's, the deans of Canterbury and Chichester, and such eminent churchmen as F. D. Maurice and Lord Lyttelton, but also representative Nonconformist clergymen—Joseph Angus (Baptist), Alexander Raleigh (Congregationalist), and J. H. Rigg (Wesleyan). The pattern of religious observances was not unlike the regime at the undenominational colleges: daily prayers from the Anglican prayerbook, and free choice on Sundays as to which place of worship, if any, students would attend. This relaxed approach inevitably drew criticism. For the *Guardian*, a High Church newspaper, there was nothing to choose between Newnham and Girton, 'both of them undenominational and non-religious'.[40] As a student in the early 1870s Constance Maynard started the 'Girton Prayer Meeting', an evangelical fore-runner of the Student Christian Movement. But the secular atmosphere of Girton Sundays prompted her own vision of a women's college where 'the name of Christ shall be loved and honoured'.[41]

Lady Margaret Hall and Westfield were, by contrast, colleges with a 'definite' church ethos, though they represented different, and controversial, styles of churchmanship. Both had Anglican governing bodies and principals and more or less compulsory religious observances and Bible-study classes. LMH was the more exclusive, adopting like Keble College the Tractarian maxim of 'education on Church principles'.[42] There was a conscience clause for students but the Hall attracted few non-Anglicans; and in 1910 it was spelt out that resident tutors should be members of the Church of England, since LMH was conceived as 'the servant and instrument of the Church'.[43] At Westfield, by contrast, there were from the start many Nonconformists among both students and staff. In Miss Maynard's eyes the essentials of Evangelical Protestantism were found in many denominations besides the Church of England. 'One may be a Presbyterian, a Methodist, a Baptist or a Quaker. Indeed, to enquire after such differences is about on a level with asking, "Do you grow your flowers in round beds or in square ones?" '[44] These colleges served niche markets within the church, and this had both advantages and drawbacks. The influential writer Charlotte M. Yonge, a

[39] Shirreff to Davies, 9 Nov. 1871; GCA, GCGB 1/3/3.
[40] Leading article, *Guardian*, (23 Apr. 1884).   [41] Firth, *C. L. Maynard*, 133 .
[42] Brock and Curthoys, *History of the University of Oxford*, vii. 171.
[43] LMH Council Minutes, 30 Apr. 1910 , LMH Archive.   [44] Firth, C. L. *Maynard*, 325.

disciple of John Keble and friend of LMH's principal Elizabeth Wordsworth, had rejected the Girton model of the women's college but supported LMH 'by way of antidote'.[45] Daughters of the higher clergy, by no means all of them Tractarian— Edith Argles, Nellie and Maggie Benson, Agnes Tait—were among its early students. But LMH's Tractarian associations did encourage the belief that it was 'a hotbed of Ritualism'.[46] As for Westfield, its Evangelical identity attracted one wealthy founding benefactor (the daughter of a London businessman, Ann Dudin Brown), and strong links were forged with the Church Missionary Society. Middle-of-the-road Anglicans, however, regarded Westfield too with some suspicion. 'Are you not all very, very pious?', Miss Maynard was asked by Lady Stanley of Alderley.[47] Both colleges had difficulty in fund-raising for scholarships and buildings.

The 1880s brought initiatives of a more official kind, presided over by Archbishop Benson, to strengthen the church's influence in the world of women's colleges and middle-class secondary schools. Formerly headmaster of Wellington College, Benson seemed just the man for the task. As a churchman he regarded himself as 'neither High, nor Low, nor Broad Church' and, although far from hostile to undenominational schools, he was a vigorous advocate of church education.[48] He also had links of family and friendship with the movement for women's higher education, which had his wholehearted support.[49] But the church's involvement with Royal Holloway College and the Church Schools Company ran into difficulties.

Royal Holloway, a handsomely endowed foundation with buildings at Egham modelled on the Château de Chambord, became—rather by chance—an experiment in non-sectarian and inclusive Anglicanism. Thomas Holloway's foundation deed required that the college should not be identified with any particular Christian denomination, but also that there should be a common religious life and religious teaching—'free from any sectarian influence', yet 'such as to inspire most forcibly in the minds of the students their individual responsibility, and their duty to God'.[50] His model was the undenominational American women's university at Vassar. It was not, however, easily transposed to the England of the 1880s. Rumour had it that this would be another 'godless' college, and that became a matter of concern when the Queen was prevailed upon (by a courtier friend of the Holloway family, Count Gleichen) to open the college in 1886.[51] Holloway's

[45] G. Battiscombe, *Charlotte Mary Yonge* (London, 1943), 146 ; C. M. Yonge to Mrs Argles (copy), 17 July 1879; Wordsworth MSS, Box 7 , bundle 1 , LMHA.

[46] E. Wordsworth, *Glimpses of the Past* (London, 1912), 168.

[47] Firth, C. L. *Maynard*, 196.

[48] A. C. Benson, *The Life of Edward White Benson* (London, 1899), i. 179; ii. 664–8.

[49] His younger sister Ada was founding headmistress of three girls' high schools, at Oxford, Norwich, and Bedford, and married the secretary of the GPDSC, Andrew McDowall; Henry Sidgwick, Newnham's founder, was Benson's brother-in-law, as was Arthur Sidgwick, a leading promoter of women's higher education at Oxford; Elizabeth Wordsworth was a close family friend.

[50] Bingham, *Royal Holloway*, 54.

[51] 'Queen Victoria and the Royal Holloway College 1885–1886: Letters and papers from the Queen's Archives at Windsor Castle', transcribed and ed L. Butler and J. Christie, 1977; typescript, Archives, Royal Holloway, University of London.

trustees, advised by the Queen's private secretary, Sir Henry Ponsonby, hastily appointed a board of governors that included Benson and the Dean of Windsor, Randall Davidson. They took on the task of fulfilling Holloway's wishes, but under the auspices of the church. The principal they appointed, Matilda Bishop, was a pious High Churchwoman, but experienced as headmistress of the GPDSC's high school in Oxford in providing religious teaching acceptable to Nonconformists. Between a quarter and a third of RHC's early students were Nonconformist, yet they seem to have been happy with the regime of compulsory morning prayers—a sung service based on the Anglican liturgy—and only the occasional Unitarian opted out from the principal's divinity lectures. [52] Sunday morning services in the chapel were Anglican but care was taken to avoid 'anything that might conduce to sectarian strife within the College walls'.[53] The college rented pews in Congregationalist and Wesleyan chapels for students who preferred Sunday worship with their own denominations.

Nonconformist protests in the press and Parliament ultimately proved fatal to this Anglican take-over. Understandably enough, it was denounced as a 'Sectarian Dodge' and a violation of the terms of the Holloway bequest.[54] From an Anglican standpoint, this was however a classic case of the 'dissidence of dissent'. Thomas Holloway's brother-in-law believed that 'our National Church' was the least sectarian of churches, and best placed to fulfil the founder's intentions.[55] Randall Davidson argued that 'the moment Governors are elected *qua* Nonconformists or *qua* Churchmen, the sectarian question comes to the front'.[56] That battle was lost in 1892 when Presbyterian and Methodist governors were appointed, and Davidson's prediction was borne out by the decision they forced through five years later allowing Nonconformists to hold Sunday services in the chapel. Miss Bishop resigned. For her this was a blow to the unity of the college and its role in sustaining Christian faith. Competition between Anglican and Nonconformist services would 'emphasise religious differences, it would foster a spirit of criticism and controversy among the students, it would make them lax and irregular in their attendance at Public Worship, it would tend to confuse their minds and weaken their hold on religious truth'.[57] A post was created for her as principal of a new church teacher-training college for women, St Gabriel's, Kennington. But the episode marked a defeat for the church in this semi-official foray into women's higher education.

In the case of the Church Schools Company (1883) the problem was not so much external opposition as divided counsels within the church itself. The CSC

---

[52] Bingham, *Royal Holloway*, 84 Principal's Reports for 1887–8 1888–9 GB/110/1, fos. 152, 240, RHUL Archives.   [53] Davidson to Clifford-Smith, 22 Feb. 1897, GB/202/1, RHUL Archives.
[54] A view with which the college's historian sympathized; Bingham, *Royal Holloway*, 73.
[55] G. M. Holloway to Davidson, 24 Feb. 1890, GB/131/41/3, RHUL Archives.
[56] Davidson to Spicer, 19 July 1889, GB/110/1, fo. 280, RHUL Archives. It was claimed that there had been no deliberate decision to exclude Nonconformist governors: the original nominees included the Congregationalist MP and philanthropist, Samuel Morley, who died in 1886.
[57] Statement by M. E. Bishop, 27 May 1897, GB/110/2, fos. 324–5, RHUL Archives.

was conceived as a 'really national movement, on Church of England lines, for middle-class education in face of the "undenominational system" '.[58] On the principle of undenominational teaching there was however a spectrum of opinions. Even among churchmen with liberal political views there were some, like Gladstone and Frederick Temple, who objected to it as a new form of ortho-doxy or modern 'syncretism'.[59] Yet many clergymen joined the local committees that promoted GPDSC schools. Some of these schools had staunch Anglican headmistresses—Ada Benson among them—and where there was local demand from parents (as in Bath and Liverpool) the company allowed visiting clergymen to provide religious instruction as an optional extra.[60] Not all Anglicans saw a need for more church secondary schools. Those who did, moreover, were divided about what form they should take. Should they be boarding or day schools; run on a charitable or commercial basis; exclusively for Anglicans; socially selective? Supporters of the Woodard Society argued for the provision of more middle-class church boarding schools, as did Elizabeth Sewell, the well-known author and sister of the founder of Radley College, who had a plan for diocesan girls' schools modelled on her own school in the Isle of Wight, St Boniface, Ventnor (1866).[61] Yet fund-raising on the scale implied by these proposals had no prospect of success.[62] The prototype chosen for the CSC was instead the church high schools founded by Canon Francis Holland and his wife in the West End of London, at Baker Street (1878) and Graham Street (1882)—proprietary day schools run on commercial principles. The Francis Holland schools, inspired by Sybilla Holland's interest in Madame de Maintenon's school at St Cyr for the daughters of the French nobility, and her belief that religion must pervade the whole curriculum if it was to be effectively taught, were however schools exclusively for Anglicans.[63]

In ruling that the CSC's schools must have a conscience clause Benson offended High Church people who wanted schools that would be, above all, 'distinctly and loyally *Church of England Schools*'.[64] The veteran Archdeacon Denison denounced the project: others objected to the company's commercial basis.[65] The

[58] Emery to Benson, 24 Aug. 1883 , Benson MSS, ii. fo. 151, Lambeth Palace Library.

[59] E. G. Sandford, *Frederick Temple: An Appreciation* (London, 1907), 167; H. C. G. Matthew (ed.), *The Gladstone Diaries* (Oxford, 1982), vii. 299.

[60] GPDSC Minutes of Council (1880), 65, 71; (1887), 14. The council did however resist an attempt by Archbishop Tait as a shareholder to require the provision of Anglican religious teaching in Croydon High School; Kamm, *Indicative Past*, 62.

[61] E. L. Sewell (ed.), *The Autobiography of Elizabeth Missing Sewell* (London, 1907), 191–4; CCR (1882), 138–9.

[62] The difficulty of making such schools pay their way is shown by the experience of the Graduated County Schools Association, an offshoot of the liberal Anglican county schools move-ment started by J. L. Brereton and Earl Fortescue—it acquired eight girls' boarding schools between 1880 and 1887 but then collapsed; J. L. de S. Honey, *Tom Brown's Universe* (London, 1977), 86–7.

[63] *Letters of Mary Sibylla Holland*, ed. B. Holland (London, 1907), 53–4, 79–80.

[64] Report of Committee on Middle Class Education from Lichfield Diocesan Conference, 1882, Benson MSS, ii. fo. 141, Lambeth Palace Library.

[65] Denison to Benson, 23 and 25 July, 6 Aug. 1883; Heywood to Benson, 12 Aug. [1883], Benson Mss, ii. fos. 124–5, 127–8, 132–3.

CSC had no hope of winning broad-based support—it remained 'an effort not of the Church but of Churchmen to meet as they think best a pressing need', and too controversial even to be worth the risk of promotion at Church Congresses.[66] Divisions of a different sort emerged, moreover, when a tailor complained that his daughters were refused admission to a CSC school in Streatham—the urban gentry's support for a church high school there was conditional on its excluding tradesmen's daughters. Benson angrily overruled the Streatham committee. A high school was 'a public school if it is anything': that principle was recognized by the GPDSC, which never refused a pupil on account of her parents' status, and to Benson it seemed 'a mockery of the word "Church" in our title to depart from it'. 'The worst that has been said of the Church, as "the Church of a class", as "no Church for the people" has been practically made the basis of our operations in Streatham'.[67]

This background of controversy does much to explain the CSC's limited success, despite the support of Dorothea Beale, Frances Buss, and Helen Gladstone, who served on its council and education committee.[68] The company's brief was to promote church high schools for both sexes, but as demand for boys' schools was largely met by the endowed grammar schools it functioned mainly as a weaker rival to the GPDSC. By the turn of the century the CSC had twenty-six girls' schools (and two schools for boys). These were mostly quite small schools and not well placed to compete with the LEA secondary schools that came into existence under the 1902 Education Act. Only twelve survived by 1939, six as independent church schools run by local committees.[69] And yet quite a number of successful church proprietary girls' schools were founded in the later nineteenth century by the same sort of local and individual initiatives that had featured in earlier decades. In some cases groups of Anglican notables took the lead—Hastings and St Leonard's Ladies' College (1883), the Higher Tranmere School for Girls (1883) in Birkenhead, the church high schools at Winchester (1884—later renamed St Swithun's School) and Edgbaston (1886). Bournemouth High School (1886, now Talbot Heath school), like NLCS, began as a private school; its founding headmistress, Mary Broad, a relative of the founders of the Ranyard Biblewomen mission, handed it over to a board of governors 'as a gift to the Church and to the town'.[70] Other schools had clerical founders. Benson himself, as bishop of the new diocese of Truro, founded a church high school (1880) which his daughters

---

[66] Emery to Moberly, 25 Aug. 1883, Benson Mss, ii. fos. 157–8.

[67] Benson to Holland, 8 and 22 May 1886, Benson MSS xxxiii., fos. 417–8 , 428–9, Lambeth Palace Library.

[68] Elizabeth Wordsworth's name appeared on the first CSC prospectus as a council member but she appears to have withdrawn; Benson Mss, xxxiii. fos. 160, 429.

[69] These schools were in Derby, Durham, Guildford, Hull, Newcastle, Northampton, Reading, St Alban's, Southampton, Sunderland, Surbiton, and York; E. Moberly Bell, *A History of the Church Schools Company, 1883–1958* (London, 1958), 84–5.

[70] *The Jubilee Book of Bournemouth High School, Talbot Heath, 1886–1946* (Bournemouth, 1946).

attended: according to A. L. Rowse it became the best girls' school in Cornwall.[71] Another headmaster-bishop Frederick Temple had a hand in starting various girls' secondary schools: a private school, The Laurels, Rugby, which educated the daughters of Rugby masters, and later became the public school Wroxall Abbey; and in the diocese of Exeter, an episcopal middle school, the endowed Exeter High School for girls (the Maynard School), and the church high school in Plymouth attended by the first High Mistress of St Paul's, Frances Ralph Gray.[72] The Revd J. S. Howson when head of the Liverpool Collegiate Institution had founded a sister school, Liverpool College for Girls (1856); he later became the founder of the Queen's School, Chester (1878), when he moved there as dean. Howson was a leading advocate of the deaconess movement, as was Edward Harold Browne, who as bishop of Winchester was the founder of one girls' school—St Catherine's, Bramley (1885)—and patron of others. [73] The founder of the Wantage sisterhood and its first two girls' secondary schools, Canon William Butler, also took the lead in starting Worcester High School (1883) as a sister school to the new cathedral school in Worcester.[74] Also active at the local level were clergymen for whom promoting girls' schools remained primarily a matter of parish organization and church extension. Charles Edward Butler, the wealthy and energetic High Church vicar of Kennington in North London, ensured that his parish acquired 'day schools for every age and class', including a church high school for girls.[75]

This list is not exhaustive, but it does indicate a burgeoning interest in *church* schools for the daughters of what were sometimes referred to as 'the educated classes'. This was not confined to day schools. Contemporaries noted a growing market for boarding schools that were more socially selective than the high schools.[76] Some older endowed schools reformed under the Endowed Schools Acts, such as Christ's Hospital and the Godolphin School, Salisbury, were now successfully taken in hand by university-educated headmistresses. A number of church boarding schools that would evolve into public schools started off as private schools before 1914, among them Malvern Girls' College (1893), Heathfield (1899), and Downe House (1905). There were of course countless other church private schools, some of them very well known at the time, that did not survive or make that transition.[77] The first English schools actually founded as girls' public

---

[71] A. K. Clarke, *The Story of Truro High School: The Benson Foundation* (Truro 1979).

[72] B. Bourke (ed.), *The Laurels, 1872–1972, Wroxall Abbey* (Wroxall Abbey, 1972); M. E. Sadler, *Report on Secondary Education in Exeter* (London, 1904); Gray, *And Gladly Wolde He Lerne.*

[73] G. W. Kitchin, *Edward Harold Browne* (London, 1895), 358, 471.

[74] V. Noake, *History of the Alice Ottley School, Worcester* (Worcester, 1952). The school was renamed after its first headmistress.

[75] A. G. Deedes (ed.), *Charles Edward Butler: A Memoir* (London, 1913), 76–7. He was also the founder of St Gabriel's Training College.

[76] See 'Girls' Schools', in J. Courtney, *Recollected in Tranquillity* (London, 1926).

[77] The most academically successful of these was Highfield, Hendon, a Low Church school founded by the Metcalfe sisters in the 1860s; a number of the more academic private boarding schools were undenominational, among them Roedean School, Prior's Field Godalming, Polam Hall, and Croham Hurst, Croydon.

boarding schools modelled on the reformed boys' public schools (rather than as day schools like CLC with some provision for boarders) were however two Anglican foundations of the 1890s: Frances Dove's Wycombe Abbey (1896) and Sherborne (1899)—that 'expensive potting shed of the English rose' remembered by one old girl, E. Arnot Robertson.[78] Similar schools with a Low Church ethos were promoted by the Church Education Corporation (1900), a somewhat less ambitious corporate venture than the CSC. It founded three girls' public boarding schools in the South of England—Sandecotes, Parkstone (1900); Uplands, St Leonard's-on-Sea (1903); and the better-known Bedgebury Park in Kent (1920)—and a women's secondary teacher-training college in Oxford, Cherwell Hall (1902), to which a day school, Milham Ford, was attached.[79]

How, then, did these processes of institution building affect Anglican opinion on the higher education of women? There are clear signs of change by the 1890s, despite some continuing controversies. A few leading clergymen like Bishop Westcott of Durham continued to regret the presence of women at Oxford and Cambridge, as did other university men whose motives were purely secular.[80] These universities still denied women degrees, and the bishops of Stepney and Hereford (both, in fact, promoters of women's education) came forward with proposals for a separate women's degree-awarding university that were all but unanimously denounced by women educationalists.[81] At Church Congresses, on the other hand, Elizabeth Wordsworth and Constance Maynard now figured as platform speakers; and—another straw in the wind, perhaps—in 1896 the dean of Rochester denounced Grant Allen's *The Woman Who Did* as an example of the low moral tone of popular fiction.[82] (As in many New Woman novels, Allen's heroine is university-educated: in this case a Girtonian, Herminia Barton—the daughter of a dean—who rejects marriage on principle, has an illegitimate daughter, and ultimately commits suicide.) The existence of church colleges became in itself an influence on conservative Anglican thinking, and the same was true of church schools. *Mothers in Council*, the Mothers' Union journal aimed at 'Mothers of the higher classes', or 'Educated Mothers', was still debating in the 1890s the case for home versus school education. One contributor frankly assumed that 'such mothers as are likely to read this paper would not send their children to other than Church High Schools, or at least to schools where the known principles of the headmistress secure that some definite religious instruction will be given'.[83]

---

[78] Graham Greene (ed.), *The Old School: Essays by Divers Hands* (London, 1934), 180.

[79] *The Church Education Corporation* (np, [1920], Bodl.G. A. Gen. Top. 4. 290/1). Cherwell Hall closed after the First World War; its principal for some years was the Herbartian educationalist Catherine Isabella Dodd.   [80] A. G. B. West, *Memories of Brooke Foss Westcott* (Cambridge, 1931), 15.

[81] G. Sutherland, 'The Plainest Principles of Justice: The University of London and the Higher Education of Women', in F. M. L. Thompson (ed.), *The University of London and the World of Learning* (London, 1990), 40–4; G. F. Browne, *The Recollections of a Bishop* (London, 1915), 309–11; W. Temple, *Life of Bishop Percival* (London, 1921), 270–6.

[82] CCR (1894), 264–8; (1895), 482–6; (1896), 448–9; (1898), 347–51, 355–8.

[83] *Mothers in Council*, 1 (Jan. 1891), 2; 2 (Apr. 1891), 109.

Across the channel in France the Catholic *bourgeoisie* were reluctant to send their daughters to secular *lycées* for girls and the state normal school for women at Sèvres.[84] Church of England schools and colleges, by contrast, played an important part in popularizing formal, academic education for the daughters of the upper middle classes. Most pupils at such schools as CLC, Wycombe Abbey, or St Paul's Girls' School before 1914 expected to be home-makers rather than to earn their own living, as did many early students at the Oxford women's colleges.[85]

Little has been said so far about Anglican debates on gender. We have seen that all parties within the church did engage with the movement for women's education; but, equally, none was free from the mid-Victorian anti-intellectualism that leading churchwomen sometimes complained of.[86] Early novels by Charlotte M. Yonge—*The Daisy Chain* (1856) and *The Clever Woman of the Family* (1865)—did no more to encourage intellectual ambition than Lord Shaftesbury's view of evangelicalism as 'exclusively the religion of the heart'.[87] It was Maurice's friend Charles Kingsley (a lecturer in English literature at Queen's College) who wrote, 'Be good, sweet maid, and let who will be clever'; and Elizabeth Wordsworth's rhyme, 'The Good and the Clever', that challenged this much-quoted maxim.[88] As Sean Gill has noted there were unresolved contradictions, and a conventional attachment to notions of 'difference', within Evangelical, Anglo-Catholic, and liberal 'theologies of womanhood'.[89] Against this background advocates of women's education used various strategies to make their case.

At one extreme was the egalitarian Girton view. While not challenging patriarchy within the family, Emily Davies claimed that 'the theory of education of our English Church recognises no distinction of sex'. The service of baptism and the catechism presented children with 'one type and exemplar, one moral law': 'the Christian theory of education implies an essential resemblance between the sexes'.[90] Miss Maynard followed that tradition when she maintained that the same attributes of character were 'of value in men and women alike'.[91] Yet there were other, less controversial, Broad church formulations of the case for equal access to a liberal education. In Maurice's understanding of the vocation of the teacher as 'an awful one', as 'the task of training an immortal spirit', there was equally no

[84] J. N. Margadant, *Madame le Professeur: Women Educators in the Third Republic* (Princeton, 1990), 55, 204.

[85] On Oxford students, see J. Howarth and M. Curthoys, 'The Political Economy of Women's Higher Education in Late-Nineteenth and Early-Twentieth century Britain', *Historical Research*, 60 (1987).

[86] Wordsworth, *Glimpses*, 168; and (for Miss Maynard's comments) M. Barlow (ed.), *The Life of William Hagger Barlow* (London, 1910), 113–15, 120–1.

[87] E. Jay, *The Religion of the Heart* (Oxford, 1979), 40.

[88] C. Kingsley, 'A Farewell', in his *Poems. Collected Edition* (London, 1878), 216; E. Wordsworth, *Poems and Plays* (London, 1931), 68. Her last verse goes: 'So friends, let it be our endeavour | To make each by each understood | For few can be good like the clever, | Or clever so well as the good'.

[89] S. Gill, *Women and the Church of England: From the Eighteenth Century to the Present* (London, 1994), 76–83.

[90] Emily Davies, *The Higher Education of Women* (1866; 2nd edn, London, 1988), 14–16, 173.

[91] CCR (1898), 349.

distinction of sex.[92] Writing at the end of the century, Dorothea Beale developed this ungendered theory of 'the task of the educator', noting its affinity to Froebelian ideas on the education of the individual child. She also deployed the much-used argument that the liberal education fitted women equally for 'the highest purposes of marriage'—that is, intellectual sympathy between husband and wife—and for other forms of 'service' in which unmarried women might find the 'satisfaction of their higher nature'.[93]

At another extreme was a High Church view that saw a place for women's higher education only within the church, seeking to reconcile it with traditional Christian notions of 'difference'. For Miss Yonge and Miss Wordsworth, the starting point remained the book of Genesis.[94] Woman was inferior and, because of the sin of Eve, rightly subordinated to man; but she was nevertheless created as a help-meet to man—that is, in the modern world, 'not merely one woman for one man... but all women for all men in just relation and degree'.[95] The modern woman did not necessarily marry and must therefore be educated for a variety of roles; but the relaxation of family disciplines made it all the more essential that she should be governed by the church. In Miss Yonge's words, 'It is only as a daughter of the Church that woman can have her place, or be satisfied as to her vocation'.[96] This was a narrower view of female education as something worthwhile only in so far as it was contained within the church; but it did not imply indifference to the *quality* of women's education or the value of educated churchwomen. Here a sermon of 1884 preached by Christopher Wordsworth, bishop of Lincoln and Elizabeth's father, repays close reading. A text from St Paul (1 Cor. 11:10) is expounded to show that women's authority depends on their deference to men and 'Christian sweetness'. The term 'higher education' is denounced if applied to training with purely intellectual rather than spiritual ends. But at the heart of the sermon is a plea to open to women the full range of university learning and welcome them to 'free fellowship with us in all these studies'. Citing women scholars honoured by the early church, and 'learned women of noble and gentle blood' in Reformation England, Wordsworth urged that 'if the Education of Women is rightly guided... they might do much to check the spread of the poison of Unbelief in modern society'.[97]

Other clerical patrons of women's education took a less conservative and church-centred view of 'difference'. One example is the head of Uppingham School, the Revd Edward Thring, who invited the Association of Head Mistresses—an undenominational body—to hold its annual conference there in

---

[92] 'Queen's College, London: Its Objects and Methods', in A. Tweedie (ed.), *The First College Open to Women: Queen's College, London* (London, 1898), 2.
[93] D. Beale, L. Soulsby, and J. F. Dove, *Work and Play in Girls' Schools* (London, 1898), 3–6.
[94] C. M. Yonge, *Womankind* (London, 1877), 1–8; E. Wordsworth, 'First Principles in Women's Education', CCR (1894), 264–8.   [95] Ibid., 266.
[96] Yonge, *Womankind*, 8.
[97] C. Wordsworth, *Christian Womanhood and Christian Sovereignty* (London, 1884), 31–5.

1887, in the 'Great Schoolroom' where the Headmasters' Conference had been founded in 1869. This was a gesture of professional 'fellowship', and appreciated as such.[98] In his address to the AHM Thring's theme was not however the equality of the sexes but the importance of women's complementary role.

Leave men to do the coarser work. Be content with the queenly life-power that moulds and rules...Woman was created to help, to make good that is the deficiencies of the world of man...to take, as it were, on themselves the part of angels on earth, ministering spirits, good Samaritans...Woman is a fellow-worker with man in an harmonious but independent sphere: man the rough shaper and fighter, woman the helper, healer and queen of the inner life.[99]

This was a Ruskinian version of the woman's sphere, at once expanded and morally dignified, that gained support in the 1880s when the church aligned itself with the purity movement (to which Thring himself was committed).[100] It was in an address on 'Purity' that Edward Benson gave women's higher education his most emphatic endorsement: 'Not one step taken thus far in woman's education and advance can be said to have led to one evil or done one mischief. Her dignity has risen steadily with her power for good'.[101] For those who took that view, there was nothing remotely controversial about Miss Beale's description of Frances Buss, in a *Guardian* obituary, as 'a great leader of that great movement by which God has called upon women in this age to arise and minister'.[102]

The Anglican contribution to the movement for women's education was cumulatively very significant. One illustration of the church's willingness to 'own' it is Dorothea Beale's tomb in Gloucester Cathedral and the ceremonial that marked her death in November 1906—simultaneous cathedral services at Gloucester and St Paul's in London, as well as services in three parish churches.[103] This essay has attempted to explore the dynamics behind church foundations. They owed much to the decentralized structure of the church and the plurality of opinions that flourished within it—two classical features of Victorian Anglicanism. Divisions within the church, while hampering its institutional effectiveness in this branch of national education, nevertheless produced a variety of initiatives that integrated the education of women and girls within all traditions of churchmanship. By degrees it emerged (in those days of single-sex schools and colleges) as a recognized female domain, with influential male patrons—offering interesting parallels with the contemporary Anglican sisterhood and deaconess movements. Many

[98] G. R. Parkin, *Edward Thring* (London, 1898), ii. 174 , 285–9.
[99] E. Thring, *An Address to the Conference of Headmistresses held at Uppingham School, June 10 1887* (Uppingham, 1887), 13, 16–17.
[100] CCR (1884), 367–72; S. Morgan, *A Passion for Purity: Ellice Hopkins and the Politics of Gender in the Late-Victorian Church* (Bristol, 1999).
[101] E. W. Benson, *Christ and his Times* (London, 1889), 104–5. For Benson's own liberal views on 'difference', see A. C. Benson's *Life* of his father, ii. 41–2.
[102] Quoted in J. Kamm, *How Different from us: A Biography of Miss Beale and Miss Buss* (London, 1958), 242.   [103] E. Raikes, *Dorothea Beale of Cheltenham* (London, 1910), 366–8.

headmistresses of the period took their religious vocation just as seriously and saw their work literally as 'ministry'. When fellow heads visited Miss Beale at Cheltenham on Sundays, according to Elizabeth Day, the prayer they said together was the 'Veni Creator Spiritus', a Pentecostal hymn that appears in the Anglican prayerbook only in the service for the ordering of priests.[104] Curiously enough, historians of women's role in the church have shown less interest in religious dimensions of the movement for women's education than historians of girls' schooling.[105] Educational work was indeed less controversial than those forms of ministry and participation in church life that challenged male authority or trespassed on male domains. All the same it belongs in the history of 'church feminism', not least as an example of the ways in which Anglican theologies of gender could adapt to accommodate change.

[104] E. Raikes, *Dorothea Beale of Cheltenham* (London, 1910), 425. The prayer was used in the service for the ordination of deaconesses in some dioceses; *The Ministry of Women: A Report by a Committee Appointed by His Grace the Lord Archbishop of Canterbury* (London, 1919), app 14, 246.

[105] See, e. g. C. Dyhouse, *Girls Growing up in Late Victorian and Edwardian England* (London, 1981), 73–8; J. S. Pedersen, *The Reform of Girls' Secondary and Higher Education in Victorian England* (London, 1987); Avery, *Best Type of Girl*, 149–71. Brian Heeney *in The Women's Movement in the Church of England* (Oxford, 1988) followed the 1919 report on *The Ministry of Women* in excluding education from his analysis of women's position within the church.

11

Protestant Histories: James Anthony Froude, Partisanship and National Identity

Jane Garnett

Froude does not even know whether he is a Catholic or a Protestant'[1]

He was perpetually upon the borderland of the Catholic Church'[2]

Two apparently paradoxical remarks about the nineteenth-century historian and critic James Anthony Froude, so often taken as the archetype of a dogmatic Protestant apologist: whether in his attitude to the Irish or in his perspective on the sixteenth century, described by modern scholars as 'a fervent and aggressive Protestant',[3] and as having portrayed the English Reformation as a 'victory over the powers of darkness'.[4] Froude is seen as a partisan in the negative sense— remembered for his savaging at the hands of the High Church historian Edward Freeman on the ground of the selective use of sources to prove his Protestant case.[5] Froude certainly believed in partisanship in the sense of devotion to a cause, but both his own experience and his historical understanding led him to be wary of partisan bigotry and alert to the sorts of conditions in which it could arise. The 1830s and 1840s—the period in which he grew to maturity—were a time in which the twin challenges of liberalism and of party spirit in both political and religious terms came to the fore, and Froude felt strongly the need to point to the interconnected dangers which they presented to national life. His particular conception of history was designed to offer the means both to counteract these

[1] J. Ruskin, 'Protestantism: The Pleasures of Truth', *The Complete Works of John Ruskin*, ed. E.T. Cook and A. Wedderburn, 39 vols. (London, 1903), xxxiii. 506.

[2] H. Belloc, introduction to Everyman edn. of J. A. Froude, *Essays in Literature and History* (London, 1906), p. xxi.

[3] J. Burrow, *A Liberal Descent: Victorian Historians and the English Past* (Cambridge, 1981), 234.

[4] A. G. Dickens and J. Tonkin, *The Reformation in Historical Thought* (Oxford, 1985), 167.

[5] W. H. Dunn, *James Anthony Froude: A Biography*, 2 vols. (Oxford, 1961 and 1963), ii. 457–70.

dangers, and to reinforce the Christian identity of the nation. Ruskin's and Belloc's observations about him thus merit interrogation in the context of recent debates about the role of history in the construction of national identity and about the part which Protestantism played in this process.

Arguments about the ways in which an overarching Protestant ideology could act to pull together diverse identities within England and Britain as a whole have, with justice, been challenged by historians who have pointed to the distinct identities within Protestantism, often defined in contradistinction to each other.[6] Yet still it is the case, for example, that an Anglican idea of Englishness could provide an ideal of the religious nation to which in particular circumstances even Protestant Dissenters and Catholics could subscribe. It is equally true that the Victorian period saw the development of a powerful national self-image (sometimes British, sometimes English) as liberal, commercial, and Protestant, an image reinforced by the passage of parliamentary reform, the triumph of free trade, and the expansion of the empire. It is clear that Protestantism could be assimilated quite readily to a predominantly progressive constitutional narrative. A schematic Protestant/Catholic binary could be invoked in its support. But such rhetorical projections were never stable or uncontested. Moreover, whilst the concept of national identity has been relentlessly problematized, in this context Protestantism is still too often treated as having a more straightforward and descriptive social and cultural reality. This remains the case even when it is subdivided denominationally. Protestantism and Anglicanism have both had distinct and historically complex stories, but as systems of Christian belief they have also represented a spiritual reality in some sense perpetually in tension with institutional identities. Particularly in the early/mid-nineteenth century the institutional rationale of the Anglican Church was in question. At the same time a generic Protestantism was all too easily being assimilated to the social and economic status quo. For many Anglicans there was a specific need to establish a new basis of authority for the national church. More broadly articulated was a need to reflect on the relationship between religious commitment and moral action in the world. Both these processes involved a challenge to ways of thinking about religious tradition. Their interrelationship had significant implications for concepts both of history and of national identity.

Froude's writings and the resonances to be drawn from shifting responses to them at different points both in his lifetime and into the early twentieth century deserve closer attention within this particular frame of reference. As was the case

---

[6] See L. Colley, *Britons* (London, 1992, 2003); J. C. D. Clark, 'Protestantism, Nationalism, and National Identity, 1660–1832, *Historical Journal*, 43 (2000), 249–76; S. Mews (ed.), *Religion and National Identity*, Studies in Church History (1982); T. Claydon and I. McBride, *Protestantism and National Identity* (London, 1998); J. Wolffe, *God and Greater Britain* (London, 1994); and, most recently, K. Kumar, *The Making of English National Identity* (Cambridge, 2003). Kumar privileges the relationship between Protestantism and British nationalism, arguing that its relationship with English nationalism was always tense (e.g. p. 114). But in many ways he wants to keep the concept of nationalism itself inherently secular.

for many of his contemporaries, the role of religious commitment in national life was Froude's central preoccupation. Yet the particular contours of this defining critical purpose have not been traced. It has too readily been assumed that the Christian faith which he retained was a vestigial one, and that his perspective on the Anglican Church was simply Erastian.[7] In fact his conviction of the dynamic nature of faith belies both these assumptions. Armed with this conviction, he returned repeatedly to reflect critically on the nature of Protestantism and to attack the ways in which the nation could either flaunt it or hide behind it as a badge of identity. In his exploration of the impact of religious mentalities on public life, in past and present, he was distinctive in stressing the interrelationship between the domestic, foreign, and imperial contexts as arenas in which national character was cultivated—and could be corrupted. The fact that his scope was so wide—his impact was as much as an essayist, and indeed as editor of *Fraser's Magazine* from 1860 to 1874—has helped to contribute to a distortion of our interpretative perspective. Within Victorian historiography he has either been identified too directly with Carlyle, or assimilated to a Liberal Anglican category which has become too capacious to be helpful.[8] Although aspects of what Duncan Forbes defined as the early nineteenth-century Liberal Anglican historical project influenced later nineteenth-century developments—Thomas Arnold's perspective on the role of religion in national life can, for example, be traced through to J. R. Seeley[9]—not all liberal Protestant history-writing conformed to the same contours. Coleridge's influence went in different directions, and F. D. Maurice was right to want to distinguish his own religious emphasis very clearly from that of Thomas Arnold and his colleagues in Oxford.[10] Froude belongs with Maurice, rather than with Arnold, and in his historical writing developed a conception of the religious history of the nation and of Protestantism in modern Britain with which Maurice closely sympathized. Historians of Ireland have tended to read only Froude's writing on Ireland; imperial historians solely (if they read it at all) his work on the colonies. Moreover, because he argued strong and often polemical positions, it has been too easy for him to be stereotyped and dismissed with the condescension of an anachronistic posterity.

Ruskin and Belloc celebrated in Froude the same critical and independent spirit which they too exercised. Both recognized the hesitations and tensions in his

[7] J. P. von Arx, *Progress and Pessimism: Religion, Politics and History in Late Nineteenth Century Britain* (Cambridge, Mass. 1985), 186.

[8] The identification with Carlyle was, of course, over-readily made at the time: see. e.g. *Edinburgh Review*, 137 (1873), 122–53, at 125 (review of Froude's *The English in Ireland in the Eighteenth Century*); Burrow, *Liberal Descent*, 243, 271 n.

[9] D. Forbes, *The Liberal Anglican Idea of History* (Cambridge, 1952); R. T. Shannon, 'John Robert Seeley and the Idea of a National Church', in R. Robson (ed.), *Ideas and Institutions of Victorian Britain* (London, 1967), 236–67.

[10] J. Tulloch, *Movements of Religious Thought in Britain during the Nineteenth Century* (1885; Leicester University Press reprint, 1971), 260. For Coleridge in this context, see M. J. Lloyd, 'The Historical Thought of S. T. Coleridge' (Oxford D.Phil., 1999).

writing, and were frustrated by what they saw as his inability to maintain an entirely consistent critical detachment from the Protestant middle-class assumptions of the day. For each of them—even for Belloc, who was confessionally Catholic—Catholicism signified less a church than a state of mind, a sense of infinitude as opposed to the narrowness of Protestantism, which in turn implied a particular attitude towards contemporary mores. Belloc saw Froude as 'perpetually striking that note of interest, of wonder, and of intellectual freedom which is the note of Catholicism'.[11] Whilst each naturally read Froude from his own vantage-point, each saw clearly the intrinsic relationship between his religious and historical sensibility, his hostility to the unreflective adoption of systems (religious or political), and his conviction of the moral importance both of the study of history and of the adoption of the right intellectual approach to the understanding of spiritual reality. There was a recognition of the fundamental sincerity and consistency of the historical method which resulted. Ruskin noted that he was 'keenly . . . and impartially, sympathetic with every kind of heroism, and mode of honesty';[12] Belloc observed that 'he despised the cowardice—for it is cowardice—that pretends to intellectual conviction and to temporal evidence of the things of the soul. He saw, and said, and he was right in saying, that the City of God is built on things incredible'.[13] This was not quite how Froude would have put it, but it pointed to his understanding of the validity of different types of truth.

The role of Froude's early life, and the development of his religious ideas in structuring both his philosophy of history and his conception of national character are fundamental, yet they have often been treated reductively. Froude arrived in Oxford in 1836, very much under the shadow of his elder brother Hurrell, the close friend of Newman and fellow promoter of the Oxford Movement, who had just died of tuberculosis. Party spirit in Oxford between different interpretations of Anglicanism was at its height. Having come from a household in which religious doctrine was never a subject of discussion, he was suddenly bombarded by theological debate, and the undogmatic certainties of his youth were undermined. There followed a period in which he struggled to regain a secure conviction of faith. In the summer of 1840 he went from Oxford to act as tutor to an Evangelical family in Ireland. He had never come across Evangelicalism before, and he later wrote that 'for the first time in my life I was in the presence of purely spiritual religion, the teaching of the New Testament adopted as a principle of life, and carried into all the details of ordinary thought and action'.[14] This provided a refreshing antidote to theological wrangling in Oxford, although even after Newman's conversion, which was in one sense liberating, Froude continued to feel

---

[11] Belloc, introduction, p. xxii.

[12] Ruskin, 'Fors Clavigera', letter 88 (March 1880), *Complete Works*, xxix. 387.

[13] Belloc, introduction, p. xxiii.

[14] Dunn, *Froude: Biography*, 64–5; cf. Froude, 'The Oxford Counter-Reformation' (1881), *Short Studies on Great Subjects*, 4 vols. (London, 1890), iv. 231–360, at 295–6.

challenged by the ways in which Newman had identified the search for intellectual conviction of faith.

It was a few years before Newman's conversion that Froude started to read Carlyle, and to feel his attraction. As he was to characterize it in his semi-autobiographical novel *The Nemesis of Faith*, this was a defining moment: 'for the first time now it was brought home to me that two men may be as sincere, as earnest, as faithful, as uncompromising, and yet hold opinions far asunder as the poles . . . it threw me at once on my own responsibility, and obliged me to look for myself at what men said, instead of simply accepting all because they said it'.[15] This realization was critical for his developing historical imagination, as it was for his approach to religious understanding. It was never conceivable that all the good could lie on one side.[16] In the immediate crisis of Anglican authority forced by Newman's secession, Froude's own religious position was in one sense fortified by adopting Carlyle's maxim that one should ask of every institution not 'Is it true?' but 'Is it alive?' But ironically he came close to the application of the test of vitality—as a mark of truth—applied by Newman in his *Essay on Development*, critical though he was of where Newman's argument led.[17] As Froude was to dramatize in *The Nemesis of Faith* (1849), he felt that the resort to the Catholic authority of the Pope represented a choice as negative as suicide.[18] In reinforcing his loyalty to the Established Church in which he had been born, he drew from his reading of the eighteenth-century apologist Joseph Butler a stance not altogether dissimilar to that argued by John Keble in his 'On the Present Position of English Churchmen' in 1844.[19] For Froude there was a sense in which he arrived at last at the Anglican faith where he had started, and knew the place for the first time. The extended metaphor of home which he developed in *The Nemesis of Faith* took its departure from a reflection on a churchyard to which men who have gone away return to be buried alongside their ancestors.[20] This image stood not just for his own personal faith but for his conviction of the place of the national church in the country's life.

Although the book was burnt as heretical in the front quad of Exeter College, and Froude was forced to resign his fellowship and his Anglican ministry, the writing of *The Nemesis of Faith* in fact revitalized Froude's Anglicanism. It was

---

[15] J. A. Froude, *The Nemesis of Faith* (2nd edn. London, 1849), 156–7.

[16] Froude, 'History: Its Use and Meaning', *Westminster Review*, ns 6 (1854), 420–48, at 438; idem, 'The Influence of the Reformation on the Scottish Character' (1865), *Short Studies*, i. 154–87, at 155; 'Condition and Prospects of Protestantism', *Short Studies*, ii. 158–9.

[17] Idem, 'Father Newman on "The Grammar of Assent"', *Short Studies*, ii. 101–45; see also J. H. Newman, 'State of Religious Parties', *British Critic and Quarterly Theological Review*, 25 (1839), 395–426, at 423; idem, *An Essay on the Development of Christian Doctrine* (London, 1845 edn.), 32–5.   [18] Froude, *Nemesis*, 214–27.

[19] J. Keble, 'Preface on the Present Position of English Churchmen', *Sermons Academical and Occasional* (Oxford, 1847), pp. i–lxxiii; for Froude's commendation of Butler, see 'Representative Men' (1850), *Short Studies*, i. 581; 'Father Newman', 110, 116; *Inaugural Address delivered to the University of St Andrews* (London, 1869), 37; *Nemesis*, 45.   [20] Froude, *Nemesis*, 101.

taken by other troubled Anglicans as inspirational—as dramatizing the destructive effects of competing systems on religious impulses. F. D. Maurice commented:

I am reviewing it in everything I am writing… it is reviewing him to show whither the habits of the religious world, its half-beliefs and no beliefs, its Jesuitisms and its open lies, are leading us. It is reviewing him to show that we are not given over to the infidelity which is the actual effect of the influences, that there is a mightier counteracting influence among us, if we will use it.[21]

Froude's conception of the Church of England had considerable affinity with Maurice's anti-systematic ideal of the Church as the embodiment of the interrelationship between spiritual and civil life. Maurice explicitly refuted the idea of the Anglican Church as either the union of the Protestant system with the Roman or a combination of elements taken from each: it was 'the faith of a Church, and has nothing to do with any system at all'[22]. Froude's perspective was more historical than Maurice's, but his imaginative ideal was very similar. As both Maurice and Charles Kingsley had, Froude came to feel the importance of considering religion less as a set of dogmas which one holds than as a reality which upholds one. For English people this reality had historical depth within the Anglican tradition, rightly conceived.

In a different but fundamentally related register, Froude argued that home as the place where religion and life are inextricably intertwined should become the model for life as a whole. His passages on this theme in *The Nemesis of Faith* do not represent a retreat into the private and domestic.[23] The imagery is nostalgic, but the purpose is combative. Froude is pointing to the need for consistency of attitude in public and private life. Home is family, affection, countryside, *patria*, church, and heaven. At home as before God, man is exposed as man, and cannot hide behind his professional role as lawyer, sailor, man of business. 'No idle, careless, thoughtless man, so long as he persists in being what he is, can endure the thought of home any more than he can endure the thought of God.'[24] This is not a commendation of the virtues of domesticity, but a reflection on the cultivation of Christian manliness and citizenship in the world. Froude's perception of an urgent national need for guidance in this respect shaped his historical and critical agenda, and his reflections on Catholicism and Protestantism. Whilst he was famously sceptical whether a focus on the lives of the saints of the early church could invigorate an active faith in the present, he underlined the strength of the Catholic tradition of exemplary lives.[25] One of his complaints about contemporary Protestantism was that it had forgotten this principle. To him it seemed to provide

---

[21] F. D. Maurice, letter (Mar. 1849) to Charles Kingsley, cited by Dunn, *Froude: Biography*, i. 142.
[22] Maurice, *The Kingdom of Christ*, 2 vols. (1853, repr. London, 1959), ii. 329; cf. Froude, 'Oxford Counter-Reformation', 237–8.
[23] *Pace* Burrow, *Liberal Descent*, 293. Burrow misses the sense of *religious* wholeness and integrity (precisely transcending a private/public distinction) for which Froude calls.
[24] Froude, *Nemesis*, 105.   [25] Froude, 'The Lives of the Saints', *Short Studies*, i. 562–3.

no models for the cultivation of national character. Theory needed to be reintegrated with practice through a sharp and vivid focus on the ethical dilemmas of modern life—through biographies of merchants, lawyers, landlords, and workmen, who carried their religious principles into their working lives.[26] Otherwise it would become increasingly easy to confine religion to the home and to the church and to lose its influence in the world. This would undermine any justification for Britain's reputation as a Protestant God-fearing nation.

Froude continued to reflect on Newman's understanding of faith as he read also in German philosophy and theology.[27] He saw the attractions of an idealist defence of Christianity, but, just as he was to feel about the difference between history and poetry, he argued that whilst there was a poetic reality in Hamlet or Ulysses, the fact that Julius Caesar existed or that Christianity had a historical reality made a difference.[28] This did not make it a reality which was more easily containable. Different kinds of truth and reality coexisted—past beliefs and legends formed part of the historical record.[29] To make the supernatural incredible (as he felt that Gibbon and Macaulay did) was to make reality unreal.[30] Equally, Froude thought it absurd to argue that the New Testament narrative could be made more credible by purging it of its miraculous elements.[31] To attempt to read the Bible in the delimited terms of human history robbed religion of its nonhistorical dimension, even as it robbed history of its religious dimension. In this sense Christian apologetic was a special case of a general truth about historical understanding—that it could never be complete, but that it needed to be pursued within a conception of an ultimate wholeness of meaning. Just as a conception of Christianity was necessarily probabilistic, 'the so-called certainties of history are but probabilities in varying degrees.'[32] In each case, such an idea of probability was not a passport to relativism but a rigorous one which could provide the condition of growth in understanding, and which was complementary to the moral certitude crucial for judgement and action. It offered a check both to the arrogance of certainty and to the sterility of scepticism.

At the same time in Oxford debate was getting under way about expansion of the syllabus—to include, for example, the study of modern history and political economy. Proponents of reform argued that this was a way in which Oxford, as one of the key Anglican institutions of the country, could reinforce the intellectual scope and hence authority of the Established Church. Froude had won the

---

[26] Idem, 'Representative Men', 580–7, 590–1.

[27] Dunn, *Froude: Biography*; cf. Froude, 'Oxford Counter-Reformation', 280–1, 284–5.

[28] Froude, *Oceana; or, England and her Colonies* (London, 1886), 27–8.

[29] Idem, 'Lives of the Saints', 552.

[30] Idem, 'History: Its Use and Meaning', 445; cf. idem, 'Origen and Celsus', *Short Studies*, iv. 431, 367; idem, 'The Scientific Method Applied to History', *Short Studies*, ii. 580.

[31] Cf. [Froude], 'A Plea for the Free Discussion of Theological Difficulties', *Fraser's Magazine*, 68 (1863), 277–91, at 287–9, where Froude criticizes Renan, Paley, and Jowett for this error.

[32] Froude, *History of England*, vii. 501. Here I contest R. Jann's interpretation of Froude's concept of fiction: *The Art and Science of Victorian History* (Columbus, OH, 1985), 109.

Chancellor's Essay Prize in 1842 for a strongly argued essay on political economy, which raised themes which were to remain central to his thinking. He argued not for opposition to political economy, but for a reconfiguration of its premises in the light of religious principle. Political economy had been left in the hands of those who stressed expediency and the goal of external prosperity. Religious men needed to engage with it, in order to challenge established norms and definitions—of productive and unproductive labour, of usefulness, of wealth.[33] Froude cited Bishop Berkeley's *Essay Towards Preventing the Ruin of Great Britain* (1721), a polemic against national corruption and loss of a proper sense of public interest, and posed the same questions. Was Britain drawing on itself the hatred of God and man? Was the human race degenerating? Like Berkeley, he concluded by rejecting any general law of deterioration—the 'old folly to make peevish complaints of the Times'.[34] There were facilities for improvement, but there were also powerful risks, which could only be averted by the exercise in public life and debate of an active religious faith.[35] Berkeley's essay was an important stimulus to Froude. Berkeley lamented that public spirit was treated like want of sense, and all respect was paid to 'cunning men, who bend and wrest the Public Interest to their own private ends'.[36] He called for the active promotion of sincerity and bravery, qualities which would follow from a right understanding of religion. True to a classical understanding of the role of history, he called for an 'Academy of ingenious Men to compile a History of Great Britain, to make discourses proper to inspire Men with a Zeal for the Public'.[37] Froude too was to conceive the teaching of history as central to the development of national character—*not*, however, in Berkeley's sense of drawing morals or plucking examples, but in the sense of stimulating an active engagement with the past. In this respect, religious apologetic was not just a special case of a historical understanding: a sense of the history of human experience was the necessary foundation for religious conviction. 'Not till the man is formed...not till all the strangeness of their own nature has broken upon them...not until they have felt the meaning of history...not till then can religion in its awfulness come out before men's minds as a thing to be thought of.'[38]

When Froude proposed the study of the *Statutes* as the basis for the planned modern history course at Oxford,[39] it was in order to introduce undergraduates to primary sources which they should read critically rather than reading modern

---

[33] Froude, *The Influence of the Science of Political Economy on the Moral and Social Welfare of a Nation* (Oxford, 1842), 13–28.

[34] [Bishop Berkeley], *An Essay towards Preventing the Ruine of Great Britain* (London, 1721), 26.

[35] Froude, *Political Economy*, 40.   [36] Berkeley, *Essay*, 22.   [37] Ibid., 20.

[38] Froude, *Nemesis*, 120.

[39] Froude, 'Suggestions on the Best Means of Teaching English History', *Oxford Essays* (Oxford, 1855), 64 fo.; see also J. B. Rye, *Froude and his Detractors* (Oxford, n.d.)—a paper delivered at the first meeting of the Froude Society, set up to rival the Stubbs Society—p. 17, in which he complains that Stubbs seized and promoted Froude's proposal without acknowledgement.

works of synthesis. He referred with scorn to the method of teaching history followed at 'popular schools':

Epitomes of Hume, or Lingard, or Sharon Turner, or Burnet or Collier, are run together on the principle of the different shades of opinion; these writers being implicitly followed when they do not contradict each other, and when they do, being either made to neutralise each other by a judicious intermixture, or else the choice between them being determined by the theological or political sympathies of the compiler.[40]

The boast of London University to teach an infinitely wider syllabus than the old universities he showed to be futile—the object of intellectual ambition becoming 'a sort of diluted omniscience'.[41] Just as he abominated religious latitudinarianism which could conduce to indifference, so he argued for the cultivation of a historical judgement which required the taking of positions and a recognition of the responsibility to do so—and to do so responsibly. A good English history could not develop whilst there was a tendency either to follow the fashions of the age, or (and here he instanced Carlyle) to 'fall into distempered antagonism to them'.[42] Nor could one pretend to Olympian detachment. Impartiality was impossible. Differences of opinion among historians were inevitable as long as there were Whigs and Tories, Catholics and Protestants, and would continue

until those tendencies towards latitudinarianism...shall have finally demolished all existing theories; and other convictions, not latitudinarian, but intense and earnest,—earnest as ever Protestantism was in the days when it went to the stake for the Gospel's sake,—shall have risen in their place. In the meantime professors and tutors may trim their sails to the many winds, to strike balances and arrive at moderate views, but they will not succeed, for they, too, are and must be partisans; and if they could succeed, the result would not be worth the labour.[43]

Not to be partisan would be to evacuate and so to betray the truth. But partisanship was always to be distinguished from the use of history simply to confirm existing opinions. This was corrupting for both writer and reader. It turned history into a meaningless relativism, 'nothing but a collection of anagrams', from which practical people would turn, preferring the so-called realities of the present 'to the dissolving views of an unapproached and unapproachable past'.[44] In the 1850s Froude saw a real danger of public loss of faith in the necessity and possibility of historical engagement.

Froude had an idiosyncratic view of the *Statute Book* as a source which treated of all great movements, political and religious, and gave access to the whole spectrum of the life of the nation.[45] He did not advocate it as a way of affirming a liberal constitutional narrative. Rather, by offering a more complex vista, it could encourage a more imaginative and sympathetic understanding of the past, which

---

[40] Froude, 'Suggestions', 48.   [41] Ibid., 51.   [42] Ibid., 78; cf. *Nemesis*, 30–6.
[43] Ibid., 59.   [44] Froude, 'History: Its Use and Meaning', 421.
[45] See e.g. Froude, *History of England*, i. 423–44.

would perforce undermine a black and white binary optic. As he provocatively observed: 'It is something more than touching to find Queen Mary's parliament, even while the fires of Smithfield were burning, engaged in preventing the manufacturers of the north from mixing devilsdust with their cloth, and the smaller tradesmen from cheating the poor consumers with adulterated articles.'[46] Such a startling juxtaposition simultaneously struck at Protestant complacency both in the present and in its attitude to the past, and underlined the importance of making historical judgements in the round. The argument followed that study of the *Statutes* would militate against oversimplified analysis of past events and the adoption of a patronizing attitude to people in the past in the belief that they were capable of actions of which we could not feel capable.[47] It was easier to deplore past failings in policy than to acknowledge present ones—and here he cited England's disinclination to take responsibility for the impact of the Irish famine, whilst deploring famines and plagues under the Tudors and Stuarts.[48] At the same time the *Statutes* would bring home the differences between the thoughts of earlier generations and of ours. There was an equal danger of distortion in seeing people in the past as too different and as too like us: 'We see them in pictures; in the pages of Chaucer and Shakespeare, so like ourselves and yet so unlike; but we have never measured the points of difference or attempted to penetrate into their hearts'.[49] Froude also considered that to base a course on the *Statute Book* (or selections from it) would also guard against the risk of theorizing out of nothing.[50] There would be a firmer basis on which historical debate could proceed, and a surer critical standard of comparison between periods—and between different religious and political perspectives.

The fact that Froude's major historical work, begun in 1850 in the wake of his religious crisis, focused on the sixteenth century, has been interpreted as the product of his need to repudiate Tractarian views of the Reformation and re-establish his Protestant orthodoxy.[51] Froude certainly wanted to demonstrate that the Reformation was the hinge on which modern history turned, but this was far from signifying a triumphalist view of it.[52] In fact his perception that at the Reformation self-consciousness set in, and history became a weapon for rival theologians, rendered its heritage a profoundly ambiguous one—hence one which needed to be prised open and explored.[53] He was very critical of the ways in which history had been used by both Protestants and Catholics to justify their positions (and especially the way in which injustices had been done by crude Protestants to

[46] Froude, 'Suggestions', 75.   [47] Ibid., 67, 71–2.
[48] Froude, 'The Dissolution of the Monasteries'(1857), *Essays in Literature and History*, 152; cf. idem, *The English in the West Indies*, 13: 'Each age would do better if it studied its own faults and endeavoured to mend them instead of comparing itself with others to its own advantage'.
[49] Froude, 'Suggestions', 73.
[50] Ibid., loc. cit.   [51] See e.g. Jann, *Art and Science*, 108, 115.
[52] As was recognized by P. R. Frothingham, 'Froude; or, The Historian as Preacher', *Harvard Theological Review*, 2 (1909), 481–99, at 491.
[53] Froude, 'Scientific Method', 591–2; cf. 'History: Its Use and Meaning', 434.

particular Catholics—Philip II and Charles V).[54] From Carlyle Froude took the conception of ages of energetic commitment and ages of decay to deny the contemporary criteria of progress. But he conceived this idea in less apocalyptic terms than Carlyle, and had more sense of the particularity of historical transitions. Carlyle imposed a structure on the past; Froude allowed for shifts of emphasis as his work developed. In the preface to the second edition of *The Nemesis of Faith*, he castigated his country and its Protestantism in the nineteenth century:

The very same symptoms meet us steadily in the decline of every great people—an old faith, withered in its shell, yet which is preserved in false show of reverence, either from cowardice, or indolence, or miserable social convenience. So Rome fell, so Greece, so Spain, so the greatness of modern Italy. Is this all which we are to expect for the England of Elizabeth and Cromwell?[55]

The positive associations of Elizabethan England were familiar to his contemporaries — although Elizabeth and Cromwell could pull in different directions.

Elizabeth's reign was seen by many Victorians as emblematic of England's pride and glory. For Matthew Arnold the Elizabethan age represented English culture at its best and most inclusive: as its principal voice Shakespeare seemed to encapsulate all the values of national culture.[56] Froude himself had contributed to this in his portraits of Elizabethan adventurers and his rhapsodic description of Elizabeth as 'the People's Sovereign' in his essay on 'England's Forgotten Worthies'.[57] Thus a twelve-volume history culminating in the defeat of the Spanish Armada could seem a straightforwardly celebratory project in this genre. Yet in the process of working on his history, Froude was to become increasingly disillusioned with Elizabeth. He saw clearly her faults and their implications, and developed a more complicated sense of the period as a whole. It has been suggested that his principal disappointment was in the nature of the religious settlement—that it left the Church of England half-Catholic and only half-Protestant.[58] Yet this is to oversimplify. He certainly felt that Elizabeth had arrested the spiritual revolution halfway through its course. This failure he saw as being rooted in her vanity and insincerity, and her lack of longer term vision. 'She insisted on conformity with an institution which she had made deliberately insincere...She constructed her Church for a present purpose, with a conscious understanding of its hollowness.'[59] Her lasting legacy to the Church, in Froude's view, was thus an institution which lacked integrity. It was this which facilitated the theological wrangling— the reactions and counter-reactions—of later centuries, and undermined the

[54] Idem, *History of England*, viii. 430–1; J. Skelton, *The Table-Talk of Shirley* (London, 1895), 198–9.   [55] Froude, *Nemesis*, pp. xii–xiii.

[56] M. Arnold, 'Heinrich Heine', *Lectures and Essays in Criticism*, ed. R. H. Super (Ann Arbor, 1962), 107–32, at 121; cf. S. Collini, introduction to *Culture and Anarchy*, (Cambridge, 1993), p. xviii.

[57] Froude, 'England's Forgotten Worthies' (1852), *Short Studies*, i. 455.

[58] Von Arx, *Progress*, 189.

[59] Froude, 'Revival of Romanism', *Short Studies*, iii. 130–206, at 168; cf. *History of England*, xi. 471–3.

spirit of Reformation. It was the same institution which in the mid-nineteenth century tried to set the clergy apart from the intellectual currents of the day behind walls of orthodoxy built out of the Thirty-Nine Articles, and reacted defensively to the posing of critical questions.[60] This was a betrayal of the ideal of the national church, which to Froude, as to Maurice, represented the religious spirit of the people.

For Froude the paradox of the sixteenth century was the fact that in many important respects it was more the end of an era than the beginning of a new one. The Elizabethan age was at the close of an age of chivalry—he noted that there were more tournaments in her reign than under Richard Cœur de Lion—and the beauty of the old was felt more and more as it was passing away.[61] A new dawn was promised, but the policies pursued permitted the retention of the worst aspects of the old system, even as they destroyed rather than reactivating some of the best aspects of it. It was the articulation of this paradox which confused Ruskin. He noted Froude's praise of the social and religious order of the Middle Ages, predicated on a sense of responsibility rather than on the selfish laws of political economy, and was perplexed by what seemed to be his inconsistent welcoming of the Reformation.[62] To Froude the two positions were not inconsistent, although the language which he used in the expression of them was often polarized. For Froude the real impulse to reform came from below. Here he drew parallels with the origins of Christianity—that the first followers of Christ were the Galilean fishermen—and indeed it is with them that he compares his Elizabethan seafarers.[63] The real spirit of the Reformation was the expression of honest men at a system which could no longer be tolerated, a revolt of the laity against clerical domination.[64] It was important that this was harnessed by those in power, and here Henry VIII's reassertion of England's independence from the papacy was crucial (and could be see in a longer historical trajectory of English Christianity—from King Alfred's defeat of the Vikings to Henry II's disposal of Becket).[65] Froude was more sympathetic to the difficulties which Henry VIII confronted than many contemporary historians, even as he was more critical of Elizabeth. The Reformation was a fundamental force for good, but in so far as it was not one process, but was made up of many parallel strands, neither its goals nor its impact could be consistently successful. Moreover, the moral impetus behind the Reformation came from the Catholic past, and although it sustained its momentum for two centuries, it was now beginning to be lost.[66]

[60] [Froude], 'A Plea for the Free Discussion of Theological Difficulties', *passim*.

[61] [Idem], 'The Morals of Queen Elizabeth: Second Paper', *Fraser's Magazine*, 48 (1853), 489–505, at 503.   [62] Ruskin, 'Fors Clavigera', letter 88, 387–9.

[63] Froude, 'England's Forgotten Worthies', 447.

[64] Idem, 'Father Newman', 144–5; *History of England*, xi. 102; 'Influence of the Reformation on the Scottish Character', 162.

[65] [Froude], 'King Alfred', *Fraser's Magazine*, 45 (1852), 74–87, at 81; idem, 'Life and Times of Thomas Becket', *Short Studies*, iv. 1–230, at 226–30.

[66] [Froude], 'History: Its Use and Meaning', p. 427; cf. 'England's Forgotten Worthies', 444–5.

It was appropriate that one of the most sympathetic reviews of Froude's *History* should have been written by F. D. Maurice, who saw very clearly what he was trying to do, and appreciated his achievement. Maurice commended Froude's disturbance of settled convictions, and his treatment of the virtues and vices of both Protestants and Catholics. He stressed that Froude was not impartial:

> there is no impartiality in *this* sense, that he looks down upon both as from a higher judgment-seat of his own; or in this sense, that he treats their differences as insignificant, such as only school controversialists would trouble themselves with. From this arrogance and frivolity, which are the great diseases of modern historians, he is ... more free than any.[67]

Nor did he follow an Anglican *via media*, 'which gives those who walk in it a title to insult the passengers on either side of the road'. Froude had illuminated the political and religious context in which dogmatizers on both sides had become persecutors and had failed to see what the results of that persecution would be. He had exposed how many of the moral abuses denounced by zealous Reformers reappeared under another name, and could find justification on Protestant as well as Catholic grounds; and how easy it was for the Reformers to undermine the genuine respect for the sacred which constituted much of the English Catholic faith. Maurice singles out those Protestants at the time who began to realize this as the real heroes of Froude's narrative. In the evocation of their difficulties lay the challenge to modern Protestants to recognize and to fight against cant and self-righteous superiority.[68]

In Froude's *History* and in his essays, many of which were collected in his popular *Short Studies on Great Subjects*, there is a constant internal debate about religious and moral vitality and the conditions in which they thrive and decay. He returned repeatedly to Calvinism, which he discussed as a historically specific theology, but even more as an ideal type of religious sincerity rooted in obedience to conscience. It is the more telling in this respect that in a lecture on Calvinism delivered in St Andrews Froude should have drawn out this latter emphasis, and should have made positive analogies with Buddhism, Zoroastrianism, and Islam, and concluded by quoting Wordsworth: as ever, his critical technique lay in going against the grain of expectation.[69] It was through engagement with Calvinism that he worked through a reconciliation of free will and determinism which took account of the individual's consciousness of his moral autonomy—and of its operation in a world where a moral order prevails.[70] In the context of the Reformation Froude had a respect for the extremists—for an intense Calvinist like John Knox who could bring about change more decisively than the intellectuals whom he also admired, Erasmus or the sixteenth-century Scottish poet and statesman Maitland of Lethington. He recognized that the fanatics went too far, but in contextualizing

[67] F. D. Maurice, 'Froude's *History*, volumes V and VI', *Macmillan's Magazine*, 2 (1860), 276–81, at 280.   [68] Ibid., 280–1.

[69] Froude, 'Calvinism', *Short Studies*, ii. 1–59.

[70] Ibid., esp. 3–14; Froude, 'Spinoza', *Short Studies*, i. 339–400, at 363–4, 394–400.

their intolerance, he wheeled round to attack the lack of intensity and inconsistency of religious behaviour of mid-Victorian Protestants. He compared the Calvinist burning of witches in the seventeenth century with the modern-day inviting of spirit mediums to dinner to conjure up dead relations: 'The first method is but excess of indignation with evil; the second is complacent toying with it.'[71] The uncomfortable comparison, and the focus on Calvinism itself, which to most of Froude's readers was a by-word for religious narrowness, helped to sharpen Froude's critique of the religious flabbiness of the present. But he was not calling for a Calvinist revival; nor did he romanticize, as Carlyle did, the Calvinist activists whom he admired—Knox or Cromwell. Calvinism stood as the type of Protestantism, in its negative and positive senses. It stood for Froude's conviction that Protestantism had an inherent tendency to support the ideal of the nation as the sphere of moral action. It also stood for the betrayal of that potential for action by biblical literalism (to which Calvinists were especially prone), by forms of modern Calvinism which represented the will as passive, by divisive sectionalism, and by a more widespread separation of precept from practice (which religious liberalism could also unintentionally encourage):

Our duty to God is not now to fear Him, and to love Him, and to walk in His ways, but to hold certain opinions about Him, to maintain the truth of certain old histories about Him. We submit to be sermonized on Sundays, provided our sermons will not interfere with enlightened prudence and political economy on week days.[72]

These various sorts of Protestant history needed to be challenged if Britain was to be an effective Protestant nation.

Froude concurred with Maurice in the need to explore civil and ecclesiastical disputes as indicative of the inner spirit of a nation, and that politics could not be understood simply by reference to theories of representation.[73] Politics could not be divorced from religion. The nation was a Christian nation, or it was nothing. Hence the importance of a focus on the sixteenth and seventeenth centuries (and a corresponding sense that loss of civil and religious energy began to be felt over the eighteenth century).[74] In itself their periodization was a radical challenge to the Whig parliamentary narrative centred on 1688 as the beginning of a benign and pacific epoch. But how could this sense of Christian responsibility be carried through, from the level of the individual citizen in daily life to the workings of the state, and to the actions of the state in the wider world? Froude's recurrent emphases were the same at each level of the argument: that the nation was corrupted, as the individual was, by feeling justified in the primary pursuit of self-interest. This

---

[71] Idem, 'Calvinism', 53; *Table-Talk of Shirley*, 202, 204.

[72] Idem, 'Condition and Prospects of Protestantism', 146–51; idem, 'Revival of Romanism', 155–6; compare [F. W. Newman], 'The Future of the National Church', *Fraser's Magazine*, 67 (1863), 549–62, at 553.   [73] Maurice, *Kingdom of Christ*, ii. 293; Froude, 'Scientific Method', 565.

[74] Froude, *The Earl of Beaconsfield* (2nd edn., London, 1890), 77; Maurice, *Kingdom of Christ*, ii. 296–8 and 302 ff.

corruption was not only morally regrettable, but politically suicidal, undermining the effectiveness of English rule at home and abroad. Froude's histories of the English in Ireland and in the West Indies have been remembered as rabidly racist—and, in the case of Ireland, anti-Catholic. He certainly shared many of the racial assumptions of his day, although not necessarily in the same terms or to the same end. He could not believe in inherent racial or religious superiority. Although he thought that the Teutonic and Protestant character had the most potential, it was far from automatically working its effect. Most striking was his consistent attack on the faults of character of the English, and his emphasis on the role of history in reinforcing cultural antagonisms. As he replied to 'a young lady' who had written to admire his work: 'I have always said that if Ireland had been colonised by angels they would have been no better by this time than its present inhabitants, with England for a master'.[75] His novel *The Two Chiefs of Dunboy* has as its two main protagonists the converted evangelical John Goring—'an Englishman of the old Puritan school'[76]—and his opponent Morty Sullivan, the Catholic who in the end murdered him. Froude's sympathies are with Goring, who was a model employer, bringing in Presbyterian labourers to work the copper mines, yet making no distinction between Catholic and Protestant tenants.[77] But he ends by observing on the one hand that it was too late for a revival of what he saw as his Cromwellian virtues, and on the other that:

when the actions of men are measured in the eternal scale, and the sins of those who had undertaken to rule Ireland and had not ruled it are seen in the full blossom of their conse-quences, the guilt of Morty, the guilt of many another desperate patriot in that ill-fated country, may be found to bear most heavily on those English statesmen whose reckless negligence was the true cause of their crimes.[78]

Froude knew Ireland much better than many of his English contemporaries, and had profoundly ambivalent feelings towards it. He conformed to the contem-porary prejudice that Catholicism inhibited the development of industry, and yet castigated both eighteenth- and early nineteenth-century government for limiting Catholic economic opportunities. He enraged Irish nationalists by his references to the weaknesses of the Celtic character, whilst he also acknowledged the attractions of it. In tracing the occupation of Ireland from the Norman period, he emphasized the catastrophic effect of English vacillation—the vicious circle of coercion, followed by conciliation, compromise, concession, rebellion, and coercion.[79]

---

[75] Oxford, Bodleian Library, MS Eng.letters e.44, fo. 138ᵛ: Froude, letter to a young lady, n.d. (but after 1879, the date of publication of his *Caesar: A Sketch*, to which he refers). This letter is cited but misinterpreted by T. W. Thompson, *James Anthony Froude on Nation and Empire: A Study in Victorian Racialism* (New York, 1987), 143.

[76] Froude, *The Two Chiefs of Dunboy* (London, 1889), 59.   [77] Ibid., 61–2.

[78] Ibid., 455. This emphasis was recognized by J. M. Hone, 'The Imperialism of Froude', *New Statesman*, 11 (1918), 172–3.

[79] Froude, *The English in Ireland in the Eighteenth Century* (London, 1872), i. 13, 36, 52; *History of England*, ii. 133; cf. *Two Lectures on South Africa* (London, 1880); *Oceana*, 59.

Justice, in the true sense, has been the last expedient to which England has had recourse in her efforts to harmonize her relations with her wayward dependency . . . How to encourage industry and honest labour, how to prevent oppression and save the working peasant from being pillaged by violence or unjust law, she has rarely troubled herself to consider.[80]

By working peasants Froude meant not just hard-working Ulster Presbyterians, but also Catholic peasants in the south, who had been given no scope for improvement of their condition. Just as Froude published in *Fraser's* a series of articles on political economy by Ruskin (after the articles which became *Unto This Last* had been discontinued in the *Cornhill Magazine*), he also gave space to the Irish political economist Cliffe Leslie who criticized from an Irish perspective the principles of free-market economics dominant in England.[81] Froude's ideal of social economy was of a land-holding peasantry, and it was the systematic removal of the rights of the Irish peasant—'under chief's law and Norman law, under Scot and Saxon, under English agent and Irish middleman'—which had bred improvidence and 'smitten one of the most beautiful countries in the world with barrenness'.[82] Landlords had also been encouraged to treat the land simply as an economic proposition, not as a matter of duty. Thus land reform in Ireland was welcomed as the consolidation of best practice, and as an act of resistance to the unthinking support of the principles of political economy.[83] To Froude the famine was a disaster created by England, and it gave rise to an enduring political problem—the emigration of large numbers of Irish to America. Froude regretted that the English government had not helped those emigrants to settle in Australia or Canada, where they would have remained loyal British subjects rather than feeling legitimately resentful of Britain from the vantage-point of the United States.[84] His lectures in the United States in the 1870s on these themes designed to undercut American support for Irish nationalism aroused a huge furore, in part because of provocative passages such as what one American commentator called his 'dauntless way of dealing with the Drogheda Massacre'. But, as the same commentator indicated, another problem was that Froude was attacking one of the sacred cows of American ideology—the right of all communities to political liberty.[85] Froude denied an automatic correlation between a sense of national identity and political independence, and challenged what he saw as the irresponsible pursuit of liberal

---

[80] Froude, *English in Ireland*, i. 120–1.

[81] e.g. T. E. Cliffe Leslie, 'Political Economy and Emigration', *Fraser's Magazine*, 77 (1868), 611–24; cf. T. Boylan and T. Foley (eds.), *Irish Political Economy*, 3 vols. (London, 2003), i. 22.

[82] Froude, *English in Ireland*, i. 131; cf. Boylan and Foley, *Political Economy and Colonial Ireland* (London, 1992), 120, on critiques of absenteeism. Cf. Froude, *The English in the West Indies; or, The Bow of Ulysses* (London, 1888), 221, on the treatment of black labour.

[83] Froude, 'Ireland since the Union', *Short Studies*, ii. 515–62, at 553–4.

[84] [Froude], 'England and her Colonies', *Fraser's Magazine*, ns 1 (1870), 1–15; 'Ireland since the Union', 546.

[85] E. L. Godkin, 'Mr Froude as a Lecturer', *Reflections and Comments 1865–1895* (Westminster and New York, 1896), 42–3. Cf. Froude, 'Reciprocal Duties of State and Subject', *Short Studies*, ii. 308–47.

nostrums. As he argued in relation to centralization under King Alfred,[86] or the failings of the Roman Republic,[87] devolution of power could only work where there was common purpose and sympathy at the local level.[88] This could not simply be conjured up by the belated exercise of good will. It needed to develop and to be developed. This was what England had failed to achieve in Ireland.

It had also failed in its responsibilities in the West Indies, and here Froude made an explicit comparison with the situation in Ireland: that if a race had been forced into unwilling subjection and treated badly, it could not be expected to prove supportive of its exploiters when its fetters were removed.[89] He observed that the black inhabitants did not speak English, were not linked to the British by senti-ment or interest, and that the white settlers refused to intermarry with them.[90] He was careful to say that he was not adducing inherent 'negro' inferiority (as Carlyle and Kingsley had—making *their* analogy with the Irish in this sense), but the impact of centuries of experience.[91] In such circumstances it was a betrayal of responsibility to impose on blacks forms of self-government which Britain had only just arrived at. It was the more absurd to expect them to be grateful when such a scheme was only being proposed out of self-interest—because Britain had decided that there was no economic justification for retaining the colonial rela-tionship. A central role in the failure of Britain to take the duties of the colonial relationship seriously was played by the Church of England, which should have helped to provide a basis for trust to develop.[92] Froude here contrasted the role of the Catholic priests in Dominica.[93] For him the future of the West Indies depended on the spiritual condition of the English, which was fundamental to the determination of a sense of duty.[94]

It was in the development of Froude's idea of commonwealth that all these themes of moral responsibility, national character, and historical understanding came together. *Oceana* (1886), which sold 75,000 copies in the first six months after publication, was an extended and reflective culmination both of his long series of writings on Ireland and the colonies and also of his thoughts on political economy and Christian apologetic. Taking his title and starting point from the seventeenth-century utopia of James Harrington, Froude identified the issue of freedom as being the fundamental challenge in maintaining an empire: that a free people would always resent the mother country having rights and liberties from which they were excluded. In the British case, the Colonial Minister was responsible to the British Parliament, and the British Parliament represented

---

[86] [Froude], 'King Alfred', 83. This article was a review of a biography of Alfred by the Prussian historian Georg Reinhold Pauli. Froude criticizes Pauli for his apparent preference for despotic cen-tral authority, and emphasizes rather that centralization was a symptom of decline. However, 'local self-government is good when there is local virtue; else it is local tyranny, local corruption, local iniq-uity'. The character of a people could not simply be restored by decentralization if conditions were not right.   [87] Froude, *Caesar: A Sketch* (London, 1879), 1, 6–7, 15–19.
[88] Froude, *English in the West Indies*, 3.   [89] Ibid., 208.   [90] Ibid., 91.
[91] Ibid., 124; cf. 126–7 on anti-negro prejudice.   [92] Ibid., 232–3.   [93] Ibid., 146.
[94] Ibid., 233–4.

British constituencies.[95] Froude argued that if colonies were to rule themselves under a constitutional system, it was inappropriate to impose English views of what was expedient—indeed he suggested that for Australia and Canada the American constitutional model might have been thought more appropriate. He advocated a united empire, but not an imperial federation dictated from Britain: 'all advances towards a closer political connection must come from their side'.[96] The context of such a recommendation was a fundamental emphasis on reciprocity of influence between mother country and colonies (as between central and local government). To effect this, there should be an interchange of governmental or legal personnel (Froude had briefly toyed with the idea of having colonial representatives in the House of Lords). On the basis that rights to self-government could only operate alongside the power of self-defence, he also advocated a federal navy.[97] The empire was not only a fertile territory for emigration and the establishment of free-holding communities; amongst the white settlers (e.g. of Australia) there were uncorrupted moral energies which could exercise a productive influence on the home country. His imaginative conception echoed that of Maurice: that in England's relations with her colonies she must not merely establish an English kingdom, politically or religiously, because that would not be a blessing to the colonists, to the natives, or to the mother country. The relationship must be presented as embodying the vitality which English Christians possessed by virtue of their status as part of the universal catholic church.[98] Froude used various organic analogies, leading up to the image of the life of a nation, like that of a tree, as lying in its extremities, and of England being already in a pollard stage. Holding the empire together was then figured as a matter of national salvation for the present and the future. It was a spiritual and moral test of the highest importance: 'once more the old choice is again before us, whether we prefer immediate money advantage, supposing that to be within our reach, by letting the empire slide away, or else our spiritual salvation. We stand at the parting of the ways.'[99]

Having expressed scepticism about democracy (in the Aristotelian sense) as a constitutional form, he concluded with the apparent paradox that the empire could only be maintained by the will of the majority, on the basis that the British nation still added up to something more than a gathering of individual producers and consumers and taxpayers.[100] But its character and bonds of sentiment needed to be cultivated. Here he underlined his criticisms of the British party system as it was currently celebrated. In Froude's view this both encouraged inconsistency and

---

[95] Froude, *Oceana*, 2–4.   [96] Ibid., 194–5.   [97] Ibid., 182–3.

[98] Maurice, *Kingdom of Christ*, ii. 319, 326; cf. Coleridge's position in relation to Harrington, which is discussed by Myfanwy Lloyd, 'Coleridge', 274; Froude, *Oceana*, 334, 170.

[99] Froude, *Oceana*, 334; cf. *English in the West Indies*, 15.

[100] Froude, *Oceana*, 134, 336–8; cf. his criticism in 'Reciprocal Duties of State and Subject', 326–8.

political manipulation at home, and had then been unthinkingly transferred to the colonial context. However, to him government by parties needed to be interpreted as the product of a particular English historical development.

Now that the transition has been accomplished, and party lines no longer correspond to natural lines, it has become doubtful whether, even among ourselves, it works with perfect success. Every wise English politician is both Radical and Conservative. He has two eyes to see with and two hands to work with, and to condemn him to one or the other is to put one eye out and to tie one hand behind his back.[101]

To apply such a system to the colonies where it had no natural appropriateness was the product of an arrogant English conviction that what was good for her must be good for all mankind, and of a wilful lack of historical imagination. References to England's self-satisfaction with her parliamentary system were juxtaposed to criticisms of a High Anglican service in Melbourne, where the sermon had gloried in England's providential role of representing the spirit of Christ: 'It was good to tell us to exhibit Christ's spirit; but was flattering our vanity the best way to bring us to it?'[102] The predominant Protestant constitutional narrative and the providential narrative of Britain's imperial mission were seen clearly to be mutually reinforcing, and to require a concerted critical challenge. Otherwise the stern, serious character type (the ideal of Protestant virtue) which could build and sustain a moral community would be corrupted.

In the introduction to *Oceana* Froude commented that 'those among us who have disbelieved all along that a great nation can venture its whole fortunes safely on the power of underselling its neighbours in calicoes and iron-work no longer address a public opinion entirely cold'.[103] He was right in this observation that by the mid-1880s there was beginning to be a more favourable climate of opinion for the reception of his writings.[104] The range of critical debate about both the policy and ideological implications of classical political economy had widened; there was increasing anxiety about the implications of home rule in Ireland; the character and justification of Britain's imperial activity had become more complicated.

In these contexts, Froude's challenges were more resonant. In historiographical terms, the intensity of party spirit within the Anglican Church had diminished, or at least the fault-lines had shifted. The nature of the debate about the scientific status of history—in part generated by the challenge of positivism—had been interwoven in Oxford especially with religious divisions and disputes about university reform. In an environment dominated by the High Churchmen Stubbs and Freeman, the substance of Froude's historical preoccupations was called into question by attacks on his historical method and the style in which he wrote.

---

[101] Ibid., 107–8.   [102] Ibid., 98.   [103] Ibid., 12.
[104] See, e.g. J. M. Hone, 'The Imperialism of Froude', 172–3; D. McCartney, 'James Anthony Froude and Ireland: A Historiographical Controversy of the Nineteenth Century', *Historical Studies*, 8 (Dublin, 1971), 171–90, at 188–9.

Froude remained the freelance writer and critic; Stubbs and Freeman vaunted their status as Professors of Modern History in Oxford, as the Liberal Anglican Seeley did at Cambridge. Only belatedly—in 1892—was Froude brought into the academy and appointed to the Regius Professorship in Oxford, for the last two years of his life. Seeley, whose *Expansion of England* (1883) owed much to Froude's arguments of the 1870s about the colonies, failed to acknowledge the debt, perhaps because he was able to dismiss him too easily with Carlyle and Kingsley as 'literary' historians.[105] On the other hand, although both believed in the educational value of the study of history, Seeley's conception of Protestant history was utterly distinct from that of Froude. In the Arnoldian tradition, he had a corporate, Erastian, and latitudinarian view of the relationship between church and state: the modern nation-state was the overarching embodiment of the moral purpose of the people. This was all too easily assimilated to a constitutionalist and progressivist narrative. Froude's preoccupation was with the intellectual and moral challenges to the individual citizen in developing an active and combative Christian identity. As a result, he was much more sceptical about national institutions. He emphasized the need for historical understanding to act both as a reinforcement of the reality of the universal Christian Church, and, as such, as a critical weapon in day-to-day moral engagement in civil society.

In a critical account of Froude's historical method from a positivist point of view, Frederic Harrison none the less felt that Froude achieved his object of capturing the public, and had done so in part because of his very lack of impartiality. He had written with a religious, social, and political purpose, and as a result 'he is read, attacked, admired, condemned. But he is not put upon the shelf, and he will not be put upon the shelf.' 'The business of the historian is to arouse an interest in the past, and if Froude has not done this, it can be asserted of no writer in the present century.'[106] Froude's combined historical and religious purpose was to get across the paradox of partiality: 'The writers of books are Protestant or Catholic, religious or atheistic, despotic or Liberal; but nature is neither one nor the other, but all in turn. Nature is not a partisan, but out of her ample treasure-house she produces children in infinite variety, of which she is equally the mother, and disowns none of them.'[107] The greatest poetry had the capacity to give insights into a higher unity, but the virtue of history was that its method conformed more closely to the habit of mind required for understanding the rule of God in nature. The ordinary human mind could not attain to a total understanding of truth, but needed to feel the conviction that there was an ultimate truth to move towards, and which could be acted upon. This could be acquired through an imaginative engagement with the forms in which such conviction had been exercised in past

[105] D. Wormell, *Sir John Seeley and the Uses of History* (Cambridge, 1980), 164.

[106] F. Harrison, 'The Historical Method of J. A. Froude', *The Nineteenth Century*, 259 (1898), 374–5, 379.

[107] Froude, *Thomas Carlyle: A History of his Life in London*, 2 vols. (London, 1890 edn.), ii. 220.

and present, by exponents of very different ideological positions. This was the only preparation for effective citizenship. The study of history through primary texts was for Froude a metaphor for understanding God:

Colours might be thrown upon it by plausible or popular lecturers, as the sunlight may seem to stain a pavement by falling through stained glass; but the substantial thing would remain unaffected in its proper simplicity, until at last the coloured glazings would disappear altogether, or the many hues blend in our intellectual prism one into the other, and the pure white light of truth at length be our only guide.[108]

Such metaphors of light came frequently to Froude. He used them to convey his belief that just as one should not look at religion itself, but at surrounding things with the help of religion,[109] so history was to be conceived as a cast of mind, rather than as a series of substantive narratives which could all too readily buttress present complacency and blunt moral understanding. Although his work found a new resonance at the turn of the twentieth century, it was ironically the case that, as Froude himself had warned, such narratives, like religious dogmas, are very difficult to dislodge, and tend perforce to be reinforced by the historical retelling of them.

[108] Idem, 'Suggestions', 78.   [109] Idem, 'Calvinism', 42.

12

Roman Candles: Catholic Converts among Authors in Late-Victorian and Edwardian England

Philip Waller

It is a great piece of courage: his [Lionel Johnson's] 'first general confession' must have been extremely disagreeable.[1]

On 7 November [1892] he was received into the Church. Immediately after his baptism he went to see Father Peter, whose 'eyes shone at the netting of this one more soul'. He clasped Ford's hands, kissed him on the cheek, slapped him gently on the shoulder, and exclaimed: 'Now you're a b——y Papist'.[2]

Then in 1900 everybody got down off his stilts; henceforth nobody drank absinthe with his black coffee; nobody went mad; nobody committed suicide; nobody joined the Catholic Church; or if they did I have forgotten.[3]

Remembering his childhood—he was born in 1883—Gerald Tyrwhitt stated that ordinary patriotic Englishmen, who did not frequent cosmopolitan society, harboured firm phobias about 'the three Rs, Russians, Radicals and Roman Catholics'.[4] Here the Russians and Radicals may be regarded as given, and explanation focus on the Romans. In condensed form, this comprises the Reformation myth which held that, by emancipation from pope and priest, the English progressively secured civil liberty, in the home as at Westminster. From such freedoms evolved personal responsibility, enterprise and moral seriousness, constitutional stability and national greatness.[5] Countries that remained Catholic

---

[1] Ernest Dowson to Arthur Moore, 25 June 1891, in *The Letters of Ernest Dowson*, Desmond Flower and Henry Maas edn. (London, 1967), 205.

[2] Max Saunders, *Ford Madox Ford: A Dual Life, i. The World Before the War* (Oxford, 1996), 54.

[3] W. B. Yeats, *The Oxford Book of Modern Verse 1892–1935* (Oxford, 1936), p. xi.

[4] Lord Berners, *First Childhood* (London, 1934; Oxford, 1983), 53.

[5] Note the matter-of-fact assumption in Matthew Arnold, *God and the Bible* (London, 1875), preface, p. xxxiv: 'M. de Laveleye is struck, as any judicious Catholic may well be struck, with the

were condemned to political and ecclesiastical absolutism, invasion of family integrity, social stagnation, economic backwardness, and national decline. The theology should not be removed from this story. For those who cared about these things, and many did, Rome was not just wrong but wicked. The antichrist, Rome, corrupted mind, body, and soul.

These were strong reasons to get agitated about Rome. Hence, conversion to that faith was judged a madness, and converts called 'perverts'. 'The convert is lost to the family', observed Conan Doyle bleakly.[6] Gladstone's perturbations about the surrender of his sister Helen are well recorded; likewise, Gladstone's shunning of Mrs Anne Ramsden Bennett, his cousin and sometime assistant, when she went the same way.[7] Nor was the Gladstone family exceptional. By 1914, few of the country's well-known families had failed to produce a Catholic cuckoo in their nest. The most decided Protestants were not immune, and the contagion set in with the Victorian age itself. In 1841–2, R. W. Sibthorp, Fellow of Magdalen, was ordained priest by Nicholas Wiseman. This was the more sensational because his brother Colonel Sibthorp was the most choleric anti-Papist in Parliament. Indeed, when in his teens R.W. first betrayed a susceptibility to Romanism, having been spellbound by Bishop Milner in Wolverhampton, 'he was brought back, under police surveillance and chancery order, by his elder brother'.[8] Where a Sibthorp slipped, it occasions little surprise later to discover a son of the archbishop of Canterbury, Benson, faltering, and a son of the Evangelical Bishop of Manchester, Edmund ('Hard') Knox. Nor were relatives of freethinkers safe, even if they had to change their name and relocate to America following the dread deed. Such was the extremity of Sister Mary Joseph of the Poor Clares, Evansville, Indiana, a descendant of Cromwell and cousin to John Morley, who once scandalized men of all faiths by conscientiously spelling 'God' with a lower case 'g'. A son of Frederic Harrison, the positivists' pope, also converted.[9]

In 1910, W. Gordon Gorman unleashed *Converts to Rome: A Biographical List of the More Notable Converts to the Catholic Church in the United Kingdom During the Last Sixty Years*. Its publication celebrated the diamond jubilee of the Catholic

superior freedom, order, stability, and even religious earnestness, of the Protestant nations as compared with the Catholic.'

[6] Sir Arthur Conan Doyle, *Memories and Adventures* (London, 1924), 20.

[7] H. C. G. Matthew, *Gladstone 1809–1874* (Oxford, 1986), 78, 89, 161, 246, and *Gladstone 1875–1898* (Oxford, 1995), 76–7.

[8] *DNB*, lii. 190–1 for R.W. Sibthorp (1792–1879). In the late 1840s, the pressure told on him again, and he applied for reinstatement as an Anglican clergyman; but he resumed the office of Catholic priest in 1865. See also Brian Fothergill, *Nicholas Wiseman* (London, 1963), 115–19, 281.

[9] W. Gordon Gorman (ed.), *Converts to Rome: A Biographical List of the More Notable Converts to the Catholic Church in the United Kingdom during the Last Sixty Years* (London, 1910 edn.), 131, 196. Bernard Harrison (1871–1956), an artist, converted in 1895. According to his brother, their father was 'surprisingly sensible' and 'even spiritually interested'. Martha S. Vogeler, *Frederic Harrison: The Vocations of a Positivist* (Oxford, 1984), 215. George Gissing was private tutor to the Harrison boys in the 1880s. On meeting them again, he entered in his diary, 24 Aug. 1896, a typically dismal assessment: 'neither strikes me as particularly intelligent. Bernard very nervous and sensitive; think I can understand his having gone over to Rome.' Pierre Coustillas (ed.), *London and the Life of Literature in Late Victorian England: The Diary of George Gissing, Novelist* (Hassocks, 1978), 420.

hierarchy's restoration; it occupied over 300 pages and included over 5,000 entries. It is common for Catholic triumphalists to herald the imminent reconversion of England by saluting celebrity converts or co-religionists who made it big in whatever capacity.[10] Correspondingly, militant anti-Papists gloat over villainous figures to exemplify Rome's reprobate character, as David Mathew wearily observed about the England of 1910 when 'the Catholic layman upon whom public interest was most concentrated...was Dr. Crippen'.[11] Gorman was undeterred. This saintly Stakhanovite produced his first edition *Rome's Recruits* in 1878, followed by nine revised editions. The original contained under 2,000 names; the 1884 edition, with over 3,000, changed the title to *Converts to Rome* 'at the request of some of the most eminent gentlemen whose names appear on the lists', presumably to demilitarize the tone. Gladstone was sent the first list and studiously welcomed its publication: 'For good, according to some, or for evil, according to others, they form as a group an event of much interest and significance.' It was Gladstone who suggested classifying the data. He proposed five categories, revealing of his concerns: '1. The number of peers. 2. Of members of titled families. 3. Of clergy. 4. Of Oxford men. 5. Of ladies.'[12] Gorman adopted a taxonomic method of presentation for the 1884 edition; but its partiality upset Gladstone who sought to establish counter-lists of converts who had recanted, of Catholic apostates and of the many Catholics, including 'most of the powerful intellects', who rejected ultramontanism.[13] Thereafter, Gorman reverted to alphabetical order, while providing summary classificatory statistics. The result was to highlight converts who belonged to what Gorman called 'the *élite*' and Gladstone had styled 'persons of weight and authority'. With numbers of converts running (according to the 1899 edition) at 'nearly 10,000 per annum', this principle of selection lightened Gorman's task; it also strengthened his claim that Rome was winning England's quality.

Gorman's treacly devotion to rank, allied to a perfect humourlessness, makes his work one of the unintended comic masterpieces of world literature. His bag by 1910 contained 29 peers, 53 peeresses, 432 other members of the nobility, 42 baronets, 25 baronets' wives, 21 knights, and 34 knightly spouses. These were Gorman's prize trophies. He also saluted the professions. Occupying pride

[10] None came bigger than the professional wrestler Giant Haystacks: see Dennis Sewell, *Catholics: Britain's Largest Minority* (London, 2001), 4.

[11] David Mathew, *Catholicism in England 1535–1935: Portrait of a Minority. Its Culture and Tradition* (London, [1936] 1938), 247. Cf. the Liverpool Protestant leader George Wise who in 1909 broadcast his belief that Jack the Ripper was a Catholic and relied on the confessional to hide his terrible guilt: P J. Waller, *Democracy and Sectarianism: A Political and Social History of Liverpool, 1868–1939* (Liverpool, 1981), 240.

[12] [W G. Gorman], *'Rome's Recruits': A List of Protestants who have Become Catholics since the Tractarian Movement* (London, 1878). Gladstone's letter, written from Hawarden and dated 11 Oct. 1878, appears after the preface, which is unpaginated.

[13] Letter to the Revd R. R. Suffield, 5 Oct. 1884, in H. C. G. Matthew (ed.), *The Gladstone Diaries, with Cabinet Minutes and Prime-Ministerial Correspondence, vol. XI, July 1883–December 1886* (Oxford, 1990), 219.

of place were clerical converts, 670 altogether: 572 Anglican clergy, 23 Church of Scotland, 12 Church of Ireland, and 13 Nonconformist ministers, and 50 Anglican sisters. Impressive though this haul was, Compton Mackenzie, an Anglo-Catholic before his conversion, was certain that 'if Cardinal Vaughan had not pressed for that declaration about the invalidity of Anglican orders, many more celibate clergymen would have made their submission to Rome'.[14] For its part, the chief Anglo-Catholic journal *The Church Review* sustained animosities by deprecating the Roman Catholic drive in England as the Italian Mission. Nevertheless, clerical converts shepherded into the Roman fold 203 wives, 350 daughters, and 269 sons. The armed services also put up a good show: 306 army and 64 naval officers, who together outgunned 192 lawyers and 92 doctors. The converts' educational background further mattered for Gorman, to underline their intellectual as well as social distinction. He identified 586 Oxford graduates (Gladstone's Christ Church led with 84), 346 from Cambridge, and 146 from other universities. There were also 425 public school men, Gladstone's Eton leading with 93.

So, what did the converts do, following their life-transforming action? Some 612 became priests, 164 nuns. The feminine party was outnumbered here but, overall, women converts formed a majority, generally obedient wives and spinsterish daughters. This perhaps explains the advertisement, at the book's end, of a home for female inebriates, 'opened at the request of His Eminence the late Cardinal Vaughan... Terms: 10s. 6d. to 3 Guineas. Apply to Mother Superior.' Authorship engaged 470 converts, the largest category after the priesthood.[15] Their output covered most genres, with a propensity for devotional works and apology, but also fiction and poetry. Again, like the nobility, it is marked how some of the country's best-known writers, where they did not themselves convert, had a relation who did. This was true of the poets Sir Edwin Arnold and Matthew Arnold[16]

---

[14] Compton Mackenzie, *My Life and Times: Octave Two 1891–1900* (London, 1963), 264. Mackenzie regarded Vaughan with awe when he first encountered him in 1900, taking tea in the unlikely setting of the Bournemouth Hydro: 'There has been no Archbishop of Westminster of comparable appearance. I see that superb figure seemingly carved from ivory as he sat there in the Hydro lounge where all the old maiden ladies goggled at him over their knitting, their chaste Protestantism thrilled to the marrow'. Idem, *Octave Three 1900–1907* (London, 1964), 16.

[15] The 1884 edn. accounted 36 names under Literature; the 1899 edn. classified 162 under a heading of Authors, Poets and Journalists. Gorman's opaque and shifting taxonomy raises questions about his statistics, which must be reckoned speculative. In the preface to the 1881 edn. of *Rome's Recruits* he recorded 'the generous assistance which he has received from the Catholic hierarchy [and] from the priesthood in general'; but in 1899 he certified that his work was unofficial and not under instruction from the Catholic hierarchy, remarking that he had sent 500 questionnaires to clergy and received only 30 replies. His chief sources were the press, converts themselves, or their families, adding, 'I am withholding hundreds of names of relatives of clergymen and of others who wish me to do so for family reasons' (preface, p. ix). His zeal inclined him to overegg the pudding; for instance, giving Gladstone a sister Lucy he never had, likewise the poet Edward FitzGerald a son he never had (Gorman, *Converts*, 104, 118).

[16] Matthew Arnold's brother Tom fathered the best-selling novelist Mrs Humphry Ward whose examinations of the crisis of faith, notably in *Robert Elsmere* (1888) and also in *The History of David*

(a brother each), the verse-playwright Sir Henry Taylor (daughter), Sir Walter Scott (niece), Rider Haggard (sister), Philip Gibbs (wife), George Grossmith (son), F. T. Palgrave (brother), 'Barry Cornwall' (three daughters),[17] Charles Reade (niece), Olive Schreiner (mother), and, most delicious of all, a daughter of Newman's principal antagonist, Charles Kingsley. She, Mary St Leger Harrison ('Lucas Malet'), herself became a famous novelist;[18] the writing gene also coursed through Dickens's granddaughter, Mary Angela Dickens, who converted in 1907.

The contribution to literature made by Catholic converts was extensive and diverse. They included Maurice Baring, whose *Landmarks in Russian Literature* (1910) complemented Constance Garnett's translations in introducing Britain's reading public to classic Russian authors. A junior of the banking family, Baring deferred his conversion until 1909, partly owing to familial objections; but his thoughts had been moving in that direction since his teens when he was 'a very militant "freethinker"—in full reaction against long years of having been dreadfully bored in church'.[19] Equally, it is fair to observe that some very queer literary fish were netted by the Church in the decades before the Great War. The Poet Laureate Alfred Austin can be discounted, not from literary demerit—admirers of his lyric poetry included Thomas Hardy[20]—but because he was a lapsed Catholic, though he sustained a curiosity about theology.[21] For the same reason,

Grieve (1892) and *Helbeck of Bannisdale* (1898), much excited Mr Gladstone. See John Sutherland, *Mrs Humphry Ward: Eminent Victorian, Pre-eminent Edwardian* (Oxford, 1990).

[17] One daughter, Adelaide Procter (1825–64), who converted in 1849, was a popular Victorian poet and hymn-writer. See Elizabeth Lee's notice in *DNB*, xlvi. 416.

[18] See Georgina Battiscombe's notice in *DNB 1931–1940*, 405–6. Battiscombe dates the conversion 1902, Gorman 1904. Harrison (1852–1931) separated from her husband (d. 1897), who had been rector of Clovelly; and marital discord was a persistent theme of her psychological fiction. To the critic William Archer in November 1902, she exclaimed: 'Puritanism is so stupidly afraid of the lessons of life as a whole, and so resolute never to learn them, that it insists on our wearing, or pretending to wear, blinkers, so as to see nothing that is inconsistent with its preconceived moral scheme. Think of the weakness, the unphilosophic quality of Puritanism, compared with Catholicism, as a basis or background for art! And then the eventual outcome of Puritanism is of necessity rationalism; and there we have the real enemy!' The similarity is marked with the author 'John Oliver Hobbes' (Pearl Craigie, 1867–1906), who converted in 1892 during the breakdown of her marriage. She also emphasized the link between the Catholic culture of confessional and a new type of introspective story-writing, saying to Archer in Mar. 1901: 'Has it ever struck you that the Church of Rome, which alone among the Churches of Western Europe enjoins and enforces continual examinations of conscience, is the real creator of modern analytical fiction?' See William Archer, *Real Conversations* (London, 1904), 61, 220; and John Morgan Richards, *The Life of John Oliver Hobbes* (London, 1911), esp. 43–5, 364–5, for her divided self between rationalism and pietism, and for Curzon's memorial address which depicted how 'in a time of trouble she found refuge in the Roman Catholic Faith . . . and a solace in its authority'.

[19] Letter, Sept. 1913, in Mackenzie, *Life and Times: Octave Four*, 201. See also Emma Letley, *Maurice Baring: A Citizen of Europe* (London, 1991), 42, 70–1.

[20] Hardy to Austin, 14 June 1891, fulsomely reporting his appreciation of *Lyrical Poems* (1891). *The Collected Letters of Thomas Hardy, i. 1840–1892*, ed. Richard Little Purdy and Michael Millgate, (Oxford, 1978), 238.

[21] Austin reported the Vatican Council, 1869–70, for *The Standard*. His trenchant criticisms of the doctrine of papal infallibility and of Cardinal Manning's ultramontanism were reprinted in *The Autobiography of Alfred Austin Poet Laureate 1835–1910* (London, 1911), i. 218–325. Grant Duff,

that he too was not a convert, we can disregard the noisiest Catholic literary figure of his day, Hilaire Belloc, whose promotion of pre-Reformation religion, splenetic anti-Semitism, and simplistic 'distributionism' created many a ripple. Belloc was 'a French clerical in English politics', living in the wrong country in the wrong century, thought A. G. Gardiner. He divided the nation into two classes, 'the British people and Mr Belloc'.[22] This ignored Belloc's exaggerated Englishness, expressed in a readiness to regale any company with his repertoire of Sussex drinking songs, though he appeared 'very woebegone' during Easter stints of teetotalism.[23] Likewise, we can technically default the other half of that zoological freak, the Chesterbelloc, because G. K. Chesterton's conversion came in 1922, which falls beyond the period focus taken here. Nevertheless, Chesterton's popular metaphysics in his Edwardian heyday, *Orthodoxy* (1908) especially, anticipate that conversion by its rejection of the agnosticism, rationalism, naturalism, and pessimism that was variously fashionable among the Victorian intelligentsia, and the theosophy, spiritualism, and occult exploration that seized the *fin de siècle* generation.

Not that many of the best-known Catholic converts among authors in the 1880–1914 period can be claimed orthodox in belief or behaviour. Max Beerbohm parodied them via Enoch Soames, his composite 1890s writer who is a Catholic Diabolist. Soames's *Negations* contains labyrinthine aphorisms of resplendent vacuousness: 'Life is web, and therein nor warp nor woof is, but web only. It is for this I am Catholick in church and in thought, yet do let swift Mood weave there what the shuttle of Mood wills.' The Preston-born Soames's speech is spattered with French phrases, and his characteristic tipple is absinthe—'la sorcière glauque'; yet he pretends to 'owe nothing to France' and, patriotically, is more decadent than the decadents Baudelaire—'a *bourgeois malgré lui*'—and Verlaine—'an *épicier malgré lui*'. When his long-anticipated slender collection of poems *Fungoids* is published, it sells, despite an approbation from the *Preston Telegraph*, only three copies, to the satisfaction of Soames who is an artist 'not a tradesman'. Soames's bedraggled state is sham—he enjoys an annuity of £300 from an aunt—and he is clandestinely hungry for posterity's praises; so, in a classic

---

whom Austin visited in 1900, 'thought he talked best when the subject was the Catholic Church, to which he belonged originally but left in his early manhood, finding it impossible to hold her dogmas though retaining the strongest regard for her'. Sir Mountstuart E. Grant Duff, *Notes from a Diary, 1896 to January 23, 1901* (London, 1905), ii. 241 (27 Aug. 1900). In 1908 Austin told Wilfrid Blunt that 'he has leanings once more towards it [Catholicism] now he is getting old'. Austin was then aged 73. Blunt, also born a Catholic, enjoyed with Austin 'long talks and discussions on theology, philosophy, and the Catholic Church. He is an acute and ready reasoner, and is well read in theology and science. It is strange that his poetry should be such poor stuff, and stranger still that he should imagine it immortal.' Wilfrid Scawen Blunt, *My Diaries* (London, 1921; New York, 1980), i. 212, 369 (5 Jan. 1896, 15 July 1900), and ii. 213 (11 Sept. 1908).

[22] A. G. Gardiner, *The Pillars of Society* (London, [1913] 1916), 312–20.

[23] Lucy Masterman, *C. F. G. Masterman* (London, [1939] 1968), 94; and Blunt, *Diaries*, ii. 243, 384 (11 Apr. 1909, 31 Mar. 1912).

scene set in a French restaurant in Soho, he sells his soul to the Devil in order to be transported a century hence, expecting to savour in the British Museum countless editions of his work and scholarly commentaries on it. Alas, he discovers that the sole evidence for his existence as a writer is Max's essay about him.[24]

Actual bohemians and decadents tended to specialize in death-bed conversions, suggesting a repentance of sorts, a need for fire-insurance or a last laugh. Personifying the older generation was George Sala who was a broken-down bore when he converted in 1895;[25] personifying the new was Aubrey Beardsley who perished at the age of 25 in 1898. The 'Fra Angelico of Satanism',[26] Beardsley was dying of consumption when coaxed to convert by John Gray, translator of Verlaine and Mallarmé. A homosexual, inevitably nicknamed Dorian, Gray too was a Catholic convert. Soon, he would become a priest, telling the world about Beardsley's spiritual rebirth and repudiation of pornographic art, giant phalluses and all.[27] Yeats, with mock impartiality, mused: 'I think that his [Beardsley's] conversion to Catholicism was sincere . . . ; and yet I am perhaps mistaken, perhaps it was merely his recognition that historical Christianity had dwindled to a box of toys, and that it might be amusing to empty the whole box on to the counterpane'.[28] Still, Beardsley's mother and sister also converted. All were sedulously listed by Gorman, as was the literary editor of the *Yellow Book* (1894–7), Henry Harland, who regularly reinvented himself. Oscar Wilde, Gorman omitted, possibly from doubt about the conversion than from other scruples. Wilde was comatose when administered the last sacraments, the priest having been summoned by Robbie Ross, himself a convert. Wilde often teased Ross about religion and, to Reggie Turner, another homosexual and wit, jested that 'the Catholic Church is for saints and sinners alone. For respectable people the Anglican Church will do.' Ross, by contrast, took his new faith seriously. He was indignant when the agent of Wilde's ruin Lord Alfred Douglas converted in 1911.[29]

Poetic licence previously brought Ernest Dowson and Lionel Johnson into the Church, although alcohol and chastity (Johnson) and alcohol and promiscuity (Dowson) held equal attractions. 'I understand that absinthe makes the tart grow fonder', reflected Dowson agreeably.[30] H. A. L. Fisher, at Winchester with

[24] Max Beerbohm, *Seven Men* (London, 1919), 3–48. One obvious model for Enoch Soames is Ernest Dowson.

[25] On Sala (1828–95), see Gorman, *Converts*, 242; John Sutherland, *The Longman Companion to Victorian Fiction* (London, 1988), 551–2; and Sidney Lee's notice in *DNB*, i. 175–8.

[26] Roger Fry, in *The Athenaeum*, (5 Nov. 1904), repr. in Roger Fry, *Vision and Design* (London, 1920; Oxford, 1981), 164.

[27] Gray's edn. of *The Last Letters of Aubrey Beardsley* (London, 1904) contained the famous letter to the publisher Leonard Smithers, postmarked 7 Mar. 1898, imploring him 'to destroy *all* copies of Lysistrata and bad drawings. . . . By all that is holy all obscene drawings', with a postscript, 'In my death agony'. G. A. Cevasco, *John Gray* (Boston, 1982), 94–101, for the context.

[28] W. B. Yeats, *Autobiographies* (London, [1955] 1980), 333–4.

[29] Maureen Borland, *Wilde's Devoted Friend: A Life of Robert Ross, 1869–1918* (Oxford, 1990), 36, 155–6; and, for Wilde's 'conversion', Blunt, *Diaries*, ii. 121–2, and Richard Ellmann, *Oscar Wilde* (London, 1987), 548.

[30] To Arthur Moore, *c.* 15 Feb. 1889, in Flower and Maas, *Dowson's Letters*, 35.

Johnson, caught a whiff of his oddity: 'A certain aura surrounded him for he was reported to be a Buddhist, to have read all the books in the school library, and to drink eau de cologne for amusement'.[31] Johnson and Dowson met at Oxford; afterwards, a 'Catholicity in every sense, including Zola and Newman', drew them closer.[32] The Zola side of Dowson would strike Francis Gribble on encountering him, staggering in the street, when his language was distinctly unpoetic;[33] and Dowson would translate *La Terre* for Lutetian Society connoisseurs. But Dowson as well as Johnson was read in Catholic apologetics and Walter Pater's aesthetics. Pater's father had lapsed from Catholicism and, though Pater himself 'never had any serious leaning towards Rome... there can be little question that the heritage of his ancestors, in their obstinate adhesion to Catholicism, had much to do with his haunting sense of the value of the sensuous emblem, the pomp of colour and melody, in the offices of religion'.[34] That this was part of Catholicism's appeal to Dowson seems clear from his decrying the vulgarity, philistinism, sentimentality, and drabness of Protestant England, not to mention rants against its middle-classes' pruriency. A repressed homosexual, Johnson was drawn more by 'asceticism, reverence for Catholic tradition, sympathy with Catholic mysticism, and a love of the niceties, rather than the splendours, of ritual—catholic Puritanism, as he called it'.[35] Both men attended services at Notre Dame de France, off Leicester Square, where for Dowson the delectation included seeing 'my special Enfant' process in a veil.[36] Here was the precipitating cause of Dowson's conversion, a fetish for under-age girls. His chief muse was a Soho Polish restaurateur's daughter, Adelaide Foltinowicz ('Missie'). She was 11 in 1889 when Dowson first glimpsed her. In 1891, anxious to declare himself and tormented that he would be rejected by her, her parents, and his friends, he embraced Rome. During these years that Dowson became absorbed in religion his iconoclasm was not suppressed. His ideal was 'to be a sort of combination of Mill and Newman with a little dash of Voltaire'.[37] To Arthur Moore, his co-author of *A Comedy of Masks* (1893), he proposed 'to give up writing, enter the Order of St. Benedict and devote my life to editing the Fathers. Will you join me? We might collaborate, with advantage, on a commentary on St. Alphonse Liguori! And we should look so charming in the Benedictine habit: not to mention the liqueur!'[38] After 1893, when Adelaide

[31] H. A. L. Fisher, *An Unfinished Autobiography* (Oxford, 1940), 37.
[32] Dowson to Charles Sayle, c. 25 Nov. 1890, in Flower and Maas, *Dowson's Letters*, 177.
[33] Francis Gribble, *Seen in Passing* (London, 1929), 221–2.
[34] (Sir) Edmund Gosse, 'Walter Pater: A Portrait' (Sept 1894), *Selected Essays (First Series)* (London, 1928), 32–3. Pater accompanied Johnson to the requiem mass for Newman at the Brompton Oratory 1890. Johnson wrote an obituary essay about Pater, *Fortnightly Review* (Sept. 1894); and his last poem was on Pater, sent to *The Academy*, (Sept. 1902), the week before he tumbled from a bar stool in the Green Dragon, Fleet St, cracked his skull, and died.
[35] Campbell Dodgson's notice in *DNB, Suppl., 1901–1911*, ii. 375.
[36] To Arthur Moore, 19 Oct. 1890, in Flower and Maas, *Dowson's Letters*, 172–3.
[37] To Victor Plarr, 5 Mar. 1891, in Flower and Maas, *Dowson's Letters*, 187.
[38] To Arthur Moore, ?4 Dec. 1890, in Flower and Maas, *Dowson's Letters*, 178.

refused his proposal of marriage, Dowson's Catholicism waned. What survived was a piteous ritual. The dishevelled Dowson 'flittered from bar to bar...and when the drink was served he would sometimes furtively take a little gold cross from his waistcoat pocket and dip it in the glass before he drank'.[39] Where Johnson would find inspiration in Celtic legend, Dowson now did in French symbolism, to produce like Verlaine 'mere sound verse, with scarcely the shadow of a sense in it'.[40] Each contributed to the first and second books of the Rhymers' Club (1892–4) as well as published individual volumes; but their print run was tiny and their work unappreciated outside a coterie. Following Johnson's death, aged 35 in 1902, the politeness was deployed that he was 'a writer's writer'.[41] Dowson's demise had occurred in 1900 at the age of 32, whereupon *The Athenaeum* coolly remarked that 'after having been ignored or misvalued during his life, he is in some danger of being overestimated simply because he is dead'.[42]

Gorman's entries for this pair of songbirds delight by their exiguity, suggesting for all the world two pillars of the establishment.

Dowson, Ernest Christopher, B.A., Queen's College, Oxford; the poet and author. (1890).

Johnson, Lionel Pigott, (1867–1902), of Winchester College; B.A., New College, Oxford; poet and critic; youngest son of Captain Johnson. (1892).[43]

Gorman's discretion then achieved genius level with:

Rolfe, Frederick William, sometime Master at Grantham Grammar School, Lincolnshire; journalist. (1887).[44]

Here was the fantasist 'Baron Corvo', Catholic convert indeed, though also an adherent of astrology. It was as 'Fr. Rolfe' that he published *Hadrian the Seventh* (1904). The 'Fr'. implied Father as much as Frederick. Twice rejected for ordination, Rolfe compensated by imagining himself pope. Notwithstanding fierce competition from other literary converts, Rolfe must be ranked indisputable champion of paranoid peculiarity. Resembling a weasel with a monk's tonsure, he wore across his chest a huge crucifix that burnished his skin, and on one finger a ring with a spur to gouge the eyes of Jesuits who, he believed, were plotting to assassinate him. Equally fiercely, he venerated the Catholic faith and abominated most Catholic institutions, clergy, and communicants. A parasite on a grand scale, Rolfe made

---

[39] Account of Dowson by Guy Thorne [C. A. E. Ranger Gull] in *T.P.'s Weekly* (July 1913), quoted in Flower and Maas, *Dowson's Letters*, 379–80.

[40] To Victor Plarr, 20 Mar. 1891, in Flower and Maas, *Dowson's Letters*, 189.

[41] *T.P.'s Weekly* (19 Dec. 1902), 169.

[42] *The Athenaeum* (12 April 1900), quoted in Desmond Flower (ed.), *The Poetical Works of Ernest Christopher Dowson* (London, [1934] 1950), 19–20. Whereas Johnson made it into *Who's Who* (in 1901), Dowson never did. Johnson was also commemorated in the *DNB Supplement* (1912); Dowson remained outcast until *DNB Missing Persons* (Oxford, 1993).

[43] Gorman, *Converts*, 89, 152. The parenthetical date after each entry was the approximate year of conversion, which for both Johnson and Dowson was actually 1891. Gorman's dubbing Dowson with a B A was supererogatory: he left Oxford without a degree.   [44] Gorman, *Converts*, 236.

the rounds of Catholic networks, always biting the hand that fed him. This included the Fabian Society, whose few Catholic converts such as Hubert Bland and his wife Edith Nesbit were also irregular in belief and habit. Bland concocted a phoney Old English Catholic CV for himself and was a serial seducer of servants and friends. His miscellaneous mistresses and offspring were superadded to the household. Nesbit, author of *The Treasure Seekers* (1899) and *The Railway Children* (1906), meanwhile maintained a lifelong credulity about ghosts and endeavoured to prove by logarithms that Bacon wrote Shakespeare. During the Great War, she upbraided the pope's neutrality; still, when she remarried in 1917 it was according to Catholic rites.[45]

Observable in the Bland ménage was 'a little group of priests and Catholic propagandists of whom Monseigneur Benson was the chief: an oratory had been specially fitted up for him in a tiny room leading off the bedroom he usually occupied'.[46] This was Hugh Benson, the late archbishop's son, who, after Eton and Trinity, Cambridge, drifted into the Anglican ministry in 1895, became an Anglican monk in 1898, and onward to Rome in 1903. Benson thereafter revelled in papal power—Pius X made him Private Chamberlain—liked the idea of the Inquisition, and, most of all, loved dressing up. He adored his biretta and purple-buttoned gown. Actual parish work he found tiresome but he became a cult figure among Cambridge undergraduates by his pulpit performances and among the public by historical romances which included dollops of Catholic polemic and mysticism. For the fan, a publisher helpfully launched *Maxims from the Writings of Mgr. Benson* in 1914, comprising snippets from his opera, one for each day of the year.[47]

Benson and Rolfe was a partnership predestined by celestial dating agency. *Hadrian the Seventh* flopped—it failed to sell six hundred copies, after which Rolfe would have been entitled to royalties—but it enraptured Benson, who gushed: 'I have read it three times, and each time the impression has grown stronger of the deep faith of it, its essential cleanness and its brilliance.'[48] Another

---

[45] Julia Briggs, *A Woman of Passion: The Life of E. Nesbit 1858–1924* (London, 1987; Oxford, 1989), 230–1, 278–84, 355–6, 376, 394, which notes, however, that Nesbit's funeral service was Anglican.

[46] Doris Langley Moore, *E. Nesbit: A Biography* (New York, 1966), 182.

[47] The publisher was R. & T. Washbourne of Paternoster Row, London, with outlets in Manchester, Birmingham, and Glasgow. *Maxims from the Writings of Mgr. Benson* was ecumenically edited by 'The Compiler of "Thoughts From Augustine Birrell", etc.'; it contained a frontispiece photograph of Benson wearing his biretta and gown. Most extracts were breathtakingly banal: this (for 24 May) from *The Sentimentalists* (1906)—'Catholicism is the sum of all religions, and the Queen of them'. Different, for the autobiographical curiosity it invites, was the extract chosen to enliven 3 Nov., from *The Conventionalists* (1908): 'If a mistaken marriage can be purgatory, mistaken celibacy is hell'. Benson's chief testimony was *Confessions of a Convert* (1913), being a revised version of articles first published in the American Catholic magazine *Ave Maria* in 1906–7. It amplified a favourite theme of his, the distinction between faith and emotion. True faith, Catholicism, being based on authority, accorded with reason; Anglicanism, being neither authoritative nor reasonable, appealed therefore to 'largely self-centred' emotions (*Confessions*, 82–3).

[48] Monsignor R. Hugh Benson to Frederick Rolfe, Feb. 1905, in A. J. A. Symons, *The Quest for Corvo* (London, [1934] 1940), 144.

billet-doux informed Rolfe that *Hadrian* was one of only three books from which Benson wanted never to be parted, although its pages dealing with the socialists' sordid deeds were so upsetting he thought of glueing them together.[49] Benson's proposal that they co-author a 'really startling novel' about St Thomas à Becket unhappily foundered, as these overtures roused Rolfe's mania about the priest-hood conspiring to entrap him.[50] An exhausted Rolfe quit life in 1913, sated by homosexual debauchery in Venice.[51] He was aged 53, ten years older than Benson who died in 1914, having grown overfond of whisky—'not for drinky but for drunky'.[52]

Rolfe and Benson did not monopolize the bizarrerie among Rome's literary recruits. Whether the heroic pornographer Sir Richard Burton qualifies for admission too is moot, because he was probably dead when a priest administered extreme unction in Trieste in 1890. Lady Burton, a zealous Catholic, drawn also to spiritualism, stagemanaged the deathbed conversion, then capped it by deposit-ing the corpse in Mortlake's Catholic cemetery in a mausoleum modelled like an Arab tent with a nine-point star on top and a crucifix at the door. Burton had derided most Christian doctrine, morality, and missionary work. If he had any belief system it was closer to Islam than anything.[53] Defiantly, widow Burton jus-tified his 'conversion' to the press, telling also how she burnt his translation of the *Scented Garden* to achieve rest for his soul. This goaded Ernest Dowson to poetic denunciation of her betrayal of Burton and worship of 'sterile Propriety'.[54] At her death in 1896, her will aimed to ban publication of Burton's writings without the 'express sanction of the secretary of the National Vigilance Society'.[55]

The conversion of Ford Hermann Hueffer (Ford Madox Ford) in 1892 also bore the hallmarks of farce. His mother encouraged it as a form of legacy-hunting, to impress their rich German Catholic relations. Fordie thought faith on the whole better than indifference, certainly for children.[56] For himself, Catholicism

---

[49] Those who have forgotten their *Hadrian* may need reminding that it contains denunciations of the 'brainless monster of socialism'; ch. 11 details a socialist conspiracy to discredit the English pope by exploiting his former landlady's crush on him; and the story climaxes with his assassination by a socialist.

[50] Miriam J. Benkovitz, *Frederick Rolfe: Baron Corvo* (New York, 1977), 188. Benson did produce *The Holy Blissful Martyr Saint Thomas of Canterbury* (London, 1910). It was a popular historical account, not a novel; and it made no acknowledgement of Rolfe. The preface highlighted the dilemma of 'God against Caesar'.

[51] Symons and Benkovitz differ about the final disintegration as revealed in Rolfe's notorious Venice letters written to Charles Masson Fox in 1909–10, Symons thinking these betray real sexual excesses, Benkovitz questioning whether they were not pornographic fantasies designed to excite both correspondents and to get money out of their recipient.

[52] David Newsome, *On the Edge of Paradise: A. C. Benson, the Diarist* (London, 1980), 297.

[53] Byron Farwell, *Burton: A Biography of Sir Richard Burton* (London, 1963).

[54] Unpublished poem, 'Against My Lady Burton', 10 Nov. 1891, in Flower, *Dowson*, 185, 287.

[55] *DNB Supplement*, i. 356.

[56] Ford Madox Ford, *Return to Yesterday* (London, [1931] 1999), 224–6, where he also admits to being 'impenitently' superstitious. Following a nervous breakdown in 1904, Ford insisted on a con-vent education for his daughters, then (in 1906) their conversion to Rome, to the regret of his wife, Elsie who remained Protestant. Thomas C. Moser, *The Life in the Fiction of Ford Madox Ford* (Princeton, 1980), 64, 302–3.

was as useful as his 'sentimental' Toryism[57] to annoy radical and rationalist friends, though it became a serious nuisance by 1909 when he itched to dump his wife and marry his mistress, Violet Hunt. Mostly, 'he was scarcely Catholic in either feeling or conduct'.[58] Ford's conversion, therefore, appears superficial. Nevertheless, the traditionalism he associated with Catholicism appealed to his colourful historical imagination, as it did to other authors. Saki drew a bead on them: 'The fashion just now is a Roman Catholic frame of mind with an Agnostic conscience: you get the medieval picturesqueness of the one with the modern conveniences of the other.'[59]

If earnestness is required to redress this picture, then Gerard Manley Hopkins's passage into the Jesuit order must be noticed; but he died largely unknown as an author in 1889, because his poetry, which struggled to express the conflicts between his (homosexual) sensuality and spirituality, was mostly withheld from publication by his literary executor Robert Bridges until 1918.[60] Bridges too had been an adolescent Puseyite, yet grew latitudinarian with age and detested Catholicism as an intellectual imprisonment. Different again among Hopkins's circle of poet correspondents was Coventry Patmore. His best-known work *The Angel in the House* (1854–63) predated his conversion in 1864. Public dismay about this threatened the poem's popularity, and Patmore brooded whether *The Angel* was in 'harmony with Catholic truth and feeling'.[61] Eventually, in 1886, he authorized Cassell's cheap editions, whereupon its sales surged past the quarter-million in the next decade. There was nothing shallow about Patmore's faith, which was systematically explored through study of Aquinas and other saints. Patmore's medievalism and mysticism were not of the camp kind; nor did his theology disregard the physical sciences, which were integrated into his writings to an extent unrivalled except by Francis Thompson in poetry and Coleridge in prose.[62] The culmination of his meditations was *The Rod, the Root and the Flower*, published in 1895, the penultimate year of his life, and which Herbert Read reckoned equal to Pascal's *Pensées*.[63] Patmore's vision reconciled earthly and heavenly love in nuptial passion; a previous treatise on this, *Sponsa Dei*, he had destroyed in 1887 after Hopkins (having consulted Bridges) deplored its eroticism and advised against publishing so 'mystical an interpretation of the significance of physical love in religion'.[64]

---

[57] 'In a mild way I should call myself a sentimental Tory and a Roman Catholic'. Ford Madox Hueffer, *Ancient Lights and Certain New Reflections, Being the Memories of a Young Man* (London, 1911), 292.

[58] Arthur Mizener, *The Saddest Story: A Biography of Ford Madox Ford* (London, 1971; New York, 1985), 19–21. Saunders, *Ford*, i. 54, accepts this verdict, while arguing that Ford broadly subscribed to the doctrine of redemption.

[59] Saki, *Reginald* (London, 1904), in Hector Hugh Munro, *The Complete Stories of Saki* (London, 1993), 10.

[60] See Robert Bernard Martin, *Gerard Manley Hopkins: A Very Private Life* (London, 1991).

[61] Quoted in Derek Patmore, *The Life and Times of Coventry Patmore* (London, 1949), 156.

[62] A point made by Frederick Page in his study of Patmore in 1933, cited in Patmore, *Patmore*, 42.

[63] Patmore, *Patmore*, 4.

[64] Quoted ibid., 199; see also Edward Thompson, *Robert Bridges 1844–1930* (Oxford, 1944), 95. Peter Gay, *The Bourgeois Experience: Victoria to Freud, ii. The Tender Passion* (Oxford, [1986] 1987), 291–7, writes of Patmore's 'erotic Christianity' and 'libidinal view of religion'.

Patmore's masterfulness is uncongenial to liberal tastes. He regarded the inequality of the sexes as preordained; therefore, the female clamour for the franchise and other freedoms he interpreted as their subliminal demonstration against modern man's inadequate manliness. At home, he ruled like a Pasha over his cowed womenfolk, according to visitors' grim accounts; but they were not the only species he exerted himself to subdue or seemed careless about offending. He was a prolific columnist under Frederick Greenwood's editorial direction of the *Pall Mall Gazette* (1865–80), *St James's Gazette* (1880–8), and *Anti-Jacobin* (1891–6), the last Patmore preferring to call *The Twopenny Damn*.[65] From this podium he denounced the diverse ways in which England was going to the dogs. 1867 he designated the Year of the Great Crime when 'false English nobles and their Jew', aka the Derby–Disraeli ministry, surrendered the vote to urban working-class householders; and he pledged £1,000, prepared ultimately to meet 'force by force', to counter Gladstone's 'treason' on further enlarging the franchise in 1884.[66] When Basil Champneys[67] told Patmore that Sargent's portrait (1894) suggested a Southern planter about to lash his slaves, its subject purred approval: 'Is that not what I have been doing all my life?'[68]

Patmore was an authoritarian who despised most authorities, ecclesiastical and political. Cardinal Manning he could not stand. The second Mrs Patmore had been bidding to become the second Mrs Manning until Manning's conversion; and Patmore resented his continuing influence over her. He also loathed Manning on account of his supposed socialism, preaching of teetotalism, and anti-tobacco crusade (Patmore was a furious smoker). If these opinions are tainted by their *ad hominem* character, then Patmore was equally idiosyncratic about other aspects of his new religion, scorning use of the rosary and having no stomach for Mariolatry. For him, women, while naturally subordinate, were as fulfilled as men through the sanctified intercourse of marriage; hence, his alarm when a daughter took the veil. Buttressed by his intricate theological system, Patmore gloried in the role of aboriginal Tory, living out the idea that Catholicism in its English manifestation was 'the religion of gentlemen'. During his country house period at Heron's Ghyll, he concealed at the rear of his bookshelves a subscriber's set of classic erotica. Simultaneously, he banned *Punch* from the home as too salacious for his daughters.[69]

---

[65] Lionel Johnson also was a contributor to the *Anti-Jacobin*.

[66] Patmore, *Patmore*, 155, 214; J. W. Robertson Scott, *The Story of the Pall Mall Gazette, of its First Editor Frederick Greenwood and of its Founder George Murray Smith* (Oxford, 1950; New York, 1971), 260; George Earle Buckle, *The Life of Benjamin Disraeli, Earl of Beaconsfield* (London, 1916), iv. 559.

[67] On Champneys (1842–1935), the architect best known for the Rylands Library, Manchester, see *DNB 1931–1940*, 168–9. He designed the St Mary Star of the Sea church at Hastings by which Patmore commemorated the death of his second wife in 1880. The third and widowed Mrs Patmore commissioned Champneys to write the official biography (it appeared in 2 vols. in 1900), in this countermanding Patmore's own choice, the literary critic Edmund Gosse. Champneys was Catholic, Gosse agnostic. In 1905, Gosse published his own study, which did much to bring Patmore's work to a new generation.

[68] James Lomax and Richard Ormond, *John Singer Sargent and the Edwardian Age* (London, 1979), 58.   [69] Patmore, *Patmore*, 119, 148.

It seems clear that Patmore dwelt in an unusual state of pretty permanent priapic excitement. In his last years, the uxorious Patmore was seized by a 'passionate heat' for Alice Meynell, no doubt attracted more by her beatitude than beauty. Capturing poets' hearts was an occupational hazard for Alice. George Meredith also had a senescent crush on her; but doyen of the doe-eyed devotees was Francis Thompson, who saw in her a Marian muse to rival the stimulation he derived from drink, drugs, and Lancashire County Cricket. Alice's goodness was legendary. Her weekly confections ('Wares of Autolycus') in the *Pall Mall Gazette* were so immaculate that Max Beerbohm considered her a 'substitute for the English sabbath'.[70] She and husband Wilfrid operated the most influential Catholic literary network in late Victorian and Edwardian England.

Born Alice Thompson in 1847, Mrs Meynell was always susceptible to poetic-cum-religious emotion. As a child she

lived upon Wordsworth... When I was about twelve I fell in love with Tennyson, and cared for nothing else until, at fifteen, I discovered first Keats and then Shelley. With Keats I celebrated a kind of wedding. The influence of Shelley upon me belongs rather to my spiritual than my mental history. I thought the whole world was changed for me thenceforth. It was by no sudden counter-revolution, but slowly and gradually that I returned to the hard old common path of submission and self-discipline which soon brought me to the gates of the Catholic Church.[71]

Her mother had already converted when, after 1868, first Alice, then her sister[72] and father, followed. In her final years—she died in 1922—she wrote to her daughter Olivia, to mark the significance of that step:

I don't at all allow that we have 'liberty' to think what we happen to choose as to right and wrong. I saw, when I was very young, that a guide in morals was even more necessary than a guide in faith. It was for this I joined the Church. Other Christian societies may legislate, but the Church *administers* legislation. Thus she is practically indispensable. I may say that I hold the administration of morals to be of such vital importance that for its sake I accepted, and now accept, dogma in matters of faith—to the last letter. To make my preachment clearer: Right and Wrong (morals) are the most important, or the only important, things men know or can know. Everything depends on them. Christian morality is infinitely the greatest of moralities. This we know by our own sense and intellect, without other guidance. The Church administers that morality, as no other sect does or can do, by

---

[70] Quoted in Viola Meynell, *Alice Meynell* (London, [1929] 1947), 127–8.

[71] Quoted ibid., 42.

[72] This sister, Elizabeth, was an acclaimed painter of military scenes, such as *The Roll Call* (1874). In 1877, she married Major (later Major-General Sir) William Butler. He had Irish Catholic gentry origins; Manning conducted the ceremony. See John Springall, ' "Up Guards and at Them!" British Imperialism and Popular Art, 1880–1914', in John M. MacKenzie (ed.), *Imperialism and Popular Culture* (Manchester, 1986), 62–8. Butler was cited as co-respondent in the Lady Colin Campbell divorce case in 1886. He refused to testify and the case was dismissed, but not before the jury recorded its opinion that, 'in not coming forward in the interests of justice, General Butler acted in a manner unworthy of an English officer and gentleman'. G. H. Fleming, *Victorian 'Sex Goddess' Lady Colin Campbell* (London, 1989; Oxford, 1990), 240.

means of moral theology. The world is far from living up to that ideal, but it is the only ideal worth living up to . . . As to the 'divine' teachings of the Genesis allegory, I cannot withdraw that word. I have to remember that all the morality worth having—the morality that led on to Christianity—had its origin in that parable.[73]

Alice's religious and literary lives were never compartmentalized. The Jesuit priest who inducted her into the Church insisted that she continue to write as a duty, while he, having fallen in love with her, disappeared abroad. The poem 'Renouncement', encapsulating her distress, who published in *Preludes* (1875), which now united her to Wilfrid Meynell who was smitten by the sonnet, 'My Heart shall be thy Garden'. He too was a convert, in 1870 after a Quaker upbringing.[74] In London, he joined St Etheldreda's mission, run by Father William Lockhart, a relation of Sir Walter Scott's biographer.[75] Wilfrid's own literary talents shone through the *Lamp: An Illustrated Catholic Journal of General Literature*, which Lockhart edited and Wilfrid progressively took over. By this, he met Manning, whom he admired for his championship of the poor, a virtue he perceived in another hero of his, Disraeli.[76] It was Manning's unflinching Catholicism in the teeth of Protestant prejudice that most enthused Wilfrid; as he put it, Manning 'fluttered a red robe in the face of John Bull'. He was disgusted by Purcell's *Life of Cardinal Manning* (1896), 'an act of biographical brigandage' which instigated Lytton Strachey to perpetrate an even greater travesty in *Eminent Victorians* (1918).[77] In 1880, when at odds with *The Tablet* (then controlled by Vaughan, his successor as primate), Manning had bought the *Weekly Register* to promote his own views; soon, he made his disciple Wilfrid Meynell proprietor-editor, a function he performed for eighteen years.[78]

---

[73] Quoted in Meynell, *Alice Meynell*, 330. The sub-text of this letter, with its rejection of Bolshevism, concerns the divisions brought to the Meynell family by the political activities of the youngest son, Francis, manager of the socialist *Herald* since 1913, a conscientious objector in the war, and a proclaimed communist following the Russian Revolution. On him, see *DNB 1971–1980*, 567–9.

[74] Viola Meynell, *Francis Thompson and Wilfrid Meynell* (London, 1952), 130, on the persistence of Quaker attributes in the Catholic Meynell.

[75] On Lockhart (1819–92) who converted in 1843, see *Oxford DNB*. Gorman, *Converts*, 175 erroneously styles him John Gibson Lockhart's son.

[76] Wilfrid Meynell published *An Unconventional Biography* of Disraeli, in 2 vols. in 1903. He was not otherwise an orthodox Conservative; for instance, sympathetic to Home Rule and Henry George's scheme of Land Reform. See Meynell, *Thompson and Meynell*, 147; and Dermot Quinn, 'Manning, Chesterton and Social Catholicism', *Chesterton Review*, 18/4 (Nov. 1992), 501–23, for the ideological context. Meynell dedicated his *Disraeli* to Wilfrid Blunt who, however, jibbed at being thought a 'Dizzy-worshipper', pointing out that though he delighted in Disraeli's wit and audacity, he was 'a hundred miles' away from him politically and aesthetically. Blunt, *Diaries*, ii. 71–2 (30 Sept. 1903).

[77] Quoted in Meynell, *Thompson and Meynell*, 65–6. Purcell's wife Jane was a convert. Gorman (*Converts*, 226) characteristically tells us that she was the 'youngest daughter of Sir Francis Desanges, the last Baronet'. Wilfrid Meynell became secretary, with the duke of Norfolk, of the Manning Memorial Committee.

[78] Manning and Vaughan disagreed over the role of the Jesuits and diplomatic relations with the Vatican. Tension existed too between the convert (Manning) and the old English Catholic (Vaughan). On this, and the Meynells' relations with Vaughan, see J. G. Snead-Cox, *The Life of Cardinal Vaughan* (London, 1910), i. 260–7, 459–68, 479–82.

The threepenny *Weekly Register*, subtitled *A Catholic Family Newspaper*, allowed little space for the Meynells' literary interests;[79] but, having use of its presses, in 1883 they started their own monthly *Merry England*. There was a Ruskinian ring about the title, but no sense of retreat to a pseudo-medieval past:

Frankly accepting the conditions of Modern England, we would have it a Merry England too...In religion, as in literature, in art and in sociology, we shall seek to fulfil Dr. Johnson's precept and 'clear our minds of cant'—the cant of commerce and the cant of capital, the cant even of chivalry and of labour, the cant of mediaevalism no less than the cant of modern days.[80]

Merry England was an intended medium for Catholic authors. Here it is necessary to remember how Catholic society was 'a thing rather apart in those days'.[81] At one gathering, hosted by Lady Herbert,[82] the then unmarried Alice met the poet Aubrey de Vere. A convert in 1851 , he was instrumental in leading Patmore to Rome in 1864 . De Vere passed Alice's poems among friends, including Patmore who signalled encouragement; later, Patmore, whose own odes Alice came to think peerless, nominated her for the laureateship on Tennyson's death, booming her as 'a woman of genius'.[83] *Merry England* aimed to supply similar patronage for other Catholic writers. As well as de Vere, Patmore, W. S. Blunt, and established names, it published some of the earliest work of Lionel Johnson, Hilaire Belloc, and his sister (Marie Belloc Lowndes); and its place in literary history became assured in 1888 when it included Francis Thompson's first published poem, 'The Passion of Mary'. The Meynells further provided sanctuary at their home and paid for what medical assistance Thompson would accept to relieve his opium addiction. The principal architects of Thompson's renown, Alice gave him

[79] On occasions, it excited wider interest, as when it disclosed that Newman's *Dream of Gerontius*, with the passages about death scored, was found among General Gordon's possessions at Khartoum. It was a classic Victorian episode, a Christian soldier's martyrdom in the cause of empire, acting out the tragic and pathetic in epic poetry.

[80] Inaugural issue quoted in Meynell, *Thompson and Meynell*, 10. Alice Meynell gave her evaluation of Ruskin's teachings in *John Ruskin* (1900). Ruskin had admired her poetry, nominating 'San Lorenzo's Mother' and the last sections of 'To a Daisy' and 'Letter from a Girl to Her Own Old Age' as 'the finest things I have yet seen or felt in modern verse'. This encomium was used as an advertising puff for Mrs Meynell's *Collected Poems*. She, like Manning and Aubrey de Vere (whom Ruskin in 1862 thought 'one of the very, very, *very* few religious men living'), had always been hopeful that Ruskin too would convert. *The Brantwood Diary of John Ruskin*, ed. Helen Gill Viljoen (New Haven, 1971), 595, 612.   [81] Meynell, *Alice Meynell*, 49.

[82] Gorman, *Converts*, 136, grandly identifies her thus: 'Herbert of Lea, The Lady, Elizabeth, daughter of General Charles Ashe A'Court, C.B.; wife of the Right Hon. Sidney Herbert, (1810–1861), first Baron Herbert of Lea, Secretary of State for War, and a great Army Reformer; mother of the fourteenth Earl of Pembroke; authoress. (1866).' In the 1890s, she took to wintering in Rome: Mathew, *Catholicism*, 234.

[83] Patmore, *Patmore*, 215. Alice Meynell's selection of Patmore's work *The Poetry of Pathos and Delight* appeared shortly before he died in 1896. It was *The Unknown Eros* (1877) rather than *The Angel in the House* by which she justified her contention that Patmore would rank among the greatest poets. 'Coventry Patmore', in Alice Meynell, *The Second Person Singular and Other Essays* (Oxford, 1921), 94–109. Max Beerbohm observed how 'the shuttlecock of praise...flashed incessantly' between the two, in an article in *To-Morrow*, quoted in Meynell, *Alice Meynell*, 128.

inspiration and Wilfrid was his literary executor.[84] *The Life of Francis Thompson* (1913) by their son Everard was a family business.

Among the leading hostesses of the age was Lady Jeune (afterwards St Helier), her receptions being prized for the social mixing between the distinguished from all walks of public life, that is, persons distinguished for ability rather than (or as well as) pedigree.[85] The Meynells could not compete in high life or free spending; but for upcoming authors, 47 Palace Court, Bayswater, was the place to be. Sunday was their At Home day which, as Charles Lewis Hind, the *Academy*'s editor explained, meant 'arriving at about half-past three, staying till midnight, and meeting in the course of the year most of the literary folk worth knowing'. In the 1890s, this included Aubrey Beardsley, Richard Le Gallienne, Lionel Johnson, H. W. Nevinson, Stephen Phillips, Herbert Trench, Katharine Tynan, William Watson, Richard Whiteing, Oscar Wilde, and W. B. Yeats.[86] Their liberality persisted through the Edwardian period. In 1909 , Sheila Kaye-Smith attended a Meynells' At Home, following her second novel *Starbrace*. Then aged 22, a doctor's daughter raised in severe Evangelical style, she had been advised by her literary agent to broaden her outlook. Now meeting other authors for the first time, she was awestruck: 'The atmosphere—artistic, cultured, casual—was entirely different from that of my own home, where Sunday supper meant the family sitting down in state to eat cold beef and prunes and talk about the evening's sermon.'[87] In 1929, together with her Anglican parson husband, Kaye-Smith would convert to Rome; but there was a republic of letters about the Meynells' At Homes which reached beyond the Catholic literary circles of which they were recognized leaders. Arthur Symons acknowledged this in 1900, telling his future wife how he was 'forcing' himself to attend because Alice's invitation carried 'some significance in one who for so long professed a pious horror of me and my works. One reason for going is that she has great influence journalistically.' Symons reckoned *Preludes* contained 'some of the most truly poetical poetry any woman has ever written'.[88]

Everything must pass. As the Meynells aged their attitudes provoked irreverence. In 1914, the Vorticists included the entire Meynell clan—all seven children as

---

[84] Brigid M. Boardman (ed.), *The Poems of Francis Thompson: A New Edition* (Boston, 2001), introduction, criticizes Wilfrid Meynell's editorial interventions in his transcriptions of Thompson's poetry and control of Thompson's papers in order to solidify his reputation as (in Alice Meynell's words) 'the poet of Catholic orthodoxy'.

[85] Lady St Helier, *Memories of Fifty Years* (London, 1909), 186–7; Ralph Nevill (ed.), *The Reminiscences of Lady Dorothy Nevill* (London, 1906; Nelson edn., n.d. [1910]), 340; and Sir Francis Burnand, *Records and Reminiscences, Personal and General* (London, 1904), ii. 285—'At "the Jeunes" you met everybody who was anybody and rarely anybody who only thought himself somebody. Not to have the *entrée* to "the Jeunes" was to argue yourself unknown.'

[86] Meynell, *Alice Meynell*, 144–5; Mrs Belloc Lowndes, *The Merry Wives of Westminster* (London, 1946), 10–11.

[87] Donald Brook, *Writers' Gallery* (London, [1944] 1970), 78. Kaye-Smith (1887–1956) is best known for her rustic novels which, like Mary Webb's and D. H. Lawrence's, were parodied in Stella Gibbons, *Cold Comfort Farm* (1932).

[88] Karl Beckson, *Arthur Symons* (Oxford, 1987), 48, 207–8.

well as Alice and Wilfrid—in their hit-list of reputations to be 'blasted'. And when Lady Cynthia Asquith visited Greatham, the Sussex estate which the Meynells acquired in 1911, she was appalled to be shown their

Holy of Holies... a room full of trophies of the elite of literature—a real little museum, calculated—if anything could—to reduce to an absurdity, Keats, Shelley, etc. A blighting, stifling cult. And, as for the family, I have never believed in the existence of such stilted preciosity. Quite incredibly like caricatures in a book—most interesting as specimens, but making one feel acutely, physically uncomfortable. Meynell himself, with a silky, reverent unctuousness, displayed literary treasure after treasure, and we had the utmost difficulty in escaping.[89]

Yet the reason Lady Cynthia visited Greatham was to see the D. H. Lawrences who were sponging off the Meynells' novelist daughter Viola.[90] Lawrence was then completing *The Rainbow*, Viola typing it up, doubtless to the Meynells' horror had they known its contents, for it was banned on publication. Still, their support of new authors, non-Catholic as well as Catholic, thus continued, however indirectly. Alice, moreover, was far from the submissive creature her 'cry baby voice' suggested.[91] She lauded Patmore as a poet, but she repudiated his reactionary politics. As a teenager, she remonstrated against limitations which custom imposed on women and, as an essayist, writing on 'Women and Books', she sought 'a kind of literary and yet feminine justice' for past women writers and the wives of literary men belittled by previous biographers and critics. Her children were taught to believe in equal rights for both sexes; indeed, Everard and Francis became militants. Alice remained constitutionalist in the suffrage campaign, but smartly refuted the distorted view of women perpetrated by Sir Almroth Wright in his 'shameful letter' to *The Times* in 1912 and amplified in the *Unexpurgated Case against Woman Suffrage* (1913).[92] Alice's clear-mindedness existed because, not in spite, of her religion. In this she resembled G. K. Chesterton, to whom— the suffrage question notwithstanding—she became close: 'If I had been a man and fat, I would have been Chesterton'.[93] They shared a delight in Dr Johnson, a virtual certificate of earthbound Englishness.[94] Even Alice's devotional writing,

[89] Lady Cynthia Asquith, *Diaries: 1915–1918* (London, [1968] 1987), 38 (5 June 1915).

[90] Janet Byrne, *A Genius for Living: The Life of Frieda Lawrence* (London, 1995), 173, 177–8. It was while staying at Greatham that Frieda Lawrence learnt of her father's death. In 1935, she only remembered having seen Alice Meynell 'as a vision in the distance, being led by Wilfred [sic] Meynell across the lawn like Beatrice being led by Dante'. Rosie Jackson, *Frieda Lawrence, including Not I, But the Wind, and Other autobiographical writings* (London, 1994), 143.

[91] The disparaging description by W. S. Blunt's daughter Judith (later Lady Lytton, then Wentworth). Blunt himself referred to Alice's 'tearful voice'; Judith went further, comparing Alice's physique to 'a ghostly bundle of dusty cobwebs tied to a stick'. Quoted in Elizabeth Longford, *A Pilgrimage of Passion: The Life of Wilfrid Scawen Blunt* (London, [1979] 1982), 226, 337.

[92] Meynell, *Alice Meynell*, 37–8, 265–7, 292–3. On Wright's intervention, Brian Harrison, *Separate Spheres: The Opposition to Women's Suffrage in Britain* (London, 1978), 63, 67–8, 193–4, and Michael Dunnill, *The Plato of Praed Street: The Life and Times of Almroth Wright* (London, 2000), ch. 7.

[93] Quoted in Maisie Ward, *Return to Chesterton* (London, 1952), 262.

[94] Alice Meynell produced *Johnson, Extracts*, with an introduction by Chesterton, in 1911.

Mary, the Mother of Jesus (1912), represented her feminism, while bearing stylistic similarities to Chesterton. This Catholic faith conferred on her an immunity against radical religious chic, such as the theosophy of Annie Besant, which impressed so many ostentatious intellectuals.[95] The permanent virtues—the certainty of God and Christ, the pleasures of nature, the delights of domesticity and children, the dedication to country—were her abiding themes. Few writers who converted to Rome had anything like her fundamental soundness or influence.

The Meynells' centrality in late Victorian and Edwardian Catholic literary life is unmistakable; yet there were other networks that historians should note, though it is less easy to read their significance. *Punch* was for twenty-six years (1880–1906) edited by Frank Burnand, a convert in 1858. It was Burnand who answered the complaint that *Punch* was not so funny as it used to be: 'It never was.' His lieutenants were the à Beckett brothers: Gilbert ('Gil') and Arthur, converts in 1869 and 1874 respectively. Their partnership places a peculiar gloss on the intelligence that *Punch* was the favourite reading in Victorian vicarages.[96] A. A. Milne, a later *Punch* regular, considered that the magazine under Burnand 'grew less intolerant of opinions with which it disagreed'.[97] By broadening its appeal, *Punch* approached the status of National Institution. Burnand was knighted in 1902, the first *Punch* writer to be gonged. His authorship was not confined to *Punch* or to spin-off series such as *Happy Thoughts* (1866), which went through twenty editions. His speciality was light comedy, that often ignored flip side of Victorian earnestness. He had discomposed Manning by confessing, after leaving Cambridge, that he had 'a vocation' for the theatre, not the priesthood. To mid-Victorian Protestants these alternatives doubtless ranked equal in degradation. Manning patiently spelt out the impropriety of thinking the stage like the priesthood; as grotesque as to suppose that shoe-mending was a vocation. To which a 'nervously inspired' Burnand replied: 'Well-er-a-a cobbler has *a great deal to do with the sole*'.[98] This little exchange supplies the clue to Burnand's facility which generated over 120 burlesques and smashed box-office records. He was master of the excruciating pun. It won for him a permanent place in Victorian affections. *Black Eye'd Susan* (1866) initially played for 800 nights at the Royalty,

[95] See her letter, Mar. 1912, after she and daughter Viola attended a lecture by Mrs Besant: Meynell, *Alice Meynell*, 275. Cf. R. H. Benson, *The Necromancers* (1909): the protagonist, a Catholic convert, gets drawn deeper into spiritualist and occult experimentation following the death of his fiancée. The story climaxes by his being saved from demonic possession by the power of prayer, symbolically on Easter Day.
[96] The illustrator Dicky Doyle—Arthur Conan Doyle's uncle—quit *Punch* in 1850 because of its anti-Popery. At the editorial vacancy caused by Tom Taylor's death in 1880, George Du Maurier, who eyed the post, reckoned a Catholic succession as impossible as that of an agnostic; yet Burnand was picked unanimously, and Arthur à Beckett shortlisted. Leonée Ormond, *George Du Maurier* (London, 1969), 166, 361–2.
[97] A. A. Milne's notice of Burnand (1836–1917) in *DNB 1912–1921*, 78. After stepping down from *Punch*, Burnand became first editor of *The Catholic Who's Who and Year-Book* (1908).
[98] Burnand, *Records*, i. 348. Burnand's italics. He had been preparing for Anglican orders at Cuddesdon before his conversion.

and was regularly revived; and *The Colonel* (1881), which packed the Prince's for a year and a half on first run, 'has never been off the stage for any very considerable spell', wrote a gratified Burnand in 1904.[99] *The Colonel* was commanded for performance at Balmoral before the Queen and Court on 4 October 1881, the first production there since Prince Albert's death twenty years before. A genial spoof of the aesthetic cult, it complemented George Du Maurier's cartoons and anticipated Gilbert's and Sullivan's *Patience* (1882). For another token of Burnand's popularity the historian can summon Frank Harris, decidedly no Catholic pietist. Harris was in the audience for *Blue Beard* (1883). Naturally, for one whose credo was that he had 'no enemy save corsets', Harris was much taken by the Gaiety girls' 'costumes that reveal every charm'; but, 'incredibly trivial' though the play was, Harris delighted in such 'a rain of the most terrible puns and verbal acrobatics ever heard on any stage—an unforgettable evening which made me put Burnand down as one of the men I must get to know'. Harris did get to know Burnand, and so embellish his tribute to 'handsome little Frank... [who] was as kindly pleasant as he was good-looking and witty', by recounting a dinner party discussion about the implication of Lord Euston in the Cleveland Street homosexual brothel scandal in 1889–90. When one purity-minded guest deplored the press for reporting indecent cases, Burnand upheld its duty to publish 'news'; moreover, he appeared blasé about Euston, for whom he invented a witty alibi.[100] Incidentally, Burnand's own circumstances offended convention. His wife, with whom he had seven children, died in 1870; four years later, he married his deceased wife's sister, and fathered another six children.

The interlocking of comic magazines and popular theatre was close in the mid- and late-Victorian period. Before switching to *Punch*, Burnand wrote for its penny rival *Fun* (*Punch* sold for threepence). Its founding editor (in 1861) was H. J. Byron, who was a theatre manager and Burnand's idol as burlesque writer.[101] Another *Fun* contributor was W. S. Gilbert, with whom Gil à Beckett co-authored *The Happy Land*.[102] Produced at the Court theatre in 1873, it ribbed Liberal principles of popular government, featuring three politicians, 'Mr. G' (Gladstone the Prime Minister), 'Mr. L' (Robert Lowe, Chancellor of the Exchequer), and 'Mr. A' (A. S. Ayrton, MP for Tower Hamlets and First Commissioner of Works).

[99] Burnand, *Records*, ii. 164; *Who's Who* (London, 1905), 229.

[100] Frank Harris, *My Life and Loves* (London, [1964] 1970), 245, 368–70. Euston, the duke of Grafton's heir, brought (and won) an action for criminal libel against Ernest Parke, editor of the *North London Press*, for publicizing his involvement. His own alibi was that he had gone to 19 Cleveland St to view *poses plastiques*—the Victorians' striptease—and indignantly left when he discovered it was a male brothel. Euston, formerly married to an actress, had convincing heterosexual form, and the suspicion was that his case was a blind to screen from exposure the homosexual Lord Arthur ('Podge') Somerset who fled abroad. See Colin Simpson, Lewis Chester, and David Leitch, *The Cleveland Street Affair* (London, 1976), ch. 8, and H. Montgomery Hyde, *The Cleveland Street Scandal* (London, 1976), ch. 3, for the trial and press reaction.

[101] Burnand, *Records*, i. 377; and *DNB*, viii. 155, for Byron (1834–84).

[102] *DNB, Supplement*, i. 7–8 for Gilbert Arthur à Beckett (1837–91); Gorman, *Converts*, 1.

Actors were dressed to resemble the subjects until the Lord Chamberlain insisted on disguise. Generally, *Fun*'s writers prioritized the pun over politics: hence their advice, upon Disraeli's 'Sanitas sanitatum' slogan, that the Conservatives be renamed 'Lava-Tories'.[103] Gil à Beckett also collaborated with Herman Merivale, another productive playwright who edited the *Annual Register* throughout the 1870s and was a friend of Lord Salisbury.[104] Having suffered bouts of insanity, Merivale converted to Catholicism a few years before his death in 1906. His first stage success was an adaptation in 1875 of Dickens's *A Tale of Two Cities* (1859), called *All For Her*, which he wrote with J. Palgrave Simpson. Simpson's output was also large, over sixty pieces, and varied, operettas as well as plays; and he served as secretary of the Dramatic Authors' Society. He converted to Catholicism in 1842.[105] The wheel comes full circle when it is observed that Simpson assisted Arthur à Beckett adapt for the stage his novel *Fallen Among Thieves* (1876). Arthur, one-time private secretary to the duke of Norfolk, genially and erratically acted as *Punch*'s editor during Burnand's absences. He also qualified for the Bar and, though he never practised, was Master of the Revels at Gray's Inn for the Queen's Jubilee in 1887. But this hardly begins to take the measure of Arthur's position in public life. His wife, Susannah, a collateral descendant of Lord Lyndhurst, three times Lord Chancellor, was a leading woman journalist, while Arthur served on the Management Committee of the Authors' Society and was president of the Institute of Journalists. He edited *The Sunday Times*, 1891–5, and the *Naval and Military Magazine*, 1896 (*Who's Who* registered his recreation: 'amateur soldiering').[106] Brother Gil meanwhile achieved immortality by inspiring Tenniel's 'Dropping the Pilot', which cartooned the Kaiser's discharge of Bismarck in 1890.[107] This image immediately lodged in the Victorian mind and has remained with historians ever since.

This web of Catholic writers connecting the stage and comic papers is incomplete without Clement Scott. As the theatre critic who in 1891 denounced Ibsen's *Ghosts* as 'an open drain', 'a dirty act done publicly', and Ibsen himself as 'a muck-ferreting dog', Scott would appear a stranger to humour or proportion.[108] Yet he also contributed to *Fun* and *Punch*, albeit sentimental verses mostly; and it is vital to spotlight him lest the impression grows that these penmen were all light-hearted types, whimsical about religion as about most else. Burnand, for instance, blushed at childhood memories of his father, whose party pieces included launching into a mock monotone of a priest chanting mass, in Latinate gobbledegook, when

[103] *Fun*, (19 Jan. 1881), quoted by Jane W. Stedman in her essay on *Fun* in Alvin Sullivan (ed.), *British Literary Magazines: The Victorian and Edwardian Age, 1837–1913* (Westport, Conn., 1984), 137.

[104] *DNB 1901–12*, ii. 616–17 for Merivale (1839–1906); Sutherland, *Companion*, 430; Gorman, *Converts*, 191.

[105] *DNB*, lii. 274–5 for Simpson (1807–87); Sutherland, *Companion*, 578–9; Gorman, *Converts*, 251.

[106] *DNB 1901–11*, i. 4–5 for Arthur William à Beckett (1844–1909); *Who's Who 1905*, 9–10; Sutherland, *Companion*, 5–6.   [107] Burnand, *Records*, ii. 230 for the attribution.

[108] George Rowell, *The Victorian Theatre 1792–1914* (2nd edn. Cambridge, 1978), 129.

their visitors were Sir Martin Archer Shee, president of the Royal Academy, and his family. The Shees, Irish Catholics, laughed, apparently uproariously rather than politely; but Burnand was troubled that his father had made fun of 'the most sacred rite of their religion'. For himself, he affirmed:

never at any period . . . have I deliberately sneered at or tried to find a subject for ridicule in anyone's professed religion, no matter whether the persons themselves either did not act up to their profession or laughed at the tenets they ought to have reverenced. Seeing the absurd side of most things, I have never been able to scoff at what appear to many as ridiculous details which are mere accidents of any form of religion, although for Tartuffes, Stigginses, Achillis, and suchlike imposters, who make a hypocritical pretence of religion as a cloak for their immoralities, the severest ridicule, the most scathing satire, and punishment the most condign is thoroughly well deserved . . . [Still], I have no sort of inclination to laugh at a Brahmin, a Mohammedan, a Hindoo, a Protestant of any denomination, on account of his creed. And, as for the Jew, directly I arrived at years of discretion I perceived very clearly that Fagin was not a representative Hebrew, and was glad to see that Dickens had made *amende honorable* by drawing that charming picture of Mr. Riah, the long-suffering servant of 'Fascination Fledgeby', the vulgar, scheming, mean, money-lending Christian.[109]

This was as clear a statement of the Victorian tolerationist ideal as historians would wish to find; and Burnand was tested to live up to it. He was exercised by George Du Maurier's brooding 'on the problems of existence—free will and determinism, the whence and why and whither of man, the origin of evil, the immortality of the soul, the futility of life, etc.', and by the seemingly rudderless speculation about Darwinism, the occult, and beliefs 'ancient and modern, Hebrew, pagan, Buddhist, Christian, Agnostic, and what not',[110] that were such features of *Peter Ibbetson* (1891) and *Trilby* (1894). Burnand accused Du Maurier of belonging to 'that tyrannical braggart school of French deism (absolute Atheism is impossible) which would in the name of Liberty of thought, burn, behead and crucify all who might venture to differ from themselves'.[111] This did not do justice to Du Maurier, but its vehemence reflected the strength of Burnand's convictions. With Clement Scott, a parade of religious certitude took on a persecuting character, as he aligned himself with the National Vigilance Association.[112] Schooled at Marlborough, a vicar's son, Scott followed the well-trodden path through Tractarianism to Catholicism in 1865. His judgement became increasingly censorious when possessed by a vision of 'the moral perils of the stage'.[113]

Playwrights were nervous of Scott. Alfred Sutro saw a 'dramatic Lord Chief Justice; the play that had his fiat flourished, the play that he condemned might

[109] Burnand, *Records*, i. 79–82. Riah appears in *Our Mutual Friend* (1865).
[110] George Du Maurier, *Peter Ibbetson* (1891), in *Novels of George Du Maurier* (London, 1947), 62–5.   [111] Letter to Henry Lucy [1894], in Ormond, *Du Maurier*, 431.
[112] Samuel Smith, *My Life-Work* (London, 1902), 452–5.
[113] T. P. O'Connor's assessment in *MAP* (2 and 9 July 1904).

just as well be withdrawn the second night'.[114] For forty years, Scott served as drama critic, variously for *The Sunday Times, Observer,* and *Illustrated London News;* above all, for *The Daily Telegraph,* his pulpit from 1871 to 1897. Throughout the 1880s he also edited a monthly, *The Theatre.* Scott's own ethical position was parlous. He had a series of mistresses during his first marriage (which produced six children) to a sister of George Du Maurier. She left him in the years before her death in 1890.[115] His role as reviewer was also compromised because he was a playwright himself, albeit of the unoriginal kind, an adapter of Sardou's comedies which flourished under the Bancrofts' production.[116] Scott's and the Bancrofts' incestuous puffery vitiated any title Scott had as disinterested critic, and his influence over the theatre fast faded after the Bancrofts' retirement in 1885. On a Cook's tour down the Nile in 1893, Canon Ainger was shown by his Arab guide a card inscribed by a previous tourist which 'he seemed much to value. He asked me if I knew the gentleman in England. I took the card and read "Mr. Clement Scott". I told him that that was his Arabic name, but that in England we pronounced it "T-ommy R-t".'[117] The 'exaggeration, gush and rhetoric' of Scott's reviews,[118] and his febrile disgust for 'Ibscene' problem plays and Society dramas in the 1890s, condemned him in the eyes of Max Beerbohm and Wilde's clique.[119] Still, it would be folly for historians to count the smart set's opinions as generally representative. Scott's comminations expressed the anxieties of a sizeable public about social impurity, whether on stage, on news stands and bookstalls, or on the streets. Pressures placed on publishers and distributors were persistent. In 1918, the Catholic Federation threatened legal action against Cassell's for publishing Arnold Bennett's *The Pretty Lady,* whose protagonist, a cocotte, was a Catholic. Boot's Library and several booksellers declined to stock it, and W. H. Smith's withdrew it. The resultant publicity inflated sales: *The Pretty Lady* cleared 30,000 copies in six months. [120] This was invariably the case. The sensation of 1913 was the circulating libraries getting fussed about Hall Caine's *The Woman Thou Gavest Me,* W. B. Maxwell's *The Devil's Garden,* and the first volume of Compton Mackenzie's *Sinister Street.* Their ban made headlines in the

---

[114] Alfred Sutro, *Celebrities and Simple Souls* (London, 1933), 36.

[115] Ormond, *Du Maurier,* 381. Perhaps indicatively, Scott did not support Mrs Ormiston Chant's campaign against the Empire music hall, where prostitutes promenaded. She expressed her crossness to George Bernard Shaw, 17 Nov. 1894, BL Add MSS 50513, fo. 60. I thank Lizzie Rayment for a transcript of this letter.

[116] See the Bancrofts, *Recollections of Sixty Years* (London, 1909), and *DNB 1901–11,* 276–7, for Scott (1841–1904). His greatest hit *Diplomacy* (1878), based on Sardou's *Dora,* was parodied by Burnand at the Strand as *Diplunacy.*

[117] Ainger to George Du Maurier, 26 Feb. 1893, in Edith Sichel, *The Life and Letters of Alfred Ainger* (London, 1906; Nelson edn.), 282.   [118] O'Connor, *MAP* (2 and 9 July 1904).

[119] Scott was Beerbohm's first satirical target after joining the *Saturday Review*: David Cecil, *Max* (London, 1964), 141–4. For jokes about Scott by Wilde's clique: Robert Hichens, *The Green Carnation* (London, [1894] 1949), 24, 70.

[120] James Hepburn (ed.), *Letters of Arnold Bennett, i. Letters to J. B. Pinker* (Oxford, 1966), 262; Margaret Drabble, *Arnold Bennett* (London, [1974] 1975), 228–9.

Daily Mail, and once more gave the books a fillip. *Sinister Street* was in its twenty-fifth thousand by the year's end. Its author was not only grateful but astonished. In his Anglo-Catholic phase Mackenzie taught Sunday School and pondered ordination; he hardly considered himself in the business of polluting the nation's morals and would convert to Rome in 1914. But the Catholic part in these vigilante actions was small. The lead was taken by Protestant groups, mainly but not exclusively of the Evangelical and fundamentalist stripe. The *Liverpool Daily Post*, whose reviewer extolled *Sinister Street*, had been hectored by Canon Cogswell of Wallasey who found: 'The very title is suggestive. The hero and heroine are quite gratuitously bastards...'. Likewise, Canon Lyttelton, headmaster of Eton and a tireless flogger, harangued *The Times* about how 'sanity and upright manliness are destroyed, not only by the reading of obscene stuff, but by a premature interest in sex matters'.[121] Usually, Nonconformists generalled these campaigns, driven by anti-metropolitan and anti-aristocratic animosity to suspect Corruption in High Places. The power of this constituency was underlined for Mackenzie by Robertson Nicoll, who, communicating his enjoyment of *Carnival* (1912), warned, 'But you mustn't expect me to say so in the *British Weekly*. It's not a book I can recommend to *my* readers.'[122] Arnold Bennett also understood this mentality. Until *The Pretty Lady*, he had not upset the libraries, only the older generation in his family. His mother would fidget when certain titles of his were mentioned—*Sacred and Profane Love* (1905) or the 'divorce novel' *Whom God Hath Joined* (1906). Best of all, his aunt burnt his first novel *A Man from the North* (1898), 'in Wesleyan horror'.[123]

Doubtless, many Catholics approved the purity crusades that were promoted largely by their sectarian adversaries. The *Tablet*'s editor, J. G. Snead-Cox, represented them before the Joint Select Committee on Stage Plays in 1909, complaining that dramatists 'habitually treat adultery as if it were the main interest in life'. The censorship was 'too lax', not too strict.[124] It was in Ireland, not England, where the Catholic ideal gained enforcement, abetted by Gaelic League and Sinn Fein fanaticism to preserve peasant piety against Anglo-European modernism. This produced the manufactured outrage against Synge's *Playboy of the Western World* (1907) at the Abbey Theatre.[125] Yet the evidence cuts both ways. On the one hand, certain authors protested against ignorant restrictions on their imaginative life. These included Catholics such as Francis Thompson,[126] who prefaced his

[121] Mackenzie, *Life and Times: Octave Four*, 192–7.   [122] Ibid., 148.
[123] James Hepburn (ed.), *Letters of Arnold Bennett, ii. 1889–1915* (Oxford, 1968), 269–70, *iv. Family Letters* (Oxford, 1986), 9, 13.
[124] Joint Select Committee on Stage Plays (Censorship), *Parliamentary Papers* (1909), viii. 451, qq. 5473–8.
[125] R. F. Foster, *W. B. Yeats: A Life, i. The Apprentice Mage 1865–1914* (Oxford, 1997), 357–67; F. S. L. Lyons, *Culture and Anarchy in Ireland 1890–1939* (Oxford, 1979), 61–71; Ruth Dudley Edwards, *Patrick Pearse* (London, [1977] 1979), 102–3.
[126] Francis Thompson was Catholic-born. It was his father, Charles, a doctor, who had converted: see Gorman, *Converts*, 269, and Everard Meynell, *The Life of Francis Thompson* (London, 1913), 1.

famous essay on Shelley by 'a fiery attack on Catholic Philistinism...driven home with all the rhetoric which I could muster...I consulted Mr. [Wilfrid] Meynell as to its suppression, but he said "Leave it in". I suspect that he thoroughly agrees with it.'[127] On the other hand, most readers seemed content with simple, uplifting stories and happy endings which did not challenge conventional behaviour. When Arnold Bennett was studying best-selling authors in the late 1890s, he was furnished by Frederick Warne & Co. with Silas K. Hocking's sales figures: 1,093,185, or an average of a thousand a week. A Methodist minister for twenty-six years, Hocking poured out fables which touched ordinary people by their naïve drama and moral purpose. They were serialized in Nonconformist periodicals, such as the *Family Circle*, of which Hocking became editor in 1894 or the *Temple Magazine* (subtitled *Silas K. Hocking's Illustrated Monthly*) which he co-founded in 1896 and which supplied approved Sunday reading for the next five years. His fame did not count in the fashionable world. A Kensington bookseller told Bennett that he never stocked Hocking's novels. In the industrial North and Midlands and in Dissent's rural and mining strongholds, things were different. In one small-town bookshop Bennett discovered 'rows of *Her Benny, God's Outcast, Ivy, For Abigail*; there, 'the literary topic of 1899 was not *A Double Thread* [the Society novel by Miss E. T. Fowler] or *The Awkward Age* [by Henry James] or the Browning Love-Letters. It was *The Day of Remembrance*, by Silas K. Hocking, with original illustrations by A. Twidle.'[128] What was true of the Dissenting reading public was, *ceteris paribus*, true of the Catholic reading public. They had no appetite or empathy for the complications of Ernest Dowson and his sort; instead, they cherished Harriet Parr, who, as 'Holme Lee', published between 1854 and 1882 about thirty novels, all 'refined in tone, somewhat sentimental, and written in an easy, unaffected style'.[129] Mudie's subscription library stocked her in quantity, and she nicely advertised her patron in *Loving and Serving* (1883): 'To gather up the books to be returned in Mudie's fortnightly box was a duty that had devolved on Mary Martha at leaving school.'[130] Parr had umpteen successors in this field of worthy fiction, among them several listed as converts by Gorman: Francesca Maria Steele, a convert

[127] Thompson to Dr Carroll, undated, in Meynell, *Thompson*, 97. The Shelley essay was rejected by the *Dublin Review* in 1889. It made amends in 1908, following Thompson's death, whereupon the essay was hailed (in a preface by George Wyndham) as 'the most important contribution to English literature for twenty years'.

[128] E. A. Bennett, *Fame and Fiction: An Enquiry into Certain Popularities* (London, 1901), 145–6.

[129] A. F. Pollard's notice of Parr (1828–1900) in *DNB Suppl.*, iii. 248. Gorman, *Converts*, 211, gives no date for her supposed conversion. In the *Oxford DNB*, Katherine Chubbuch's revision of Pollard's notice observes that Parr 'was often mistaken for a Sister on Mercy' of the Isle of Wight, 'where she taught Sunday School and acted as a ministering angel to the local population.' Gorman further styles her Mrs whereas the *DNB* accounts her unmarried, and he misspells her pseudonym as 'Holm Lee'. Parr published under her own name *The Life and Death of Jeanne d'Arc, Called The Maid*, (2 vols. 1866), in which she saw herself as pulling no punches: 'my endeavour has been to represent her true to nature and to evidence, sure that the truth of a nature so loyal, religious, and pure is more touching with its rudenesses and its shadows upon it, than with any glosses overlaying them, or any evasions striving to deny them' (preface, pp. v–vi).

[130] Holme Lee, *Loving and Serving* (London, 1883), i. 60.

in 1887, who as 'Darley Dale' wrote over thirty children's and adults' stories and under her own name published works on the convents and monasteries of Britain and Ireland (1902–3) and *The Life and Visions of St Hildegarde* (1914);[131] and Jean Middlemass, author of some forty 'harmless sentimental melodramas' from 1872, climaxing with *At the Altar Steps* (1910), the first chapter of which sees alpha male Dr Trevor, 'with a masterful physique and masterful stroke', rescue from drowning Elsie Morant, 'daughter of a well-known financier.'[132]

The best-seller market before 1914 was characterized by this type of fiction. Queen of the crop was Marie Corelli, whose heroine Mavis Clare—a narcissistic self-portrait—in *The Sorrows of Satan* (1895) writes healthy Christian fiction. Her popularity and virtuousness earn the sneers of corrupt and envious reviewers. Undaunted, Mavis exposes Society's sins, upholds Christian truth, and, quite literally, repels the Devil. Corelli was a favourite with Anglican clergy, declared one authority on 'England's Taste in Literature'.[133] Her description of the Resurrection in *Barabbas* (1893) was recited by the Dean in Westminster Abbey on Easter Sunday.[134] Nonconformist ministers and purity campaigners, among them Hugh Price Hughes, also commended her work. So did Catholic priests; and Clement Scott, as editor of *The Theatre*, was the first to publish an effusion from her pen.[135] These associations became embarrassing in 1900 when Corelli's *The Master-Christian* dominated the bookstalls. It was permeated by anti-Romanism, albeit presented as an attack on ecclesiastical institutions rather than on the Catholic faith. According to Corelli's semi-official biographers, her views were transmitted through the character Aubrey Leigh: 'I have never denied the beauty, romance, or mysticism of the Roman Catholic Faith. If it were purified from the accumulated superstition of ages, and freed from intolerance and bigotry, it would perhaps be the grandest form of Christianity in the world. But the rats are in the house, and the rooms want cleaning.'[136] Corelli expressed herself plainly enough in press articles, collated as *Free Opinions* (1905). Romanism she denounced as 'an intolerant system of secret Government'; and she scorned ' "fairy-lamp" churches, with various altar-bobbings and other foolish ceremonies, caring nothing for the *Spirit* of the faith'.[137] Corelli relished crossing swords with Cardinal Vaughan, in an Open Letter lambasting his conduct in the Mivart case. This she compared to

---

[131] Sandra Kemp, Charlotte Mitchell, and David Trotter (ed.), *Edwardian Fiction: An Oxford Companion* (Oxford, 1997), 88, for Steele (1848–1931). Gorman, *Converts*, 258, gives her surname 'Steel'.

[132] Jean Middlemass, *At the Altar Steps* (London, 1910), 8–9. Kemp et al., *Edwardian Fiction*, 280, for Middlemass (1834–1919). Gorman, *Converts*, 192, gives no date for her conversion.

[133] Raymond Blathwayt, 'England's Taste in Literature', *Fortnightly Review*, 91 (Jan. 1912), 160–71.   [134] Bertha Vyver, *Memoirs of Marie Corelli* (London, 1930), 166.

[135] See Corelli's entry in *Who's Who, 1905*, 347.

[136] Thomas F. G. Coates and R. S. Warren Bell, *Marie Corelli: The Writer and the Woman* (London, 1903), 211–12. For the quotation and context: Marie Corelli, *The Master-Christian* (London, 1900), 320.

[137] Marie Corelli, *Free Opinions, Freely Expressed on Certain Phases of Modern Social Life and Conduct* (London, 1905), 32, 53.

'the blind stupidity which arraigned glorious Galileo, and the fiendish cruelty which supported Torquemada'.[138] She ardently opposed Vaughan's campaign to purge the Coronation Oath of its anti-Catholic strictures;[139] and in 1906 she inveighed against the ' "perversion" to Rome' of Queen Victoria's granddaughter Princess Ena of Battenberg, as the price of her marrying King Alfonso XIII of Spain.[140]

To Catholics' dismay, therefore, anti–Romanism remained a recipe for popular success. When Conan Doyle contested Edinburgh Central in 1900, he was overwhelmed by posters exposing him as 'a Papist conspirator, a Jesuit emissary, and a Subverter of the Protestant Faith'.[141] This was rather hard on Doyle because, he told the press, schooling at Stonyhurst cured him of Catholicism. He was now an enemy of all dogmatic religion, and attended the Theistic church at Swallow Street, Piccadilly. This proved only a transit stage en route to Spiritualism, to which he formally attested in 1916.[142] Roads thus continued to lead from as well as to Rome. It was small consolation that in 1910 Doyle added his voice to those wanting to rid the Coronation Oath of its 'medieval rancours' against Romanism, because he did so out of simple courtesy to avoid alienating otherwise dutiful subjects. Later, his hostility to his former church resurfaced when he declaimed against the confessional and enticement of young girls into nunneries.[143] What always animated Doyle was a fervent patriotism. It was his justification of Britain's action in the Boer War, not his creation of Sherlock Holmes, that caused Joseph Chamberlain to recommend his knighthood in 1902. Likewise, it is their Anglicism, whether commonplace or eccentric, which continued generally to mark the miscellany of converts among authors in this period. Especially, many shared objections to the *Roman* organization of Catholicism that typified their Protestant countrymen. In a curious way Gorman got it right. Not so much in his boastfulness that the roll-call of converts 'speaks eloquently for the vitality of the Church', as in his concern to deflect customary suspicions, which led him to aver that 'in yielding allegiance to the Old Faith the convert becomes no less loyal to his native country. His Gracious Majesty King George V has not in the thousands

[138] Quoted in Coates and Bell, *Corelli*, 213. For Vaughan's position, see Snead–Cox, *Vaughan*, ii. 300–3. Dr Mivart, who died in 1900 (*DNB Suppl.*, iii. 79), was a biologist, initially denied a Catholic burial by Vaughan who had inhibited him for publishing scientific theories considered heretical by the Church. The 1899 edn. of Gorman, *Converts to Rome*, included Mivart (converted, 1844) together with his wife (1856), mother and brother (both 1846); the 1910 edn. quietly dropped Mivart while retaining the other three.   [139] Corelli, *Free Opinions*, 54–64, 70–2.
[140] *Pall Mall Gazette* (14 Apr. 1906).
[141] Doyle's letter to *The Scotsman*, (16 Oct. 1900), in *The Unknown Conan Doyle: Letters to the Press*, ed. John Michael Gibson and Richard Lancelyn Green (London, 1986), 67–8; R. D. Blumenfeld, *R.D.B.'s Diary* (London, 1930), 93 (14 Oct. 1900).
[142] Conan Doyle, *Memories and Adventures*, 14–17, 31–2, 395–408; Martin Booth, *The Doctor, the Detective and Arthur Conan Doyle* (London, 1997), 309. Doyle's mother also drifted away from Catholicism, in her case to Anglicanism.
[143] Booth, *Doyle*, 268–9. Owen Dudley Edwards, *The Quest for Sherlock Holmes: A Biographical Study of Sir Arthur Conan Doyle* (London, 1983; 1984), 19, remarks that Doyle 'retained his admiration for certain parts of Roman Catholic doctrine such as the cult of the Virgin Mary'.

enumerated in these pages lost a single subject; rather has he gained, for loyalty like all the virtues only grows stronger in the fuller life.'[144]

What other common threads can be detected? Personal crises, often of a sexual nature, are well represented in the reasons several sought refuge in Catholicism and absolution thereby. That this was a period of Catholic aggression against modernism and materialism also explains its allure to writers of a certain disposition, drawn to salute authority on spiritual and ethical questions and to cherish beauty and tradition. A final irony deserves notice. Protestantism and individualism were long considered twin; yet, in an overwhelmingly Protestant country, conversion to Catholicism appealed as the supreme assertion of singularity.

[144] Gorman, *Converts*, pp. ix–x. Likewise, the 1st edn. of *The Catholic Who's Who and Year-Book* (London, 1908), p. iii, contained a lavish dedication by Sir Francis Burnand 'to our gracious Sovereign, *Rex et Imperator*, King Edward VII, in plain, straightforward token of the firmly-founded devotion of all British Catholics to His Majesty's person and throne. Loyalty is the true note of Catholic life . . . GOD SAVE THE KING!' Note, however, Benson, *Holy Blissful Martyr*, 4–5: 'no Christian would dispute that St. Peter was right in his defiance of Nero; no English Catholic would deny that it is his own duty to be an obedient subject of Edward VII. Yet somewhere between those respective duties comes a dividing line where the territories meet, and where a conscientious man is forced to choose on which side he will stand.'

13

Scenes from Professional Life: Medicine, Moral Conduct, and Interconnectedness in *Middlemarch*

Margaret Pelling

One of the many merits of *Middlemarch* is that it shows the inadequacy of all other less arduous short cuts to the reformation of society.

(Edith Simcox, 1873)[1]

Middlemarch explores the theme of interconnectedness between differing spheres in life, which has been identified by some commentators as a set of variations around community and society, and by others as a reflection of organicist theories of both mind and body.[2] I like to think it is appropriate to my subject as well as to the purpose of this volume to mention some personal connections, before discussing the evolving relationship between medicine and literature in general. This essay was first presented to a general audience, a form of outreach of which Colin Matthew approved. When I mentioned it to him, he stressed the contemporary significance of *Middlemarch*, saying that Gladstone had recorded his reactions to the book.[3] I tried to reciprocate by providing him with a copy of *The Fortunes of*

Early versions of this chapter were given at the Department of External Studies, University of Oxford, in 1985, and at the Wellcome Unit, Oxford, in 1992. An extract was published in *Middlemarch: A Viewer's Guide*, ed. J. Barron (BBC Education, London, 1994), 22– 3. A shortened version was presented at the Memorial Conference for Colin Matthew held in 2002. I am grateful to these audiences, to the editors and to Boyd Hilton; and to Rosemary Ashton for commenting on the submitted version, and in particular for information on John Chapman.

[1] Gordon S. Haight, *A Century of George Eliot Criticism* (London, 1966), 78.

[2] Cf. e.g. Suzanne Graver, *George Eliot and Community: A Study in Social Theory and Fictional Form* (Berkeley, Calif., 1984); Tess Cosslett, *The 'Scientific Movement' and Victorian Literature* (Brighton, 1982), 74–100; Sally Shuttleworth, *George Eliot and Nineteenth-Century Science: The Make-Believe of a Beginning* (Cambridge, 1986). Graver (e.g. p. 203) stresses Eliot's sense of 'separateness' in society.

[3] See H. C. G. Matthew, *Gladstone 1809–1874* (Oxford, 1986), 61, 231, 247.

Richard Mahony (1917–29), a powerful novel in the Victorian tradition written
by another female author using a male pseudonym, the Australian Henry Handel
Richardson. Like Eliot and yet unlike her, Richardson chose a medical man as her
main character, and dealt with some of the same issues, taking the colonies where
Eliot had used the provinces as a setting for the moral failure of the central male
character.[4]

On the same occasion, Colin made sure that I did not overlook the fact that as
long ago as 1948, before the 'rediscovery' of Eliot as a novelist, Asa Briggs had
pointed to the interest of *Middlemarch*'s portrayal of doctors and of science.[5] The
figure of the medical practitioner[6] has been a part of literature from Chaucer
onwards and the relationship between medicine, science, and literature in any
given culture is one which is now approached quite readily by historians. Literary
scholars in particular continue to go boldly, exploring *Middlemarch* in terms of
gender as well as contemporary natural philosophy and political science.[7]
However the main focus has been on scientific ideas or research rather than either
the art or practice of medicine (except for illustrative purposes), or medicine in its
public aspect.[8] Still in this context, slight but honourable mention should be
given to those medical men who have always been appreciative, if not proprietorial,
of the connections between medicine and literature, which they see as an aspect of
the humane and liberal side of medicine. These connections have, of course, long
been asserted at a different, more political level, to help substantiate the claim of
medicine to join the ranks of the learned professions.

In some ways the most enduring connections between medicine and literature
have been more prosaic, that is, occupational. Given the large numbers of medical
practitioners in pre-industrial society, it is not surprising that some of them, like
Rabelais, are major literary figures as well; nor is it surprising that many literary fig-
ures, confirmed (as Hilaire Belloc tells us) 'in their instinctive guess | That literature

[4] *Middlemarch* was serialized in the *Australasian* (published in Melbourne) from Feb. 1872 to
Mar. 1873: Gordon S. Haight (ed.), *The George Eliot Letters*, 9 vols. (London, 1954–78), v. 298.
Ethel Florence Lindesay Richardson (1870–1946), born in Melbourne, drew on her own experience,
her father (d. 1879) being an Irish doctor educated in Edinburgh.
[5] Asa Briggs, ' "Middlemarch" and the Doctors', *Cambridge Journal*, 1 (1948), 749–62. Cf. Louis
Cazamian, *The Social Novel in England 1830–1850* (1903), tr. M. Fido (London, 1973), for whom
Eliot represented 'intellectual compassion' rather than 'impassioned sympathy' (p. 299).
[6] The term is preferable to 'doctor' as being broader, and as not implying distinctions in medical
practice which were more often political than real when applied to the profession as a whole.
[7] See e.g. Nancy L. Paxton, *George Eliot and Herbert Spencer: Feminism, Evolutionism, and the
Reconstruction of Gender* (Princeton, 1991), esp. ch. 8; Anne E. Patrick, 'Rosamond Rescued: George
Eliot's Critique of Sexism in *Middlemarch*', *Journal of Religion*, 67 (1987), 220–38; E. A. McCobb,
'Of Women and Doctors: *Middlemarch* and Wilhelmine von Hillern's *Ein Artz der Seele*',
Neophilologus, 68 (1984), 571–86. For a representative collection, see John Peck (ed.), *Middlemarch:
George Eliot* (Houndmills, Basingstoke, 1992).
[8] See e.g. Robert A. Greenberg, 'Plexuses and Ganglia: Scientific Allusion in *Middlemarch*',
Nineteenth Century Fiction, 30 (1975), 33–52. Lilian R. Furst, *Between Doctors and Patients: The
Changing Balance of Power* (Charlottesville, Va., 1998), ch. 3, is an interesting exception, but not
wholly reliable on medical theory and practice.

breeds distress', turned to medicine to make a living. Two relevant examples from Eliot's own circle are John Chapman, the unlicensed surgeon and later physician and publisher with whom Eliot edited the *Westminster Review*; and her life partner George Henry Lewes, who got as far as walking the hospital wards as a young man before turning elsewhere.[9] This is of course to stress the role of medicine less as a vocation than as a means of getting a living. However, the economic importance of medicine is still often underplayed in historical reconstructions, as are its insecurities and its relationship with other areas of economic life, largely because, as Eliot's medical protagonist Lydgate himself found, economic aspects are in practice inseparable from other aspects of society, even though they are apparently remote from the scientific or vocational credentials of medicine.[10]

At the same time, we should not overlook a broader cultural aspect, namely the subject-matter shared by medicine and literature, where both are fundamentally concerned with the daily drama of human existence. The interest that Eliot found in ordinary lives in an ordinary setting is also the interest that many find in medicine. The use of a word like drama in this context is more than metaphorical. Medicine has had connections with plays and players from an early period, partly because both could be itinerant; and there is a histrionic role demanded in medical practice exemplified by some of Lydgate's emotional responses, which are represented as more acquired than innate. George Lewes, having turned away from medicine, contemplated going on the stage, and other examples can be found of interchange between these two seemingly disparate occupations.[11] Interestingly, however, and in striking contrast to law, the histrionics of medicine have rarely translated into the arena of politics, and Lydgate is portrayed as wishing to remain aloof from all forms of political activity.[12]

The varying connections between medicine and literature, as well as the perceived autonomy of science, are well illustrated by the library catalogue of that leader and teacher of the medical profession, in Oxford as well as the United States,

---

[9] Gordon Haight, *George Eliot and John Chapman: With Chapman's Diaries* (2nd edn., Hamden, Conn., 1969), 93 ff., 269–71; Rosemary Ashton, *G. H. Lewes: A Life* (Oxford, 1991), 14, 331.

[10] Recent widespread deployment of the 'medical marketplace', a concept well applied by Harold Cook (*The Decline of the Old Medical Regime in Stuart London*, Ithaca, NY, 1986) has tended to be superficial in economic terms and has been used mainly to imply a failure of cognitive authority within medicine itself. However, see, for Eliot's period, Irvine Loudon, *Medical Care and the General Practitioner 1750–1850* (Oxford, 1986); Anne Digby, *Making a Medical Living: Doctors and Patients in the English Market for Medicine, 1720–1911* (Cambridge, 1994).   [11] Ashton, *G. H. Lewes*, 75–85.

[12] See e.g. George Eliot, *Middlemarch*, ed. W. J. Harvey (Harmondsworth, 1978), ch. 46 (504). All references below are to this Penguin edn. On the relationship between medicine and politics, see Dorothy Porter and Roy Porter (eds.), *Doctors, Politics and Society: Historical Essays* (Amsterdam, 1993); Pelling, 'Politics, Medicine and Masculinity: Physicians and Office-Bearing in Early Modern England', in Margaret Pelling and Scott Mandelbrote (eds.), *The Practice of Reform in Health, Medicine, and Science 1500–2000* (Ashgate, forthcoming). I hope to take this further in a longer study. Cf. James F. Scott, who suggests a case for Lydgate as a representative, albeit flawed, of a Comtean elite, citing his 'social purpose': 'George Eliot, Positivism, and the Social Vision of "Middlemarch" ', *Victorian Studies*, 16 (1972), 70.

Sir William Osler. He devised his own catalogue and divided it into three principal parts. The first, Bibliotheca Prima, consisted of a chronology of the few works
over the centuries which Osler regarded as the essential literature of medicine, in
which the writings of William Harvey took pride of place. The second and largest
section covered works not of the first rank; and a third main category, called
Bibliotheca Litteraria, included what Osler called 'medicated novels' and medical
works by laymen.[13] *Middlemarch* appears in the Litteraria section, with a long
note by Osler himself, a note which goes some way to explain why Eliot's portrait
of Lydgate has been both highly respected and misunderstood. Writing just after
the First World War, Osler asserted that if he was to 'ask the opinion of a dozen
medical men upon the novel in which the doctor is best described ... a majority
will say "Middlemarch" '. For Osler, Lydgate was both an example and a warning,
but primarily a 'man of the highest type', whose scientific interest took the form of
professional enthusiasm. It should be noted here that Osler was above all a clini-
cian, renowned for his bedside teaching and for balancing the active life of medical practice with the contemplative life of the library and the laboratory bench.
He went on to attribute Lydgate's decline to factors outside himself and his high
medical ideals: 'the warning in his case is plain—not to marry a fool with a pretty
face!' 'Would', he added, 'that the Lydgates existed only in fiction!'[14]

Thus, for Osler and his contemporaries, Lydgate had come to summarize the
circumstances holding back the nineteenth century's realization of an ideal of professional autonomy based primarily on scientific qualifications. Lydgate's concern
for his profession was enough to ensure his high scientific quality, and should have
earned him independence from worldly restrictions. Some worldly factors were of
course in his favour: Osler noted approvingly that Lydgate was 'well born, well
bred, and well trained', all of which should have increased his right to autonomy.[15]
Lydgate's role is thus that of the Prometheus of professionalization, a process which
for medicine was accelerating at the end of the nineteenth century, pointing
towards a high level of success in the twentieth. And indeed Osler's view had at least
the merit of recognizing Lydgate's active commitment to medical reform, even if he
made Lydgate's own mistake of exaggerating science's rights to autonomy.

Yet under this interpretation, Lydgate becomes a peculiarly isolated figure in a
moral and political sense. It can be argued that this is precisely what Eliot did not
mean, and that her real intentions are better represented by the approach of social
history, which sees medicine and science as connected, even in their content, with
other aspects of society; and in which medical practitioners necessarily share in the

---

[13] William Osler, *Bibliotheca Osleriana: A Catalogue of Books Illustrating the History of Medicine
and Science ... Bequeathed to McGill University* (Oxford, 1929), editors' preface, p. xi. The literature
on Osler is enormous, but see *DNB*, and the contemporary life by Harvey Cushing, *The Life of Sir
William Osler*, 2 vols. (Oxford, 1929; special facs. edn., Birmingham, Ala. 1982), esp. i. 371, 461–3.
[14] Osler, *Bibliotheca Osleriana*, 430. On the attitudes of physicians to marriage, see M. Pelling,
'The Women of the Family? Speculations around Early Modern British Physicians', *Social History of
Medicine*, 8 (1995), 383–401.   [15] Osler, *Bibliotheca Osleriana*, 430.

intellectual and moral world of their contemporaries. Regardless of her allegedly
singular interest in medicine and science, it is perhaps significant that Eliot, as
already indicated, found it impossible to pursue a 'vocational' version of the novel
in which Lydgate and Fred Vincy were the main characters.[16] Later in the project's
long-drawn-out history, she combined this early attempt with the initially separate story of Miss Brooke.[17] The reviewers of the time, who dealt in character
rather than text, were particularly taken with Dorothea, whose pet name, Dodo, is
surely a gesture of ironical affection on the part of the author towards her vanished
younger self, as well as a most human application of a current scientific—and literary—fact.[18] The reviewers' reaction to Lydgate varied. Some resented him because
his story lacked a happy ending; because his sacrifices had no redemptive effect;
and because they found the book's concluding chapters unfairly melancholy after
a humorous start. Others objected because they saw Lydgate rather than Will
Ladislaw as the masculine counterpart of the idealist Dorothea, with his propor-
tions of head and heart suitably reversed when compared with hers. Dorothea and
Lydgate should have come together rather than Dorothea and Ladislaw.[19]
However, such alternative marriage plans undoubtedly underestimate Eliot's
compassionate but critical notion of Lydgate's character.[20] Eliot was praised by
contemporaries for her 'masculine breadth' of intellect and grasp over space and
time, but for these reviewers, what Dorothea and Ladislaw shared, and what Eliot
apparently and perversely endorsed, was in essence feminine. One such reviewer
described Ladislaw as a 'clever, mercurial, petulant young politician'; for Henry
James, he was a 'woman's man'.[21] By contrast Lydgate's merits, like science itself,
were properly masculine attributes which they saw as wasted or betrayed. Other
reviewers found Lydgate and his money problems simply distasteful and could not
understand how he came to be a hero at all.[22]

[16] On the concept of vocation in *Middlemarch*, see Alan Mintz, *George Eliot and the Novel of
Vocation* (Cambridge, Mass., 1978).

[17] Jerome Beaty, *Middlemarch from Notebook to Novel: A Study of George Eliot's Creative Method*
(Urbana, Ill., 1960). Stanton Millet, 'The Union of "Miss Brooke" and "Middlemarch": A Study of
the Manuscript', *Journal of English and Germanic Philology*, 79 (1980), 32–57, argues that the union
brought Lydgate forward as a major character in tandem with Dorothea.

[18] The dodo, *Raphus cucullatus*, of Mauritius, was made extinct in the late 17th cent. but was rein-
terpreted in the 19th: see Pietro Corsi, *The Age of Lamarck: Evolutionary Theories in France
1790–1830*, rev. edn., tr. J. Mandelbaum (Berkeley, Calif., 1988), 228; R. F. Ovenell, 'The Tradescant
Dodo', *Archives of Natural History*, 19 (1992), 145–52. I am grateful to Pietro Corsi for the latter
reference. See also Lewis Carroll's *Alice in Wonderland* (1865).

[19] John Holmstrom and L. Lerner (eds.), *George Eliot and her Readers: A Selection of Contemporary
Reviews* (London, 1966), 96.

[20] For one modern version of the urge to pair Lydgate and Dorothea, see Lloyd Fernando, 'Special
Pleading and Art in "Middlemarch": The Relations between the Sexes', *Modern Language Review*, 67
(1972), 44–9.

[21] R. H. Hutton (1873), in William Baker (ed.), *Critics on George Eliot: Readings in Literary Criticism*
(London, 1973), 28; Henry James (1873) in Holmstrom and Lerner, *George Eliot and her Readers*, 111.

[22] Modern critics have echoed some of these responses. Cf. James D. Benson, ' "Sympathetic"
Criticism: George Eliot's Response to Contemporary Reviewing', *Nineteenth-Century Fiction*,
29 (1974–5), 428–40; Baker, *Critics on George Eliot*, 27, 28, 30, 31; Haight, *A Century of George Eliot*

In general, contemporaries reacted strongly to what they saw as the scientific content of the book. Some found it oppressive and an unnecessary parade of undesirably up-to-date ideas; others saw it, more accurately, as a vision of the closer but sadder brotherhood of man (and woman) revealed by the biological philosophies of the second half of the century. 'Melancholy' was the word most often used to summarize the book, by which many reviewers meant Eliot's apparent abandonment of both the positivist project of the perfectibility of man through knowledge, as well as the prospect of consolation in the next world. Gladstone's verdict was that it was 'an extraordinary, to me a very jarring, book'.[23] When he wrote this comment he was 65, ten years older than Eliot herself. It occurs mid-way through a course of reading Eliot's novels, poems, and essays which had begun in 1859, with her first major success, *Adam Bede*, and ended in 1889, nine years after her death, with Mathilde Blind's account of her life in a series on eminent women. Gladstone recorded his admiration for *The Mill on the Floss*, which he read in 1884, long after its publication, and also for *Silas Marner*, read almost immediately afterwards; but his only other extended comment was on *Felix Holt, The Radical*, read when first published in 1866, which he also, but more predictably, found 'a most inharmonious book. It jars and discomposes me.'[24] For their part, both Eliot and Lewes had by the 1870s distanced themselves from party politics and especially from liberalism. Eliot described herself in 1874 as 'no believer in Salvation by Ballot', and castigated Gladstone himself as an example of 'imbecile literary vanity in high places'.[25]

Gladstone's brief comment on *Middlemarch* suggests his sense that others might not respond as he had done. One aspect of professional development at the end of the century was that it would become an article of faith that, while medical men could still understand and be nurtured upon the humanities, the laity could no longer have any adequate share of medical knowledge. Medicine had become, at least at the top of the professional pyramid, far more technical and increasingly specialized and so 'disconnected'—the latter feature being one that was frequently deplored by Osler among others. However limited the achievements of medical reform, the perceived balance of power within the doctor–patient relationship had been successfully shifted. This awareness of the increasing distance between the medical man and the lay person meant that Eliot's contemporaries in the 1870s expressed amazement that she could portray medical matters, even of a period forty years earlier, with any degree of authenticity.

Criticism, 316, 343, 351; Holmstrom and Lerner, *George Eliot and her Readers*, 78 ff., 86, 90,102, 118, 119; Richard Ellmann, 'Dorothea's Husbands: Some Biographical Speculations', *Times Literary Supplement* (16 Feb. 1973).

[23] William Ewart Gladstone, *The Gladstone Diaries*, ed. M. R. D. Foot and H. C. G. Matthew, 14 vols. (Oxford, 1968–94), viii. 555. [24] Ibid., xii. 250; xi. 126, 138; vi. 456–7.
[25] *The Letters of George Henry Lewes*, ed. W. Baker, 3 vols. (Victoria, BC, 1995–9), iii. 127; Haight, *George Eliot Letters*, ii. 25; iv. 236; v. 386; vi. 14, 21–2; vii. 47. Cf. Eliot's view of Disraeli (and his literary efforts): Haight, *George Eliot Letters*, ix. 282 (1879).

In the same way, Asa Briggs was not alone among later commentators in singling out medicine as the aspect of the novel most likely to require comment and historical information for the benefit of the reader.[26] Where such commentary has been provided, it is mostly in relation to changing forms of professional qualification.[27] Some interest has been taken in the prototypes on which Eliot may have drawn for the figure of Lydgate, but in general this has been left to medical enthusiasts. There is now a very large body of commentary on Eliot and on *Middlemarch* in particular, deriving primarily from literary sources, but Lydgate has attracted far less attention than Casaubon or Dorothea.[28] Some commentators, perhaps tired of the Casaubon/Pattison controversy, have tended to follow the lead of Eliot herself, and of Lewes on her behalf, in deprecating the search for originals of *Middlemarch* characters, and it is true that this can be simplistic.[29] However, in dealing with Eliot's medical sources and contacts, and with the possible sources among her acquaintance for the character of Lydgate, I hope to correct some entrenched misconceptions, and also to explore further the theme of interconnectedness.

G. H. Lewes raised the value and mystique of Eliot's achievement by asserting that she had never known a surgeon intimately; that she had no acquaintance 'in any degree' resembling Lydgate, and that her *direct* knowledge of the medical area had originally been very slight. This was partly in response to an opinion offered by the prominent surgeon Sir James Paget, who was also Lewes's and Eliot's medical adviser and might have been seen as an authoritative source.[30] Paget's comment, a rather typical one among medical readers of literature, was that *Middlemarch*'s insight into medical life was so deep that it could only have been acquired by direct personal experience: there must have been a 'biographical foundation' for Lydgate's career.[31] Lewes may have covered himself according to the letter rather than the spirit when he used the term 'surgeon' rather than the more general 'practitioner', but in itself his denial on Eliot's behalf was not worth a great deal, even if this quashing of the hunt for originals of *Middlemarch* characters, something which had been encouraged by the popular idea of the

---

[26] Eliot, *Middlemarch*, Introduction (19).

[27] See e.g. the now outdated C. L. Cline, 'Qualifications of the Medical Practitioners of *Middlemarch*', in Clyde de L. Ryals (ed.), *Nineteenth-Century Literary Perspectives: Essays in Honor of Lionel Stevenson* (Durham, NC, 1974), 271–81, who also takes an Oslerian view of Lydgate and Dorothea.

[28] See Karen L. Pangallo, *George Eliot: A Reference Guide 1972–1987* (Boston, 1990). For some, Lydgate does not qualify as a principal character in the novel: Fernando, 'Special Pleading', 44.

[29] See Gordon S. Haight, 'George Eliot's Originals', in R. C. Rathburn and Martin Steinmann, Jun. (eds.), *From Jane Austen to Joseph Conrad: Essays Collected in Memory of James T. Hillhouse* (Minneapolis, 1958), 177–93.

[30] Frederick Karl, *George Eliot: A Biography* (London, 1995), 453, 516, 517, 601, 620; Rosemary Ashton, *George Eliot: A Life* (London, 1996), 300, 364, 373; Haight, *George Eliot Letters*, vi. 196.

[31] Ashton, *George Eliot*, 314–15. On the Pagets, see M. Jeanne Petersen, 'Gentlemen and Medical Men: The Problem of Professional Recruitment', *Bulletin of the History of Medicine*, 58 (1984), 457–73; idem, *Family, Love, and Work in the Lives of Victorian Gentlewomen* (Bloomington, Ind., 1989).

novel as a gallery of figures who were like a series of photographs from life, placed justifiable stress on Eliot's intelligence and creative capacities.

In fact the relatively copious records left by Eliot of her activity as a novelist show her deliberately acquiring medical knowledge for the purposes of the novel. The *Quarry for Middlemarch* indicates that her sources were sensible though relatively restricted.[32] She paid particular attention to the *Lancet*, a fairly conventional medical journal by the 1870s but a wild and scurrilous reforming organ in the decades in question. Eliot apparently did not consult the *Provincial Medico-Chirurgical Journal*, later to become the *British Medical Journal*, which represented provincial practitioners from about 1828, but then the *Lancet* spilled the professional beans much more thoroughly than any other source of the time. She also, very sensibly, read, or read about, the authors of the standard textbooks who between them dominated the century: William Cullen, of Glasgow and Edinburgh, whose clinical textbooks first evolved in the 1760s and were still being published in 1831; and Cullen's effective successor, Thomas Watson, whose *Principles and Practice of Physic* began as a lecture series in the early 1840s and was only displaced in the 1870s. (It would ultimately be succeeded as a clinical bible by the work of William Osler.) These textbooks were of high quality but their durability is an apt reflection of the comparative stability of medical practice even in the nineteenth century.[33]

Both Cullen and Watson were particularly interested in fever, both as a fundamental pathological process and in its different specific manifestations. Watson was unusual among the leaders of the profession in his responsiveness to the work of younger men, especially in areas with implications for practice, and in his willingness to change his mind on important subjects related to fever and epidemic disease.[34] The nature of fever was, as Eliot detected, a major issue in the early nineteenth century, a point at which French investigators appeared to be in the lead. On the practical side, it was an underlying feature of many of the major causes of mortality, that is, the infectious diseases. However, being a condition affecting the body as a whole, it also seemed to contain within its phenomena more basic information about bodily mechanisms and how the body became diseased in the first place. Eliot was thus making an excellent choice of an area of medical controversy with both theoretical and practical implications, which could create dilemmas for Lydgate, his more empirical colleagues, the proponents of different forms of institutional provision, and the households of the patients themselves.[35]

[32] *Quarry for Middlemarch, by George Eliot*, ed. Anna T. Kitchel (Berkeley, Calif., 1950). See also J. C. Pratt and V. A. Neufeldt (eds.), *George Eliot's Middlemarch Notebooks: A Transcription* (Los Angeles, 1979).
[33] For Cullen and Watson, see *DNB*; Margaret Pelling, *Cholera, Fever and English Medicine 1825–1865* (Oxford, 1978), 14, 271; A. Doig *et al.* (eds.), *William Cullen and the Eighteenth Century Medical World* (Edinburgh, 1993), esp. 34–9, 141–5.   [34] Pelling, *Cholera*, 271–2, 274, 292.
[35] *Quarry for Middlemarch*, 9, 29–31; Pelling, *Cholera*, esp. ch. 1; W. F. Bynum and V. Nutton (eds.), *Theories of Fever from Antiquity to the Enlightenment, Medical History*, suppl. 1 (London, 1981).

In addition, fever, especially the 'continued' fevers including typhoid and typhus, was the primary concern of the sanitary reformers, including the associate of Bentham and Chadwick, Thomas Southwood Smith, who was the main author of official doctrine on sanitary matters in its theoretical aspect. Lewes had known Southwood Smith as a young man, and Smith's 'adopted' granddaughter and biographer, Gertrude Hill the sister of Octavia Hill, married Charles Lewes, who as the surviving son of George Lewes became George Eliot's heir.[36] The emerging distinctions between different fevers, and the methods for controlling them, could qualify as a justification for Eliot's selection of a 'better understanding of disease' as one measure of recent progress making a difference between her time of writing and forty years earlier. Her comments to this effect have been comparatively neglected.[37] As we shall see, among Eliot's medical contacts it was those concerned with medicine in its public aspect who predominated. The views ascribed to Lydgate are not those of the Utilitarian sanitary reformers; rather, for Eliot as for Southwood Smith and his associates, fever was an expression of the intimate relationship between human beings and their environment. Like Eliot, they stressed 'the gradual action of ordinary causes' as having greater importance than the remote or exotic causes that might lie behind sporadic imported diseases such as cholera.[38]

It is worth noting that neither Eliot nor Lewes enjoyed good health, and that their families had their share of illness and death. Much of the medical byplay in *Middlemarch* is actually generated by patients rather than practitioners, and was therefore within common observation, as well as being relatively timeless. However, it is also important that Eliot was of a class and status to know certain sections of the medical profession socially as well as professionally. One of her sisters married a surgeon, who has been suggested as the original for Lydgate, largely on the grounds that he was well-born and ended as a bankrupt.[39] More significantly, one advantage of Eliot's irregular marital position was that she was much more likely to meet professional men directly rather than to be confined to the round of visiting among a group of women.

Medical men were of course as variable as any other group. By and large Eliot's acquaintances among medical practitioners were of the more interesting sort.[40]

[36] Pelling, *Cholera*, esp. chs. 1 and 2; F. N. L. Poynter, 'Thomas Southwood Smith—the Man (1788–1861)', *Proceedings of the Royal Society of Medicine (Sect. Hist. Med.)*, 55 (1962), 381–92; R. K. Webb, 'Southwood Smith: The Intellectual Sources of Public Service', in Porter and Porter, *Doctors, Politics and Society*, 46–80; Ashton, *G. H. Lewes*, 27, 32, 88; Karl, *George Eliot: A Biography*, 643. Pratt and Neufeldt, *George Eliot's Middlemarch Notebooks*, 1, 142–3, show Eliot's reading of Smith on fever but I would disagree with their inferences.

[37] Thomas Pinney, 'More Leaves from George Eliot's Notebook', *Huntington Library Quarterly*, 29 (1966), 372–3.

[38] Haight, *George Eliot Letters*, v. 168; Pelling, *Cholera*, 21 ff., 46 ff.; Pelling, 'Epidemics in Nineteenth-Century Towns: How Important was Cholera?', *Transactions of the Liverpool Medical Institution* (1983–4), 28 ff. Two of Southwood Smith's other concerns of relevance here were the provision of bodies for anatomical instruction, and model housing, which Eliot made the favourite (and most practical) pursuit of Dorothea.   [39] Haight, 'George Eliot's Originals', 190.

[40] For one encounter with a well-meaning physician, see Haight, *George Eliot Letters*, v. 24 (1869). Rosamond, it will be recalled, married 'an elderly and wealthy physician' after Lydgate's death: Eliot, *Middlemarch*, Finale (893).

The apparently unlicensed Chapman, an important figure in her early adult life obscured by her friends and first biographers, was no mid-Victorian stereotype, though he was probably less unusual than he sounds. After studying medicine in Paris and London, following a period as a watchmaker, he seems to have begun as an unlicensed surgeon and to have taken out a Scottish MD rather later, when his activities as a publisher became too precarious.[41] At this earlier period in her life Eliot also knew major figures in what would come to be called alternative medicine, like the phrenologist George Combe. Chapman too was interested in phrenology. However, people such as Combe held wider philosophical and political views of which the implications for medicine were only a part;[42] but none of the medical figures in *Middlemarch* was allowed this kind of intellectual wholeness. In later life too, Lewes's and Eliot's friends included many practitioners of wider interests and functions, notably John Simon, head of government public health administration from the 1850s to the 1870s, whose background and career Eliot may well have found suggestive. Of Huguenot extraction, Simon was a surgeon whose early interests in pathological anatomy were absorbed into his political role. He and his wife were active members of a literary and artistic circle that included Ruskin and other Pre-Raphaelites, and with which Eliot and Lewes also had close links.[43]

Of the proto-Lydgates, attention has been focused on Clifford Allbutt, described by Osler as 'my brother Regius of Cambridge'. There are obvious circumstantial reasons for mentioning Allbutt in this context, but it is probably only medical authors who would see him, a younger man, as influencing Eliot rather than the other way about. Nevertheless, Allbutt's candidature remains alive.[44] However, the notion of his resembling Lydgate shows a forgetfulness not only of Lydgate's attributes in the novel but of the medical reform positions of the 1820s and 1830s, and also of Eliot's awareness of the dead hand of the medical colleges and English universities in this context. As a physician and graduate of Cambridge, Allbutt was one of a tiny minority, less than 4 per cent, of orthodox nineteenth-century medical practitioners.[45] In the 1860s, he became, with little difficulty, physician to the three main medical institutions of Leeds, where he had family connections—the general infirmary, the house of recovery or fever hospital,

[41] Haight, *George Eliot and John Chapman*, 4–5, 95 ff.; *DNB*, art. 'Chapman, John'. F. N. L. Poynter, 'John Chapman (1821–1894): Publisher, Physician, and Medical Reformer', *Journal of the History of Medicine*, 5 (1950), 1–22, offers some corrections to Haight. One of Chapman's medical instructors in London was George Budd, brother of William. Chapman's medical works were later favourably reviewed by Clifford Allbutt and other friends of Eliot (ibid., 10, 16–17).
[42] See Roger Cooter, *The Cultural Meaning of Popular Science: Phrenology and the Organization of Consent in Nineteenth-Century Britain* (Cambridge, 1984).
[43] Royston Lambert, *Sir John Simon 1816–1904 and English Social Administration* (London, 1963); Pelling, *Cholera*, 229–37 and *passim*; Haight, *George Eliot Letters*, iii. 69 (1859), v. 148, vii. 16, 23, viii. 196.
[44] Osler, *Bibliotheca Osleriana*, 430. This claim was made by Sir Humphry Rolleston (also a Cambridge Regius) in the *DNB* article on Allbutt. Cf. *Quarry for Middlemarch*, 2–5; Karl, *George Eliot: A Biography*, 439, 514; Ashton, *George Eliot*, 304–6.
[45] *Quarry for Middlemarch*, 27–8; Pelling, *Cholera*, 5n.

and the dispensary. He produced his multi-volume *System of Medicine* in the
1890s, as Regius Professor of Physic at Cambridge. He was undeniably interested
in fever: he introduced the standard use of a new convenient short thermometer,
and, during an epidemic in 1865–6, tried to introduce the management of fever
patients along open-air lines in a kind of pavilion system.[46] However, the
application of both thermometry and of ventilation to the management of fever in
urban environments were topics dating from the previous century.[47] Allbutt's own
qualified awareness of the distinction between typhoid and typhus, established for
the English profession in the 1850s by William Jenner on clinical rather than
pathological grounds, would not of itself have been informative for Eliot unless he
had been fully aware of the earlier debates which had taken place largely, but not
wholly, outside the English context. It is this earlier debate, and its methodologies,
that Lydgate brought back with him from Paris.[48]

Allbutt and Lewes were already friends, both having an interest in positivism,
which Allbutt claimed had directed his attention towards medicine and science.[49]
Eliot visited Allbutt in Leeds in August 1869, when she had already embarked on
the Lydgate/Middlemarch story. She later agreed that this visit had given her
'suggestions': this may sound definite, but for her suggestions were 'subtle, shad-
owy'. Eliot and Lewes were taken by Allbutt over the Leeds infirmary, where she
applauded the fact that wards were beginning to be ornamented by their physicians with chromo-lithographs and other objects likely to soothe the sick. Eliot's
other comment on the infirmary and its inmates was rather less sympathetic—
although reported rather than first-hand—and illustrates her inclination to stay
away from the industrial realities of the larger, newer towns.[50] It is noticeable in
Middlemarch that the inmates of Bulstrode's new hospital, as well as those of the
infirmary, are entirely notional, and that their presence is not necessary for the
workings of the plot.

It is then perfectly possible, as others have found, to find medical men of the right
period who fit the Lydgate reforming mould more nearly than Allbutt, and I would
like to offer my own suggestion.[51] Moreover, the career, ideas, and sensibilities of
this candidate—the physician and epidemiologist William Budd, of Devon and
Bristol—have a relevance not just to the technical aspects of the novel but,

[46] On Allbutt (1836–1925), see *DNB*; Humphry Rolleston, *The Right Honourable Sir Thomas
Clifford Allbutt—A Memoir* (London, 1929), esp. 18, 30, 32–6, 39, 43, 55, 59–62.
[47] See in general John Pickstone, *Medicine and Industrial Society: A History of Hospital
Development in Manchester and its Region, 1752–1946* (Manchester, 1985).
[48] The most comprehensive source for shifts in views on fever among the English profession is
Charles Murchison, *A Treatise on the Continued Fevers of Great Britain* (London, 1862; 2nd edn.,
1873; 3rd edn., ed. W. Cayley, 1884). See Pelling, *Cholera*, 287–91.
[49] Ashton, *G. H. Lewes*, 280; Rolleston, *Allbutt*, 12, 60. It is unclear when Lewes and Allbutt first
met: *Quarry for Middlemarch*, 2. See in general Scott, 'George Eliot, Positivism, and the Social
Vision', esp. 69 ff.
[50] Haight, *George Eliot Letters*, vi. 476 (1868); Haight, 'George Eliot's Originals', 182.
[51] Haight, 'George Eliot's Originals', puts the claims of Charles Benjamin Nankivell (MD Pisa),
who came to Coventry in 1831, above those of Allbutt.

perhaps more importantly, to its moral life and its metaphors.[52] Lewes met Budd at least once, having dinner with him and other artistic and scientific friends, including John Tyndall, in April 1871, a date when Eliot was still writing *Middlemarch*: Lewes describes it as advancing slowly.[53] In 1871 Budd, already in declining health, was on the verge of publishing his major work on continued fever, which was an amalgam of the papers he had published or written on the subject since imbibing the views of his French teachers on fevers in the late 1820s and 1830s.[54] Like Lydgate, Budd 'knew Broussais',[55] and was influenced by Pierre-Charles-Alexandre Louis, although neither Budd nor Lydgate adopted Louis's quantitative methodology.[56] Besides a possible direct contact, Eliot could have heard about Budd via a number of other routes over an extended period: through John Tyndall, Henry Holland, William Benjamin Carpenter, or John Simon, or else the writings of Watson.

Simon knew, and was partly persuaded by, Budd's writings about infectious diseases in their combined theoretical and public aspect.[57] One of the more remarkable of these was Budd's tract on the cattle plague, which Gladstone read in 1865. Gladstone of course read everything—around 21,000 titles by over 4,500 authors, to quote his editor—but Budd's tract bore upon pressing political issues, not dissimilar to those arising in late twentieth-century Britain from the foot and mouth epidemic.[58] Budd's work also illuminated the fates of individuals. Another of the subjects on which he published was diphtheria, which Eliot made the cause of Lydgate's premature death. Both these events, the actual and the fictional, took place in mid-century. Diphtheria was then a relatively newly defined disease. Although Eliot was not so crude as to make it explicit, she may have wished to imply that Lydgate's death was something of a real martyrdom. Medical practitioners were well known to have died from diphtheria, contracted either from closely examining a coughing patient, or more heroically, when attempting to remove the suffocating membrane in the throat by a method of suction.[59]

---

[52] For what follows on Budd, see Pelling, *Cholera*, esp. ch. 7. See also *DNB*.

[53] Haight, *George Eliot Letters*, v. 144.

[54] William Budd, *Typhoid Fever: Its Nature, Mode of Spreading and Prevention* (London, 1873); Pelling, *Cholera*, 274, 281–94. For Budd's early views on fever, see also William Budd, *On the Causes of Fevers (1839)*, ed. Dale C. Smith (Baltimore, 1984).

[55] Eliot, *Middlemarch*, ch. 10 (118); Pelling, *Cholera*, 15–16, 265–6. On François Joseph Victor Broussais (1772–1838), see also essays by W. R. Albury and Jacalyn Duffin in C. Hannaway and A. La Berge (eds.), *Constructing Paris Medicine* (Amsterdam, 1998).

[56] Murchison, on the other hand, did. See Eliot, *Middlemarch*, ch. 16 (193); Alfred J. Bollet, 'Pierre Louis: The Numerical Method and the Foundation of Quantitative Medicine', *American Journal of the Medical Sciences*, 266 (1973), 93–101; Pelling, *Cholera*, 256, 289–90; J. Rosser Matthews, *Quantification and the Quest for Medical Certainty* (Princeton, 1995), chs. 2 and 4.   [57] Pelling, *Cholera*, 274, 292.

[58] Eliot, William Budd, *The Siberian Cattle-Plague; or, The Typhoid Fever of the Ox* (Bristol, 1865); idem, 'On the Cattle Plague', *British Medical Journal* (1865/ii), 205–6; Pelling, *Cholera*, 237, 256, 274; Gladstone, *Diaries*, vi. 403, xiv. p. xi. See also Haight, *George Eliot Letters*, iv. 236, where Eliot combines reference to the cattle plague and the Reform Bill (1866).

[59] William Budd, 'Diphtheria', *British Medical Journal* (1861/i), 575–9; Pelling, *Cholera*, 98, 251, 258; Eliot, *Middlemarch*, Finale (893); Anne Hardy, *The Epidemic Streets: Infectious Disease and the*

Like Lydgate, Budd was a product of Edinburgh, London, and Paris, who decided against London in favour of the provinces. The arena in which he struggled for recognition, Bristol, was larger, more cosmopolitan, more radical, and more blatantly insanitary than the fictional Middlemarch, but still it was an old corporate town experiencing religious and political divisions and gradually losing ground in competition with industrial centres like Liverpool.[60] Bristol was, moreover, a town which succeeded in establishing a medical school in the teeth of metropolitan opposition, just as Lydgate somewhat unconvincingly envisaged for Middlemarch. Unlike Lydgate, Budd took the MD, and was one of a small minority of well-qualified Bristol practitioners prepared to use new methods and techniques.[61] Eliot effectively simplified her contrasts by having Lydgate qualify (but not practise) as a surgeon in opposition to conventional physicians, signifying his sense of status by distinguishing him from the pre-existing model of the general practitioner, the surgeon-apothecary.[62]

At most, Bristol, like Leeds, might have provided Eliot with 'suggestions'. More to the point are Budd's epidemiological investigations in other, smaller localities, which may have appealed to Eliot as providing analogies with the close interconnections, often unsuspected but often fateful, which she saw in human affairs and depicted in rural areas and smaller towns. As in the case of the French investigators by whom he was influenced, Budd's most striking investigations into typhoid fever were carried out in a number of small rural communities in his home county, Devon. With an intimate knowledge of these communities and the intercourse between them, Budd was able to trace cases of fever from one to another in a way that was impossible in larger populations. Both the environment and personal contacts were involved. As in the case of many of the human events depicted by Eliot, the transfer of infection in typhoid fever is commonly indirect, by means of contaminated water sources.[63] Thus, an event affecting a family in one hamlet could bring about death in another downstream, with the connection between the two events invisible except to the omniscient observer.[64] Although the truths so obtained were general in their meaning and application, both Eliot and Budd were best able to demonstrate their case on a restricted canvas.

There is, finally, another aspect of Budd's life and work which may have appealed to Eliot: his sensitivity to suffering. Lewes had given up medicine

---

Rise of Preventive Medicine, 1856–1900 (Oxford, 1993), ch. 4, esp. 80–3, 87. The first influential descriptions of this disease, like the disease itself, can also be traced to France.

[60] For an effective contrast between types of town in this period, see Hilary Marland, *Medicine and Society in Wakefield and Huddersfield 1780–1870* (Cambridge, 1987).

[61] Pelling, *Cholera*, 156 ff.

[62] Eliot, *Middlemarch*, ch. 15 (176), cf. ch. 70 (768). See in general Loudon, *Medical Care and the General Practitioner*.   [63] Pelling, *Cholera*, 266–7, 277–8.

[64] Metaphors and meanings deriving from water are of course an ancient literary resource, but had a peculiar salience for both Eliot and her century: Shuttleworth, *George Eliot*, 158, 162, 165; Pelling, *Cholera*, esp. chs. 5 and 6; Bill Luckin, *Pollution and Control: A Social History of the Thames in the Nineteenth Century* (Bristol, 1986); Jean-Pierre Goubert, *The Conquest of Water: The Advent of Health in the Industrial Age*, tr. A. Wilson (Cambridge, 1989).

because the spectacle of pain affected him too deeply. Budd was also, if anything, too sensitive to the sufferings of his patients, and this same sensitivity led him, in his early career in the 1820s and 1830s, to reject the experimentation on live animals which was then a major feature of French physiological investigation. This aversion probably changed the course of Budd's own research interests towards the chemically based physiology of the famous German chemist Justus von Liebig, whom both Budd and Lewes met and admired early in their respective careers.[65] Lydgate, it will be recalled, had a strong man's tenderness towards his patients, which plays a crucial role in his betrothal to Rosamund. On the other hand, Eliot has the student Lydgate conducting experiments on live animals, without qualms but apparently without extending this to vivisection.[66] With respect to the direction of their respective researches, Budd was ultimately vindicated as a precursor of the bacteriological revolution, but recognition came late and his experiences included some humiliation in the 'cholera fungus controversy' of 1849. His intervention in this controversy was, however, based on the latest methods, including microscopy. The credit and then discredit experienced by the Bristol microscopists provide an apt demonstration of the problems arising from the value placed on visual perception in the period: Lewes may have been among those concerned that the Bristol controversy would cast doubt on microscopy as a mode of investigation, due to the difficulties in sharing and validating its results.[67] Like Lydgate, Budd had begun with extremely ambitious aims in basic research which he was unable to fulfil, in spite of his achievements in other areas, and this may have been caused in part by massive financial losses incurred by some form of speculation in the 1840s, possibly investment in a water company.[68]

Lydgate's favourite topics were minute and pathological anatomy and the structures of development. He is shown as researching just in advance of the cell theory, and along lines established by Bichat.[69] In terms of the direction of Lydgate's research, Eliot seems most concerned with historical precision, with a view to suggesting that her character had the intention, and possibly the ability, to make a significant contribution. As with Dorothea, Lydgate's ideals were necessarily at an early stage of formulation. What is important to the novel is less his current views than the potential power and apparent legitimacy of his methodology in the context

[65] Ashton, *G. H. Lewes*, 14, 191; Pelling, *Cholera*, 125–30, 261, 269–70; John E. Lesch, *Science and Medicine in France: The Emergence of Experimental Physiology, 1790–1855* (Cambridge, Mass., 1984); Richard D. French, *Antivivisection and Medical Science in Victorian Society* (Princeton, 1975), 18–23.   [66] Eliot, *Middlemarch*, ch. 15 (173 ff., 180); ch. 31 (336).

[67] Pelling, *Cholera*, ch. 5; Mark Wormald, 'Microscopy and Semiotic in *Middlemarch*', *Nineteenth-Century Literature*, 50 (1996), 501–4; George Levine, *The Realistic Imagination: English Fiction from Frankenstein to Lady Chatterley* (Chicago, 1981), ch. 11.

[68] Pelling, *Cholera*, 267 ff.; idem, *The Common Lot: Sickness, Medical Occupations and the Urban Poor in Early Modern England* (London, 1998), 257.

[69] Eliot, *Middlemarch*, ch. 15 (177); *Quarry for Middlemarch*, 25–6, 31; W. J. Harvey, 'The Intellectual Background of the Novel: Casaubon and Lydgate', in Barbara Hardy (ed.), *Middlemarch: Critical Approaches to the Novel* (London, 1967), 35–6. On Marie-François-Xavier Bichat (1771–1802), see *Dictionary of Scientific Biography*; Lesch, *Science and Medicine in France*.

of that more hopeful period.[70] None of this appears in the later life to which Lydgate has to resign himself, where his patients are those wealthy enough to travel to continental spas and to develop gout, a condition of the individual constitution redolent of the previous, unreformed century.[71] In scientific terms, the fate of Lydgate—and perhaps also Budd—is also a symbol of the imperviousness of English society to continental influences, and of the limited adoption of the principle of meritocracy urged by the Philosophical Radicals after the French example. In constantly referring to Middlemarch as a kind of lost world, a world supposedly on the brink of the major reforms of the 1830s and 1840s, Eliot is (paradoxically) also pointing to the degree to which change, whether political, moral, or scientific, did not occur at all.

Overall, the main interest of the comparison between Budd and Lydgate lies in the fact that the former's work bore directly on the theme of interconnectedness, with a precision and intricacy greater than that of the Utilitarian sanitary reformers. Thus Budd's work on infectious disease was strongly marked by its reliance on analogy to 'unify and define'.[72] Epidemiology might be defined as the medical science of interconnectedness, and the negative and threatening aspects of this form of physical continuity, as well as its inevitability, are as much present in *Middlemarch* as is any perspective taken from the nascent social sciences or from physiology. At one level of course, the interchangeability of sin and suffering was highly traditional. In the novel Fred Vincy, having kept bad company in sordid places, is punished—but *not* purified—by a life-threatening fever.[73] However, the sanitary movement of the first half of the nineteenth century had as its mission the need to remind contemporaries, with all the moral and political force at its command, that no spatial distance between rich and poor would preserve the rich from the poor's diseases—nor, just as pertinently, from the economic and social effects of the deaths of breadwinners among the labouring class. That is, the rich could no longer retain the illusion of living 'apart on their stations up the mountain', in a 'rarefied social air'.[74] The diseases which defined the sanitarian cause were not the blatantly contagious infections, like smallpox, but the insidious, so-called 'doubtful' diseases, notably the continued fevers, which appeared to relate as much to a shared environment as to the individual. William Budd's views belonged to the other end of the theoretical spectrum from official sanitarian doctrine, but still he can be regarded as a major participant in the sanitary movement, stressing the role of individuals as well as the environment.

[70] Eliot, *Middlemarch*, ch. 15 (175–6, 178); ch. 16 (193–4). Cf. M. Y. Mason, '*Middlemarch* and Science: Problems of Life and Mind', *Review of English Studies*, 22 (1971), 162 ff.; Paxton, *George Eliot and Herbert Spencer*, 174–5, 178; Cosslett, *Scientific Movement*, 87; Harvey, 'The Intellectual Background', 35–6; Shuttleworth, *George Eliot*, 145.

[71] Eliot, *Middlemarch*, Finale (892–3). On gout, see Roy Porter and George S. Rousseau, *Gout: The Patrician Malady* (New Haven, 1998).

[72] David R. Carroll, 'Unity through Analogy: An Interpretation of *Middlemarch*', *Victorian Studies*, 2 (1959), 305–16, esp. 316; Pelling, *Cholera*, ch. 7.   [73] Eliot, *Middlemarch*, ch. 26.

[74] Ibid., ch. 34 (360).

My conclusion would be that Eliot was not on the side of the later commentators who saw Lydgate as an ideal type defeated, at least for a time, by a reactionary environment and extraneous social obligations. In this novel at least, Eliot, however respectful of basic research, is not endorsing the science of the laboratory but is rather pointing to the inevitability of a natural history—or epidemiology—of society, as the very English natural historian Mr Farebrother so fittingly describes it.[75] Lydgate's rival practitioners, whatever their defects, have an intimate sense of their society. Lydgate by contrast is markedly scornful of the small change of communal life. As has recently been pointed out, in his intellectual work he searches for the intimate connections and resemblances in living matter, but in his social and moral life this vision of the truth is disregarded. Being well born, he does not feel himself to be of the same material as other men. Eliot comments pointedly on this, using a deliberate paradox in naming 'commonness' as Lydgate's main defect.[76] In this he is contrasted with Will Ladislaw, whose origins are strikingly motley, although only 'low' according to a provincial outlook. Eliot sidesteps issues of class and nationality by allowing Ladislaw to say of himself, 'I never had any caste'.[77] Lydgate's ability to communicate with lower class patients—which is described rather than exemplified—is only a learned behaviour; Will Ladislaw by contrast instinctively treats everyone alike, even poor children, less as a political principle than as an expression of the unity of emotion and intellect he shares with Dorothea, and which (as we saw) some reviewers condemned as feminine when compared with the masculinity of Lydgate.

It is important that Lydgate's downfall is not ascribed to his defence of any scientific or medical principle. This possibility is rigorously excluded from his dilemma over the death of Raffles.[78] In this Eliot's treatment may be contrasted with Ibsen's *Enemy of the People* (1882), in which a scientific belief about epidemic disease, albeit one of immediate social significance, is made the crux of the play. Similarly, Lydgate's casting vote in the election of a chaplain for the infirmary is not a symbol of the control of such institutions by medical men—which Eliot knew was not the case—but rather a stroke of fate and of his own pride whereby a net of small circumstances leads to substantial results.[79] Lydgate's fineness of mind is limited to his intellectual qualities. Eliot accepted the existence and even the goodness of such minds, while insisting on their limitations and unequal development. Medical men in general, and the French experimental physiologists in particular, were frequently suspected of scepticism, and Eliot gives suggestions in Lydgate's research interests as well as in his character of a tendency to materialism.[80]

---

[75] See e.g. Nancy Henry, 'George Eliot, George Henry Lewes, and Comparative Anatomy', in John Rignall (ed.), *George Eliot and Europe* (Aldershot, 1997), 44–63. For conflicting views on natural history in *Middlemarch*, see Mason, '*Middlemarch* and Science', 164 ff.; Shuttleworth, *George Eliot*, 143 ff. Farebrother is however appropriate to his period.　　　　　　[76] Eliot, *Middlemarch*, ch. 15 (179).

[77] Ibid., ch. 46 (502); Scott, 'George Eliot, Positivism, and the Social Vision', 74 ff.

[78] Eliot, *Middlemarch*, ch. 70.　　　　　[79] Ibid., ch. 18.

[80] See e.g. ibid., ch. 18 (211), ch. 31 (330).

Of course, Eliot's own religious views shocked her contemporaries, Gladstone probably included; but materialism would contradict what she described to Allbutt as her 'yearning affection towards the great religions of the world which have reflected the struggles and needs of mankind'.[81] The materialism of Lydgate's medical colleagues is literal and venal, but in Lydgate it is more dangerous, at least to himself. It is a metaphor for the lack of spirituality which sets him apart from Dorothea and which she shares with Ladislaw. Ladislaw's intellectual interests were eclectic, not to say kaleidoscopic, but were ultimately drawn together by the idea of public service; it is he, rather than the comparatively focused, 'private' Lydgate, whose character resembles that of Lewes, the man seen by Shuttleworth and others as the source of many of Eliot's biological ideas. In summary then, it seems to me that, although the idea of the scientific mentality upholding its own criteria of judgement independent of society is one which develops in the course of the nineteenth century, Eliot herself arguably did not believe in this idea, and certainly did not convey it in *Middlemarch*.

[81] Haight, *George Eliot Letters*, iv. 472 (1868).

14

Victorian Interpretations of Thomas Hobbes

Jose Harris

I

Two decades ago Professor John Burrow in *Whigs and Liberals* cautioned his readers against taking Victorian references to Hobbes too seriously. Virtually nobody in nineteenth-century England, he suggested, had employed a conception of human nature or reasoned about 'man in society' in terms closely derived from the philosophy of Thomas Hobbes. This warning was aimed at certain historians in the 1960s who had too readily identified Hobbes with the liberalism of Herbert Spencer and Mill.[1] Subsequent historians of nineteenth-century thought have mostly followed Burrow's advice, and have either ignored the Victorian resurgence of interest in Hobbes, or treated it merely as a matter of literary or antiquarian significance. Many Victorian commentators themselves took a similar view, discussing Hobbes's works—if noticed at all—simply as part of the wider explosion of interest in seventeenth-century history. Some, however, portrayed Hobbes in a rather different light: as a thinker who offered important clues to the political, philosophical, and theological trends of their own era. This more engaged perspective found a voice among both admirers and antagonists of Hobbesian ideas. It was expressed by some who found in Hobbes's works an attractive prototype for modern law reform, rational theology, natural science, and the growth of civil society; and by others who saw the resurgence of Hobbesian themes as an insidious force behind the decline of ancient communities, the waning of supernatural religion, and the invasion of English liberties by the rise and concentration of the modern 'absolute' state.

This latter theme—of Hobbes, not as the ancestor of nineteenth-century liberalism, but as a malevolent mastermind behind the rise of modern tyranny—has been pursued in a number of recent investigations of the Victorian Hobbesian

---

[1] J. W. Burrow, *Whigs and Liberals: Continuity and Change in English Political Thought* (Oxford, 1988), 3–5.

revival. These studies have varied in detail, but have concurred in claiming that arguments derived from Hobbes were systematically deployed by Victorian theorists, not just for purposes of abstract speculation, but in order to resist the rise of democracy and to foster new forms of state power on a scale undreamt of by 'absolutist' rulers of Hobbes's own era. One such account by Mark Francis ascribed this process to the growth of legal positivism: the school of thought, rooted in Hobbes's theory of sovereignty, whereby law was defined simply as the 'command' of whoever happened to be the *de facto* ruler of a commonwealth, unencumbered by morality, intrinsic justice, hereditary entitlement, or individual rights. As elaborated by Jeremy Bentham and John Austin, and even more markedly by later Victorian jurists headed by Sir Frederick Pollock, this 'despotic theory of right based on the personal authority of the ruler' had evolved into a covert bid for the restoration of unlimited monarchical power. Supposedly 'scientific' debates about sovereignty were used by these theorists (who 'loathed' democracy and 'doted on' Hobbes) to justify authoritarian resistance to democratic rights, both in Britain itself and throughout the empire. Hobbes's 'unashamed defence of tyranny' was thus 'tamed and turned into a support for Victorian conservatism'.[2] A study by C. D. Tarleton laid less emphasis on the capture of Hobbes's thought by authoritarian conservatives, and more on the 'sanitizing' role of well-meaning but deluded Victorian liberals. In this account the English liberal had tradition sought to detach Hobbes from his despotic roots, to credit him with an 'idealist' theory of moral obligation, and to harness his doctrine of sovereignty 'to the great democratic idea of self-government'. 'More or less since Bentham', Tarleton concluded, political commentators had 'concealed, ignored, misinterpreted or rewritten despotism right out of Hobbes', and perversely reclaimed him as a moderate liberal constitutionalist.[3] A third perspective was suggested by David Nicholls, who focused not just on Hobbes's secular thought but on his political theology. Nicholls acknowledged that Hobbes's 'sovereign' might in principle be anything from a solitary ruler to an elective mass democracy. But democracy so derived was no less prone to arbitrary 'domination' than a personal monarch or oligarchic elite. The heart of the problem was Hobbes's vision of secular government as directly analogous to the role of the deity in Augustinian and Calvinist theology. This portrayal of an all-powerful, utterly transcendent Godhead at the apex of human affairs had gripped the Victorian political imagination and provided a subliminal model for the growth of the modern, all-embracing, 'sovereign' state: a state geared, Nicholls concluded, to Hobbesian goals of security and order, rather than to 'human' goals of freedom, diversity, and individual rights.[4]

[2] M. Francis, 'The Nineteenth Century Theory of Sovereignty and Thomas Hobbes', *History of Political Thought*, 1/3, (1980), 517–29.

[3] C. D. Tarleton, 'The Despotical Doctrine of Hobbes, Parts I and II', *History of Political Thought*, 22/4 (2001), 587–618, and 23/1 (2002), 61–89.

[4] D. Nicholls, *Deity and Domination, vol. 1, Images of God and the State in the Nineteenth and Twentieth Centuries* (London, 1989).

These are ambitious claims, which make large and contentious assumptions about the ideas of Hobbes himself, as well as those of his Victorian interpreters. The present essay is concerned less with Hobbes's own thought than with the many different strands in his nineteenth-century revival. I shall take account, not just of the reception of Hobbes's *political* thought (central as that must be), but of the engagement with his ideas among Victorian scientists, philosophers, theologians, and students of language and literature. Can the various 'authoritarian conspiracy' interpretations mentioned above be sustained? Or was interest in Hobbes simply part of a widespread Victorian passion for the details of English history, doubtless of some cultural and imaginative significance, but not to be taken too literally as a pointer to contemporary attitudes and beliefs?

II

By the 1890s Hobbes was widely referred to, even by those who disliked his ideas, as England's 'greatest' political philosopher. His most important work, *Leviathan*, was portrayed as 'one of the English bibles', 'the first great fountain of original ideas', and 'nothing less than the cornerstone of the science of politics'.[5] Yet it had not always been thus. After his death in 1679 detailed knowledge of Hobbes's life and thought had largely disappeared from the mainstream of intellectual debate in Britain for well over a century. Apart from his commentaries on Aristotle's *Rhetoric* and on Thucydides' *History of the Peloponnesian War*, none of Hobbes's major works had been republished in English throughout the eighteenth century. This was in marked contrast to the many translations of his writings that had appeared on the continent, where his ideas were well-known to both Enlightenment rulers and proponents of revolution.[6] Although never a wholly forgotten book, the *Leviathan* had been widely dismissed in Britain as 'the gospel of cold-headed and hard-hearted unbelievers';[7] while Hobbes's philosophical and scientific views, rooted in geometry, mechanics, and syllogistic logic, had found little favour among schools of thought that favoured natural theology, intuitionism, and theories of 'common sense'. When Hobbes was mentioned by eighteenth-century moralists it was with rare exceptions as a supporter of tyranny, a 'scoffer', and an ignoble trimmer and turncoat. He was equally despised in more popular writings, numerous editions of *The Visions of John Bunyan* portraying him as eloquently but unavailingly repenting in Hell.[8]

---

[5] *Saturday Review* (27 Feb. 1886), 308; W. Graham, *English Political Philosophy from Hobbes to Maine* (1899), pp. xix, xxxi; W. A. Dunning, 'Jean Bodin on Sovereignty', *Political Science Quarterly*, 11 (1896), 84.

[6] These included Dutch, Russian, Swiss, and French translations of Hobbes's *De Cive*, and numerous commentaries on Hobbes's works, though no translation of *Leviathan* before the 1790s: C. Hinnant, *Thomas Hobbes: A Reference Guide* (Boston, 1980), 18–43.

[7] Macaulay, cited in A. W. Benn, *A History of Modern Philosophy* (London, 1912), 28.

[8] *The visions of heaven, and the glories thereof: likewise, visions of hell, and the torments of the damned; being the last remains of Mr John Bunyan* (London, repr. 1750, 1790, 1803, 1812).

This indifference or active hostility to Hobbes's thought was to survive well into the Victorian age. A memorable vignette in Macaulay's *The History of England* in 1848 juxtaposed Hobbes's mental brilliance and reputed atheism with the licentiousness and immorality of the Restoration era, subtly conveying the impression that the former had been a direct cause of the latter.[9] Nevertheless, from the second decade of the nineteenth century individual works by Hobbes began slowly to re-appear, initially from back-street printing houses on the radical fringes of public debate in the wake of 1789. A new edition of Hobbes's philosophical treatises *On Human Nature* and *Of Liberty and Necessity* appeared in 1812, with an introduction that highlighted his teachings on the unity of 'physics and politics', and on personal liberty not as an adjunct of 'free will' but as the mere absence of external constraints.[10] The colourful memoirs of Hobbes's life composed by John Aubrey and Anthony à Wood were reissued in 1813, and an anthologized version of *Behemoth* in 1815. All these works were taken up and publicized by the essayist William Hazlitt, whose popular lectures at the Russell institution were the conduit by which Hobbes's life and thought would become better known among a wider metropolitan audience, including Coleridge, James Mill, and other philosophical radicals.[11] A 'modernized' version of Hobbes's *Thucydides* was published in 1829, and was prescribed for undergraduates studying classical literature at Oxford (where it was read, apparently with some distaste, by the young William Gladstone).[12] Not until 1839–45, however, did the publication of a substantial sixteen-volume library edition of Hobbes's English and Latin works, edited by the radical MP Sir William Molesworth, make the bulk of his writings potentially available for scholarly and public consumption.[13]

This renewed interest in Hobbes's thought at first percolated only slowly. Indeed, lengthy reviews of the Molesworth edition were still trickling into the Victorian periodicals twenty, thirty (and in one case even forty) years after publication. Not a few Victorian authors who made use of Hobbesian language and ideas did so without attribution, perhaps fearing the continued taint of despotism and blasphemy. But the 1860s saw the beginnings of scholarly commentary on Hobbes among philosophers and theologians in English and Scottish universities, while mid-Victorian Comtean positivists hailed him as having made 'the only real improvement to social science which had been accomplished since the time of Aristotle'.[14] From the 1870s the work of the young German scholar Ferdinand

[9] T. B. Macaulay, *The History of England from the Accession of James the Second* (London, 1848); (1864 edn.), 86.

[10] T. Hobbes, *The Treatise on Human Nature: And that on Liberty and Necessity*, ed. Philip Mallet (London, 1812).

[11] 'Fragments of Lectures on Philosophy' (1812), in *The Collected Works of William Hazlitt* ed. A. R. Waller and A. Glover (London, 1904), 25–74.

[12] H. C. G. Matthew, *Gladstone, 1809–1874* (Oxford, 1986), 20.

[13] *The English Works of Thomas Hobbes of Malmesbury*, ed. Sir W. Molesworth (i–xi); and *Opera Philosophica*, i–v (London, 1839–45).

[14] J. Morley, 'Thomas Hobbes's, *Westminster Review* (1867), 345; A. Comte, *A System of Positive Polity*, tr. F. Harrison, E. Beesley, and R. Congreve (1875), ii. 246–8, iv. 483.

Tönnies in tracking down manuscript versions of previously unknown writings by Hobbes, initiated what would eventually become a large-scale international enterprise of Hobbesian textual scholarship.[15] And in 1886, after twenty years of research, George Croom Robertson, professor of philosophy at University College London, produced the first full-length scholarly study of Hobbes's political, philosophical, and scientific thought in the English language.[16] Between 1880 and 1910 no less than seven British publishing houses issued editions of the *Leviathan*, of which the Dent's Universal Library version, edited by Henry Morley, was reprinted eight times.[17] Hobbes's writings on legal, moral, and political philosophy also appeared for the first time on university curricula. *Leviathan* was prescribed for the Cambridge Moral Sciences tripos from 1874, for the Oxford school of jurisprudence from 1877, and from the mid-1880s was being used as a set text for courses on 'political science' and 'theories of the state' introduced by the history schools in both the ancient universities. In 1886 the Oxford faculty of Literae Humaniores introduced a new special subject on 'The History of English Moral Philosophy' with particular reference to the 'ethical works' of Hobbes and David Hume. Scottish universities had long made use of Hobbes's handbooks on logic and rhetoric, but now for the first time they also offered courses on his major political texts. Thus Hobbes achieved some two hundred years after his death what had been a burning but thwarted ambition during his lifetime: the adoption of his writings on 'civil philosophy' as manuals of instruction for the future leaders of the nation.[18] At a wider level this was replicated by mass sales of Hobbes's *A Brief of the Art of Rhetoric*, which served the needs of large numbers of Victorian citizens actively involved in a burgeoning public culture of debating societies, local 'parliaments', open-air meetings, and other fora of articulate and often impassioned political debate.[19]

This resurgence of interest in Hobbes's ideas was, moreover, no mere British peculiarity: indeed, French and German scholarship on Hobbes ran far ahead of its counterpart in Britain, and significantly influenced many strands in the Anglophone Hobbesian revival. Auguste Comte's *Cours de Philosophie Positif*, published in Paris in the 1830s and 1840s, repeatedly identified Hobbes as 'the true father of revolutionary philosophy', and he was allotted his own 'saint's day'

[15] 'Some Newly-Discovered Letters of Hobbes', *Mind*, 15 (July 1890), 440–8.

[16] George Croom Robertson, *Hobbes* (London, 1886).

[17] In addition to John Bohn and Longmans, who issued the Molesworth volumes, edns. of *Leviathan* were published by Thorntons of Oxford, Routledge, Dent, Clarendon Press, and Cambridge University Press.

[18] *Cambridge University Examination Statutes*, (1876–1912); *Oxford University Examination Statutes* (1870–1899 and 1900–1920); S. Collini, D. Winch, and J. Burrow, *That Noble Science of Politics* (Cambridge, 1983), ch. 11.

[19] This was by far the best-selling of Hobbes's works, being reissued in various edns. at least seventeen times over the Victorian era. On the popular demand for 'rhetoric', see H. C. G. Matthew, 'Rhetoric and Politics in Great Britain, 1860–1950', in P. Waller (ed.) *Politics and Social Change in Modern Britain* (Bnghton, 1987), 34–58.

Jose Harris

in the Positivist Calendar.[20] For Comte, Hobbes provided the missing link between an early-modern epoch of monotheistic metaphysics and the modern era of scientific positivism (the latter characterized by its treatment of politics, morals, and human behaviour generally, as indistinguishable from the study of natural phenomena). This view was reiterated from a neo-Kantian viewpoint by F. A. Lange's influential *History of Materialism*, which appeared in a widely read English translation in 1877–80.[21] Leopold Ranke claimed that the fundamental truths of Hobbes's analysis of state power were becoming even clearer in the nineteenth century than they had been in the seventeenth; while Tönnies's *Gemeinschaft und Gesellschaft* (1887) used Hobbes's dichotomy of 'natural' and 'civil' society as a sociological template from which to decipher the hidden dynamics of modern civilization.[22] From the 1880s such writings were supplemented by the growth of Hobbes studies in the new 'political science' faculties of North America, where not only political thought but the 'history of political thought' was emerging for the first time as a specialist academic discipline. Moreover, fascination with Hobbes was by no means confined to formal scholarship. John Shorthouse's much-acclaimed Restoration novel of the 1880s, *John Inglesant* (reviewed and greatly admired by Gladstone), portrayed Hobbes as the genial voice of Anglican theological sanity that had saved the eponymous hero from Jesuitism and Popery. R. D. Blackmore's 'romance of Exmoor', *Lorna Doone*, set out to illustrate Hobbes's claim that 'in all places, where men have lived by small families, to rob and spoil one another, has been a trade . . . and the greater the spoils they gained, the greater was their honour'. And the best-sellers of the late-Victorian pulp novelist Pearl Craigie were inspired by her joint hero-worship of Thomas Hobbes and Oliver Cromwell (embodied in her professional *nom de plume*, John Oliver Hobbes).[23]

This resurgence of interest in Hobbes's thought was never as wide-ranging as, for example, the Victorian cult of Plato, and even among 'empiricists' Hobbes was never so universally admired as Bacon, Locke, and Hume. The very nature of Hobbes's writings—difficult in subject-matter, and densely packed with biblical and classical allusions—meant that he could never be a 'popular' writer, even in an age that had no difficulty reading Ruskin or Carlyle. Nevertheless, by 1900 Hobbes's standing as a national literary icon and as a point of reference in many aspects of 'modern' thought contrasted strikingly with his obscurity of a hundred years before. How and why had this revival come about? And what if anything

[20] A. Comte, *Cours de Philosophie Positive*, 1833–45 (Libraire Schlesicher Frères, Paris, 1908), v. 375–84, 391, vi. 420–1, *The Positive Philosophy of Auguste Comte*, freely translated by H. Martineau, 1853 (1896 edn.), iii. 185–94, 358.
[21] F. A. Lange, *History of Materialism and Criticism of its Present Importance* (English trs. E. C. Thomas, London, 1877–80), i. 270–90.
[22] L. von Ranke, *A History of England principally in the Seventeenth Century* (1859–68; English tr., Oxford, 1875), iii. 76; F. Tönnies, *Community and Civil Society* (1887; English tr., Cambridge, 2001), pp. xxv–xxvi, 122–3.
[23] J. H. Shorthouse, *John Inglesant: A Romance* (1885), ch. 5; R. D. Blackmore, *Lorna Doone: A Romance of Exmoor* (1869): for Pearl Craigie, see above P. Waller, 'Roman Candles: Catholic Converts among Authors in Late-Victorian and Edwardian Britain', Ch. 12 this vol.

does it reveal about the ideas and beliefs of the Victorians? One seemingly obvious answer to these questions is that Hobbes's writings engaged with certain core issues that lay at the heart of Victorian political, intellectual, and imaginative life: the armed balance of power between nations; clashes between church and state; 'civilized' encounters with 'backward' and 'savage' peoples; and the prolonged although (except in Ireland) largely peaceful struggles over the location, extent, and character of political power within the United Kingdom. At the most banal level a culture that discovered the biological principles of 'natural selection' and 'survival of the fittest' could scarcely fail to feel some interest in a philosopher who had diagnosed the natural state of mankind as 'the war of all against all' (a comparison reiterated to the point of cliché by social analysts, ranging from Marx to Nietzsche, from Walter Bagehot to David Ritchie).[24] And a political system that found itself almost by accident managing the affairs of a quarter of mankind could scarcely avoid engagement with such Hobbesian themes as competition for scarce resources, the principles of government and law, the subversive effects of inspirational religion, and relations between the 'sovereign' power and other lesser or intermediate agencies of human association.

None the less, at second glance both the timing and content of the Hobbesian revival seem more than a little surprising, since many aspects of Hobbes's thought appear considerably *less* in tune with British political culture in the 'age of reform', than with the much more coercive, turbulent, and confessionally exclusive society of a hundred years before (when his works had been largely forgotten). Moreover, there is an obvious puzzle in the fact that Hobbesian thought came back into intellectual currency, not simply at a time of expanding democracy, but through the medium of theorists and polemicists many of whom were, by the standards of their day, advanced radical democrats and critics of state power. Likewise, despite his cult following among Comteans and positivists, Hobbes's almost total lack of interest in the role of such factors as class, race, custom, climate, and moral character[25] in explaining the affairs of any particular polity, seems to mark him off even from those many Victorian theorists who shared his belief that the study of human behaviour could be treated as an exact science. And though Hobbes constantly invoked the image of 'the body' as an allegory or prototype of political affairs, it was of a mechanical or celestial body operating by 'wheels and pulleys' rather than the living, growing, evolving, 'organic' body envisaged by progressive and conservative theorists in the later nineteenth and early twentieth centuries.[26] There can likewise be little doubt that many religious trends in mid-nineteenth-century

[24] D. McLellan, *Karl Marx: His Life and Thought* (London, 1973), 423; F. Nietzsche, *Untimely Meditations*, tr. R. J. Hollingdale (London, 1983), 30; D. G. Ritchie, *Darwinism and Politics* (1889: London, 1895 edn.), 21–2.

[25] On Hobbes's neglect of 'character', see W. L. Courtney, 'Thomas Hobbes's, *Edinburgh Review*, 165 (1887), 98–9.

[26] Ibid., 89; W. H. Campion, *Outlines of Lectures on Political Science: Being Mainly a Review of the Political Theories of Thomas Hobbes* (1892; London, 1911 edn.), 12; A. W. Benn, *A History of Modern Philosophy* (London, 1912), 24.

Britain—the growth of Nonconformity, religious revivalism both inside and out-side the Anglican Church, the restoration of the Roman Catholic hierarchy, and the drift towards disestablishment—would have seemed to Hobbes distasteful and undesirable if not positively dangerous. Hobbes's entry into the university curriculum appears equally paradoxical, since it occurred at a moment when Platonic and Hegelian 'idealism', the intuitionism of Henry Sidgwick, and the ethical altruism of Bishop Butler (one of Hobbes's most forceful critics) have gen-erally been portrayed as the ascendant fashions in political and moral philosophy. Perhaps most puzzling of all is the rise of Hobbes's reputation as England's 'great-est political philosopher' during an era and within a political culture that prized various models of personal 'liberty' as the distinctive and transcendent national virtue. How could John Stuart Mill, the national prophet of liberty and champion of private conscience, be a lifelong admirer of an author so closely identified with determinism, censorship, doctrinal conformity, and monopolistic state power? And how could the supposedly 'minimal state' of the early Victorian era, the 'moral-purpose' state of late-Victorian philosophical idealism, or the national cult of self-governing voluntary associations cherished by liberal pluralists throughout the period, be reconciled with the absolutism, amoralism, and mechanistic indi-vidualism ascribed to the author of *Leviathan*? An adequate treatment of these issues would require many volumes of detailed study; here a few tentative lines of enquiry must suffice.

III

One key to these contradictions lay in the fact that the nineteenth-century rediscovery of Hobbes's works occurred not on one single front, but many: in philosophical, scientific, and religious spheres, as well as legal and political. Hobbes himself had maintained that his system was an integrated whole and that 'the last principles of Physics are conjoined with the first principles of Politics'.[27] But though the quest for such unity was one that many nineteenth-century intellectuals found attractive, it was nevertheless extremely rare for Victorian readers of Hobbes to endorse or condemn his system on every front. As we have seen, the earliest promoters of his rehabilitation had been men who held no brief whatso-ever for his theories of state power, but were willing to pardon 'his services to Despotism' in consideration of 'his services to Philosophy'. These figures had included such avowed enemies of authoritarianism as the Unitarian scientist Joseph Priestley, the anarchist William Godwin, and the radical orator and civil liberties campaigner John Horne Tooke. It was these fierce critics of Hanoverian government who first brought Hobbes's name back into circulation, not as a

---

[27] P. Mallet, introduction to Hobbes, *The Treatise on Human Nature: And that on Liberty and Necessity* (London, 1812), 52–3.

theorist of state power, but as a 'natural philosopher' who had written extensively on questions of mind, logic, language, sensation, and scientific method. Priestley drew attention to Hobbes's teachings on the unity of mind and matter, on the role of 'invariance' or 'necessity' in determining physical motion, and on the 'association of ideas' (as distinct from *a priori* or innate ideas) as the key to human conduct.[28] William Godwin's novel *Caleb Williams* was designed to demonstrate how Hobbes's account of the mechanical interplay of individual rational calculation (including what would now be known as 'the prisoner's dilemma') governed even the minutest relations of everyday life.[29] Horne Tooke was a passionate disciple of Hobbes's theory of language, which held that meaning lay in 'words' rather than 'things'; that 'truth' was a property of statements rather than phenomena; and that thought was impossible without the prior invention of 'names', 'marks', and 'signs'.[30]

These doctrines would be of central importance in the early decades of the nineteenth century in developing a radical critique of prevailing 'common sense' or 'intuitionist' conceptions of mind; and it was in these fields—psychology, logic, and language—that Hobbes's name was first reabsorbed into the mainstream of intellectual debate. The enthusiasms of Priestley and Tooke were taken over in the 1820s by James Mill, leader of the Benthamite radicals, who saw in Hobbes a doughty ally in his private war against the 'muddled' reasoning and metaphysical preconceptions exemplified by such eminent contemporaries as Dr Thomas Brown. Mill's *Essay on Education* (1823) gave a central role to Hobbes's 'sensationalist' theory of perception, a theme developed in much greater detail in his *Analysis of the Phenomena of the Human Mind* (1829). Mill's famous *Essay on Government* (1820) mentioned Hobbes only briefly by name, but nevertheless applied his 'geometric' method to the study of institutions (i.e. reasoning from axioms, rather than from observation of particular historical examples).[31] Mill's polemical *Fragment on Mackintosh* likewise defended Hobbes's syllogistic reasoning, universalist deontology, and sensory theory of perception, against the imputed charges of Sir James Mackintosh that Hobbes's system of ideas was dogmatic and immoral.[32] Mill was not himself a flamboyant publicist, but his views were to be transmitted much more widely through the circle of philosophical radicals (among them Sir William Molesworth and his mentor, George Grote) and through the programme of education that he devised for his eldest son. John Stuart Mill's daily

[28] J. Priestley, *Works*, iii. 45.

[29] W. Godwin, *Things as they are: or, The Adventures of Caleb Williams* (London, 1794); M. Philp, *Godwin's Political Justice* (London, 1986), 109–10.

[30] J. Horne Tooke, *The Diversions of Purley* (London, 1798, 1805 edn.); W. Hazlitt, 'On Tooke's *Diversions of Purley*' (1812), in *Collected Works of William Hazlitt* (London, 1904), xi. 119–32.

[31] T. Ball (ed.), *James Mill's Political Writings* (Cambridge, 1992), 10–11, 147–8, 152–3.

[32] James Mill, *Fragment on Mackintosh*, 28–55. Mackintosh was in fact far more generous to Hobbes than Mill allowed, comparing him with Aristotle and Kant as the 'only persons who united in the highest degree the great faculties of comprehension and discrimination', *Dissertation on the Progress of Ethical Philosophy* (London, 1836), 115–33.

tasks from the age of 12 included intensive study of Hobbes on logic and rhetoric, and throughout adult life the younger Mill was to display an unusually detailed familiarity with the problems in formal logic posed by Hobbes's writings. Hobbes's doctrine of necessity was to be a continuing (and constraining) presence in all Mill's attempts to construct a systematic social science; while critical engagement with his treatment of propositions, predication, truth-statements, syllogisms, deduction and induction was evident in many of the most technical passages of Mill's magnum opus, *A System of Logic*.[33] Hobbes's treatise *Computatio sive Logica* was also adopted as a philosophy text at the Benthamite foundation, University College, London, where it would influence the mid-century revolution in mathematical and syllogistic logic brought about by Augustus de Morgan, George Bentham, and George Boole.[34]

Hobbesian ideas also permeated the mass of early and mid-Victorian studies on perception and association, produced by James Mill's devoted disciples: G. H. Lewes, Alexander Bain, and other 'mental philosophers' at the universities of London, Edinburgh, Glasgow, and St Andrews, where Hobbes was viewed as having 'more distinctly than any other' pioneered the view that mind was part of the natural world.[35] The project of fusing together Hobbes's theories of perception, logic, and language was further carried on in the work of George Croom Robertson, who—as well as being the first comprehensive expositor of Hobbes's ideas—was also a co-founder and first editor of the journal *Mind*, which was to maintain a strongly 'posivitist' bent in British academic philosophy against the current of late-Victorian idealism.[36] Moreover, although interest in Hobbes's philosophical and scientific ideas was particularly evident among positivists and utilitarians, it was by no means confined to them. F. D. Maurice's *Modern Philosophy* (1862) portrayed Hobbes as the champion of logic and 'ratiocination' over mere factual knowledge; while Henry Hallam's *Introduction to the Literature of Europe* (1837–9), though deploring Hobbes's 'heartless indifference to right', nevertheless portrayed him as the precursor of Berkeley's theory of vision, of Hume's critique of causality, and of the recent revival of syllogistic logic—and did so in a much more accessible style than the stilted prose of James Mill.[37] Many reviewers of Molesworth were similarly no less interested in Hobbes's contribution to the history of science and philosophy than in his politics. And from the 1860s onwards Hobbes was also

[33] J. S. Mill, *Collected Works of John Start Mill*, ed. J. M. Robson (Toronto, 1965–96), i. 20–1, 124–5, 165–7, 567–8; v, 715; vii. 24–5, 79–80, 90–101, 144–5, 176–7, viii. 827, 889, 1011, 1024, 1046; xiii. 530, 581, 638–9.

[34] Ibid., xiii. 366; A. de Morgan, *On the Syllogism and Other Logical Writings* ed. P. Heath (London, 1965), 184, 226, 318–9; J. Passmore, 'New Developments in Logic', in *A Hundred Years of Philosophy* (London, 1957), 130–1.

[35] G. H. Lewes, *The History of Philosophy from Thales to Comte* (1845–6; London, 1867 edn.), 227–53; A. Bain, *The Mental and Moral Science: A Compendium of Psychology and Ethics* (London, 1868), 411–13, 543–56.   [36] Croom Robertson,*Hobbes*, 124.

[37] F. D. Maurice, *Modern Philosophy; or, A Treatise of Moral and Metaphysical Philosophy* (London, 1862), 242–4; H. Hallam, *Introduction to the Literature of Europe*, iii. 306, 338 , iv. 275, 308–9.

widely identified in more populist writings as a precursor of evolutionary thought, of scientific approaches to biblical criticism, of the discovery of notions of 'relativity', and of the 'molecular structure of matter'.[38] In 1874 he figured as one of the heroic godfathers of positivist natural science in John Tyndall's famous Belfast address to the British Association; while Leslie Stephen's study in the *Dictionary of National Biography*, subsequently elaborated into his full-scale 'life' of Hobbes (1904), identified his subject as the generator of a 'ferment in English thought not surpassed until the advent of Darwinism'.[39] Even Hobbes's claim that society was based on force was seen by some as a maxim of physics rather than politics, the union of unstable particles being 'resolved into an equilibrium . . . by violent pressure from without'.[40]

So in many quarters Hobbes's reputation as a philosopher and forerunner of modern scientific thought was at least as great as his standing as an authority on politics and law. Equally contentious, though more difficult to interpret, were his views on religion. In early Victorian religious pamphleteering Hobbes's name continued to be associated both with atheism and blasphemy, and with the institutional privileges of an Established Church. His notorious 'last sayings' (among them that religious belief was a 'bitter pill that must be swallowed whole') still gave offence to many, by implying that religion was simply a useful discipline, whose precise theological content didn't really matter.[41] His picture of the Holy Trinity— as three actors each playing a representational role—was again seen as startlingly heretical.[42] When in 1838 the young William Gladstone defended the principle of a religious establishment in *The State in its Relations with the Church*, he explicitly rejected the model of establishment set out in the *Leviathan*, which turned the 'church and her doctrines' into 'mere creatures' of the secular power.[43] Dr Pusey likewise condemned Hobbes's 'social contract' account of the origins of human society as an 'unbelieving theory'; and the growing 'catholic' revival within the Church of England increasingly discredited Hobbes's doctrine that priestly authority was vested by God in the holder of secular power.[44] Reviewers of the Molesworth volumes gave vent to many expressions of distaste at Hobbes's

[38] *Westminster Review* (1867), 361–2, 367–9; J. Hunt, 'Thomas Hobbes of Malmesbury', *Contemporary Review*, (1868), 192–3; J. F. Stephen *Horae Sabbaticae*, 2nd ser. (1892), 51.

[39] G. Basalla, W. Coleman, and R. Kargon (eds.), *Victorian Science: A Self-Portrait from the Presidential Addresses of the British Association* (New York, 1970), 446, 448; L. Stephen, 'Hobbes', *DNB* (1885).

[40] A. W. Benn, 'The Relation of Greek Philosophy to Modern Thought', *Mind*, 726 (Apr. 1882), 232.

[41] *The Last Sayings or Dying Legacy of Mr Thomas Hobbes of Malmesbury* from *Tracts during the reign of Charles II*, arranged by Sir Walter Scott, vii. (2nd edn., London 1812); J. Hunt, 'Thomas Hobbes of Malmesbury', *Contemporary Review*, 7 (1868), 192.

[42] J. Hunt, 'Thomas Hobbes of Malmesbury', *Contemporary Review*, 7 (1868), 194. W. R. Sorley, 'Hobbes and Contemporary Philosophy', *Cambridge History of English Literature* (1912–20), x. 296.

[43] W. E. Gladstone, *The State in its Relations with the Church* (1838; 4th edn. London, 1841), 31.

[44] S. A. Skinner, *Tractarians and the 'Condition of England': The Social and Political Thought of the Oxford Movement* (Oxford, 2004), 127.

'irreverence' and religious 'despotism', including the hope that Providence would 'use Hobbes for good' by provoking opposition to his 'strange farrago of contradictory heresies'.[45] Sir William Molesworth himself was mobbed by a demonstration of the Anti-State Church Association, shouting 'No Obbes', when he stood as parliamentary candidate for the London borough of Southwark at the general election of 1845.[46]

Yet what Hobbes's heresies really amounted to remained a matter of great uncertainty.[47] To some it seemed that the very fact of his materialism and contemptuous denial of the 'airy things we call infinite' was tantamount to atheism, whereas to others his insistence on the unity of mind and matter was entirely in accord with the historic creeds of the church.[48] Hobbes's insistence on the 'unknowability' of God likewise appeared to many as a denial of Christian revelation; yet this doctrine was also endorsed by some of the most powerful mid-Victorian exponents of Christian metaphysics (among them Dean Mansel and the Scottish Kantian philosopher Sir William Hamilton).[49] Hobbes's depiction of human nature as inherently calculating and selfish was frequently cited as evidence of his own grossly un-Christian outlook. But to the incarnationalist theologian F. D. Maurice it suggested precisely the opposite: that Hobbes's doctrine of man was surprisingly 'orthodox', and that Hobbes had performed a signal service to Christian readers by reminding them of the appalling 'savagery' of human life, unregulated by either civil government or the Kingdom of God.[50] Even rationalists and agnostics could not agree on the nature of Hobbes's opinions. In the earlier nineteenth century he was frequently portrayed as a deist, whereas later in the century he was more often claimed as a pioneer of 'pantheistic naturalism', 'humanism', or the 'religion of science'.[51] Yet J. S. Mill—as deeply acquainted as anyone with Hobbes's writings—thought otherwise: Hobbes, he claimed in 1871, 'never speaks otherwise than as a believer in God, and even in Christianity'.[52] Mill himself in the 1840s had made use of Hobbes's method of logic to attack what he saw as the 'vacuous ontology' of the Anglican intelligentsia.[53] But Leslie and Fitzjames Stephen, themselves victims of classic mid-century crises of orthodox faith, both came to the conclusion that Hobbes's views were largely

[45] *Christian Remembrancer* (1845), 94; *British Quarterly*, 6 (1847), 187; *Contemporary Review*, 7 (1868), 193–5.

[46] M. Fawcett, *Life of the Right Hon. Sir William Holdsworth, Bart. M.P., FRS* (London, 1901), 251–4.

[47] J. Hunt, *Religious Thought in England from the Reformation to the End of the Last Century* (London, 1869), i. 409–10.

[48] A. Bain, *Mind and Body: The Theories of their Relation* (London, 1873), 184, 196.

[49] A. Ryan, introduction to J. S. Mill, *An examination of Sir William Hamilton's Philosophy*, in J. S. Mill, CW, ix: H. L. Mansel, *The Philosophy of the Conditioned* (London, 1866).

[50] Maurice, *Moral Philosophy*, 262–4.

[51] Morley, 'Thomas Hobbes', 374; A. W. Benn, *The History of English Rationalism in the Nineteenth Century* (London, 1906), i. 94; Mary Whiton Calkins (ed.) *The Metaphysical System of Thomas Hobbes* (Religion of Science Library, 57; Chicago, 1906); J. M. Robertson, *Pioneers of Humanism* (London, 1908), 115–46.   [52] J. S. Mill, CW, xi. 466.

[53] Ibid., xiii. 529–32.

indistinguishable from long-term shifts of religious belief within the Anglican Church.[54] Again, to one reviewer of Molesworth it was not lack of belief but 'faintness of belief'—the 'weakness of his sense of Providence' and his indifference to doctrinal detail—that characterized Hobbes's pronouncements on religious matters. To this extent Hobbes's thought epitomized, and was perhaps even partly responsible for, the long-drawn-out transformation of religious thought in England from the theological intensity of the 1830s and 1840s to the not 'irreligious' but more 'agnostic' Christianity of the 1890s.[55]

IV

Uncertainty and faintness in religious belief hardly accord with those recent accounts of Victorian Hobbism, cited above, which link the growth of modern state power to Hobbes's vision of a punitive omnipotent deity. This aspect of his theology may have supplied the template for theories of state absolutism in the 1650s, but such a link seems much less tenable for the Victorian era, when those attracted to Hobbes's theories of government largely ignored or actively dissented from a Calvinistic construction of the sovereignty of God. Nevertheless, the question remains as to how and why Hobbes's political thought came to be, as never before in Britain, the subject of sustained intellectual debate. The adoption in the 1870s and 1880s of Hobbes's political works as prescribed texts for courses in the major universities was undoubtedly a significant moment. But the meaning of this development can easily be misinterpreted, since many of those who devised such courses were far from being unqualified disciples. Of the academics who lectured on Hobbes at Oxford in the 1880s and 1890s, W. Pogson Smith was a Hegelian idealist who revered Hobbes as a technical philosopher but regarded his politics as 'rotten to the core'. D. G. Ritchie likened Hobbes to Glaucon and Thrasymachus (the champions of utility and physical force outsmarted by Socrates in Plato's *The Republic*); while W. J. Campion was a Christian Socialist and contributor to *Lux Mundi*, who favoured an equal division of sovereignty between church and state (Hobbes's *bête noire*).[56] Henry Sidgwick in Cambridge portrayed Hobbes appreciatively as a harbinger of 'modern thought', yet rejected his view that politics could be rooted in rational self-interest; while J. R. Seeley, who as a realist and positivist might have been expected to relish Hobbism, in fact advocated an inductionist methodology of the kind Hobbes

[54] J. F Stephen, 'Hobbes on Government', *Horae Sabbaticae*, 2nd ser. (1892), 6; Leslie Stephen, *Hobbes* (London, 1904), 234–6.

[55] G. P. Gooch, *Political Thought in England from Bacon to Halifax* (London, 1915), 56–7.

[56] W. Pogson Smith, 'The Philosophy of Hobbes', in *Hobbes's Leviathan* (Oxford, 1909), p. xvii; D. G. Ritchie, 'Contributions to the History of Social Contract Theory', *Political Science Quarterly*, 6 (1891), 656–7, and *Natural Rights* (London, 1895), 24–5; W. J. H. Campion, 'Christianity and Politics', in C. Gore (ed.) *Lux Mundi. A Series of Studies on the Religion of the Incarnation* (London, 1890), 437–64.

had dismissed as peculiarly futile.[57] In fact *Leviathan* appears to have been selected as a student text, not for its substantive doctrines but for quite different reasons. It was seen as a classic English 'literary' text; it was believed to exemplify the 'analytical' (as opposed to historical) approach to politics; and it offered a methodological foil to the inductive, relativistic, classificatory method expounded in the other great text of late Victorian 'political science' courses, Aristotle's *Politics*. It was primarily for its deductive method, its system of logic, and its rhetorical and polemical skills, not its moral and political teachings, that *Leviathan* was seen as supplying a unique intellectual whetstone for training the minds of future citizens and rulers of the early twentieth century.[58]

This did not mean, of course, that Victorian interpretations of Hobbesian political thought involved nothing more than disinterested academic analysis. Quite the contrary. Academics (with one exception, considered below) came late on the scene, and for much of the earlier period covered here the prime arena for discussion of political ideas in Britain remained periodicals, polemical works, and public platforms rather than textbooks. Moreover, as with his ideas on science and religion, interpretations of Hobbes's political thought were extremely diverse. Thus, while some saw Hobbes as 'the deadliest enemy of individualism', others saw him as an archetypal 'individualist' (both in the 'solitary' sense implied by his 'state of nature', and as a precursor of the culture of autonomy, diversity, and heightened self-awareness that increasingly characterized 'modern' civilization).[59] Some saw Hobbes's commonwealth as strictly hierarchical, while others noted that he was 'one of the greatest opponents of hierarchical rule that ever existed'.[60] The progressive Rainbow Circle criticized Hobbes's thought as fundamentally 'anti-social', whereas James Fitzjames Stephen claimed that, without the framework of a Hobbesian-style commonwealth, 'there would be no such thing as society among men'.[61] Hobbes was both the epitome of the 'selfish philosophy', and also the epitome of 'the good of the whole as the supreme rule of conduct'.[62] His portrayal of sovereign states in international relations—armed to the teeth in an irredeemable 'state of nature'—was viewed by some as a recipe for violence and armed conflict; whereas for others it seemed that the whole rationale of his political philosophy was fine-tuned calculation for the strategic avoidance of war.[63]

[57] H. Sidgwick, *The Development of the European Polity* (London, 1903), 349–50; J. B. Schneewind, *Sidgwick's Ethics and Victorian Moral Philosophy* (Oxford, 1977), 35–5, 355, 420; J. R. Seeley, *Introduction to Political Science* (London, 1895), 20–4.

[58] Graham, *English Political Philosophy*, 28–30; Pogson Smith, 'Philosophy', pp. xvii–xviii.

[59] H. W. Hoare, 'Thomas Hobbes', *Fortnightly Review*, 42 (1884), 227; W. L. Courtney, 'Thomas Hobbes', *Edinburgh Review*, 165 (Jan. 1887), 93; C. E. Vaughan, *Studies in the History of Political Philosophy* (London, 1925), 22–3.   [60] W. J. H. Campion (citing Ranke) in *Outlines of Lectures*, 24.

[61] *Minutes of the Rainbow Circle* 1894–1924, ed. M. Freeden (Camden Society, 4th ser. 38; London, 1989), 85; J. F. Stephen, *Horae Sabbaticae*, 2nd ser. (1892), 6.

[62] Morley, 'Thomas Hobbes', 381; Alfred W. Benn, 'The Relation of Greek Philosophy to Modern Thought', *Mind*, 726 (1882), 232.

[63] J. A. Hobson, 'The Ethics of Internationalism', *International Journal of Ethics*, 171 (1906), 25–6; A. D. Lindsay, introduction to *Leviathan* (London, 1908), p. xxii.

There was thus no single Victorian stereotype of Hobbes's political doctrines, and this diversity increased as his works, particularly *Leviathan*, became more widely read. Yet there remained areas of tacit agreement about what Hobbes's political thought implied, and these are of some significance in reflecting the assumptions of the Victorian epoch. Despite Hobbes's depiction of mankind as insatiably acquisitive, no Victorian writer interpreted the *Leviathan* as primarily a machine for protecting market capitalism or bourgeois private property. On the contrary, it was generally assumed (by both J. S. Mill and F. D. Maurice, for example) that it was the restraint and regulation of human competitive instincts, not their unleashing, that constituted the primary agenda of the Hobbesian state (a view that drew credence from the fact that most of the economic policies recommended by Hobbes could well have come from the pages of Ruskin or Carlyle).[64] Hobbes's model of the 'social contract', which portrayed subjects but not rulers as bound by covenant to obey the law, was dismissed by most Victorian authors as either historically inaccurate or conceptually absurd. There were also certain points on which his theories might have been expected to attract attention, but didn't. No Victorian feminist, for example, ever referred to Hobbes's doctrine that under the 'law of nature' dominion over children lay with the mother. And Victorian socialists (unlike their German counterparts) made no use of his assumption of 'natural equality', nor of his portrayal of private property as something that was dependent on, and ultimately at the disposal of, the prevailing sovereign power.

All these areas of debate could be treated in much greater detail than there is space for here. More must be said, however, about two themes that have figured prominently in recent discussion of Hobbes's place in Victorian political thought, namely sovereignty and personal liberty. As is well known, Hobbes had argued that the essence of 'sovereignty' in any civil commonwealth, whether rooted in conquest or popular consent, was the effective power for getting orders obeyed, if necessary by force. Such a power might be decently veiled in ritual and convention; but 'in matter of government, when nothing else is turned up, clubs are trumps'.[65] Law likewise was characterized in the last resort solely by enforceability: even the English common law, though notionally evolved out of custom and precedent, was in Hobbes's view simply the consolidated sum of the sovereign's commands.[66] Such a notion of sovereignty had been current in European political thought since the sixteenth century. But it acquired new potency after 1789, as nation-states asserted themselves against international empires; secular governments against the Catholic Church; bureaucratic regimes against ancient communities and self-governing corporations; and as popular movements throughout Europe struggled to turn traditional 'sovereignty' on its head by asserting the new-found doctrine of the sovereignty of the people.

[64] F. D. Maurice, *Modern Philosophy* (London, 1862), 259; J. S. Mill, *CW*, v. 749; Stephen, *Horae Sabbaticae*, 2nd ser. (1892), 16, 30; Graham, *English Political Philosophy*, 40–1.
[65] T. Hobbes, *A Dialogue of the Common Laws* (Molesworth edn., 1840), 122.   [66] Ibid., 5–6.

It was against this background that Professor John Austin, disciple of Bentham and James Mill, gave the course of lectures in 1828 at the newly founded University College, London, that was to restore Hobbes's account of law and the state to a central role in English political theory. Like most nineteenth-century critics, Austin dismissed Hobbes's 'social contract' ideas as irrelevant and outmoded. But he followed Hobbes closely in arguing that the defining characteristic of 'law' was not 'right' but 'habitual obedience' to a sovereign power; and that sovereignty was by definition both unitary and 'absolute' (the term 'absolute' meaning, not just legally but linguistically, 'free from any bounds or limits'). Though sovereigns ought to pursue their subjects' welfare, there were no higher sanctions that could ensure this (metaphysical codes such as natural law being not true laws at all but mere moral guidelines, or what Hobbes had called 'theorems'). Laws, properly-so-called, were simply whatever the sovereign power commanded. Hence, Hobbes's sinister-sounding dictum that 'no law can be unjust' was, in Austin's view, 'neither pernicious or paradoxical' but 'merely a truism put in unguarded terms'.[67]

It was doctrines such as these that gave rise to the anxieties, voiced by reviewers of Molesworth and Croom Robertson, that rehabilitation of Hobbes was no mere scholarly exercise, but part of a wider agenda for reconstructing the historic society and polity of Britain according to principles of 'utility' and positive law.[68] As noted above, recent historical writings have echoed this view, and have credited Austin, Mill, Molesworth, Pollock, and others with favouring autocratic monarchy, 'democratic despotism', and a massive extension of the discretionary powers of the state.[69] Of these various charges, the suggestion that 'sovereignty' was part of an orchestrated conspiracy to restore royal autocracy in Britain may quickly be discounted. Although several leading utilitarians from time to time commented wistfully on the merits of 'good stout despotism' over the muddles of corrupt aristocracy, the evidence of their writings lends little support to any serious monarchical agenda.[70] On the contrary, Austin's lectures, published in the year of the 1832 Reform Act, explicitly condemned the false equation of 'sovereignty' with 'monarchy', and claimed that sovereign power in Britain was currently shared by king, peers, and the 'electoral body of the commons' (the king himself, in relation to this composite sovereign, being no less a 'subject' than any other citizen).[71] The two Mills, though neither was a strictly capitational democrat, nevertheless propounded models of political representation that their contemporaries found startlingly democratic. Frederick Pollock (portrayed in recent historiography as the great high priest of late Victorian Hobbism), likewise gave no sign of favouring a return to 'absolute' monarchy. Indeed, far from 'doting on' Hobbes, he was

---

[67] J. Austin, *The Province of Jurisprudence determined* (1832), ed. H. L. A. Hart (London, 1954), 215–85.

[68] *Christian Remembrancer* (1845), 98–9; [James Dennery], 'Hobbes of Malmesbury, *Quarterly Review*, 327 (June 1887), 425–6.   [69] See above, 238–9.

[70] J. S. Mill, *CW*, xii. 365.   [71] Austin, *Province*, 230–1, 266–8.

highly critical of the 'dogmatic assumption that sovereignty is illimitable and indivisible'.[72]

More plausible is the suggestion that the Hobbesian revival implicitly favoured enhancement of the powers of the Victorian state. Following Hobbes, Austin had argued that any sovereign body, be it a monarchy or a mass democracy or (if such were to exist) an overarching international authority, was both legally and logically 'despotic' and could innovate as it pleased. In popular Victorian discourse this topic was often confused with the quantitative expansion of government into new areas of public responsibility, such as education and public health. But although in practice they might overlap, the problem of sovereignty was in principle something quite different from that of 'state intervention'. Regardless of whether the *scope* of government was large or small, sovereignty posed a dilemma about its *nature*: how far could the ruling body in any given polity could be tamed, limited, and legalized without thereby transferring authority to some other, higher, lower, or coexistent, but no less 'absolute' final power?

For those who viewed Hobbes's analysis as an expression of 'positivist' legal science, this latter question was meaningless. What characterized sovereignty was not its good or bad effects, but that its existence in some form or another was simply a fact of life in any organized society. In the striking metaphor of James Fitzjames Stephen, the operation of sovereignty within a political body was as inescapable as gravity within a physical one, regardless of the content of specific acts of policy.[73] For others, however, a possible route out of this dilemma—of how to limit the unlimited—was the identification of sovereignty with the 'will of the people'. Hobbes himself had been well aware that his model of sovereignty could in principle be applied to a popular assembly or 'multitude'; and some of his Victorian interpreters carried this conception to its widest conclusions, portraying 'sovereignty' as stemming, not just from Parliament or electorate, but from the populace as a whole, including those as-yet-unenfranchised classes who were a part of the elusive but increasingly all-encompassing force known as 'public opinion'. For some this enlarged conception of sovereignty effectively solved the problem, since 'the will of the people' was both a good in its own right and self-evidently the final court of appeal in all human affairs. Even a thinker so closely associated with doctrines of reified 'state absolutism' as Bernard Bosanquet could be found arguing that 'sovereignty' was not located in formal governing institutions but dispersed among all citizens.[74] Yet for many others mere civic universalism was no automatic safeguard against the spectre of 'democratic despotism' (where, in Hobbes's own phrase, there were 'as many Neros as orators'). A.V. Dicey, for example, conscientiously applied Hobbesian categories to the analysis of Victorian

---

[72] *The Pollock–Holmes Letters: Correspondence of Sir Frederick Pollock and Mr Justice Holmes 1874–1932*, ed. M. DeWolfe Howe (Cambridge, 1942), ii. 26–7, 201.

[73] J. F. Stephen, *Horea Sabbaticae*, 2nd ser., 16, 30.

[74] B. Bosanquet, *The Philosophical Theory of the State* (London, 1899), 232, 282–3.

constitutional and political change, whilst at the same time deeply deploring many of the populist, illiberal, and 'state-interventionist' consequences that he perceived those changes as bringing in their train.[75]

Numerous commentators grappled with these issues. Among them were many who, even when acknowledging the force of 'sovereignty' as an analytical formula, nevertheless questioned its claim to be all-embracing. Sir Henry Maine claimed that Hobbes's account grossly oversimplified the relation between the sovereign and the vast mass of lesser self-governing institutions that existed in any function- ing society: such lesser bodies were not 'worms in the entrails of the body politic', but 'primary cells out of which the whole human body has been built up'. Nor was 'sovereignty' an adequate guide to the inner logic of the English common law, but an alien category superimposed by theorists drawing upon the continental 'Roman' or 'publicist' tradition.[76] Frederic Harrison, the famous barrister and leading spokesman of late-Victorian positivism, endorsed the Hobbes–Austin model of *legal* sovereignty as a 'truism', but denied its literal application to politics and government. The legislative power of Parliament might in principle be a 'phenomenon without limit', but nevertheless, in Harrison's view, 'a law of outrageous injustice and cruelty' would be 'universally defied'.[77] Lord Salmond, the leading turn-of-the-century expert on commonwealth law, criticized the Hobbes–Austin model of sovereignty even when applied purely in a legal context: the self-governing British dominions demonstrated the empirical fact of 'shared sovereignty', despite the 'unitary sovereignty' notionally vested in the British crown.[78] And throughout the period before 1914 Anglo-Catholic, Nonconformist, and Roman Catholic apologists waged recurrent guerrilla warfare against claims to exclu- sive sovereignty made on behalf of either a church–state establishment or a purely secular state.[79] Most critical of all was the legal historian (and close collaborator of Pollock), Frederick Maitland, whose writings and lectures on constitutional history portrayed the legacy of Hobbes's theory of sovereignty as a major force behind the creeping erosion of local and group rights (religious and secular, corporate and com- munitarian), which he identified as a powerful hidden leitmotiv of modern British history. Maitland's personal influence (powerfully reinforced by his studies of Gierke and the German 'law of association') was to be of major importance in gener- ating an Edwardian pluralist critique of the doctrine of unitary sovereignty, for which *Leviathan* was commonly cited as the *locus classicus*.[80]

[75] A.V. Dicey, *Law and Opinion in England* (1905; 2nd edn. London, 1914), 305–6, 310; *The Law of the Constitution* (1885, 8th edn., London, 1915), xxiii–xxv.

[76] H. Maine, *Early Institutions* (1874; London, 1892 edn.,), 363–4, 393–66.

[77] F. Harrison, 'The English School of Jurisprudence', *Fortnightly Review*, NS., 24 (July–Dec. 1878), 487, 491. Cf. Dicey, *Law of the Constitution*, 73.

[78] J. W. Salmond, *The Theory of Law* (London,1902), 628–37. Dicey likewise referred to 'this more or less fictitious omnipotence': *Law of the Constitution* (1915 edn.), p. xxvii.

[79] H. Laski, *Studies in the Problem of Sovereignty* (New Haven and Oxford, 1917), chs. 1–4.

[80] F. W. Maitland, *The Constitutional History of England* (London,1908), 408–9; *Collected Papers of Frederick William Maitland*, ed. Fisher (Cambridge, 1911), 310–11; J. N. Figgis, *Churches in the*

Hobbes's writings, both political and 'scientific', defined 'liberty' as simply the absence of external restraint, and some of Hobbes's most biting sarcasms had been aimed against the classical–republican view that liberty was indissolubly bound up with some degree of civic 'self-government'.[81] On the contrary, in Hobbes's account the unlimited right to order their own affairs that individuals enjoyed in the state of 'nature' was deemed to have been transferred *en bloc* to the sovereign power at the (timeless) moment when men contracted to enter 'civil society'. And in the purely private sphere, much of what passed for 'freedom of choice' or 'free will' was in Hobbes's view merely an expression of the 'appetites' or 'passions', which were governed like all other physical entities by the laws of 'matter' and 'motion'. The very notion of free will was derided by Hobbes as on a par with a 'round quadrangle' or 'immaterial substances', i.e. a logical absurdity.[82]

Such 'necessitarian' doctrines seemed startlingly at odds with the visions of personal liberty cherished by ordinary nineteenth-century Englishmen as a unique and enduring keynote of their national culture. Readers of the Molesworth volumes, including those broadly sympathetic to other aspects of Hobbesian thought, were virtually unanimous in their condemnation of Hobbes's account of 'liberty and necessity'. In the words of one reviewer of Croom Robertson, it was 'a stage army' of 'silly ideas', hostile alike to Christianity, common sense, and secular morality; while others commented that the very idea of absence of free will was to most people simply unintelligible.[83] Many aspects of the political essays of John Stuart Mill—with their support for civic activism and popular self-government, their critique of 'collective tyranny', and their exaltation of 'conscience' and 'character' over the natural passions—could be read as an assault on Hobbes's doctrines on this issue. (Indeed, the opening sentences of Mill's *On Liberty* could well have been composed with Hobbes in mind!) A generation later the idealist philosopher T. H. Green explicitly identified Hobbes as the purveyor of a 'false notion of rights', and the 'chief enemy' of new conceptions of 'positive liberty'; conceptions that entailed, not mere negative 'freedom from restraint', but growth towards 'consciouness of a common good' and a 'common interest on the part of members of a society'.[84]

Yet despite this chorus of criticism, traces of a Hobbesian presence in nineteenth-century understandings of liberty were more widely pervasive than many even of Hobbes's defenders seemed aware. It was perhaps no coincidence that some of the most prominent champions of the principle of habeas corpus (a national icon of

---

Modern State (1913; London, 1914 edn.), 56–7, 79, 82, 185; Colin Matthew, *The Nineteenth Century* (Oxford, 2000), 94.

[81] *Leviathan*, ch. 21.   [82] Ibid., ch. 5.

[83] [J. Dennery], review of Croom Robertson's *Hobbes* in *Quarterly Review*, 327 (June 1887), 415–44.

[84] T. H. Green, *Lectures on the Principles of Moral and Political Obligation* (1886; London, 1911 edn.), 44–8; H. A. Prichard, 'Green: Political Obligation', in J. MacAdam (ed.), *Moral Writings: H. A. Prichard* (Oxford, 2002), 246–8.

negative liberty) were also among the earliest promoters of the revival of interest in Thomas Hobbes. And, despite Hobbes's reputation for 'despotism', his personal views on the question of 'freedom of thought'—which combined support for absolute liberty of private conscience with extensive public censorship over views deemed subversive of public morality and order—corresponded closely with the conventional wisdom and legal practice of the Victorian age. Though Herbert Spencer claimed to abhor Hobbes's writings, there were some who interpreted Spencer's own theory of politics (based on extensive personal freedom guaranteed by stern enforcement of law) as having much in common with that of Thomas Hobbes.[85] Again, J. S. Mill's core principle—that society might interfere with private behaviour only when such behaviour caused harm to others—was much more in tune with Hobbes's ideas than was commonly supposed. Hobbes doubtless would have not have shared Mill's indignation at the case of the 'unfortunate' blasphemer, Thomas Pooley (championed in *On Liberty*), but this would have been a disagreement of fact about what constituted public harm rather than about the principle of private conscience. Moreover, as Henry Hallam (approvingly) and T. H. Green (disapprovingly) observed, Hobbes's account of the relinquishing of 'natural liberty' within the confines of civil society was far from all-embracing, since it explicitly envisaged that sensible sovereigns would keep laws to a minimum, permitting their subjects to be free to do anything that was not explicitly forbidden ('unnecessary' laws being mere 'traps for money').[86] In contrast to Hobbes's views on 'free will' and 'necessity', this negative emphasis on 'absence of constraint' and 'the silence of the laws', was seen by many liberally minded Victorians as the very core and essence of English freedom. But, in Green's view, this attitude had encouraged a 'false notion of rights' and fostered a national culture that treated political and moral obligation as passive, privatized, and crudely instrumental. It was to be seen, he complained, 'in the irreverence of the individual towards the state, in the assumption that he has rights against society irrespectively of his fulfilment of any duties to society, that all "powers that be" are restraints upon his natural freedom which he may rightly defy as far as he safely can'.[87]

V

By 1900, Hobbes's ideas were incomparably more respected and respectable than they had been at the start of the Victorian era. Some knowledge of the *Leviathan* had become part of the mental frame of reference of any educated person, on a par with *Pilgrim's Progress* and *Gulliver's Travels*. There was no longer a sense (as there

[85] David Duncan, *Life and Letters of Herbert Spencer* (London,1908), 416–17; A. E. Taylor, *Hobbes* (London, 1908), 27–8; Salmond, *Theory of Law*, 185.
[86] *Leviathan* (Oxford, 1957), 145, 227–8.   [87] Green, *Principles*, 67.

had certainly been when the Molesworth volumes appeared in the 1840s) that Hobbes's religious and philosophical views, as well as his political thought, were implicitly subversive and dangerous. The ideas of the philosophical radicals, who had originally promoted Hobbes's works for their own polemical purposes, now seemed to many people somewhat staid and outdated, whereas Hobbes himself was viewed as startlingly 'modern'. His early twentieth-century admirers included such diverse figures as Bertrand Russell, William James, Harald Hoffding, John Dewey, and H. G. Wells; while admirers and critics alike were also prominently represented among those close-knit family networks known as the English 'intellectual aristocracy'.[88] Moreover, in Britain, Europe, and North America his political and philosophical writings—including new translations of his Latin works—now took their place alongside the writings of Plato and Aristotle as canonical texts of political science. (Only Rousseau among post-classical political theorists had a comparable standing.) His works were entrenched in undergraduate courses on law, philosophy, politics, and history; and serious writing and scholarship on Hobbes's thought had now largely migrated into the universities (often, particularly in North America, with interesting and unusual results).[89]

What was the significance of this long-drawn-out revolution in Hobbes's reputation for the politics and culture of Victorian Britain? The question of whether Hobbesian ideas actively shaped political institutions and events lies largely beyond the scope of this chapter. Maitland, Figgis, and Laski certainly thought that they did, and that the intellectual legacy of Hobbes was at least partly responsible for the overwhelmingly 'unitary' and 'monistic' character of the late-Victorian British state. To Maine, Sidgwick, and Ranke, on the other hand, it seemed that certain monopolistic trends generic to modern states, which had been starkly perceived in outline by Hobbes in the seventeenth century, were now progressively working themselves out in the nineteenth century, regardless of any direct causal input from political or legal theory. Popular writing on Hobbes inclined to the latter view, usually citing foreign rather than British examples: Bonapartism in France, the federal victory in the American Civil War, Bismarck's campaigns against Roman Catholics and socialists in the German empire.[90] Nevertheless, primary research on a far wider scale than has been possible here—into such themes as property rights, church autonomy, the governance of corporate bodies, and constitutional relations within the United Kingdom—would be required to establish just how far Hobbesian thought was a significant element in the shaping of 'real' politics.

My conclusions must be largely confined to an assessment of Hobbes's *intellectual* impact on Victorian critics and disciples. One such conclusion is that, though

[88] Croom Robertson, Frederick Pollock, Leslie and Fitzjames Stephen, A. V. Dicey, F. W. Maitland, Henry Sidgwick, e.g. all belonged to the circles classifed in this way by Noel Annan.

[89] e.g *The Metaphysical System of Thomas Hobbes*, selected by Mary Whiton Calkins (Religion of Science Library, 57; Chicago, 1906); and Calkins, *Persistent Problems of Philosophy* (New York, 1907).

[90] Stephen, *Horae Sabbaticae*, 2nd ser., 61; 'The "Sovereignty" in America, France and England', *Spectator* (25 June 1898), 900–1; Dennery, *Quarterly Review* (1887).

serious engagement with Hobbes's thought was more widespread than allowed for in *Whigs and Liberals*, John Burrow was nevertheless right to stress the pitfalls and absurdities that ensue if such engagement is abstracted from its immediate linguistic and historical context. Of the authors mentioned above, most took Hobbes's ideas seriously, but they did so selectively and used them in different and unpredictable ways.[91] If there were 'conspiracies' at work to promote Hobbesian policies and ways of thought, as some have supposed, then they were working not in one direction but many. Hobbes's works were initially promoted by radicals sympathetic to revolutionary France who loathed his views on the absolute state, but saw his philosophical and scientific ideas as leading in directions that were profoundly *subversive* of established authority. Slightly later, the more moderate 'philosophical' radicals (identified in recent writing as prime mediators of Hobbesist authoritarianism) greatly differed among themselves about the import of Hobbes's doctrines for politics and government. James Mill believed as firmly as Hobbes himself that natural science and the study of politics were one and the same; but his son could never quite reconcile the two (and he strongly emphasized those ethical and 'civic' dimensions of politics that Hobbes had largely discounted). George Grote, the inspiration behind the Molesworth edition, believed in the 'Greek' ideal of freedom as passionately as Hobbes had despised it.[92] George Croom Robertson likewise concluded, after twenty years of research, that—despite the claims of the positivists—there was no real congruity in Hobbes's thought between 'laws' governing the natural world and 'laws' in the sense of the arbitrary 'command of the sovereign' (the latter in fact being specifically designed to 'put an end to' the former).[93] Despite his alleged links with 'despotism', throughout the nineteenth century commentators of all complexions almost invariably linked Hobbes with liberal, radical, populist, and even 'revolutionary' causes. Contrary to one account cited above, virtually no Victorian conservatives admired Hobbes, and the few who did so usually misinterpreted his key ideas: for example, they imagined that Hobbes was a believer in natural inequality and the principle of aristocracy.[94] Paradoxically, as his reputation soared, academic writing on Hobbes's political thought became increasingly detached and critical. And throughout the Victorian era there were many who read *Leviathan* simply out of curiosity, or as a historical document, without in the least being swept away by its substantive political doctrines.[95]

Another conclusion is that though Hobbes's political thought, particularly his notion of sovereignty, aroused extensive debate, this was not the paramount theme in the Hobbesian revival. From Priestly and Horne Took, through to

---

[91] For a useful résumé of contemporary views, see Frederick Pollock's Oxford University extension lecture on 'Hobbes', 11 Aug. 1894, *National and English Review*, 24 (1894), 29–41.

[92] [W. L. Courteney] 'Thomas Hobbes', *Edinburgh Review*, 165 (1887), 89.

[93] Robertson, *Hobbes*, 138–46.

[94] Anthony Ludovici, *A Defence of Aristocracy: A Textbook for Tories* (London, 1915), 9–15, 25.

[95] *Saturday Review* (27 Feb. 1886), 308.

Croom Robertson and the founding of *Mind*, the prime concern of many of Hobbes's most engaged disciples was not with his politics as such, but with the philosophical ideas lying behind them. Throughout the century Hobbes's system would be used as a major point of reference in combating successive schools of thought—natural theology, 'common sense', Kantian *a priorism*, intuitionism, idealism—which their critics saw as infected by the 'poison' of supernaturalism. Within this ongoing war of ideas Hobbes's reflections on the material basis of mind, syllogistic reasoning, the 'artificial' character of language, the priority of words over ideas, and 'truth' as signifying 'logical consistency' were powerful weapons. It was in these fields, rather than in political thought *per se*, that Hobbes's writings most powerfully shaped the mind of the young John Stuart Mill; and the same was to be true half a century later of his impact on the young Bertrand Russell.[96] And even in law and political science, it was arguably through such methodological routes—formal logic, linguistic positivism, and moral 'calculus'—that Hobbes would most profoundly influence the academic culture and mental outlook of the early twentieth century.

A final point is that Victorian debates on Thomas Hobbes raised many more questions than they answered. Many of the big issues about Hobbes's ideas that were to be fought out on the battlegrounds of international scholarship during the twentieth century had already been anticipated over the previous hundred years. Whether Hobbes was an authoritarian or libertarian, an enforcer or subverter of the rule of law, a selfish individualist or champion of the public good, an autocrat or ultra-democrat, an exponent of crude force or of fine-tuned rational calculation—all had been advanced from some quarter or another during the Victorian era. Whether Hobbes was the 'founder of sociology', or whether on the contrary his philosophy was fundamentally hostile to 'sociological' thought, was a recurrent bone of contention.[97] Despite the claims of positivists (Comtean and otherwise) that Hobbes was one of their number, there were others who doubted this, noting that he had portrayed knowledge of all kinds, even in geometry, as inherently contingent and uncertain.[98] Indeed, the Victorian story of Thomas Hobbes comes to an end just at a point when, having been safely bedded down for two decades in academic curricula, Hobbesian themes were once again about to burst upon the political arena. The Edwardian arms race, Irish Home Rule, industrial syndicalism, the 1911 Parliament Act, sectarian and secular pluralism, were all to generate a new wave of popular writing on the issue of sovereignty; while the First World War itself, bringing in its train conscription, requisitioning, and the threat of violent death, was to fan traditional stereotypes of Hobbism back into fashion.[99] But in 1915 it was imperial Germany not wartime Britain that was seen as the site

---

96 *The Collected Papers of Bertrand Russell*, Vol. 1 (London, 1983), 156–61, 170–1, 186–92.

97 Graham, *English Political Philosophy*, xxxi. 45–6.

98 G. Croom Robertson, 'Hobbes', *Encyclopedia Britannica*, 1875.

99 J. A. Hobson, 'The War and British Liberties: The Claims of the State upon the Individual', *Nation* (10 June 1916); G. P. Gooch, *Political Thought in England from Bacon to Halifax* (London,

of the so-called *New Leviathan*. 'Current German political thought is infected with a taint of Hobbism', pronounced the Scots economist Alexander Gray. '(On) all current German theorisings about freedom lies the heavy hand of Hobbism... we in this country gave our final answer to Hobbism in all its forms in 1688'.[100] 'Hobbes is now revealed as the first philosopher of Prussianism... and the bitter foe of individualism', echoed the literary critic Ivor Brown. 'His conception of complete unity between the State and the citizen... is really good Hegelian doc-trine'.[101] So despite a greatly enhanced intellectual reputation, Hobbes's Victorian resurrection concluded even more ambiguously than it had begun. Admired by some unusual and important thinkers and firmly established in the curriculum of all major universities, he still had the 'taint' of absolutism and unfreedom attached to his name.

1914–15), 49–57; C. E. Vaughan, *Studies in the History of Political Philosophy* (Manchester, 1925), 21–55. (Though not published till 1925, Vaughan's polemic against Hobbes was written in 1917.)

[100] A. Gray, *The New Leviathan: Some Illustrations of Current German Political Theories* (London, 1915). In 1942, in another work of the same name, R. G. Collingwood argued the exact opposite: it was not despotism and tyranny, but the idea of a 'civilized society', which was the core of Hobbes's political philosophy: R. G. Collingwood, *The New Leviathan* (Oxford, 1942), and *Essays in Political Philosophy*, ed. David Boucher (Oxford, 1989), 228.

[101] Ivor Brown, *English Political Theory* (London, 1920), 48–51.

Index